Murder in
Retrospect

Murder in Retrospect

A Selective Guide to Historical Mystery Fiction

MICHAEL BURGESS AND
JILL H. VASSILAKOS

UNLIMITED

A Member of the Greenwood Publishing Group

Westport, Connecticut • London

Library of Congress Cataloging-in-Publication Data

Burgess, Michael, 1948–
    Murder in retrospect : a selective guide to historical mystery fiction / by Michael
Burgess and Jill H. Vassilakos.
      p. cm.
    Includes bibliographical references and indexes.
    ISBN 1–59158–087–0 (alk. paper)
    1. Detective and mystery stories, English—Handbooks, manuals, etc. 2. Detective and
mystery stories, American—Handbooks, manuals, etc. 3. Historical fiction, English—
Handbooks, manuals, etc. 4. Historical fiction, American—Handbooks, manuals, etc.
5. Detective and mystery stories, English—Bibliography. 6. Detective and mystery
stories, American—Bibliography. 7. Historical fiction, English—Bibliography.
8. Historical fiction, American—Bibliography. I. Vassilakos, Jill H. II. Title.
PR830.D4B85 2005
  823'.087209—dc22   2005047488

British Library Cataloguing in Publication Data is available.

Library of Congress Catalog Card Number: 2005047488
ISBN: 1–59158–087–0

First published in 2005

Libraries Unlimited, 88 Post Road West, Westport, CT 06881
A Member of the Greenwood Publishing Group, Inc.
www.lu.com

Printed in the United States of America

The paper used in this book complies with the
Permanent Paper Standard issued by the National
Information Standards Organization (Z39.48–1984).

10 9 8 7 6 5 4 3 2 1

For Our Parents—
Walt & Betty Burgess
Demetrios & Marion Vassilakos
—And the Mystery of History

Contents

Introduction

Detecting the Past

Murder in Retrospect is the first annotated guide to a popular subgenre of the modern detective story. Although historical mysteries have existed almost from the beginning of the field (e.g., see Agatha Christie's *Death Comes as the End* [1944], with its setting in Ancient Egypt), they became popular (and common) only in the last quarter of the twentieth century, as writers began turning to historical *milieux* to provide exotic locales and characters for their literary crimes. Interest in the field increased through the 1980s with the popularity of the Ellis Peters novels featuring Brother Cadfael. It continued to increase through the 1990s, spurring the publication of a series of anthologies edited by Mike Ashley for Robinson Publishing (U.K.) and Carroll & Graf (U.S.) which allowed readers to sample a variety of authors active in the genre. Interest continues to rise in the new millennium; historical mysteries are more popular than ever both in print and onscreen.

This popularity has led to the publication of a large number of historical series, series that are not always published in chronological order; as well as to the publication of anthologies and collections of short stories, many of which are actually related to existing series. Fans will want to read a series in chronological order, from beginning to end, including those "cases" that were related in short stories.

Purpose:

We designed *Murder in Retrospect* to help readers track down the entries in major historical mystery series and to assist fans who wish to read the stories in order. It will be of use to librarians doing reader's advisory, allowing them to help patrons find materials set in specific eras, and will also be of use to those who are building collections of historical mysteries.

Scope:

We regard a mystery as historical if its backdrop is set in a time period at least fifty years before its date of composition; however, we have in any case excluded all stories set after World War II. Since we would have had to quintuple the size of this book to cover all known historical detective stories, we have limited its scope to those specific works of fiction with significance to the development of this field, as well as to those authors who seem to be the most popular exemplars of their art or who seem to have the largest fan following. We have mostly not covered the vast array of novels based around real-life historical personages as detectives, with a few exceptions to provide examples of those fictions (e.g., the Nate Heller books of Max Allan Collins or the Elliott Roosevelt series based on the exploits of his mother, Eleanor Roosevelt, FDR's wife). Many of these types of works lack basic credibility as stories, since their protagonists could not have possibly been so thoroughly involved in solving crimes on an ongoing basis without being discovered by the press or by historians. We also have not featured works with fantasy or science fiction elements, even those with historical settings, feeling that such fictions really deserve coverage in a book of their own.

How to use this book:

Each entry includes the author's name, series name, background information on the series and its leading characters, comments and criticism of the basic premise and its realization within the context of the series, and detailed entries for the major books (and selected short stories) in the series. Whenever possible, entries are listed in chronological order by the year in which the story is set; in some instances where the time setting of particular entries in the series is not clear, the materials may be listed in chronological order by publication date. Collections of short stories and associational works (describing the series or works that impinge upon, but are not directly part of, the series) are listed after all the other entries. Additional notes may be included where appropriate. A specific title entry provides series number, title, alternate title, publication in which a shorter work appeared, publication data, the place and setting where most of the action occurs, a plot summary, and a list of "Associates" (names of characters other than the principals who appear on a recurring basis) and/or "Historical Figures" (actual individuals from history making their appearance in the narrative).

Indexes provide access by:

- author
- series
- title
- major character
- setting (date and location)

and are cross-referenced to entry page number.

Special thanks are due to Mary Wickizer Burgess and Marion White-Vassilakos for their assistance in finding and reviewing some of these materials and for providing much encouragement and sustenance during this book's birthing—and another tip of the hat to Mary for indexing the book. Thanks, too, to the Interlibrary Loan Department of the John M. Pfau Library, California State University, San Bernardino (particularly to Lee Bayer and Annemarie Hopkins), for their heroic efforts on our behalf; and also to the following institutions: the San Bernardino Public Library, the San Bernardino County Library, and the Riverside Public Library. Thanks also to Johnnie Ann Ralph for her forbearance while this book was under way, and to Barbara Ittner, our editor at Libraries Unlimited, for her good advice and patience.

We hope that this volume will appeal to fans, general readers, and librarians, as well as to all lovers of mysteries everywhere, particularly of the historical variety. Of course, we hope to provide updated editions in the future. We look forward to receiving your comments and suggestions, c/o Libraries Unlimited.

—Michael Burgess and Jill H. Vassilakos
California State University, San Bernardino

ALEXANDER, Bruce (1932–2003). American.

SIR JOHN FIELDING AND JEREMY PROCTOR SERIES

Scene of the Crime: England, beginning in 1768.

Detective: Sir John Fielding (1721–1780), the detective in this series, actually served as a magistrate in London; despite having been blinded at the age of nineteen, it was said that he could recognize over 3,000 thieves by their voices. John was the half brother of the novelist Henry Fielding, who preceded him as a magistrate, and together they founded the first English police force, the Bow Street Runners. (A story of how Sir John was blinded is related in *Watery Grave*.)

Known Associates: Jeremy Proctor, who acts as narrator of the series. He was thirteen years old when he was brought before Sir John's court framed for theft; Sir John saw through the plot, made him a ward of the court, and took him into his own household. The intention was to find Jeremy an apprenticeship at a printer's, that being the work for which he had been trained; however, on the eve of his apprenticeship every member of the printing establishment was murdered, and Sir John decided that Jeremy should remain in his care. Other members of the household include Sir John's wife, Kitty, who dies of a wasting illness in *Blind Justice*. In *Murder in Grub Street* Sir John marries Katherine Durham, a widow who has fallen on hard times. Katherine has one son, Tom. Mrs. Gredge is the Fieldings' housekeeper and cook until she falls ill in *Watery Grave*, when she is pensioned off. Annie Oakum, who was first met in *Blind Justice*, is hired as her replacement but leaves for a career in the theater before the events recounted in *Smuggler's Moon*. Molly Sarten takes the job of cook-housekeeper in *An Experiment in Treason*. Clarissa Roundtree is taken in as a ward by the Fieldings at the end of *Jack, Knave, and Fool* and becomes Lady Fielding's secretary. Sir John works extensively with the Bow Street Runners, Benjamin Bailey being their Captain. The Lord Chief Justice, Lord Mansfield, is Sir John's superior and sometimes involves him in investigations. In the course of his inqueries Sir John may need information on the seamier sides of London; this is provided by Black Jack Bilbo, who was once a privateer, and by a (soon reformed) pickpocket named Jimmie Bunkins.

Premise: A blind judge in London solves crimes and administers justice with the help of his ward.

Comment: Jeremy Proctor's father was a printer. To demonstrate his skills, Mr. Proctor printed a controversial pamphlet, a translation of some Voltaire. The leader of the local congregation took exception to the book and argued about it with Mr. Proctor. Mr. Proctor defended his work and was denounced by the churchman. The congregation broke into the print shop, destroyed the machinery, and stole what they might, then dragged Mr. Proctor to the stocks. Filth and stones were thrown at him, and after a space of days he was dead, "pelted to death," meaning either that a stone struck him and caused his death or that mud and ordure so covered his face that he suffocated. His son Jeremy fled from the town and took the road to London, hoping to find employment with a printer. Within hours of entering London he was caught in a trap by two rogues and framed for theft. He was taken before the court of Sir John Fielding, who realized that he was innocent and dismissed all charges against him. Sir John declared Jeremy a ward of the court and took him into his household. Jeremy makes himself useful by assisting with the work of everyone on Sir John's staff and eventually is included in Sir John's investigations. At the onset of the series he is twelve years of age but turns thirteen before he enters London. The great abilities of Sir John Fielding have been well documented in history. His social conscience was manifest in his works, and the plight of the poor, coupled with the harshness of the justice system of the time, forced Sir John to be inventive in his judgments, which at times are worthy indeed of Solomon.

Literary Crimes & Chimes: This fascinating series shows the excitement, color, and brutality of eighteenth-century London by employing a naïve narrator, who is seeing it all for the first time. The series is written from Jeremy's point of view; he is a capable Watson, and it is reasonable that a boy in his position would not be privy to every thought of the detective. In most of the books the reader will guess the villain fairly early in the story; the thrill lies in seeing how Sir John will use the law to render justice. In some cases, he cannot do justice to the situation (in *Watery Grave*, for instance), and that knowledge adds to the reader's suspense.

THE CASES

1. *Blind Justice.* New York: G. P. Putnam's Sons, 1994, 254 p.

LONDON, ENGLAND, 1768. The odious Lord Goodhope, having gambled away a great deal of his fortune and destroyed his good name, is found dead, apparently a suicide. Jeremy notices that, although the side of his face is blackened with gunpowder, his hands are clean. Sir John Fielding, having had the scene described to him, remarks that it is unlikely that such a wound would be self-inflicted by a man who was left-handed, as was Lord Goodhope. Associates: Mr. Gabriel Donnelly; Moll Caulfield; Peg Button; Annie; Meg. Historical Figures: Dr. Samuel "Dictionary" Johnson; David Garrick; James Boswell.

2. *Murder in Grub Street.* New York: G. P. Putnam's Sons, 1995, 276 p.

LONDON, ENGLAND, 1768. The night before Jeremy is to begin his printer's apprenticeship, every person in the printer's household is viciously murdered; that is, every person but one, and that one was found standing over the bodies holding a bloody ax. The man (a poet) claims that he remembers nothing of the crimes, but Sir John discovers that more than one "soul" (personality) resides within this individual. If he is not guilty, then all three of his identities must be innocent, and the murderer is still on the loose. Associates: Constable Cowley; Amos Carr; Moll Caufield; Peg Button; Raker; Rabbi Gershon. Historical Figure: Dr. Samuel "Dictionary" Johnson.

3. *Watery Grave.* New York: G. P. Putnam's Sons, 1996, 265 p.

LONDON, ENGLAND, 1769. Tom Durham (Lady Fielding's son) returns from sea, where he was posted to the frigate the H.M.S. *Adventure*. Many crimes were committed aboard this ship, but most members of the crew believe that the charges of murder lodged against Lieutenant William Landon are false. Sir John is called in to help with the investigation, and finds that there are crimes that the navy considers too scandalous to prosecute. Associates: Tom Durham; Constable Cowley; Sir Robert; Raker. Historical Figure: Thomas Churchill.

4. *Person or Persons Unknown.* New York: G. P. Putnam's Sons, 1997, 279 p.

ENGLAND, 1770. A series of murders, the victims of which are prostitutes, takes place near Covent Garden. Jeremy has just conceived a passion for a fallen woman, and he wishes to gain not only her safety but eventually her freedom. He eagerly takes up a risky task to try to trap a madman. Associates: Mariah; Raker; Mr. Gabriel Donnelly; Rabbi Gershon; Constable Cowley; Constable Perkins; Mr. Tolliver; Robert Burnham; Jackie Carver. Historical Figure: Oliver Goldsmith.

5. *Jack, Knave, and Fool.* New York: G. P. Putnam's Sons, 1998, 279 p.

LONDON, ENGLAND, 1771. Lord Lanningham, patron to the Academy of Ancient Music, drops his bottle of wine and falls, dead, upon the stage. Sir John sends Jeremy around the stage to find the bottle of wine, but it has mysteriously disappeared. Sir John is convinced that Lord Lanningham was poisoned, and subsequent mysterious deaths put the matter beyond question. Associates: Mr. Gabriel Donnelly; Mr. Wills; Robert Burnham; Constable Cowley; Constable Perkins; Dr. Isaac Diller; Thomas Trezavant; Jackie Carver. Historical Figures: David Garrick; Oliver Goldsmith.

6. *Death of a Colonial.* New York: G. P. Putnam's Sons, 1999, 275 p.

LONDON AND BATH, ENGLAND, 1771. Under English law, when the last of a noble line meets his death, the family lands and possessions revert to the Crown. In such a situation, Sir John helps convict a man for murder; he's also the last-known heir to the estate, and the King intends to bestow the country manor on the Prince of Wales (currently nine years of age). When a long-lost brother of the hanged man returns to England to claim both title and fortune, Sir John is one of those called forward to investigate. Note: This book was inspired by the case of the Tichborne Claimant, one of the most famous examples under old English law. Associates: Mr. Archibald Talley; Thomas Trezavant; Mr. Gabriel Donnelly; Constable Cowley.

7. "The Episode of the Water Closet," in *Crime through Time III*, ed. by Sharan Newman. New York: Berkley Prime Crime, 2000, p. 162–171.

LONDON, ENGLAND, 1771. Prince Govinda, Maharajah of Bangalore, has recently arrived in London and been dazzling and amusing high society. Sir John is invited to a dinner given in the Maharajah's honor by Lork Kilcoyne. When Lady Kilcoyne's emerald pendant is stolen, Sir John steps in to investigate.

8. *The Color of Death.* New York: G. P. Putnam's Sons, 2000, 279 p.

LONDON, ENGLAND, 1772. A gang of murderous robbers is terrorizing London. London's mobs are ready to lynch any men of the same skin color as the robbers. Sir John is badly injured, and seventeen-year-old Jeremy must lead the investigation. Associates: Mr. Burnham; Mr. Gabriel Donnelly; Thomas Trezavant; Frank Barber; Constable Patley; Mr. Moses Martinez. Historical Figure: Dr. Samuel "Dictionary" Johnson.

9. *Smuggler's Moon.* New York: G. P. Putnam's Sons, 2001, 247 p.

KENT, ENGLAND, 1773. Lord Mansfield used his influence to have Albert Sarton appointed as magistrate in Kent. Then he hears that Mr. Sarton is unacceptably lenient with smugglers, and rumor has it that he is on the criminals' payroll. Lord Mansfield sends Sir John to investigate. The crimes take a darker turn, from smuggling to murder, soon after Sir John, Jeremy, and Clarissa arrive in Kent. Associates: Constable Perkins; Sir Simon Grenville; Constable Patley; Marie-Helene; Clarissa.

10. *Experiment in Treason.* New York: G. P. Putnam's Sons, 2002, 274 p.

LONDON, ENGLAND, 1773. Sir John is asked to investigate an odd burglary; the thieves gained access to the locked house too easily, they knew just where their prize was located, the dogs did not bark at their entrance, and the homeowner, Lord Hillsborough, Secretary of State for the American colonies, refuses to speak about what was stolen. Eventually, the victim of the crime sees that Sir John must be given some information if he is to be of any help, and the judge is told that politically sensitive letters were pinched. Sir John surmises that letters held by the colonies' Secretary of State and worth a man's life must relate to the highest crime—treason! Note: This story is based on the affair of the Hutchinson letters. Associates: Mr. Gabriel Donnelly; Marie-Helene; Constable Perkins; Arthur Lee; Tom Durham; Annie Oakum; Harold, Earl of Bardwell. Historical Figures: Benjamin Franklin; Dr. Samuel "Dictionary" Johnson; David Garrick; Oliver Goldsmith.

11. *The Price of Murder.* New York: G. P. Putnam's Sons, 2003, 257 p.

LONDON, ENGLAND, 1774. The discovery of the body of an eight-year-old girl leads Sir John into an investigation of child-selling, kidnapping, prostitution, and murder. The final novel in the series, *Rules of Engagement*, was published posthumously in 2005. Associates: Elizabeth Hooker; Mr. Gabriel Donnelly; Deuteronomy Plummer; Constable Patley.

ASHLEY, Mike (i.e., Michael Raymond Donald) (1948–). British.

MAMMOTH BOOK HISTORICAL ANTHOLOGY SERIES

Scene of the Crime: Various.

Detective: Various.

Known Associates: Various.

Premise: Ashley gathers together anthologies of stories on different periods in history by the well-known authors in the field.

Comment: After his early retirement from a British Civil Service post, Ashley began a new career as a reference book writer and as an anthologist for Robinson Publishing in Great Britain, with the latter volumes being reprinted by Carroll & Graf in the United States. The first few books in Ashley's series were collections of tales with historical settings from a variety of periods. These proved to be widely popular in the mid-1990s and, together with the Brother Cadfael novels of Ellis Peters, helped put the historical mystery genre on a firm footing with its fan audience. Later books in the sequence began to focus on particular time periods, following the pattern of the novels then being produced in the subgenre.

Literary Crimes & Chimes: All of these books are very well edited and presented and filled with high-quality stories, the vast bulk of which are publications original to the anthologies in question. Ashley demonstrates a partial bias toward British writers and stories. The least successful books in the series are the two volumes focusing on William Shakespeare and his fictional creations; the tales in these anthologies mostly employ settings from Shakespeare's dramas, producing in many cases a fantasy effect that works against the mystery elements in these tales. The most successful publications are the initial pair of volumes, both of which contain an exceptional selection of stories. The later books generally feature a good variety of tales by capable writers, although not penned quite to the level of the materials in books one and two. Overall, however, this series has consistently provided the best (and longest-lasting) of the historical anthology collections available. All but the Shakespeare books are highly recommended and should belong on the bookshelves of every fan of the historical mystery tale.

THE CASES

1. *The Mammoth Book of Historical Whodunnits.* London: Robinson Publishing; New York: Carroll & Graf, 1993, 522 p. As: *Historical Whodunnits.* New York: Barnes & Noble, 1997, 522 p.

   An anthology of historical detective stories set in a variety of eras. CONTENTS: "Introduction: The Chronicles of Crime," by Mike Ashley; "Foreword," by Ellis Peters. Part I: The Ancient World: 1. "The Locked Tomb Mystery," by Elizabeth Peters; 2. "The Thief Versus King Rhampsinitus," by Herodotus; 3. "Socrates Solves a Murder," by Brèni James; 4. "Mightier than the Sword," by John Maddox Roberts; 5. "The Treasury Thefts," by Wallace Nichols; 6. "A Byzantine Mystery," by Mary Reed and Eric Mayer; 7. "He Came with the Rain," by Robert van Gulik; 8. "The High King's

Sword," by Peter Tremayne. Part II: The Middle Ages: 9. "The Price of Light," by Ellis Peters; 10. "The Confession of Brother Athelstan," by Paul Harding; 11. "The Witch's Tale," by Margaret Frazer; 12. "Father Hugh and the Deadly Scythe," by Mary Monica Pulver; 13. "Leonardo Da Vinci, Detective," by Theodore Mathieson; 14. "A Sad and Bloody Hour," by Joe Gores. Part III: Regency and Gaslight: 15. "The Christmas Masque," by S. S. Rafferty; 16. "Murder Lock'd In," by Lillian de la Torre; 17. "Captain Nash and the Wroth Inheritance," by Raymond Butler; 18. "The Doomdorf Mystery," by Melville Davisson Post; 19. "Murder in the Rue Royale," by Michael Harrison; 20. "The Gentleman from Paris," by John Dickson Carr; 21. "The Golden Nugget Poker Game," by Edward D. Hoch. Part IV: Holmes and Beyond: 22. "The Case of the Deptford Horror," by Adrian Conan Doyle; 23. "Five Rings in Reno," by R. L. Stevens; "Afterword: Old-Time Detection," by Arthur Griffiths; "Appendix: Chroniclers of Crime."

2. *The Mammoth Book of Historical Detectives.* London: Robinson Publishing; New York: Carroll & Graf, 1995, 532 p. As: ***Historical Detectives.*** Edison, NJ: Castle Books, 2002, 532 p.

A second anthology of historical detective stories set in different eras. CONTENTS: "Introduction: The Second Book of Chronicles," by Mike Ashley. Part I: The Ancient World: 1. "Death in the Dawntime," by F. Gwynplaine MacIntyre; 2. "The Judgement of Daniel" (Bible); 3. "Death Wears a Mask," by Steven Saylor; 4. "The King of Sacrifices," by John Maddox Roberts; 5. "The Three Travellers," by R. L. Stevens; 6. "The Case of the Murdered Senator," by Wallace Nichols; 7. "A Mithraic Mystery," by Mary Reed & Eric Mayer; 8. "Abbey Sinister," by Peter Tremayne; 9. "The Two Beggars," by Robert van Gulik. Part II: The Middle Ages: 10. "The Investigation of Things," by Charles Ardai; 11. "The Midwife's Tale," by Margaret Frazer; 12. "The Duchess and the Doll," by Edith Pargeter (Ellis Peters); 13. "Ordeal by Fire," by Mary Monica Pulver; 14. "The Chapman and the Tree of Doom," by Kate Sedley. Part III: The Age of Discovery: 15. "The Murder of Innocence," by P. C. Doherty; 16. "Cassandra's Castle," by J. F. Peirce; 17. "Man's Inherited Death," by Keith Heller; 18. "The Curse of the Connecticut Clock," by S. S. Rafferty; 19. "The Scent of Murder," by Theodore Mathieson; 20. "The Inn of the Black Crow," by William Hope Hodgson; 21. "The Spirit of the '76," by Lillian de la Torre. Part IV: Regency and Gaslight: 22. "Deadly Will and Testament," by Ron Burns; 23. "The God of the Hills," by Melville Davisson Post; 24. "The Admiral's Lady," by Joan Aiken; 25. "The Eye of Shiva," by Peter MacAlan; 26. "The Trail of the Bells," by Edward D. Hoch; 27. "Murdering Mr Boodle," by Amy Myers. Part V: Holmes and Beyond: 28. "The Phantom Pistol," by Jack Adrian; 29. "The Adventure of the Frightened Governess," by Basil Copper.

3. *Classical Whodunnits: Murder and Mystery from Ancient Rome and Greece.* London: Robinson Publishing, 1996; New York: Carroll & Graf, 1997, 374 p.

An anthology of historical detective stories with settings in ancient Rome and Greece. CONTENTS: "Introduction," by Mike Ashley; "Preface: A Murder, Now and Then . . ." by Steven Saylor; "Aphrodite's Trojan Horse," by Amy Myers; "Investigating the Silvius Boys," by Lindsey Davis; "The Gateway to Death," by Brèni James; "Death of the King," by Theodore Mathieson; "The Favour of a Tyrant," by Keith Taylor; "The White Fawn," by Steven Saylor; "The Statuette of Rhodes," by John Maddox Roberts; "The Things That Are Caesar's," by Edward D. Hoch; "Murderer, Farewell," by Ron Burns; "A Pomegranate for Pluto," by Claire Griffen; "The Gardens of Tantalus," by Brian Stableford; "A Green Boy," by Anthony Price; "Mosaic," by Rosemary Aitken; "The Brother in the Tree," by Keith Heller; "The Ass's Head," by Phyllis Ann Karr; "The Nest of Evil," by Wallace Nichols; "In This Sign, Conquer," by Nina-Gail Anderson and Simon Clark; "Last Things," by Darrell Schweitzer; "Beauty More Stealthy," by Mary Reed and Eric Mayer; "The Poisoned Chalice," by Peter Tremayne; "Sources and Acknowledgements."

4. *Shakespearean Whodunnits.* London: Robinson Publishing; New York: Carroll & Graf, 1997, 422 p.

An anthology of historical detective stories focusing on William Shakespeare and his literary creations. CONTENTS: "Introduction: Shakespeare's Mysteries," by Mike Ashley; "King John: When the Dead Rise Up," by John T. Aquino; "Richard II: The Death of Kings," by Margaret Frazer; "Henry IV: A Villainous Company," by Susanna Gregory; "Henry V: The Death of Falstaff," by Darrell Schweitzer; "Henry VI: A Serious Matter," by Derek Wilson; "Richard III: A Shadow That Dies," by Mary Reed and Eric Mayer; "Coriolanus: Mother of Rome," by Molly Brown; "Timon of Athens: Buried Fortune," by Peter T. Garratt; "Julius Caesar: Cinna the Poet," by Tom Holt; "Cymbeline: Imogen," by Paul Barnett; "King Lear: Serpent's Tooth," by Martin Edwards; "Macbeth: Toil and Trouble," by Edward D. Hoch; "Hamlet: A Sea of Troubles," by Steve Lockley; "A Midsummer-Night's Dream: A Midsummer Eclipse," by Stephen Baxter; "Much Ado about Nothing: Much Ado about Something," by Susan B. Kelly; "The Winter's Tale: Who Killed Mamillius?" by Amy Myers; "Twelfth Night: This Is Illyria, Lady," by Kim Newman; "Romeo and Juliet: Star-Crossed," by Patricia A. McKillip; "The Two Gentlemen of Verona: The Banished Men," by Keith Taylor; "The Taming of the Shrew: The Shrewd Taming of Lord Thomas," by Mary Monica Pulver; "Othello: Not Wisely, but Too Well," by Louise Cooper; "As You Like It: Murder as You Like It," by F. Gwynplaine MacIntyre; "The Merchant of Venice: The House of Rimmon," by Cherity Baldry; "Epilogue: All Is True: An Ensuing Evil," by Peter Tremayne; "All the Plays: The Collaborator," by Rosemary Aitken; "The Contributors."

5. **The Mammoth Book of New Sherlock Holmes Adventures.** London: Robinson Publishing; New York: Carroll & Graf, 1997, 524 p.

An anthology of mystery stories focusing on the fictional protagonist, Sherlock Holmes. CONTENTS: "The Bothersome Business of the Dutch Nativity," by Derek Wilson; "The Affray at the Kildare Street Club," by Peter Tremayne; "The Case of the Incumbent Invalid," by Claire Griffen; "The Adventure of Vittoria the Circus Belle," by Edward D. Hoch; "The Darlington Substitution Scandal," by David Stuart Davies; "The Adventure of the Suspect Servant," by Barbara Roden; "The Adventure of the Amateur Mendicant Society," by John Betancourt; "The Adventure of the Silver Buckle," by Denis O. Smith; "The Case of the Sporting Squire," by Guy N. Smith; "The Vanishing of the Atkinsons," by Eric Brown; "The Adventure of the Fallen Star," by Simon Clark; "The Adventure of the Dorset Street Lodger," by Michael Moorcock; "The Mystery of the Addleton Curse," by Barrie Roberts; "The Adventure of the Parisian Gentleman," by Robert Weinberg and Lois H. Gresh; "The Adventure of the Inertial Adjustor," by Stephen Baxter; "The Adventure of the Touch of God," by Peter Crowther.

6. **Shakespearean Detectives.** London: Robinson Publishing; New York: Carroll & Graf, 1998, 440 p.

A second anthology of historical detective stories focusing on William Shakespeare and his literary creations. CONTENTS: "Introduction," by Edward Marston; "Edmund Ironside: War Hath Made All Friends," by Edward Marston; "Edward III: A Gift for Killing," by Susanna Gregory; "Henry IV: The Chimes at Midnight," by Cherith Baldry; "The Merry Wives of Windsor: A Man of Middle-Earth," by Gail-Nina Anderson; "Henry VIII: All Is True," by Stephen Baxter; "The Two Noble Kinsmen: Murdered by Love," by Darrell Schweitzer; "Troilus and Cressida: The Wine-Dark Cup," by Claire Griffen; "The Rape of Lucrece: The Fire That Burneth Here," by Anne Gay; "Pericles: As Near to Lust as Flame to Smoke," by Andy Lane; "The Comedy of Errors: Stolen Affections," by Lawrence Schimel and Jeffrey Marks; "Julius Caesar: Three Meetings and a Funeral," by Lois Gresh and Robert Weinberg; "Antony and Cleopatra: A Good Report of the Worm," by Tom Holt; "Twelfth Night: A Kind of Wild Justice," by Ron Tiner; "Measure for Measure: The Duke of Dark Corners," by Gail-Nina Anderson; "Love's Labour's Lost: Love's Labour's Discover'd," by Phyllis Ann Karr; "The Tempest: As Strange a Maze as E'er Men Trod," by David Langford; "We Are for the Dark," by Stan Nicholls;

"Arden of Feversham: Footsteps in the Snow," by Amy Myers; "Venus and Adonis: The Price of Virginity," by Paul Barnett; "Titus Andronicus: That Same Pit," by Margaret Frazer; "Murder Most Foul," by Richard Butler; "Love's Labour's Won: Love Labour's, Lost?" by Peter T. Garratt; "Beneath Which Hour?" by Peter Valentine Timlett; "All's Well That Ends Well: Methought You Saw a Serpent," by Peter Tremayne; "Othello: Desdemona's Daughter," by Edward D. Hoch; "A Yorkshire Tragedy: Conspiracy Theory," by Tina and Tony Rath; "The Name-Catcher's Tale," by John T. Aquino; "The Sonnets: Master Eld, His Wayzgoose," by Chaz Brenchley; "Fortune's Other Steward," by Mary Reed and Eric Mayer; "The Contributors."

7. **Royal Whodunnits.** London: Robinson Publishing; New York: Carroll & Graf, 1999, 434 p.

An anthology of historical detective stories focusing on kings, queens, princes, and other royals. CONTENTS: "Foreword," by Paul C. Doherty; "The Snows of Saint Stephen," by M. G. Owen; "Night's Black Agents," by Peter Tremayne; "Even Kings Die," by Mary Reed and Eric Mayer; "Accidental Death," by Tom Holt; "The White Ship Murders," by Susanna Gregory; "Who Killed Fair Rosamund?" by Tina and Tony Rath; "Provenance," by Liz Holliday; "To Whom the Victory?" by Mary Monica Pulver; "A Frail Young Life," by Renée Vink; "A Stone of Destiny," by Jean Davidson; "Perfect Shadows," by Edward Marston; "The Friar's Tale," by Cherith Baldry; "Neither Pity, Love Nor Fear," by Margaret Frazer; "Happy the Man . . ." by Amy Myers; "Borgia by Blood," by Claire Griffen; "The Curse of the Unborn Dead," by Derek Wilson; "Two Dead Men," by Paul Barnett; "A Secret Murder," by Robert Franks; "The Gaze of the Falcon," by Andrew Lane; "The Mysterious Death of the Shadow Man," by John T. Aquino; "The Day the Dogs Died," by Edward D. Hoch; "Natural Causes," by Martin Edwards; "The Modern Cyrano," by Stephen Baxter; "News from New Providence," by Richard A. Lupoff; "Woman in a Wheelchair," by Morgan Llywelyn; "The Contributors."

8. **The Mammoth Book of Historical Whodunnits: Brand New Collection.** London: Robinson Publishing, 2001, 500 p. As: **The Mammoth Book of More Historical Whodunnits.** New York: Carroll & Graf, 2001, 500 p.

A third generic anthology of historical mystery stories set in different eras. CONTENTS: "Introduction: Past Crimes," by Mike Ashley; "Poppy and the Poisoned Cake," by Steven Saylor; "Blind Justice," by Michael Kurland; "A Payment to the Gods," by Rosemary Rowe; "The Last Legion," by Richard Butler; "And All That He Calls Family," by Mary Reed and Eric Mayer; "Death of an Icon," by Peter Tremayne; "King Hereafter," by Philip Gooden; "The Death Toll," by Susanna Gregory; "The Isle of Saints," by

Kate Ellis; "A Perfect Crime," by Derek Wilson; "On Wings of Love," by Carol Anne Davis; "A Lion Rampant," by Jean Davidson; "The Amorous Armourer," by Michael Jecks; "Benefit of Clergy," by Keith Taylor; "The Pilgrim's Tale," by Cherith Baldry; "And What Can They Show, or What Reasons Give?" by Mat Coward; "Heretical Murder," by Margaret Frazer; "A Moon for Columbus," by Edward D. Hoch; "House of the Moon," by Claire Griffen; "Flibbertigibbet," by Paul Finch; "The Vasty Deep," by Peter T. Garratt; "A Taste for Burning," by Marilyn Todd.

9. *The Mammoth Book of Egyptian Whodunnits.* London: Robinson Publishing; New York: Carroll & Graf, 2002, 496 p.

An anthology of historical detective stories with an ancient Egyptian setting. CONTENTS: "Foreword: The Sands of Crime," by Mike Ashley; "Introduction," by Elizabeth Peters; "Set in Stone," by Deirdre Counihan; "Serpent at the Feast," by Claire Griffen; "The Sorrow of Senusert the Mighty," by Keith Taylor; "The Execration," by Noreen Doyle; "No-Name," by R. H. Stewart; " 'Or You Can Drink the Wine . . . ?' " by Paul C. Doherty; "Murder in the Land of Wawat," by Lauren Haney; "The Locked Room Mystery," by Elizabeth Peters; "Heretic's Dagger," by Lynda S. Robinson; "Scorpion's Kiss," by Anton Gill; "Claws of the Wind," by Suzanne Frank; "The Weighing of the Heart," by F. Gwynplaine MacIntyre; "Chosen of the Nile," by Mary Reed and Eric Mayer; "The Justice of Isis," by Gillian Bradshaw; "The Wings of Isis," by Marilyn Todd; "Bringing the Foot," by Kate Ellis; "Unrolling the Dead," by Ian Morson; "Heart Scarab," by Gillian Linscott; "Made in Egypt," by Michael Pearce.

10. *The Mammoth Book of Roman Whodunnits.* London: Robinson Publishing; New York: Carroll & Graf, 2003, 526 p.

An anthology of historical detective stories with an ancient Roman setting. CONTENTS: "Introduction: 'The Long Reach of Rome,' " by Steven Saylor; "Never Forget," by Tom Holt; "A Gladiator Dies Only Once," by Steven Saylor; "The Hostage to Fortune," by Michael Jecks; "De Crimine," by Miriam Allen deFord; "The Will," by John Maddox Roberts; "Honey Moon," by Marilyn Todd; "Damnum Fatale," by Philip Boast; "Heads You Lose," by Simon Scarrow; "Great Caesar's Ghost," by Michael Kurland; "The Cleopatra Game," by Jane Finnis; "Bread and Circuses," by Caroline Lawrence; "The Missing Centurion" (Anonymous); "Some Unpublished Correspondence of the Younger Pliny," by Darrell Schweitzer; "A Golden Opportunity," by Jean Davidson; "Caveat Emptor," by Rosemary Rowe; "Sunshine and Shadow," by R. H. Stewart; "The Case of His Own Abduction," by Wallace Nichols; "The Malice of the Anicii," by Gillian Bradshaw; "The Finger of Aphrodite," by Mary Reed and Eric Mayer; "The Lost Eagle," by Peter Tremayne.

11. *The Mammoth Book of Roaring Twenties Whodunnits.* London: Robinson Publishing; New York: Carroll & Graf, 2004, 534 p.

An anthology of historical mystery stories set in the 1920s. CONTENTS: "Foreword: The Crazy Age," by Mike Ashley; "Timor Mortis," by Annette Meyers; "Brave New Murder," by H.R.F. Keating; "So Beautiful, So Dead," by Robert J. Randisi; "'There Would Have Been Murder,'" by Ian Morson; "Someone," by Michael Collins; "Kiss the Razor's Edge," by Mike Stotter; "Thoroughly Modern Millinery," by Marilyn Todd; "The Day of Two Cars," by Gillian Linscott; "The Hope of the World," by Mat Coward; "Bullets," by Peter Lovesey; "He Couldn't Fly," by Michael Kurland; "Putting Crime Over," by Hulbert Footner; "Valentino's Valediction," by Amy Myers; "Skip," by Edward Marston; "The Broadcast Murder," by Grenville Robbins; "For the Benefit of Mr Means," by Christine Matthews; "Without Fire," by Tom Holt; "The Austin Murder Case," by Jon L. Breen; "The Man Who Scared the Bank," by Archibald Pechey; "A Pebble for Papa," by Max Allan Collins and Matthew V. Clemens; "Beyond the Call of Beauty," by Will Murray; "The Problem of the Tin Goose," by Edward D. Hoch; "I'll Never Play Detective Again," by Cornell Woolrich.

BARRON, Stephanie (pseud. of Francine Stephanie Barron Mathews) (1963–). American.

JANE AUSTEN SERIES

Scene of the Crime: Great Britain, beginning in 1802.

Detective: Jane Austen, the well-known British novelist (1775–1817).

Known Associates: Lord Harold Trowbridge, brother of the Duke of Wilborough, who is mysteriously connected with the British government; Cassandra Austen, Jane's sister and her most trusted confidante; James, Frank, Edward, Charles and Henry Austen, Jane's brothers; Jane's parents, Mr. and Mrs. Austen; Henry Austen's wife, Eliza, Comtesse de Feuillide.

Premise: A British novelist solves crimes in early nineteenth-century England.

Comment: "Stephanie Barron," a history buff with an interest in detective fiction, visits her good friends, Paul and Lucy Westmoreland, in the spring of 1995. The Westmorelands, who trace their lineage to a founder of the state of Maryland, and their Baltimore home, Dunready Manor, to the Georgian period, are in the process of renovating an old coal cellar on the property. They discover several hidden boxes of old family records. On further investigation the three realize that the boxes contain "no less than an entire series of manuscripts we believed had been written by Jane Austen, a distant relative of the Westmoreland line." The trio ponder what to do with the treasure trove, and Barron suggests that the best editor would be an Austen scholar. "The Westmorelands demurred. Knowing of my own interest in detective fiction and feeling that the manuscripts' discovery was in part my own, they asked that I undertake the task of editing the notebooks for publication." She adds at the end of the preface to the first book in the series: "To edit Austen is daunting. I do not pretend to her skill. I only hope that the essential spirit of the original manuscripts blazes forth from these new pages, with all the power of that remarkable mind." Writer Francine Mathews, a lifelong Jane Austen admirer who lives and works in Colorado, used her middle and maiden names to create the pseudonym "Stephanie Barron," which is also the name of her alter ego, who plays a major role in this series. As the co-discoverer of the hidden Austen manuscripts, "Stephanie" prefaces each of Austen's tales she "edits" with a current-day framing device designed to enlighten the reader as to the historical events and other factors in Austen's personal life that may have motivated her writing.

Literary Crimes & Chimes: Such "collaborations" with better-known authors are a tempting device, but to undertake such a demanding task, the "collaborator" must tread carefully to be certain she remains faithful to the original writer's vision and style. The framing device is innovative and lends a certain credibility to the project. Barron's interpolation of herself as Austen's "editor" also mitigates somewhat against any false notes she might sound inadvertently. The text contains occasional footnotes, as the "editor's" attempt to elucidate further on what was going on in "Austen's" life at the time. Since little is known of the real Austen's personal life (most of her letters to her sister Cassandra were destroyed after her death), such extrapolations are possible but lead to an almost jarring duality when the reader begins to wade through what is fact and what is fiction—and what is "fact" within a secondhand "fictional" account of supposedly factual events! Skip the schizophrenia and enjoy the series as a lighthearted romp, but don't take the "fictional/factual" framework of these books too seriously.

THE CASES

1. *Jane and the Unpleasantness at Scargrave Manor: Being the First Jane Austen Mystery.* New York: Bantam Books, 1996, 289 p.

SCARGRAVE MANOR, ENGLAND, DECEMBER 1802. On a visit to the estate of her friend, the young and beautiful Isobel Payne, Countess of Scargrave, Jane bears witness to a tragedy. Isobel's husband, a gentleman of mature years, is felled by a mysterious and agonizing ailment. The Earl's death seems a cruel blow of fate for the newly married Isobel. Yet the bereaved widow soon finds that it's only the beginning of her misfortune, as she receives a sinister missive accusing her and the Earl's nephew of adultery—and murder. Desperately afraid that the letter will expose her to the worst sort of scandal, Isobel begs Jane for help. Jane finds herself embroiled in a perilous investigation that will soon have her following a trail of clues that leads all the way to Newgate Prison and the House of Lords—a trail that may well place Jane's own person in the gravest jeopardy. Associates: Isobel Payne, Countess of Scargrave; Fitzroy, Viscount Payne, the Earl's nephew and heir; Lord Harold Trowbridge, brother of the Duke of Wilborough; Henry Austen and his wife Eliza, Comtesse de Feuillide; Mr. Cranley, attorney for the defense.

2. *Jane and the Man of the Cloth: Being the Second Jane Austen Mystery*.
New York: Bantam Books, 1997, 274 p.

LYME REGIS, DORSET, ENGLAND, SEPTEMBER 1804. Jane and her family are looking forward to a peaceful holiday in the seaside village of Lyme Regis. On the outskirts of town an overturned carriage forces the shaken travelers to take refuge at a nearby manor house. There Jane meets the darkly forbidding, yet strangely attractive, Mr. Geoffrey Sidmouth. What murky secrets does the brooding Mr. Sidmouth seek to hide? Jane suspects the worst, but her attention is swiftly diverted when a man is discovered hanged from a makeshift gibbet by the sea. The worthies of Lyme are certain his death is the work of "the Reverend," the ringleader of the midnight smuggling trade whose true identity is the town's paramount mystery. It falls to Jane to entrap and expose the notorious Reverend, even if the evidence points to the last person on earth she wants to suspect, a man who already may have won her heart. Associates: Mr. and Mrs. Austen; Cassandra; Lord Harold Trowbridge.

3. *Jane and the Wandering Eye: Being the Third Jane Austen Mystery*.
New York: Bantam Books, 1998, 262 p.

BATH, ENGLAND, DECEMBER 1804. As Christmas approaches, Jane Austen finds herself "insupportably *bored* with Bath, and the littleness of a town." It is with relief that she accepts a peculiar commission from her Gentleman Rogue, Lord Harold Trowbridge: to shadow his niece, Lady Desdemona, who has fled to Bath to avoid the attentions of the unsavory Earl of Swithin. But Jane's idle diversion turns deadly when a man is discovered stabbed to death in the Theatre Royal. Adding to the mystery is an unusual object found on the victim's body—a pendant that contains a portrait of an eye! As Jane's fascination with scandal leads her deeper into the investigation, it becomes clear that she will not uncover the truth without some dangerous play-acting of her own. Associates: Lord Harold Trowbridge; Lady Desdemona, his niece; Jane's friend, Anne Lefroy; Cassandra; Henry and Eliza.

4. *Jane and the Genius of the Place: Being the Fourth Jane Austen Mystery.* New York: Bantam Books, 1999, 290 p.

CANTERBURY, ENGLAND, AUGUST 1805. In the waning days of summer, Jane Austen is off to the Canterbury Races, where the rich and fashionable gamble away their fortunes. It is an atmosphere ripe for scandal, but even Jane is unprepared for the shocking drama that unfolds. A flamboyant French beauty known for her brazen behavior is found gruesomely strangled in a shabby chaise. While many urge the arrest of a known scoundrel who had eyes for the victim, Jane looks further afield and finds a number of acquaintances behaving oddly. As rumors spread like wildfire that Napoléon's fleet is bound for Kent, Jane begins to suspect that the murder was an act of war rather than a crime of passion. Suddenly, the peaceful fields of Kent are a very dangerous place, and Jane's thirst for justice may exact the steepest price of all—her life. Associates: Cassandra; Edward "Neddie" Austen; Henry and "Lizzy" Austen; Anne Sharpe, governess to some of the Austen children; Lord Harold Trowbridge.

5. *Jane and the Stillroom Maid: Being the Fifth Jane Austen Mystery.* New York: Bantam Books, 2000, 277 p.

DERBYSHIRE, ENGLAND, AUGUST 1806. Jane Austen is enjoying Derbyshire's craggy peaks, sparkling streams, and cavernous gorges, that is, until she discovers the corpse of a young gentleman whose blond curls and delicate features suggest the face of an angel. More shocking still is the coroner's revelation: the deceased is no man at all, but a maidservant clad in the garb of her master, Mr. Charles Danforth of Penfolds Hall. Tess Arnold had ruled the stillroom at Penfolds for many years, until she was labeled a witch and dismissed for indiscretion. Was Tess the prey of a madman loose in the hills or perchance the cast-off impediment to a gentleman's marriage? As usual, Jane's acute perception and her nose for trouble place her supremely at risk, from a killer who may strike as violently by day as he once did by night. Associate: Lord Harold Trowbridge.

6. *Jane and the Prisoner of Wool House: Being the Sixth Jane Austen Mystery.* New York: Bantam Books, 2001, 291 p.

SOUTHAMPTON, ENGLAND, FEBRUARY 1807. On a raw winter morning, Jane Austen first learns of the case of Captain Tom Seagrave, who faces execution for a murder he swears he didn't commit. Together, she and her brother Frank, a post captain in the Royal Navy, set out to uncover the truth. It is a journey that leads from the troubled heart of Seagrave's family, through the seaport's worse sinkholes, and finally to the prison of Wool House. Risking contagion or worse, Jane comes away with more questions than answers. Did one of Seagrave's jealous colleagues frame the unpopular captain? Was a veiled political foe at work? And what of the sealed orders under which Seagrave embarked that fateful night on his ship, the *Stella Maris*? Then death surfaces again, and Jane must race to untangle the final knot, before she, too, is caught in a killer's embrace. Associates: Captain Frank Austen; Charles Austen; Eustace.

7. *Jane and the Ghosts of Netley: Being the Seventh Jane Austen Mystery.*
   New York: Bantam Books, 2003, 294 p.

SOUTHAMPTON, ENGLAND, OCTOBER 1808. Jane is visiting Netley Abbey in the company of her nephews, George and Edward Austen, whose mother has just died. She is approached by Orlando, a strange man in a cloak, who is acting for his master, Lord Harold. Harold's mother, the Duchess of Wilborough, has also just perished. Trowbridge works as an agent for the British government, and he asks Jane to assist him in watching Sophia Challoner, a spy for Napoléon, whom he thinks responsible for firing a British ship moored to the docks. Harold is accused of the murder of a local maidservant, and his aide, Orlando, promptly disappears. Jane must find the real killer to save her good friend, but by the time she does, the reader scarcely cares. This series has the feel of finally playing out, alas. Hokum and humbug! Associates: George and Edward Austen, sons of Jane's brother Edward; Frank Austen; Lord Harold Trowbridge; Henry and Eliza Austen; Orlando. Historical Figures: Marie Fitzherbert; George Prince of Wales, later British King George IV.

BOWEN, Rhys (pseud. of Janet Quin-Harkin) (1941–). British.

MOLLY MURPHY SERIES

Scene of the Crime: New York, New York, beginning in 1901.

Detective: Molly Murphy, an Irish immigrant, has a slim figure, red hair, and a ready temper. At the start of this series she is one week shy of her twenty-third birthday. She's always had a quick wit (her mother was sure it would get her in trouble). Molly was educated above her station when the landowner's wife took a liking to her. She solves her first case to help a friend, using dogged persistence and flashes of insight to find the truth and save him from being deported back to Ireland. In *Death of Riley* she manages to get work at P. Riley Investigations, but her boss is murdered before she learns much about detection. By *For the Love of Mike* Molly, as the only remaining employee of P. Riley Investigations, has taken over the firm.

Known Associates: Kathleen O'Connor helps Molly when the police are closing in; she asks Molly to assume her place and take her children, Seamus and Bridie, to their father in America. (Kathleen has just discovered that she has tuberculosis and thus will not clear the immigration office.) Molly meets Michael Larkin onboard the ship to America; he soon regards her as an older sister. She also meets Captain Daniel Sullivan at Ellis Island and forms a (possibly unfortunate) attachment to him. Seamus O'Connor meets her when she brings his children to him; he's been staying with his horrible relations, Nuala and Finbar. In *Death of Riley* Molly is apprenticed to an investigator, Paddy Riley, and moves to Greenwich Village to share a house with two young bluestockings, Gus and Sid. In *For the Love of Mike* Molly becomes involved with labor leader Jacob Singer.

Premise: A young Irish immigrant solves crimes in early-twentieth-century America.

Comment: Molly Murphy came to America's shores under an assumed name, on the lam for killing a rich landowner's son. She has great sympathy for those fleeing English oppression; when a young man she met aboard ship is accused of murder, she tries to convince the police to look elsewhere. She eventually uncovers the killer and decides to set herself up as an investigator. No one takes her seriously, but her persistence wins her a cleaning job at P. Riley Investigations. Riley shows her a little of the work, and she's hoping to be made his apprentice, when he is suddenly and brutally murdered. Once again, when she sees that the police have little interest in finding the culprit, she takes matters into her own hands. In the course of *Death of Riley*, she makes herself an associate in the firm of P. Riley Investigations, since she's the only employee left in the firm. *Murphy's Law* won the 2002 Agatha Award for Best Mystery Novel of the Year and the 2002 Herodotus Award for Best First U.S. Historical Mystery Novel. *Death of Riley* was a finalist for the 2003 Agatha Award for Best Mystery Novel. *For the Love of Mike* won the 2004 Bruce Alexander Historical Mystery Award and the 2004 Anthony for Best Historical Mystery. The rich backdrop of New York in the 1910s includes Tammany Hall politics, women's rights, and anarchy.

Literary Crimes & Chimes: These books convey a sense of a very different time and place, even though they are set in a world that features some modern trappings of technology. Electricity is a wonder to Molly, since it did not exist in the small village where she grew up. Skyscrapers are again a marvel to a small-town woman. The subway is being built, and the men who work on it feel that they are part of something new and great. The society of urban America in 1901 is a very different one from today; men who die while digging the subway tunnels leave no benefits to their families;

workers who are maimed on the job have no health care. Many of the immigrants regard America as the land of opportunity; they had no hope of a better life in the old country and believe that, with hard work, anything is possible in the United States. The inhabitants of Greenwich Village are throwing off the conventions of their parents. Molly is trying to get a job that would normally be held by a man. In many ways the entire society seems poised on a knife's edge between the Old World and the New.

THE CASES

1. *Murphy's Law: A Molly Murphy Mystery*. New York: St. Martin's Press, 2001, 226 p.

IRELAND, AND NEW YORK, NEW YORK, FEBRUARY 1901. Molly is accosted in her family's kitchen by the landowner's son, who tells her that he owns her as well as the land she lives on. He assaults her, and during the ensuing struggle he falls, striking his head and dying from his wound. Molly is forced to flee to avoid being hanged for his supposed murder. Another Irishwoman, one who knows the injustice of English law, helps Molly to escape to America. Onboard the ship Molly befriends a young man who becomes the chief suspect when another passenger is murdered at Ellis Island, New York. Molly investigates, trying to save him from being deported and handed over to English law. Associates: Michael; Captain Sullivan; Kathleen; Seamus; Bridie.

2. *Death of Riley*. New York: St. Martin's Minotaur, 2002, 275 p.

NEW YORK, NEW YORK, SEPTEMBER 1901. Through sheer determination Molly has gained a position as a cleaning lady with a detective agency; Molly hopes later to be made an apprentice to the owner, Paddy Riley. Then Riley is murdered, and Molly surprises the killer ransacking the office. When it becomes obvious that the police will not make much of an effort to find the killer, Molly takes on the investigation. Associates: Paddy; Miss Van Woekem; Ryan O'Hare; Lennie Coleman. Historical Figures: Emma Goldman; Leon Czolgosz.

3. *For the Love of Mike*. New York: St. Martin's Minotaur, 2003, 322 p.

NEW YORK, NEW YORK, OCTOBER 1901. Molly swears off criminal cases, deciding that she needs to take jobs that are less dangerous and more uplifting. She is hired to investigate the theft of certain designs from the house of a New York couturier and as part of the case begins doing piecework as a seamstress in various sweatshops. The horrible and dangerous working conditions are more than she can bear, and she becomes part of the labor movement, an activity that is more dangerous than she knows. Associates: Jacob Singer; Katherine Kelly (née Faversham); Rose Levy; Sadie Blum; Miss Van Woekem. Historical Figure: Samuel Clemens (Mark Twain).

BUCKLEY, Fiona (pseud. of Valerie May Florence Anand) (1937–). British.

URSULA BLANCHARD SERIES

Scene of the Crime: England, Scotland, and France, beginning in 1560.

Detective: At the outset of the series Ursula Blanchard is twenty-six years of age, with black hair, long hazel eyes, and a "shield shaped" face. Widowed with a young daughter, she is in desperate straits financially. Her husband, Gerald Blanchard, displeased his family by marrying her, and so Ursula and their daughter cannot go to them. She was never better than an unpaid servant to what is left of her own family. (Her mother was sent home from Court, pregnant and in disgrace, and after her mother's death Ursula was treated shamefully.) Ursula appeals to the Queen, who, for her own reasons, believes that Ursula will be a trustworthy ally and gives her a position as Lady of the Queen's Presence Chamber.

Known Associates: In *To Shield the Queen* Sir William Cecil, Queen Elizabeth's Secretary of State, becomes Ursula's friend and patron. He was Gerald's employer when Gerald acted as an agent for England; by the end of the first book he is employing Ursula in a similar capacity. To join the court Ursula must leave her daughter, Meg, in the care of Meg's nurse, Bridget Lemmon. The cost of Bridget's hire and of a cottage to house them consumes most of the wages Ursula garners from being a simple Lady of the Presence Chamber, so the extra money for tasks as Cecil's agent are most welcome. Ursula travels with her maidservant, Fran Dale, and hires Mr. Brockley as a manservant in *To Shield the Queen*. Fran and Mr. Brockley marry before the events recounted in *The Doublet Affair*. Gladys Morgan joins her household in *To Ruin a Queen*.

Premise: A woman solves crimes and acts as an agent in early Elizabethan England.

Comment: Queen Elizabeth I has a tenuous hold on the country. Her cousin, Mary, has proclaimed herself Queen of Scotland, England, and France, and English Catholics would prefer to see Mary on England's throne. Elizabeth knows the truth about Ursula's parentage and determines to trust her. Ursula gradually proves herself to be quick-thinking, brave, and determined. She has amazing political instincts and is good at hiding her reactions. Her fealty is absolute, but there are times when Ursula tries to return to private life and must be lured back into service. The author does an excellent job of portraying the political stakes, the societal pressures, and the religious divisions in England during the beginning of Elizabeth I's reign.

Ursula's memories of the horrors perpetrated by Mary, and the measured response Elizabeth has used with staunch Catholics, are both depicted honestly. The absolute expectation that women must marry is both implicit and explicit in these books. While the unusual strength and clarity of vision that Elizabeth brought to her rule comes through clearly, the Queen is always shown as a wholly believable individual. The relationship the monarch develops with Ursula allows the latter to become one of the few people who could glimpse moments of uncertainty and thus develop her own set of believable explanations for the strength of Elizabeth's character.

Literary Crimes & Chimes: This well-researched series focuses on the various tensions within Elizabethan England, which include the sometimes vicious byplay at court, with political intrigue and family matters vying with religious policy. At each level of society the themes play out, and the reader is shown through example how the decisions required of Elizabeth affected the daily lives of her subjects. The passion, determination, and at times, fanaticism of Catholic factions within the realm also are depicted extraordinarily well.

THE CASES

1. *The Robsart Mystery.* London: Orion, 1997, 278 p. As: *To Shield the Queen: A Mystery at Queen Elizabeth I's Court: Introducing Ursula Blanchard.* New York: Charles Scribner's Sons, 1997, 278 p.
ENGLAND, 1560. Lady Amy Dudley is gravely ill and expected to die; the political ramifications of her death are many. On the surface, her death will simply free her husband, Robin, to become Queen Elizabeth's consort; but her death might also lead to scandal, with the Queen (or Robin) suspected of murder. To forestall this possibility, Robin hires Ursula to act as a companion to his wife, to be her friend as well as a disinterested observer, and thus able to testify that Amy's illness (and eventual death) are due to entirely natural causes. Unfortunately, Ursula finds that the symptoms of Amy's "illness" sound suspiciously like poisoning. Associates: John Wilton; Aunt Tabitha; Uncle Hubert; Master Matthew de la Roche; Leonard Mason; Ann Mason. Historical Figures: Robin Dudley; Queen Elizabeth I; Sir William Cecil.
2. *The Doublet Affair.* London: Orion, 1998, 294 p.
ENGLAND, 1562. The final message of a murdered agent has put Cecil, Elizabeth I's Secretary of State, on the trail of traitors who would seize England's throne for Mary Stuart. The message implicates people known to Ursula, people she protected in the aftermath of her first case. Cecil convinces Ursula to trade on her friendship and visit these individuals to gather information, either to clear their names or to get to the bottom of their traitorous plot. Associates: Rob Henderson; Master Matthew de la Roche as

Mark Lenoir; Father Ignatius Wilkins; Leonard Mason; Ann Mason. Historical Figures: Sir William Cecil; Queen Elizabeth I.

3. *Queen's Ransom: An Ursula Blanchard Mystery at Queen Elizabeth I's Court.* New York: Charles Scribner's Sons, 2000, 348 p.

ENGLAND, 1562–1564. With France on the brink of a civil war between the Protestants and the Catholics, Ursula is sent on a journey that combines a mission of mercy with one of intrigue. She must help her father-in-law rescue a young woman and bring her back to England, and she must deliver a secret message from the Protestant Queen Elizabeth I to the Catholic Catherine de Médicis, Queen of France. Associates: Master Luke Blanchard; Helene; Master Matthew de la Roche; Father Ignatius Wilkins; Master Anthony Jenkinson. Historical Figures: Queen Elizabeth I, Sir William Cecil.

4. *To Ruin a Queen: An Ursula Blanchard Mystery at Queen Elizabeth I's Court.* New York: Charles Scribner's Sons, 2000, 287 p.

ENGLAND AND FRANCE, 1564. Philip Mortimer has been hinting that he has within his power the ability to blackmail Queen Elizabeth I into offering him both lands and offices. The Queen offers Ursula the estate of Withysham Abbey if she will spend just two weeks evaluating this threat to the throne. In the course of her investigation Ursula encounters young lovers (and decides that a life of the mind would suit her well), ghosts (and connives at impersonating one), and a witch (who becomes part of Ursula's household). Associates: Master Matthew de la Roche; Rob Henderson. Historical Figures: Elizabeth I of England; Sir William Cecil.

5. *Queen of Ambition: An Ursula Blanchard Mystery at Queen Elizabeth I's Court.* New York: Charles Scribner's Sons, 2002, 286 p.

ENGLAND, 1564. Ursula is commanded to accompany an advance party of official harbingers to Cambridge, where they are making ready for the Queen's progress. Sir William Cecil is concerned that there is more behind the plans for some staged horseplay than has been revealed. When one of the students involved meets with an odd accident, Ursula begins to believe that Cecil was right. Associates: Rob Henderson; Sybil Jester. Historical Figures: Sir William Cecil; Queen Elizabeth I.

6. *A Pawn for a Queen: An Ursula Blanchard Mystery at Queen Elizabeth I's Court.* New York: Charles Scribner's Sons, 2002, 279 p.

ENGLAND AND SCOTLAND, JANUARY 1565. Ursula's cousin Edward had continued to act as Mary Stuart's agent, unbeknownst to Ursula. When he disappears while conveying a list of her English supporters, his family tells Ursula everything; for the sake of his pregnant wife, Ursula goes after him on horseback. Ursula traces his steps while posing as a supporter of Mary, being believed because her dead husband, Matthew, was known as one of Mary's agents. She finds Edward dead and must search Mary's court for his killer out of loyalty to her own family and to her Queen. Associates: Uncle Herbert; Aunt Tabitha; Helene; Hugh Stannard; Master John and Mistress Euphemia Thursby; Master and Mistress Bycroft; Sir Brian Dormbois; Rob Henderson. Historical Figures: Mary Stuart, Queen of Scots; Henry, Lord Darnley; James Hepburn, Earl of Bothwell; Master Knox.

7. *The Fugitive Queen: An Ursula Blanchard Mystery at Queen Elizabeth I's Court.* New York: Charles Scribner's Sons, 2003, 277 p.

ENGLAND, 1568. Ursula is sent with her husband, her daughter, and her ward (Penelope Mason) ostensibly to inspect a property that Robin Dudley has offered to provide as dowry for Penelope; her clandestine mission is to deliver a message from Queen Elizabeth to the captive Queen Mary. Ursula well knows that plots swirl around Mary, but she cannot deny Queen Elizabeth, and so she goes forward into danger, murder, and treachery. Associates: Ann Mason; Penelope Mason; Sybil Jester. Historical Figures: Robin Dudley; Queen Elizabeth I; Mary, Queen of Scots.

8. *The Siren Queen: An Ursula Blanchard Mystery at Queen Elizabeth I's Court.* New York: Charles Scribner's Sons, 2004, 288 p.

LONDON, ENGLAND, 1568. Ursula uncovers a plot linking the Duke of Norfolk with Mary Queen of Scots, who covets the British throne of her cousin, Queen Elizabeth I. When the messenger is found murdered, and the bodies begin piling up, Ursula is drawn to an Italian banker, Roberto Ridolfi, who is apparently acting as a middleman in the conspiracy. Ursula, acting on behalf of the British government, must help defuse the situation before the English nobles take matters into their own hands. Associates: Meg; Gladys. Historical Figures: Lord Cecil; Mary, Queen of Scots; Robert Ridolfi; Duke of Norfolk.

CARR, Caleb (1955–). American.

THE ALIENIST SERIES

Scene of the Crime: New York, New York, beginning in 1896.

Detective: Doctor Laszlo Kreizler, an alienist specializing in the analysis of the criminal psyche, and head of the Kreizler Institute for Children.

Known Associates: Theodore Roosevelt, President of the Board of Commissioners of the New York City Police Department, later Governor of New York, later President of the United States; Stevie Taggert, Kreizler's young ward, whom he saved from physical and psychological abuse, and narrator of *The Angel of Darkness*; Sara Howard, Secretary to Commissioner Roosevelt; John Schuyler Moore, reporter for the *New York Times* and narrator of *The Alienist*; Cyrus Montrose, Kreizler's driver; New York Police Detective Sergeants (and brothers) Lucius and Marcus Isaacson.

Premise: An alienist puts his theories of criminal psychology to the test in Gay Nineties New York.

Comment: The initial premise for *The Alienist* is superb: the first application of the science of criminal psychology to tracking a brutal serial killer. Carr gets the historical details of New York City in the Gay Nineties just right, and his characters are all fully fleshed out. Doctor Kreizler is an eccentric, but brilliant, practitioner, who attempts in real life to help young children who have been traumatized by physical or psychological abuse. Appropriately, the slayings in this novel are all focused on young boys, most of whom have been sexually molested before attaining their horrible fates. The "I was there," first-person recitation of John Schuyler Moore, the newspaper reporter, lends exactly the right touch of both distance and immediacy to the hunt for the killer. The second book in the sequence, *The Angel of Darkness*, is set a year after the first and is told by Stevie Taggert, one of the junior characters in the first novel, after he has grown into an adult, from the persective of 1919. But the voice here is far less compelling than in the first novel, and the story as whole seems a mere shadow of the original.

Literary Crimes & Chimes: It's clear that the author found one really good idea in *The Alienist* and felt obliged by market realities to follow the initial novel with a second offering that is not nearly as well thought out or conceived or executed. Stevie has lost all of his charm, and so has the scribbling of the writer's pen. The rooftop *dénouement* is utterly ridiculous. Forget that *The Angel of Darkness* even exists and reread *The Alienist* instead.

THE CASES

1. *The Alienist.* New York: Random House, 1994, 496 p.
NEW YORK, NEW YORK, MARCH 1896 (the frame is dated January 1919). A serial killer is murdering young men and boys in New York City, carving each up like butchered animals. The police are thoroughly baffled, so Commissioner Theodore Roosevelt, who has already been sweeping corrupt officers out of the Police Force by the dozens, enlists Dr. Kreizler and his radical new ideas of psychoanalysis to find and stop the brutal murderer. Together with the narrator, John Moore, and their small group of friends, they pursue the killer through the slums of New York and finally bring the monster to justice. A superior work of historical detection in every respect. Associates: Kreizler; Stevie; Sara; John (the narrator); Cyrus; Lucius; Marcus. Historical Figure: Theodore Roosevelt.

2. *The Angel of Darkness.* New York: Random House, 1997, 629 p.
NEW YORK, NEW YORK, JUNE 1897 (the frame is dated June 1919). The fourteen-month-old daughter of the private secretary to the Spanish consul in New York is abducted, but Señor Narciso Linares refuses to take action. His wife, Isabella, has seen the girl in the company of a white woman and begs Sara (now head of the Howard Agency: Research Services for Women) and Kreizler to take action to recover her child. Their investigation finally uncovers a series of child abductions and killings, apparently perpetrated by the same individual. Both Darrow and Roosevelt (now Assistant Secretary of the Navy) become involved as the case progresses. In the end, the murderer is cornered on a New York rooftop but refuses to surrender. The way the killer is brought to justice is a real pain in the neck! Associates: Stevie Taggert (the narrator); Sara; John; Kreizler; Lucius; Marcus; Cyrus. Historical Figures: Clarence Darrow; Theodore Roosevelt.

CARR, John Dickson (1906–1977). American.

MISCELLANEOUS SERIES

Scene of the Crime: Various.

Detective: Various.

Known Associates: Various.

Premise: Various.

Comment: Carr was one of the first mystery writers to employ historical settings in his books, and he did so with great skill and imagination, thus helping to popularize the incipient genre. Some of his novels, such as *The Devil in Velvet* and *Fire, Burn!*, are actually time-travel fantasies in which the detective journeys from a contemporary setting into the past (and back again), usually without explanation, and so are not covered here. The books listed below are arranged in chronological order by date of setting.

Literary Crimes & Chimes: At his best, Carr is exceptional at evoking the feel of British life of an earlier era. His books are filled with humor, pathos, and well-crafted plots, often revolving around closed-door or other classic puzzle scenarios. The author has clearly done his research; most of his books feature four or five pages of commentary at the end of the novel indicating his primary sources, the actual events into which the plot is linked, and some background information on the historical figures mentioned in the narratives. However, Carr also has a tendency to play so much with the reader's sensibilities, to have so much fun on the page, that his fictions, particularly the later books, deteriorate into frothy pabulum that make little sense either as stories or as mysteries. Typical of these is his final novel, *The Hungry Goblin*, written when he was already seriously ill. Still, most of these works are entertaining at the least and well worth the reader's attention, even today. The historical mysteries penned by Carr have dated very little, unlike his many contemporary detective novels. Also, unlike the writer's more modern works, the historicals were never series-driven but always independent one-shots. This makes them somewhat more believable and ultimately much more fun.

THE CASES

1. *Devil Kinsmere*, as "Roger Fairbairn." New York: Harper & Brothers, 1934, 319 p. Rewritten as: *Most Secret*, as "Roger Fairbairn." New York: Harper & Row, 1964, 235 p. As: *Most Secret*, as "John Dickson Carr." London: Hamish Hamilton, 1964, 283 p.

ENGLAND, MAY 1670. Roderick "Rowdy" Kinsmere, the son of a deceased cavalier, comes to London to claim his mother's inheritance from the banker to whom it has been entrusted, Roger Stainley. His father's fortune had been lost to Cromwell, and the young man's only legacy a beautiful blue ring given to old Kinsmere by the first King Charles. Rowdy quickly is swept up in a conspiracy against King Charles II; he and Bygones Abraham capture one of the conspirators, Captain Pembroke Harker, who is promptly murdered before he can reveal any details of the plot. The King then delegates Rowdy and Bygones to carry the halves of a secret treaty document to King Louis XIV of France. Rowdy is captured at Dover by Salvation Gaines, another conspirator, and it appears that all is lost. But the King is more wily than any of the plodding plotters, and two British warships are waiting in the English Channel to sweep up the lot. The treaty is delivered, and all is right once again. The author's first historical mystery is rather windy and plodding at times. Historical Figure: King Charles II.

2. Captain Cut-Throat. New York: Harper & Brothers, 1955, 306 p.

PARIS, FRANCE, AUGUST 1805. A serial killer is wreaking havoc among the Emperor Napoléon's Grande Armée. Five times he has struck in the night, stabbing each victim through the heart. He signs his murders "Captain Cut-Throat," and all the evidence suggests that he is English. The encampment is demoralized and on the verge of panic. Minister of Police Joseph Fouché is ordered to solve the killings and stop the rampage. He decides to set a spy to catch a spy, in the person of an Englishman named Alan Hepburn, who has recently been captured by the French. Hepburn has just one chance to stay alive: find and capture Captain Cut-Throat within five days, or face the firing squad himself! Historical Figure: Joseph Fouché, Duc d'Orante.

3. The Demoniacs. New York: Harper & Row, 1962, 238 p.

LONDON, ENGLAND, SEPTEMBER 1757. The houses that have lined London Bridge for hundreds of years are scheduled to be demolished in a few days. There Jeffrey Wynne, a so-called thief-taker (self-employed policeman), discovers the recently murdered body of a woman who had once been fancied by Wynne's grandfather and on whom he had bestowed a fortune in jewels. Wynne has been hired to escort Margaret "Peg" Ralston, a former paramour, back to her "uncle," Sir Mortimer Ralston, but the wayward and headstrong lady flees the scene, and the baronet issues a warrant for her arrest through Sir John Fielding, the blind magistrate of the Bow Street Court. Peg is caught and jailed in Newgate Prison but escapes her captivity again. What is the link between Margaret and the murdered woman? Can true love finally find its course? The portrait here of Sir John Fielding as a scheming, devious manipulator of both friend and foe alike provides an interesting contrast with the image created by Bruce Alexander in his history mystery series (*q.v.*). Historical Figures: Justice Sir John Fielding; writer Laurence Sterne.

4. *The Bride of Newgate.* New York: Harper & Brothers, 1950, 308 p.

LONDON, ENGLAND, JUNE 1815. Dick Darwent has been wrongly condemned to death for a murder that he didn't commit and is scheduled to be hanged at Newgate Prison. Across the street, the heiress Caroline Ross is plotting with her attorney to take advantage of the situation. Her grandfather's will specifies that she will inherit her fortune on her twenty-fourth birthday (several months hence), but only if she has been legally married by that time. The only exception allowed is a state of natural widowhood. She proposes to marry the condemned man, knowing that he will be executed shortly thereafter. Dick agrees to do the deed to provide a small amount of money for his beloved Dolly, a common actress. Then comes the news of Waterloo, and suddenly Darwent is a Marquess, his sentence automatically being rendered invalid. Dick sets out to find the villains who kidnapped and framed him for the crime and simultaneously must deal with his beautiful, but coldhearted, new wife. One of the author's best books, featuring a great premise and an action-filled plot. Historical Figures: Reverend Horace Cotton; Beau Brummell; Lord Alvanley.

5. *Scandal at High Chimneys: A Victorian Melodrama.* New York: Harper & Brothers, 1959, 230 p.

LONDON AND BERKSHIRE, ENGLAND, OCTOBER 1865. Clive Strickland, a writer of popular magazine mystery serials, is beseeched by his friend Victor Damon to carry a proposal of marriage on behalf of Lord Albert "Tress" Tressider to Victor's sister, Celia, at their country home, High Chimneys. Victor's father, Matthew Damon, has become increasingly moody of late, and Victor wishes to facilitate the exit from their estate of both Celia and her younger sister, Kate, both now of marriageable age. But when Clive approaches the elder Damon, Matthew indicates that he has uncovered a dread secret about his family. He's on the verge of telling the writer when he's shot dead in front of Strickland's eyes. The local police can make nothing of the crime, so retired Inspector Whicher is brought in to assess the case. Meanwhile, Clive is becoming increasingly involved with the pretty, dark-haired girl, Kate, and he begins to worry that she might have been a bastard child of her father or that either he or Kate might be accused by the county constabulary of the murder. It takes all of Whicher's perceptive insight to unravel the tangle. Historical Figure: former Police Inspector Jonathan Whicher.

6. *The Hungry Goblin: A Victorian Detective Novel.* New York: Harper & Row, 1972, 290 p.

LONDON, AND ELSEWHERE IN ENGLAND, OCTOBER 1869. Christopher "Kit" Farrell, foreign correspondent in America for the *London Evening Clarion*, has come home for the first time in nine years. Meeting him is his old friend, Nigel "Nige" Seagrave, whose country estate, Udolpho, had been named for the old Gothic novel character. Kit also encounters a former girlfriend, Patricia "Pat" Denbigh. Nigel, a famous African explorer whose recent expedition nearly proved to be his last, has a strange tale to tell: since returning home, he's come to believe that his beautiful wife, Muriel, is an impostor. Little things about her just don't add up. He asks the reluctant Kit to visit the manor and judge for himself. But scarcely has Farrell arrived when Nigel is shot by an unseen assailant. After meeting Muriel, Kit agrees with Nigel that she doesn't seem to have the encyclopedic knowledge of English literature that the real Muriel possessed. But if she's a substitute, to what end?—and what has happened to Seagrave's real wife? Mystery writer Wilkie Collins assists in elucidating the mystery. The author's last book is a bit of a muddle, although entertaining enough if the reader can find some way to leave his or her eyes wide shut. Historical Figures: Wilkie Collins; Colonel Sir Edmund Henderson.

7. *The Witch of the Low-Tide: An Edwardian Melodrama.* New York: Harper & Brothers, 1961, 215 p.

LONDON AND FAIRFIELD-ON-SEA, ENGLAND, JUNE 1907. Doctor David Garth, a specialist in the budding science of neurology (psychology), is enamored of the beautiful Lady Betty Calder, widow of the elderly Governor of Jamaica. But when Betty's scheming lowlife sister, Glynis, is found strangled in a beach hut, Betty immediately becomes the prime suspect, with Garth fingered as her chief assistant. David is frantic to find a way out of his conundrum, but at every turn he seems thwarted by the efforts of Detective-Inspector Twigg, who hates everything that the upper-class physician stands for. Only the uncovering of the real culprit can save the day, before Betty and David are arrested and charged for the crime. Carr tried to mix the nascent science of psychology into a drawing-room-style mystery, but everything here is old hat, and a rather worn old hat at that. One to skip.

8. *The Ghosts' High Noon: A Detective Novel.* New York: Harper & Row, 1969, 255 p.

NEW ORLEANS, OCTOBER 1912. Jim Blake, a successful journalist for *Harper's Weekly* and a best-selling novelist, is sent on assignment to New Orleans to cover the congressional campaign of another James Blake (called "Clay"). Both Blakes become involved in the intrigue of Louisiana politics, and when sexual indiscretion, a phantom Clay Blake, and murder are added

of that corruption is frighteningly believable, and the measures that he takes against it are realistically slow and painful and sometimes surprisingly amusing. The knowledge that many of the schemes outlined in the books were, at one time or another, crimes that actually took place along the borders adds to the reader's enjoyment.

THE CASES

1. *A Famine of Horses: A Sir Robert Carey Mystery.* New York: Walker and Co., 1995, 270 p.

CARLISLE, ENGLAND, JUNE 1592. Sir Robert Carey takes up his command and finds his posting in disarray. One of his Captains works more for the reivers than for the Queen, the stores of gunpowder and weapons are missing, and the Warden is so anxious to avoid trouble that he has practically abdicated his authority. Into all of this, the killing of Jock of the Peartree's favorite son will inevitably set off a bloodbath. Associates: Daniel Swanders; Jock of the Peartree.

2. *A Season of Knives: A Sir Robert Carey Mystery.* New York: Walker and Co., 1996, 231 p.

CARLISLE, ENGLAND, JULY 1592. When Jemmy Atkinson, the corrupt paymaster that Carey had dismissed, is murdered, his wife knows she will be suspected of petty treason and could be burned at the stake; her only hope is that she knows justice is for sale at a price she can afford. Unfortunately, a search for other likely culprits turns up Carey himself! Associates: Sergeant Nixon; Archibald Bell; Aglionby.

3. *A Surfeit of Guns: A Sir Robert Carey Mystery.* New York: Walker and Co., 1997, 234 p.

ENGLAND AND SCOTLAND, JULY 1592. While on night patrol one of Carey's company is badly hurt by a misfiring gun; further investigation proves that a good many fine weapons have been replaced with firearms of such poor quality that they are more likely to maim the hunter than the prey. When those weapons go missing as well, Carey is sent forth to search for all the missing guns, with the dubious comfort of knowing that when he finds the thieves, they will be armed to the teeth. Associates: Emilia Bonnetti; Giovanni Bonnetti; Sir Henry Widdrington; Roger Widdrington. Historical Figures: Scottish King James VI; Sir John Carmichael; Lord Maxwell; Lord Spynie.

4. *A Plague of Angels: A Sir Robert Carey Mystery.* Scottsdale, AZ: Poisoned Pen Press, 2000, 252 p.

LONDON, ENGLAND, AUGUST 1592. Carey's father summons him and Dodd to London to account for themselves. Reports have been sent forward by Richard Lowther, who hates Carey, which have included accusations against them. London abounds with other problems, from a missing brother to a family infected with plague, from creditors to murderers. Associate: Mistress Bassano. Historical Figures: Lord Hunsdon; Vice-Chamberlain Heneage; William Shakespeare; Greene; Christopher Marlowe.

CHRISTIE, Agatha (Mary Clarissa) (1890–1973). British.

RENISENB SERIES

Scene of the Crime: Ancient Egypt, circa 2000 BC.

Detective: Renisenb, a young widow and the daughter of Imhotep, a mortuary priest and major plantation owner.

Known Associates: Hori, Imhotep's handsome steward; Esa, Imhotep's elderly mother.

Premise: Following the death of her husband, Renisenb returns home to the sanctuary of her father's estate, where her innocence is suddenly shattered by a series of brutal murders. In the limited universe of plantation life, one of the family or their servants must be the killer—but which one? The puzzle deepens as all the usual suspects themselves become victims.

Comment: Christie, the wife of the well-known archeologist, Sir Max Mallowan, accompanied her husband on a number of his expeditions to the Middle East during the 1930s and later used her experiences as the basis for several mysteries employing the backdrop of Mesopotamia and Egypt. *Death Comes as the End* was her only novel, however, actually to be set in the ancient world. Although not wholly successful in its premise and not Christie's most popular work, the book's importance as a precursor fiction penned by a best-selling mystery writer cannot be overstated. More than any other crime novel of its period, this book states unequivocally that literary murder can be committed—and solved—at any time and in any place.

Literary Crimes & Chimes: Christie employs the device of the universally hated character—Nofret, the new and pretty young concubine of Imhotep—as well as the psychological stress and strain of a family group of strong-minded women and weak-willed men forced to live together for long periods of time in unnaturally close quarters, in order to generate numerous suspects for the killer. Renisenb does not act as a traditional detective, but as the rather naïve member of the society into which she was born. Gradually, as the story unfolds, she becomes aware that not everyone around her is telling the truth. Together with her friend and confidant Hori, she uncovers the reasons behind the series of murders and finds surcease and justice at the end. Christie is faithful to the Egyptian society of the period, but the pettiness and close-mindedness of the ensemble ultimately become rather wearisome.

THE CASE

1. ***Death Comes as the End.*** New York: Dodd, Mead, 1944, 223 p.
   EGYPT, CIRCA 2000 BC. See commentary in this series.

CLEVERLY, Barbara. British.

<u>JOSEPH SANDILANDS SERIES</u>

Scene of the Crime: India, 1922.

Detective: Commander Joseph Sandilands, awarded the Distinguished Service Order (DSO), Royal Scots Fusiliers, ex-Military Intelligence, now of Scotland Yard.

Known Associates: Sir George Jardine, Acting Governor of Bengal.

Premise: Scotland Yard Detective on temporary assignment to India finds himself co-opted by the Acting Governor of Bengal, Sir George Jardine.

Comment: These books are especially fascinating when they explore the Indian way of life. Concepts such as *Pukhtunwali* (the Pathan code of honor) that demands that an insult be avenged even to the third and fourth generation; and *Melmastia* (the Pathan code of hospitality) that demands that a host offer everything from food to absolute protection give the reader windows into different culture. Mrs. Cleverly ascribes her fascination for the setting to bundles of photographs, journals and other mementos of her husband's great uncle, which she and her husband found in an old tin trunk in their attic. Brigadier Harold Sandilands had been General Office Commanding in Peshawar on the North West Frontier. He'd made friends with local tribesmen and had moved among the warlike Afridi tribe. This man was the inspiration for Commander Joe Sandilands.

Literary Crimes & Chimes: Each book begins with a scene that precedes Commander Sandilands' involvement in the case. This technique gives the reader an edge in solving the mystery and makes the progress of the investigation easier to follow. Joseph Sandilands doggedly unravels each case in a logical manner spiced with flashes of empathy-inspired insight. At times he sets traps for the person he knows is guilty, because at times that would be the only way to gain enough proof to bring charges. All the cases take place in 1922, *Ragtime in Simla* creates a sort of frame around the action of the last two books in the series, since the main action of *Ragtime in Simla*'s plot is set before those books, in Spring of 1922, while the last chapter involves Joe leaving India in Summer of 1922. *The Damascened Blade* won the 2004 Ellis Peters Historical Dagger, given by the Crime Writers' Association.

THE CASES

1. ***The Last Kashmiri Rose: Murder and Mystery in the Final Days of the Raj.*** New York: Carroll & Graf Publishers, 2001, 288 p.

PANIKHAT, CALCUTTA, AND LASRA KOT, INDIA, 1922 (includes flashback to Panikhat in 1910). The wives of the Bengal Grey's regiment have been dying, murdered. Five women have died; they've all died in March, but in different years. The regiment's wives have figured out the pattern but they cannot get officials to listen. Then the niece of Sir George Jardine asks her uncle for help and Joe Sandilands is assigned to the case. Joe agrees that they have identified a pattern; he just has to find out who has the motive, the means, and the opportunities to capture a ruthless murderer before the next woman is killed. Associates: Naurung Singh; Nancy Drummond; Andrew Drummond, her husband; Police Superintendent Bulstrode; Kitty, Mrs. Kitson-Masters; Major Prentice; Midge Prentice.

2. ***Ragtime in Simla.*** New York: Carroll & Graf, 2003, 287 p.

SIMLA, 1922 (includes flashback to Paris in 1919). Commander Sandilands was fascinated by the world of Simla depicted in Kipling's *Kim* and is anxious to visit and play tourist. He offers a ride to an affable fellow traveler, Feodor Korsovsky, and is stunned when the man is gunned-down before his eyes. Sir George Jardine, Joe's host, asks him to get to the bottom of the murder and Joe finds himself embroiled in a case involving everything from a woman scorned to gunrunning to a Lazarus who rose from the dead. It takes assistance from those in the world of the living, those who have crossed over, and those who are in between to get to the bottom of the case. Associates: Police Superintendent Charlie Carter; Alice Conyers; Reggie Sharpe; Rheza Khan; Marie-Jeanne Pitiot; Maisie Freeman; Madame Flora; Edgar Troop; Isobel Newton; Captain Colin Simpson.

3. ***The Damascened Blade.*** New York: Carroll & Graf, 2004, 287 p.

PESHAWAR, 1922 (includes flashback to the North West Frontier in 1910). Commander Sandilands travels to the front line fort of Gor Khatri to visit an old army buddy, James Lindsay. The relative peace of the fort is destroyed when the military orders Lindsay to play host to a group of visitors. It is a motley collection including a Pathan prince, a rich American girl, the chairman of the West India Trading Company, and a doctor who has devoted her life to helping the people of India. When the Pathan prince is killed, it is up to Joe to find the murderer. Pathan law demands a life for a life, and a friend of the Prince has taken hostages to ensure that the killer will be turned over to the Pathans, Joe must not only find the murderer, but also secure the safety of the hostages. Associates: Major James Lindsay; Betty Lindsay; Minto; Lily Coblenz; Lady Holland; Edward Dalrymple-Webster; Nick Carstairs; Police Superintendent Charlie Carter; Sir Edwin Burroughs; Dr. Grace Holbrook; Lord Rathmore; Fred Moore-Simpson; Zeman Khan; Muhammed Iskander Khan.

4. *The Palace Tiger.* London: Constable, 2004, 304 p.

RANIPUR, 1922. Something is stalking the people of Ranipur, a tiger that has developed a taste for human flesh. Something more human, but no less dangerous, is stalking the royal house of Ranipur. When the oldest prince is killed, Sir George Jardine sends Commander Sandilands to investigate and report. Joe cannot make an arrest, he has no authority to do so in Maharaja Udai Singh's kingdom; he does not legally even have the right to investigate. When the second prince is killed Claude Vyvyan, Britain's man in Ranipur's palace, asks Joe to hunt a murderer. Associates: Edgar Troop; Maharaja Udai Singh of the Principality of Ranipur; Prithvi Singh, Udai's second son; Madeleine, Prithvi's wife; Captain Stuart Mercer, Madeleine's brother; Bahadur Singh, Udai's third son; Zalim Singh, Udai's brother; Claude Vyvyan, British Resident; Lois Vyvyan, his wife; Colin O'Connor; Lizzie Macarthur; Shubhada, Udai's third wife; Sir Hector Munro.

COLLINS, Max Allan (1948–). American.

NATHAN HELLER SERIES

Scene of the Crime: Chicago, Illinois, beginning in 1932 and continuing into the 1960s.

Detective: Nathan "Nate" Samuel Heller (born 1905), formerly a Chicago policeman, later (from *True Detective*) a private investigator and owner of the A-1 Detective Agency; he was twice married, had one son, Nathan Jr., and eventually retired to Boca Raton, Florida, by 1970. He was still living there as late as 1992 (*Blood and Thunder*).

Known Associates: Many historical figures living in Chicago and elsewhere during the Great Depression, including politicians, police, federal officials, and gangsters; Barney Ross, Heller's friend and first landlord.

Premise: A private investigator rights wrongs and solves crimes in depression-era Chicago.

Comment: This is the real thing, a series of gritty private-eye tales told in an "I was there" style, intersprinkled with real-life events, locales, and individuals. Collins has clearly done his research: the settings are meticulously correct to their time and place, and the actions and motivations of his hero correspondingly true-to-life. Not many characters, real or imagined, escape the unvarnished, jaundiced scrutiny of Collins' pen. The corruption inherent in American life is exposed for all to see, and sometimes the gangsters seem more honorable than the politicians and crooked cops. There's also plenty of action in these books, enough blood and guts to satisfy the most jaded of readers. Most of the novels have tailpieces providing background information on the real-life history of the events being described, plus biographical data on the historical characters encountered. Two of the books in the series won Shamus Awards as best private-eye novels of the year.

Literary Crimes & Chimes: When all's said and done, these are basically "gimmick" novels, centered around real-life events and real-life characters, and they work only as well as the reader allows them to in his or her own imagination, in comparing the actual historical accounts of crimes and criminals and the movers and shakers of society with the writer's depictions of same. This absence of artistic freedom is less noticeable in the early books in the series, but it tends to become a bit wearisome after two or three novels. How many of these major events and personages and crimes could Heller actually have influenced? The author requires a suspension of disbelief that at times borders on fantasy, solving the Lindbergh kidnapping and murder, the disappearance of Amelia Earhart, and the Roswell unidentified flying object (UFO) scare, among others. You betcha! Make no mistake: the plotting here is superb, the characters well drawn. But there's something amiss in Chicagoland, an absence of freshness and vitality that marks great fiction. And that's a pity indeed, because the writer clearly has the talent to do much better.

THE CASES

1. *Stolen Away: A Novel of the Lindbergh Kidnapping.* New York: Bantam Books, 1991, 514 p.

    CHICAGO, ILLINOIS, AND NEW JERSEY, MARCH–APRIL 1932, MARCH–APRIL 1936. Policeman Nathan Heller is made liaison between the Chicago Police Department and the New Jersey State Police during their 1932 investigation of the kidnapping and murder of aviator Charles Lindbergh's young son. The combined efforts of the law enforcement agencies, while resulting in the capture, trial, and sentencing of the supposed killer, Bruno Hauptmann, result in a terrible tragedy for the Lindbergh family. But Nate has not been satisfied with the investigation, and four years later, when asked by the Governor of New Jersey to do a pre-execution examination of the facts, he comes to believe that the Lindbergh child might still be alive. Can he find the boy before Hauptmann is executed for a crime that he may not have committed? Historical Figures: Charles Lindbergh; Anne Lindbergh; Eliot Ness; Al Capone; Bruno Hauptmann; Frank Nitti; New Jersey Governor Harold Hoffman; Elmer Irey; Frank J. Wilson. Winner of the Shamus Award for best private detective novel of the year.

2. *Damned in Paradise: A Nathan Heller Novel.* New York: A Dutton Book, 1996, 308 p.

HONOLULU, HAWAII, APRIL–MAY 1932. Heller is asked by Clarence Darrow to investigate the abduction and rape of Thalia Massie in Hawaii and so takes a leave of absence from the Chicago Police Department. Massie, the wife of a Naval Lieutenant, has accused five natives of the crime, but Heller begins to doubt certain aspects of her story as he investigates her past. In the end, he puts together enough pieces of the truth to paint a very different picture of the injured woman than the one presented by her to the court. Historical Figures: Clarence Darrow, Thalia Massie.

3. *True Detective.* New York: St. Martin's Press, 1983, 358 p.

CHICAGO, ILLINOIS, AND MIAMI, FLORIDA, DECEMBER 1932–SEPTEMBER 1933. Chicago cop Nathan Heller is forced to participate in the illegal shooting of gangster Frank Nitti and throws down his badge in protest, before setting himself up as a private investigator. His first client is the imprisoned boss of bosses, Al Capone, who wants Nate to save the worthless life of corrupt Chicago mayor Anton Cermak. Heller fails to prevent Cermak from being assassinated in Miami while the latter is visiting President-elect Roosevelt. Upon his return to the Windy City, Nate becomes involved in locating the long-vanished brother of his new girlfriend and finds himself enmeshed once again in gangland and real-life politics. The first novel written in the Heller sequence. Associate: Barney. Historical Figures: Eliot Ness; Frank Nitti; Al Capone; Mayor Anton Cermak; Ronald "Dutch" Reagan; former Vice President Charles Dawes; Walter Winchell; George Raft; President-elect Franklin D. Roosevelt. Winner of the Shamus Award for best private detective novel of the year.

4. *True Crime.* New York: St. Martin's Press, 1984, 357 p.

CHICAGO, ILLINOIS, JULY–SEPTEMBER 1934. Heller finds himself facing gangsters Ma Barker, Baby Face Nelson, and John Dillinger—if the latter was really the man who was shot down by the Federal Bureau of Investigation (FBI) in the alleyway next to the Biograph Theater. Heller's search for the truth of Dillinger's supposed passing leads him into a confrontation with J. Edgar Hoover himself, but not before the streets of Chicago run red with gangster blood. Associate: Barney. Historical Figures: Ma Barker; Baby Face Nelson; John Dillinger; J. Edgar Hoover; Sally Rand; Melvin Purvis.

5. *Blood and Thunder: A Nathan Heller Novel.* New York: Dutton, 1995, 320 p.

OKLAHOMA CITY, OKLAHOMA, NEW YORK, NEW YORK, BATON ROUGE AND NEW ORLEANS, LOUISIANA, AUGUST–SEPTEMBER 1935, OCTOBER– NOVEMBER 1936. Heller has been hired by Senator Huey P. Long's trusted adviser to present the politician with a bulletproof vest. Long's enemies are legion, the threats against his life too numerous to count, but Huey refuses to wear the bulky garment. Nate then does his best to save his client, but the Senator is murdered anyway by physician Carl Weiss. A year after the fact, Long's widow Rose hires the detective to investigate the circumstances of her husband's death, hoping to collect some extra insurance money. The policy contained a clause voiding any supplemental payments if he was murdered. On the other hand, if the fusillade launched by Long's guards against his assassin actually killed the Senator—accidentally, so to speak—then his widow can collect a very tidy sum. As usual, the deeper that Nate digs, the more humid the environment becomes—filled with corruption, dirty politics, and mixed motives. Historical Figures: Huey Long; Dr. Carl Weiss; Earl Long; Seymour Weiss.

6. *Flying Blind: A Novel of Amelia Earhart.* New York: Dutton, 1998, 343 p.

CHICAGO, ILLINOIS, AND SAIPAN, MARCH–MAY 1935, MARCH–JULY 1937, MAY–JUNE 1940 (the Prologue is dated February 1970, the Epilogue March 1970). In 1970 a stranger approaches Nathan Heller, now living semiretired in Boca Raton, Florida. He wants the detective to return with him to Saipan to search for the remains of downed aviatrix Amelia Earhart. Heller had encountered the flyer thirty-five years earlier, when her husband had hired him to uncover the source of several threatening letters. His path crosses hers again in 1940 in the South Pacific, where she's being held prisoner on Saipan by the Japanese. But their escape attempt is botched, and Amelia is left behind, apparently killed by the Japanese. Now Nate must discover whether or not his friend survived the horrors of war, or whether he's just chasing another wild goose. Historical Figures: Amelia Earhart; Ed Noonan; Robert Myers; G. P. Putnam.

7. *Caribbean Blues: The Most Novel Novel in the History of the Mystery,* with Mary Higgins Clark, Molly Cochran, Gregory Mcdonald, Richard S. Meyers, Warren Murphy, Bill Palmer, Karen Palmer, and Robert J. Randisi. Toronto, Canada: PaperJacks, 1988, 295 p.

AT SEA ON THE S.S. *COUNTESS*, MAY 1938. "Lady Hannah," the wealthy owner of a major Cuban resort, the Perfumed Garden, is traveling about the Cunard *Countess* with a group of private investigators, among them Nathan Heller, Chico Mangini, "The Solution," Ph.D. "Phil" Phlem, Andy Baltimore, Devlin Tracy, Leslie Dither, and Jack Miles. Shortly after their departure from San Juan, Puerto Rico, Lady Hannah is found dead, and her three priceless gems, the so-called Caribbean Blues, are missing. The detectives band together their resources to solve the crime and recover the jewels. Collins wrote Chapters 4 and 12 of this round-robin novel, and coauthored Chapter 18 with the Palmers; Heller is mentioned throughout, however. A book notable only for its scarcity.

8. *The Million-Dollar Wound.* New York: St. Martin's Press, 1986, 335 p.

CHICAGO, ILLINOIS, NOVEMBER 1939 AND MARCH 1943; CONGRESS HEIGHTS, MARYLAND, NOVEMBER 1942–FEBRUARY 1943; GUADALCANAL IN THE PACIFIC, NOVEMBER 1942. Heller joins the marines with his pal, Barney Ross, and they wind up together on the jungle island of Guadalcanal. Nate is rendered an unconscious amnesiac during a Japanese attack and is flown back to the States for treatment. There he slowly recovers and remembers and is finally told that Barney didn't make it. When he returns to Chicago, the murder of a high-priced call girl ignites the final violent days of mobster Frank Nitti, Heller's old nemesis, forcing Heller once again to reassess his life. Nicely illustrated with period photographs. Associate: Barney. Historical Figures: Frank Nitti; Robert Montgomery; Sally Rand; Eliot Ness; William Drury.

9. *Carnal Hours: A Nathan Heller Novel.* New York: A Dutton Book, 1994, 324 p.

CHICAGO, ILLINOIS, AND NASSAU, BAHAMA ISLANDS, JULY 1943. The brutal murder of multimillionaire Sir Harry Oakes in Nassau, the Bahamas, shocks the world. Oakes had lured Heller to the islands to uncover dirt on French playboy Count Freddie de Marigny, the fortune hunter who married Harry's beautiful teenaged daughter. When the Count is arrested for the crime, Nate is ready to return home, but Nancy Oakes de Marigny begs him to take the case. Soon the detective finds that the Bahamas are a jungle of duplicity, where the mob hobnobs with British royalty, and voodoo priests intermingle with Nazi spies. Heller muscles his way through a case riddled with inconsistencies and cover-ups, with the private investigator (PI) becoming the killer's next target! Historical Figures: Edward, Duke of Windsor; Wallis, Duchess of Windsor; Ian Fleming; Meyer Lansky; Sally Rand; Erle Stanley Gardner.

10. *Neon Mirage.* New York: A Thomas Dunne Book, St. Martin's Press, 1988, 275 p.

CHICAGO, ILLINOIS, AND LAS VEGAS, NEVADA, JUNE 1946–JUNE 1947. An underground war is raging in Chicago. Heller is caught in the middle when the man he has been hired to protect is gunned down before his eyes. Nate must quickly determine who ordered the hit, Jake "Greasy Thumb" Guzik or Ben "Bugsy" Siegel. The detective's quest eventually takes him to the West Coast and the desert train stop called Las Vegas, where Siegel is using his ill-gotten gains to build a fabulous gambling casino. Nate gets involved with Bugsy's girlfriend, Virginia Hill, and the body count continues to mount. Illustrated with contemporary photographs. Historical Figures: Jake Guzik; Bugsy Siegel; Virginia Hill; James Ragen; Meyer Lansky; George Raft.

11. *Angel in Black: A Nathan Heller Novel.* New York: New American Library, 2001, 340 p.

LOS ANGELES, CALIFORNIA, JANUARY 1947 (the Afterword is dated January 1982). Heller is visiting Los Angeles to establish the West Coast branch of his A-1 Detective Agency (and also to celebrate the one-month anniversary of his short-lived marriage to Peggy Hogan), when news hound Bill Foley drags him into the murder case of Elizabeth Short, better known as the Black Dahlia. Nate is astonished to realize that he had known Short back in Chicago. His own investigation of the brutal killing starts with what he knows of the doomed starlet, with the crazed phone call that he had received from her just days before her death. But delving into her past means reopening old personal wounds and revealing more than a few secrets of his own! Historical Figures: Eliot Ness; Finis Brown.

12. *Majic Man: A Nathan Heller Novel.* New York: A Dutton Book, 1999, 293 p.

WASHINGTON, DC, AND ROSWELL, NEW MEXICO, MARCH–MAY 1949 (the Prologue is dated September 1940). With World War II over and President Truman in power, Heller is called to the nation's capital by his friend Jim Forrestal, the recently deposed first Secretary of Defense. Forrestal believes that someone or some agency wants him dead and hires Heller to find out who and why. Nate's investigation leads him to the desert town of Roswell, New Mexico, where a UFO is reported to have landed two years earlier, the incident having been covered up by a mysterious military group called Majestic Twelve. When Forrestal supposedly commits suicide shortly thereafter, Heller smells something rotten in the halls of American government and strongly suspects murder! Historical Figures: James V. Forrestal; President Harry S. Truman; Drew Pearson; Teddy Kollek.

13. *Chicago Confidential: A Nathan Heller Novel.* New York: New American Library, 2002, 292 p.

LOS ANGELES, CALIFORNIA, AND CHICAGO, ILLINOIS, SEPTEMBER 1950. Congress decides to investigate organized crime, and Nathan Heller is one of the few individuals who know where all the bodies are buried, his having put a few of the hoods into their graves himself. Nate has no intention of blabbing; he prefers to stay alive and remain in business. But the mob is not so sure of his discretion, particularly since Heller's partner, former cop Bill Drury, is cooperating with the feds. Soon the detective finds himself at the center of a federal squeeze, as Senator Joe McCarthy weighs in with his own Red-baiting agenda. When Drury is murdered by the Syndicate, and a troubled showgirl is sadistically victimized, Nate must make his own stand against the hoods, not in court but on the rough streets of Chicago. Historical Figures: Frank Sinatra; Jayne Mansfield; Sam Giancana; the Fischetti Brothers; Senator Joseph McCarthy; William Drury; Estes Kefauver; Drew Pearson.

14. ***Dying in the Post-War World: A Nathan Heller Casebook.*** Woodstock, VT: Foul Play Press, 1991, 251 p.

CHICAGO, ILLINOIS, AND CLEVELAND, OHIO, 1933–1947. The first collection of stories featuring Nathan Heller. CONTENTS: "Foreword: Raising Heller," by Ed Gorman; "Dying in the Post-War World" (Chicago, July 1947; Sam Flood, aka Giancana; Jerry Lapps); "Private Consultation" (Chicago, December 1933); "House Call" (Chicago, January 1936); "Marble Mildred" (Chicago, June 1936); "The Strawberry Teardrop" (Cleveland, Ohio, August 1938; Eliot Ness); "Scrap" (Chicago, December 1939; Jack Ruby); "I Owe Them One" (Afterword).

15. ***Kisses of Death: A Nathan Heller Casebook.*** Norfolk, VA: Crippen & Landru Publishers, 2001, 206 p.

CHICAGO, ILLINOIS, AND ELSEWHERE, 1933–1961. The second collection of stories featuring Nathan Heller. CONTENTS: "Introduction"; "Kisses of Death" (Chicago, 1954; Marilyn Monroe); "Kaddish for the Kid" (Chicago, Summer 1933); "The Perfect Crime" (Hollywood, California, October–December 193?, Thelma Todd); "Natural Death, Inc." (Cleveland, Ohio, March 1939; Eliot Ness); "Screwball" (Miami Beach, Florida, May 1941); "Shoot-Out on Sunset" (Hollywood, California, Summer 1949); "Strike Zone" (Chicago, Illinois, June 1961); "Afterword: I Owe Them One"; "A Max Allan Collins Checklist."

ELIOT NESS SERIES

Scene of the Crime: Cleveland, Ohio, beginning in 1935, and continuing through 1939.

Detective: Real-life Treasury Agent Eliot Ness, now Director of Public Safety in Cleveland, Ohio (from December 1935).

Known Associates: Real-life politicians and mobsters.

Premise: Having cleaned up Chicago and put away Al Capone for life, former U.S. Treasury Agent Eliot Ness now moves to Cleveland to mop up another crooked town.

Comment: As in the Nathan Heller series, where Ness makes an occasional appearance, these books have been meticulously researched by the author and are filled with authentic depictions of the actual persons, places, and crimes that took place in this Ohio city during the Great Depression. Real names are used much of the time. Ness is the one incorruptible cop in this mess of deceit, bribery, and backstabbing. His crusade against wrongdoers everywhere is utterly merciless.

Literary Crimes & Chimes: Because the incidents and historical characters featured in this series are much less known to the average reader, the books tend to work better on the whole than do their counterparts in the Nathan Heller sequence. On the other hand, Ness is a much less inviting figure than Heller, being somewhat dour and holier-than-thou in his attitude. He bloody well *will* get his man, every bloody time. We wait in almighty anticipation for him to stumble and fall like a real person, but it never happens. Rats.

THE CASES

1. *The Dark City: An Eliot Ness Novel.* New York: Bantam Books, 1987, 233 p.
CLEVELAND, OHIO, DECEMBER 1935–MAY 1936. Ness has been called to Cleveland to clean up an anonymous ring of bent cops that specializes in vice, graft, gambling, and labor racketeering. Their leader, the so-called Outside Chief, deliberately keeps a low profile, becoming visible only through his criminal activities. Caught between corrupt politicians, jealous colleagues, a parasitic reporter, and two blondes, Ness seems to be in over his head—until the "Outside Chief" finally makes his move, and Ness moves just a little bit faster! Historical Figures: Mayor Harold Burton; Prosecutor Frank Cullitan; Police Chief George Matowitz.

2. *Butcher's Dozen: An Eliot Ness Novel.* New York: Bantam Books, 1988, 215 p.
CLEVELAND, OHIO, JULY 1937–AUGUST 1938 (the Prologue is dated 1935). Eliot Ness investigates the notorious Cleveland serial murderer, the Mad Butcher of Kingsbury Run, who specializes in killing young women and hacking up their bodies. Ness eventually stops the killings, but the Butcher is never prosecuted, and Eliot must be content with the knowledge of having ended the reign of terror, while the public remains ignorant of the actual outcome. Historical Figures: Mayor Harold Burton; Coroner

Samuel Gerber; Police Chief George Matowitz; Assistant Safety Director Robert Chamberlin; the Butcher.

3. ***Bullet Proof: An Eliot Ness Novel.*** New York: Bantam Books, 1989, 197 p.

CLEVELAND, OHIO, JULY–SEPTEMBER 1937 (the action takes place within a six-week gap in the chronology of *Butcher's Dozen*). Eliot Ness must fight a Cleveland extortion ring putting the squeeze on organized labor. Everyone seems to be on the take, from city officials to union leaders, everyone except Ness, of course. Eliot is hell-bent on cleaning up his adopted home, but he's a sitting duck for a mob triggerman with a tommy gun who plans to blow Ness and his pals sky-high. Only fast action will save the day! Historical Figures: Mayor Harold Burton; Prosecutor Frank Cullitan; Police Captain John Savage; Police Chief George Matowitz; Assistant Safety Director Robert Chamberlin.

4. ***Murder by the Numbers: An Eliot Ness Novel.*** New York: St. Martin's Press, 1993, 210 p.

CLEVELAND, OHIO, SEPTEMBER 1938–MAY 1939 (the Prologue is set in 1933, the Epilogue in 1941). Eliot Ness is drawn into a gang war between the Cleveland Mafia and the black mobsters who rule the "Bucket of Blood," a notorious slum. The blacks have a lock on the city's numbers racket and have traditionally depended on their political connections for protection. The mob, however, wants a piece of the action and is not above using force to gain that action. The city's large African American population is poised on the brink of explosion when Ness intervenes. Historical Figures: Mayor Harold Burton; Prosecutor Frank Cullitan; Police Chief George Matowitz; Assistant Safety Director Robert Chamberlin; Chester Himes.

LITERARY DETECTIVE (OR DISASTER MYSTERY) SERIES

Scene of the Crime: Various.

Detective: Various.

Known Associates: Various.

Premise: Various detective writers become involved in solving real-life crimes during periods of intense crisis or emergency.

Comment: As with the other two Collins series covered here, this sequence of historical mysteries is basically "gimmick" fiction, centered on real-life mystery writers placed in situations of crisis where they must solve murders that resemble or foreshadow real-life crimes. The books are meticulously researched, as always with this author's fictions, and even though the basic situation, that a writer could somehow become involved in actual criminous investigations, is ludicrous, Collins mostly pulls it off. The sixth book mentioned here, *Road to Perdition*, is one of the author's best books, an original creation loosely adapted from his previous researches into Chicago mob life during the depression era. It was made into an equally popular motion picture, with a number of plot changes.

Literary Crimes & Chimes: When Collins was just starting his career, he wrote a number of mysteries with contemporary settings that were first-rate in every respect, filled with fresh ideas, dynamic plots and action, and engaging characters. It's unfortunate that the author has been forced into writing this kind of derivative fiction—or somehow believes that it advances his art. The books are light and engaging, and that's about all that can be said for them, with one great exception: *Road to Perdition* makes up for all the rest. This is the book that Max Allan Collins was intended to write all those years. A graphic novel filled with graphic violence, it nonetheless puts together all of the finer elements of Collins' fiction and is unreservedly recommended.

THE CASES

1. *The Titanic Murders*. New York: Berkley Prime Crime, 1999, 258 p.

AT SEA ON BOARD THE S.S. *TITANIC*, APRIL 1912, and 1999. As the wreck of the *Titanic* is explored by modern-day deep-sea submersibles, two carefully wrapped bodies are found in the vessel's cold storage compartment. Shortly thereafter, Collins is contacted by the elderly daughter of well-known American detective writer, Jacques Futrelle. The Futrelles had sailed on the ship's maiden voyage. According to Virginia Futrelle, supposedly repeating a story told her by her mother May, her father, Jacques, had been called in to investigate two murders that occurred on the *Titanic* shortly after it sailed from England. Futrelle used his deductive reasoning ability (previously demonstrated by his literary character, the "Thinking Machine") to uncover the murderer. Just hours later, however, the *Titanic* struck an iceberg and very shortly sank, and Futrelle went down with the ship, although his family survived to tell the tale. Historical Figures: John Jacob Astor; Maggie Brown; Ship's Captain Smith; W. T. Stead; Benjamin Guggenheim; Thomas Andrews; Robert Ballard; May Futrelle; Virginia Futrelle.

2. *The Lusitania Murders*. New York: Berkley Prime Crime, 2002, 254 p.

AT SEA ON BOARD THE S.S. *LUSITANIA*, APRIL–MAY 1915. American critic and journalist Willard Wright, aka the well-known mystery writer "S. S. Van Dine," accepts an assignment under his pseudonym to interview the

Lusitania's rich and famous passengers. Simultaneously, however, he has also been asked to investigate the possible transportation of munitions for the war effort. When six of the travelers receive telegrams warning them of the impending destruction of the liner, Wright knows that this will be no ordinary voyage, and he must work feverishly to stop the vessel's sabotage by German agents. Ultimately, of course, he fails. Historical Figure: Ship's Captain Bill Turner.

3. *The Hindenburg Murders.* New York: Berkley Prime Crime, 2000, 257 p.

IN FLIGHT ON BOARD THE DIRIGIBLE *HINDENBURG*, MAY 1937. Well-known British mystery writer Leslie Charteris is traveling on the great German dirigible, the *Hindenburg*, from Frankfurt, Germany, to Lakehurst, New Jersey. Charteris is puzzled by the high level of security on boarding the airship and disturbed by the overt presence of Nazi military officers. When an undercover Gestapo agent suddenly disappears, it becomes evident to the author that his apprehension is not misplaced. Asked to investigate, Charteris soon uncovers a series of dangerous secrets. But as the *Hindenburg* prepares to dock in New Jersey, events suddenly reach their peak, and in the end only the writer knows what really sparked the explosion that sent the dirigible down in flames. Historical Figures: Eric Spehl; Colonel Oberst "Fritz" Erdmann; Captain Ernst Lehmann; Captain Max Pruss.

4. *The Pearl Harbor Murders.* New York: Berkley Prime Crime, 2001, 254 p.

PEARL HARBOR, HAWAII, DECEMBER 1941. In the waning days of 1941, many believe that war with Japan is inevitable, but Edgar Rice Burroughs, the well-known American author, is too busy tanning in the Hawaiian sun to pay them any mind. With him is his son, Hulbert "Hully" Burroughs. Then they find the body of Pearl Harada, a popular Japanese American singer, lying murdered on the beach. Soon the islands are buzzing with speculation. Was one of Pearl's many ex-boyfriends involved in the killing? Could the murder have been racially related? Burroughs comes to believe that Pearl died because she knew too much about an impending Japanese attack. But before he can solve the mystery, bombs begin falling on Pearl Harbor on the morning of December 7, and the war has started. Historical Figures: Admiral Kimmel; General Short.

5. *The London Blitz Murder.* New York: Berkley Prime Crime, 2004, 360 p.

LONDON, ENGLAND, FEBRUARY 1942. In blitz-ravaged London, British mystery writer Agatha Christie is called upon to help solve a modern-day Jack the Ripper's rampage, assisting Sir Bernard Spilsbury, the renowned pathologist, in his official investigation of the crimes. But her experience with literary criminals has scarcely prepared her for the gory impact of viewing real-life murder victims. This novel is based on the actual crimes of the so-called Blackout Ripper. Historical Figures: Sir Bernard Spilsbury; Inspector Edward Greeno; the Blackout Ripper.

6. ***Road to Perdition,*** with artwork by Richard Piers Raynor. New York: Paradox Press, 1998, 294 p.

THE TRI-CITIES (ROCK ISLAND, MOLINE, DAVENPORT), ILLINOIS AND IOWA, NEW MEXICO, CHICAGO, ILLINOIS, AND ELSEWHERE, WINTER 1930. Michael O'Sullivan works as a hit man and enforcer for gangland boss John Looney. One day his son, Michael Jr., witnesses a mob execution conducted by his father and by Connor Looney, John's son. Afraid that O'Sullivan will betray him, Connor arranges for the murder of his family, including O'Sullivan's wife and second son. Michael Jr. escapes, and father and son must flee the city. O'Sullivan petitions Frank Nitti, Looney's senior in the crime organization, for redress, but Nitti refuses, citing business concerns. A one-man war erupts, with Michael Sr. holding up mob-controlled banks to pressure Nitti and Capone to give up Connor. Finally the bosses relent, and Connor is killed, but Michael Sr. must ultimately pay the price himself for crossing the Capone gang. Only his son escapes, shooting down his father's assassin and eventually becoming a priest to atone for the family's sins. Simply outstanding in every respect, from storyline to artwork. Graphic novel. Historical Figures: Eliot Ness; Al Capone; Frank Nitti.

CORNWELL, Bernard (pseud. of Bernard Wiggins) (1944–). British.

SERIES

Scene of the Crime: London and elsewhere in England in 1817.

Detective: Captain Rider Sandman, formerly an officer in His Majesty's Fifty-Second Regiment of Foot, British Army, during the Napoleonic Wars.

Known Associates: Sergeant Berrigan, formerly a noncommissioned officer in His Majesty's First Foot Guards, British Army, during the Napoleonic Wars, and now an employee of the exclusive Seraphim Club in London.

Premise: An ex-military officer investigates a murder on behalf of the British government and refuses to sell his integrity to the devil of expediency.

Comment: The painter and portrait artist Charles Corday has been tried and convicted of murdering and raping one of his clients, the Countess of Avebury. He proclaims his innocence but is sentenced to death and is awaiting execution in Newgate Prison in London. His mother, a seamstress to Queen Charlotte, has petitioned that lady to have the case reopened. The

Home Secretary, Henry Addington, Viscount Sidmouth, appoints an official Investigator in the person of Captain Sandman, whose father gambled away the family inheritance before committing suicide. Now Sandman is forced to dwell in one of London's worst slums. The retired military officer takes his duties seriously, despite the offer of bribes, threats, and inducements by the establishment's rich and powerful upper crust. In particular, his investigations take him to the Seraphim Club, an organization peopled by the sybaritic offspring of the noble classes, spoiled young men who feel that they can commit any act without ever being called to account. There he finds a former army sergeant, Berrigan, who eventually helps him resolve the case and save the homosexual painter. They later go into partnership with each other to import Spanish cigars to sell to the wealthy individuals who can afford them.

Literary Crimes & Chimes: Cornwell is best known for his long series of historical novels dealing with Richard Sharpe and his adventures during the Napoleonic Wars, mostly in Spain. His portrait of London social life in the Regency Period is absolutely impeccable. The story itself aptly reflects the snobbishness of British society of the time and the mercilessness of the British judicial system, which routinely sentenced individuals to death for crimes that we would now consider misdemeanors at best. In his Afterword, Cornwell points out that many of these death sentences were not actually carried out, being commuted to transportation to Australia. Nonetheless, the inherent brutality of the system and the overt favoring of the rich and influential members of society are not glossed over here or "prettified" to make them more palatable to modern sensibilities. We come to admire Captain Sandman simply because he does have a code of ethics, a code that he strictly follows, even when the consequences affect him in the pocketbook quite adversely. A superior work in every respect.

THE CASE

1. *Gallows Thief.* London: HarperCollins, 2001, 280 p.
   ENGLAND, 1817. See commentary in this series.

CRICHTON, (John) Michael (1942–). American.

MISCELLANEOUS SERIES

Scene of the Crime: Various.

Detective: Various.

Known Associates: Various.

Premise: Various.

Comment: Crichton always writes an entertaining novel, but his later works have tended to focus on cutting-edge issues of society or technology, with plenty of flash and polish but relatively little character development. These two early novels, both based around actual historical curiosities, are without such accoutrements but have about them a freshness sometimes lacking in Crichton's deliberately crafted bestsellers. Both were made into popular movies.

Literary Crimes & Chimes: *The Great Train Robbery* uses the events of that real-life crime to fashion a commentary on the early industrial era of the Victorian period in Britain. That a fast-moving train, the symbol of all that was progress in the nation, could be robbed while moving at full speed down the track, shocked the establishment to its core and disabused champions of the benefits of technology of the notion that scientific progress per se would reduce or eliminate crime. When asked at the end of his trial why he did the awful deed, Pierce laconically responds, "I wanted the money." *Eaters of the Dead* is a very different kind of book, telling of the discovery during the Dark Ages of a remnant of another human species in Iceland. The commentator, a sophisticated Arab from the most cultured society then in existence in the world, is shocked by the state of the filthy and unlettered men with whom he travels. He fights to protect the Vikings from the attacks of the cannibalistic barbarians, who are, after all, only following their nature. Ahmad ibn Fadlan actually existed, and he did write a commentary about his travels into Scandinavia; Crichton's account, however, is wholly fictitious but highly entertaining nonetheless.

THE CASES

1. ***Eaters of the Dead: The Manuscript of Ibn Fadlan, Relating His Experiences with the Northmen in AD 922.*** New York: Alfred A. Knopf, 1976, 193 p.

SCANDINAVIA, 922. A refined Arab courier, representing the Caliph of Bagdad, encounters and joins a party of Viking warriors on their journey homeward to the barbaric North. At Rothgar they are set upon by strange creatures, and several of their party are killed. They decide to pursue the manlike beasts into their caves, and they slaughter all that they can find. The creatures appear to be a primitive kind of human, and their battle with the Northmen is an age-old conflict that they are on the verge of losing. With the mystery of the killings solved, ibn Fadlan heads south again.

2. ***The Great Train Robbery.*** New York: Alfred A. Knopf, 1975, 266 p.

ON THE SOUTH EASTERN RAILWAY, AND LONDON, ENGLAND, MAY 1854–AUGUST 1857. The debonair Edward Pierce meticulously plans and executes a robbery of gold bullion from the South Eastern Railway, circumventing all of the sophisticated locks and other security devices used to block such thievery. He carries out the plan without a hitch and is caught only by accident several years later. Pierce and his cohorts are tried and convicted of the crime, but Pierce escapes while being transported from the court. He is never recaptured, and the stolen gold is never recovered.

DAVIS, Lindsey (1949–). British.

MARCUS DIDIUS FALCO SERIES

Scene of the Crime: The Roman Empire, beginning in AD 66.

Detective: Marcus Didius Falco was born in AD 41, the sixth of seven children of Junilla Tacita and Marcus Didius "Geminus" Favonius. Geminus abandoned his family, and Junilla Tacita raised them on her own. Falco was born a plebeian and rises to the equestrian rank in *One Virgin Too Many*, in which he is appointed Procurator of Poultry for the Senate and the People of Rome. His family includes his wife, Helena Justina; his daughters, Julia (born AD 73 in *A Dying Light in Corduba*), and Favonia (born AD 75, the story of her birth being recounted in *A Body in the Bath House*). Other clan members include Falco's five sisters, all of whom have married men whom he despises. Falco's only brother died heroically in the wars. Falco's service was very different from his brother's. Most Roman men take pride in their military service. Falco and Petronius remember theirs with anger, misery, and shame. They are both veterans of the infamous Second Augusta Legion. Their Prefect held the Second Augusta back from joining other legions to quell Queen Boudicca's rebellion in Britannia. The men who served in that legion must live with a disgrace that they did nothing to earn. The experience left Falco with a deep distrust of authority, an unfortunate lack of funds, and an embarrassing (to him) drive to protect and defend the underdog. The contrasts in Falco's character—the outward show of being mercenary coupled with the secret altruism, the public bravado covering up the self-doubt, and the vocal cynicism masking the powerful idealism—combine to create an interesting and sympathetic protagonist.

Known Associates: Petronius Longus, a friend from his days in the military; Maia, Falco's favorite sister; Smaractus, Falco's landlord; Lenia, proprietress of the Eagle laundry; Anacrites, a palace informer, jealous of Falco's imperial commissions; Decimus Camillus Verus, an impoverished senator, and Julia Justa, his wife; Aelianus Camillus Justinus, Verus' eldest son; Quintus Camillus Justinus, Verus' youngest son; the Emperor Vespasian; his older son and heir, Titus Caesar, Falco's friend; his younger son, Domitian Caesar, Falco's enemy.

Premise: A plebeian investigates crimes and acts as an agent for the Emperor Vespasian in first-century Rome.

Comment: "Down these mean streets a man must go . . ." Marcus Didius Falco is the Philip Marlowe of Ancient Rome. He works as an informer (*delator*), a despised profession. Society considers him a sort of private spy for hire. Everyone expects that his conscience can be purchased; a man who would stoop to snooping into the business of his countrymen can have no morals. Falco's sneaking passion for justice is the albatross around his neck; it prevents him from accepting bribes to look the other way. In interviews with the author, Davis has stated that her interest in archeology started her writing about Ancient Rome. New archeological finds are regularly incorporated into her novels. The research here is solid, and Davis' speculations about the period are great fun.

Literary Crimes & Chimes: These stories do not follow a formula; you can read the entire *oeuvre* without becoming bored. The stories include everything from police procedurals, to courtroom dramas, to classic whodunnits. Villains range from serial killers, to patriots, to traitors, to garden-variety criminals. One of the great joys of the series is watching the protagonist develop: Falco is a cynic with a heart of gold. He struggles with his conscience and (occasionally) succeeds, forms attachments, and sees his family grow, all providing an interesting backbone to the series. Rumor hath it that Davis changed her mind about the identity of the villain partway through the writing of *The Silver Pigs*, and the red herrings are all the better for it. Just as a side-note, Davis must have had some very interesting experiences with home builders—unscrupulous, even criminal contractors and remodelers are a recurring theme in the series. One of the better historical detective series set in the ancient world.

THE CASES

1. *The Silver Pigs: A Novel*. New York: Crown Publishers, 1989, 258 p.

ROME AND BRITANNIA, AD 70. Falco parlays his rescue of a young woman into a job to keep her safe. He suspects that she was grabbed by an importunate suitor; before he realizes his mistake, he's in way too deep, somehow winding up investigating treason against the Empire. Associates: Gaius Flavius Hilaris, Imperial Procurator of Finance in Britain; Aelia Camilla, his wife; Helena Justina.

2. *Shadows in Bronze: A Marcus Didius Falco Novel*. New York: Crown Publishers, 1990, 341 p.

ITALY, AD 71. Falco is deputized to get rid of the corpse of a man whose treasonous plot he had uncovered in *The Silver Pigs*. That gruesome task turns out to be the easier part of cleaning up the remains of the conspiracy. At least he makes some money utilizing the spoils from his last case while going undercover for this investigation. Falco knows that Emperor Vespasian is so frugal that the detective will never get wealthy working for the government. Associates: Tullia; Helena Justina. Historical Figure: Roman Emperor Vespasian.

3. *Venus in Copper: A Marcus Didius Falco Novel*. New York: Crown Publishers, 1991, 277 p.

ROME, AD 71. Falco's luck never changes. Realizing that he can never get ahead while working for the stingy Emperor Vespasian, he becomes a private investigator once more. This time he's hired as a bodyguard and, true to form, is soon attending the funeral of his client. Unfortunately, one of the people looking to hire him to uncover the murderer is also his chief suspect! At least this time maybe he'll make some money. Associate: Thalia. Historical Figure: Roman Emperor Vespasian.

4. *The Iron Hand of Mars*. New York: Crown Publishers, 1992, 305 p.

ROME, GAUL, AND GERMANIA, AD 71. Titus Caesar has taken an active interest in Falco's girlfriend, believing that she could do better with Imperial company. Falco knows that the lucrative job in Germany that has been offered to him is partly just to get the detective out of the way, but he needs the money and seems to have lost his girl. His task is to make a discreet inspection of the Fourteenth Gemina, a historically unruly legion. Not only are the soldiers rioting, but they have a habit of rewriting their own orders. So Falco's assignment is not an easy one, and neither is the journey: he's well aware that if the chieftains in Germania rip him from limb from limb, Titus will be relieved of any competition for Helena's company, and Vespasian will be relieved of the obligation to pay him! Historical Figures: Roman Emperor Vespasian; Titus Caesar.

5. *Poseidon's Gold: A Marcus Didius Falco Mystery.* New York: Crown Publishers, 1994, 336 p.

ROME, AD 72. Falco returns from Germania to find his apartment ransacked and his mother upset by rumors blackening the name of Falco's dead brother, Marcus Didius Festus (the family hero). Falco is desperate to find a lucrative case so that he can earn the money it would take to raise him in rank and to marry the woman he loves, but family loyalty demands that he clear Festus' name first. What begins as a financial problem ends up involving a murder, and Falco himself becomes the prime suspect! Associates: Marcus Didius Favonius, Falco's father; Festus; Helena Justina.

6. *Last Act in Palmyra.* New York: Mysterious Press, 1994, 476 p.

ROME, NABATAEA, AND PALMYRA, AD 72. Falco is suspicious when Anacrites, Vespasian's chief spy, who sees Falco as a rival, offers him a job, but any commission that takes him away from Rome now seems appealing. There's a woman in Rome who's causing Falco endless grief; and so, of course, when he accepts the commission, she decides to tag along. They join a traveling acting troupe in Palmyra, but their problems are compounded when they discover a murdered playwright, and Falco has to take over his scriptwriting. Associates: Thalia; Helena Justina; Anacrites. Historical Figure: Roman Emperor Vespasian.

7. *Time to Depart.* New York: Mysterious Press, 1997, 400 p.

ROME, AD 72. For six years Petronius has worked to find enough information to convict one of the dirtiest underworld organizers in Rome. Convicted criminals can choose either exile or death, and Balbinus chooses the former; but his departure does not close down his criminal enterprises. They rise again when his lieutenants and competitors fight among themselves for control. And that's not the worst of it! Everyone is wondering when Balbinus will return to seek revenge against Petronius and Falco. Associates: Helena Justina; Petronius; Balbinus Pius, a businessman; Milvia, his daughter; Florius, her husband.

8. *A Dying Light in Corduba.* New York: Mysterious Press, 1998, 428 p.

HISPANIA, AD 73. Falco attends the feast for the Society of Olive Oil Producers of Baetica; amazingly, no one is murdered, at least not until after the banquet, when an attempt is made on the life of Falco's old rival, Anacrites. The Imperial Palace wants Falco to investigate, but he's promised his wife to remain by her side until their child is delivered. She solves the problem by accompanying him as he trails the would-be assassin across the Iberian Peninsula. Associates: Helena Justina; Anacrites; Claudia Ruffina, a young woman who will inherit a fortune; Julia. Historical Figure: Roman Emperor Vespasian.

9. *Three Hands in the Fountain.* New York: Mysterious Press, 1999, 351 p.

ROME, AD 73. A plumber finally fixes the fountain in Tailor's Lane—by removing the severed hand blocking the pipe! Falco and Petronius are horrified, but the man assures them that body parts are spewed forth from the aqueducts on a regular basis. Their subsequent investigation proves this truism, partly because a serial killer in Rome has been murdering and dismembering young women for years. The book includes an interesting tour of Rome's aqueduct system. Associates: Helena Justina; Petronius; Milvia; Florius; Claudia Ruffina.

10. *Two for the Lions.* New York: Mysterious Press, 1999, 390 p.

ROME, TRIPOLITANIA, AND CYRENAICA, AD 74. Falco has finally found lucrative work, albeit a job that is even more despised than that of informer. He's turned his investigative skills to working for the census, auditing taxes. In inventorying Calliopus' holdings, Falco finds that he owns a menagerie in Africa as well as a lion in Rome. When the lion is murdered, Falco wants to investigate, but the crime is so bizarre, what possible motive could there be? Next to die is a glamorous gladiator, and motives and opportunities suddenly start multiplying! Associates: Helena Justina; Famia, Falco's brother-in-law; Thalia; Claudia Ruffina.

11. *One Virgin Too Many.* New York: Mysterious Press, 2000, 356 p.

ROME, AD 74. Just as Falco is appointed Procurator for the Sacred Geese, strange and deadly events begin to occur among the priests and priestesses of Rome. Aelianus falls over a body at a feast in the Sacred Grove. He is so rattled by the event that he flees rather than calling for help, and when he and Falco return to the scene, the corpse has disappeared. Of more immediate distress to Falco is the disappearance of a six-year-old girl who had tried to hire Falco to prevent her death at the hands of her family. He had thought her overly imaginative, and when she vanishes, the detective is wracked with guilt and determined to give the girl some measure of justice. Associates: Terentia Paulla; Gloccus; Cotta; Helena Justina.

12. *Ode to a Banker.* New York: Mysterious Press, 2001, 372 p.

ROME, AD 74. Falco is thrilled when a publisher expresses an interest in his writing. Then he finds out that the man is running a vanity press. Furious at being expected to pay to see his work in print, Falco quarrels with the man. When the publisher is found murdered, Falco immediately becomes the prime suspect, and feels that he must solve the case in order to exonerate himself. Associates: Helen Justina; Rutilius Gallicus; Gloccus; Cotta.

13. *A Body in the Bathhouse.* New York: Mysterious Press, 2002, 354 p.

BRITANNIA, AD 75. Falco's problems with building contractors go from bad (their general incompetence) to worse (their murderous inclinations), when he discovers a corpse under his new bathhouse floor. Then the Emperor asks Falco to audit a public building project, a house being erected for a favored chieftain in Britannia. At first Falco refuses, but when he learns that his errant builders have already left Rome to construct the Great King's House in Britannia, Falco sees an opportunity to combine gainful (more or less) employment with his own interests. He also has to solve a crime that may have taken place within his own home. Associates: King Togidubnus, a powerful chieftain in the British Isles; Helena Justina; Favonia; Larius; Gloccus; Cotta. Historical Figure: Roman Emperor Vespasian.

14. *The Jupiter Myth.* New York: Mysterious Press, 2002, 323 p.

LONDINIUM, BRITANNIA, AD 75. Londinium, located on the far edge of civilization, is a place filled with individuals who have given up on life and those who see an opportunity to get something started. Inevitably, the city attracts numerous gangs of criminals. Falco, blamelessly trying to visit relatives on his journey home from his last mission, finds himself drawn once more into state service, investigating the murder of a man who should not have been there! Associates: Albia, a foundling; Flavius Hilaris; Aelia Camilla; Chloris; Florius; King Togidubnus; Helena Justina.

15. *The Accusers.* New York: Mysterious Press, 2003, 368 p.

ROME, AD 75. Under Roman law, when a man of property is accused and convicted of a major crime, his estate is confiscated and sold, and those who prosecuted him share in the proceeds; one way to avert a family's financial ruin is for the disgraced individual to commit suicide before the verdict. Falco is pleased to be offered a job soon after he returns to Rome but soon realizes that he is in over his head when he finds himself going up against professional informers, men who have litigated and won unscrupulous cases, men of immense wealth and larger power. All Falco has left are his principles, his brothers-in-law, and a strong suspicion that Paccius Africanus' client's death was not actually a suicide. Associates: Albia; Helena Justina. Historical Figures: Paccius Africanus; Silius Italicus.

16. *Scandal Takes a Holiday.* New York: Mysterious Press, 2004, 352 p.

OSTIA, AD 76. Falco is hired to find a man who writes scandalous bits for the local *Daily Gazette* under the pen name of "Infamia." He soon realizes that Infamia had aspirations of becoming an investigative reporter and breaking a major story. The trail uncovers deeds more deadly than gossip, including piracy, dangerous villains, and unscrupulous contractors! Associate: Albia.

DeANDREA, William L(ouis) (1952–1996). American.

THEODORE ROOSEVELT SERIES

Scene of the Crime: New York, New York, in 1896.

Detective: Dennis Muldoon, a New York City policeman.

Known Associates: Theodore Roosevelt, Police Commissioner of the City of New York, later President of the United States. Other Historical Figures: newspaper moguls (and rivals) William Randolph Hearst and Joseph Pulitzer; Democratic Presidential candidate William Jennings Bryan.

Premise: A cop teams up with his politically savvy mentor, Theodore Roosevelt, to solve crimes in the big city.

Comment: When New York City policeman Dennis Muldoon discovers a beautiful young woman, Cleo, bound and gagged in a hotel room, he proceeds to release her but can't help noticing the strange, ankh-like birthmark on her inner thigh. Then Muldoon falls in with Commissioner Roosevelt, who is attempting to wean the New York Police Department (NYPD) of its corrupt elements and who finds the Irish cop a useful adjunct to his crusade. At the same time, anarchists have targeted William Jennings Bryan, the Democratic candidate for president, and plan to assassinate him during the wedding of a supporter. Somehow the lovely Cleo is involved peripherally in all of these shenanigans, and Dennis must elucidate the names and purposes of the different levels of rogues, both in and out of the NYPD. Well-written and remarkably entertaining.

Literary Crimes & Chimes: It is interesting to compare this novel to Caleb Carr's later and much larger work, *The Alienist* (*q.v.*). Both books feature a younger version of Teddy Roosevelt cleaning up crime in Manhattan, but the feel of each series is vastly different. DeAndrea presents an interesting mystery to be solved by a local policeman, Dennis Muldoon, and while the book contains all of the flavor of the big city, Carr's more ambitious work focuses on the psychological underpinnings of modern society and how the filth and corruption of large urban areas undercut the very basis for civilized behavior. Both fictions remain very good reads. DeAndrea may have intended at some point to continue the series, since the Prologue notes that in 1898, when Roosevelt was elected Governor of New York, Muldoon, who by then had relocated to Washington, DC, "returned to New York City and opened a private enquiry agency, at which he prospered. He and Roosevelt continued to be friends, and spent much time visiting each other."

THE CASE

1. *The Lunatic Fringe: A Novel Wherein Theodore Roosevelt Meets the Pink Angel.* New York: M. Evans & Co., 1980, 287 p.
NEW YORK, NEW YORK, AUGUST 1896. See commentary in this series.

LOBO BLACKE AND QUINN BOOKER SERIES

Scene of the Crime: Le Four, Wyoming, circa 1890.

Detective: Louis Bowman "Lobo" Blacke, age fifty, a former soldier in the Civil War and later a federal marshal, who has been left paralyzed from the waist down after being shot in the back by an unknown assailant. He now owns and publishes a small newspaper in Wyoming.

Known Associates: Quinn Booker, an Easterner of good upbringing who entertains himself by writing dime novels, especially those about his western hero, Lobo Blacke, and who also narrates these accounts; Merton Mayhew, fourteen-year-old son of the local doctor, part-time employee at the *Witness*; Clayton Henry, photographer and engraver at the *Witness*; Rebecca Payson, former prostitute, now business manager of the *Witness* and sometime nurse to Lobo; Sheriff Asa Harlan.

Premise: A crippled newspaper publisher and a dime story novelist combine forces to solve crimes in late nineteenth-century Wyoming.

Comment: Quinn Booker, an Eastern dime novelist of elite upbringing, has created a western hero in the form of Lobo Blacke, a real-life former federal marshal who has been permanently crippled in a gunfight and who is now confined to a wheelchair. Lobo takes his share of the proceeds from Quinn's books and purchases a newspaper, the *Black Hills Witness*, in the small Wyoming town of Le Four. He then asks Quinn to give up his comfortable life in the East and come to Wyoming to assist him in running the newspaper, and, of even more importance to Lobo, to become his legs in the ongoing search for the criminal who maimed him. His attention is focused particularly on Lucius Jenkins, the wealthiest rancher in the area, and a former lawman and ex-associate of Lobo. DeAndrea provides interesting characterizations in a series very reminiscent of the *Ironside* television series. The stories are told by the dime novelist himself, the educated Quinn Booker, who takes a very jaundiced view of the West and is always concerned about the integrity of his own backside. His humorous asides greatly enliven the ongoing repartee. The relationship between Lobo Blacke and Quinn Booker has been compared to that of Nero Wolfe and Archie Goodwin in the Rex Stout series, and DeAndrea has identified Stout's work as one of the sources for his fiction. But it's Lobo who does the actual thinking here, solving otherwise impenetrable crimes that would have been resolved by the local populace in more straightforward ways had not the newspaperman intervened.

Literary Crimes & Chimes: It's unfortunate that DeAndrea did not live long enough to develop this series any further. There are obvious future story points embedded into the two books, including the ongoing battle of wits between Lobo and his chief nemesis, Lucius Jenkins. Although the material is light and sometimes humorous, the characters are interesting enough to engage fans of both the mystery and western genres, and the mix works exceedingly well. The date of the series is never clearly established, although the suggestion that Lobo served in the American Civil War and is, at the time of *Written in Fire*, fifty years of age, would suggest a period of about 1890–1895.

THE CASES

1. *Written in Fire: A Lobo Blacke/Quinn Booker Mystery.* New York: Walker & Co., 1995, 163 p.

WYOMING, NOVEMBER 1890?–JANUARY 1891? Quinn Booker turned his back on his father's West Point background and his mother's elite upbringing to become a writer. And Louis Bowman "Lobo" Blacke is the lawman Booker has made famous in a series of dime novels. Lobo, a former federal marshal and man of action had been shot in a gunfight and is now permanently wheelchair-bound. With his share of the earnings from Quinn's books, Lobo has purchased a Wyoming newspaper, the *Witness*, and has dedicated his spare time to identifying and capturing the man who crippled him. Frustrated by his immobility, he convinces Booker to give up his eastern creature comforts and come to Wyoming Territory to write for the paper—and at the same time serve as Lobo's "legs" in the investigation. Booker is barely off the train before trouble tracks him into the boomtown of Le Four, in the form of drunken cowboys whom he manages to best in a standoff. When the photographer who captures the scene on film is later found shot to death, Lobo suspects the killer is the same man who crippled him and begins to issue orders to Booker about the investigation. It doesn't take long for Booker to decide that writing about criminals is one thing, but actually chasing them is something else again. And a man can't get started unless he learns a few basics—like what to do in a gunfight. This definitely wasn't what Booker was raised to do, but working with Lobo Blacke is decidedly what he was born to do.

2. *Fatal Elixir: A Lobo Blacke/Quinn Booker Mystery.* New York: Walker & Co., 1997, 246 p.

LE FOUR, WYOMING, MAY 1891? (Six months after the events in *Written in Fire*.) Someone has doctored Dr. Herkimer's Ozono, a patent medicine remedy for gout, cancer, excessive wind, heart palpitations, and numerous other complaints and conditions. The potion doesn't have much of anything good in it, but it has never killed anyone—before now. For Lobo, a paralyzed former marshal, the death is a puzzle. Why would Herkimer kill the goose that's laying the golden egg? When Le Four's sheriff becomes one of the potion's victims, Lobo's associate, Quinn Booker, finds the badge pinned to his own shirt and must somehow prevent the angry townspeople from lynching the unfortunate Herkimer. In the meantime, Lobo and Quinn learn that Paul Muller, the last man arrested by Lobo before he was crippled, has escaped from prison and is making his way back to Le Four, both to take his revenge and to make contact with Lucius Jenkins, a wealthy rancher who may have profited from Muller's criminal activities. One complication after another confronts the duo as they seek to solve old murders and prevent new ones. This is the last book DeAndrea wrote before his untimely death from a blood infection. Associates: Merton; Asa; Rebecca; Clayton; Lucius.

DE LA TORRE, Lillian (pseud. of Lillian Bueno McCue) (1902–1993). American.

DR. SAM JOHNSON SERIES

Scene of the Crime: London, second half of the eighteenth century.

Detective: Dr. Sam Johnson is a real-life historical figure (1709–1784), a noted essayist, critic, poet, one of England's greatest men of letters. His *A Dictionary of the English Language* was enormously influential. He was a friend of David Garrick and of the magistrate Sir John Fielding (known as the "Blind Beak of Bow Street") and showed an interest in crime. Boswell (also a real-life historical figure) recorded that Johnson spent most of one winter sitting in on Bow Street interrogations of criminals. Johnson was a large man, powerfully built, with a face scarred from childhood scrofula.

Known Associates: The narrator of these stories is James Boswell, Johnson's friend and biographer in real life. His personality comes through in the narration as well as in the dialogue.

Premise: A man of letters and his associate solve crimes in eighteenth-century Britain.

Comment: As was probably true in real life, the fictional Dr. Johnson is welcome everywhere. In the fictional series, when crimes take place before his eyes, he investigates until he finds the answers. Having become (in these stories) known for his investigative abilities, he is also sought out by friends of innocent men who are under suspicion, and his compassionate nature moves him to help. At times he finds the truth, at time he manufactures evidence, but his goal is always to provide justice. These tales are great fun. Boswell often provides one (or many) possible solutions to the crime, while Johnson carefully works toward an understanding of the facts. The personalities of the two friends are portrayed beautifully, with humor and a marked generosity of spirit. The narrative includes some of the mannerisms that have made historians wonder if Johnson might have been obsessive-compulsive.

Literary Crimes & Chimes: In the preface to the International Polygonics edition of *The Return of Dr. Sam: Johnson, Detector*, Lillian de la Torre recounts her inspiration for the series. She writes of a number of incidents in which Johnson showed an inordinate interest in crime and detection. Examples include attending the interrogation of criminals, his writing of the "Last Dying Speech and Confession" of the forger Dr. Dodd, and his denouncing of a fraudulent literary find. Both the real and the fictional Dr. Johnson are renowned for their perspicacity and wit. The author takes pains to explain at the beginning of the series that the events in these books are fiction and that she has worked to make the tone, the speech, the attitudes, and even the actions of the characters as true to Johnson's and Boswell's real-life personas as possible. Many of the stories are followed by author's notes delineating the historical basis on which each is grounded. The language of these tales harks back to the writing style of the time, peppered with the use of some archaic spellings. This adds to the historical flavor of the works, which also employ beautiful language and imagery. For instance, "Soon we drew rein before the tent of the court-martial. 'Twas a brave sight in full sun, with the company standard waving before it, and the red of its peak repeated in a bed of flowers sparkling beside it like a pool of blood, a wave of full-blooded ruffled blooms like scarlet silk, with blackness at the heart."—from "The Stroke of Thirteen," in *The Detections of Dr. Sam: Johnson*.

THE CASES

1. ***Dr. Sam: Johnson, Detector: Being a Light-Hearted Collection of Recently Reveal'd Episodes in the Career of the Great Lexicographer Narrated as from the Pen of James Boswell.*** New York: Alfred A. Knopf, 1946, 257 p.

ENGLAND, 1770s. The first collection of Sam Johnson tales. CONTENTS: "The Wax-Work Cadaver"; "The Second Sight of Dr. Sam: Johnson"; "The Flying Highwayman"; "The Monboddo Ape Boy"; "The Manifestations in Mincing Lane"; "Prince Charlie's Ruby"; "The Stolen Christmas Box"; "The Conveyance of Emelina Grange"; "The Great Seal of England."

2. *The Detections of Dr. Sam: Johnson.* Garden City, NY: Published for the Crime Club by Doubleday, 1960, 190 p.

ENGLAND, 1770s. The second collection of Sam Johnson tales. CONTENTS: "The Tontine Curse"; "The Stroke of Thirteen"; "The Viotti Stradivarius"; "The Black Stone of Dr. Dee"; "The Frantick Rebel"; "Saint-Germain the Deathless"; "The Missing Shakespeare Manuscript"; "The Triple-Lock'd Room."

3. *The Return of Dr. Sam. Johnson, Detector: As Told by James Boswell.* New York: International Polygonics, 1985, 191 p.

ENGLAND, 1770s. The third collection of Sam Johnson tales. CONTENTS: "Murder Lock'd In"; "The Bedlam Bam"; "The Disappearing Servant Wench"; "The Blackamoor Unchain'd"; "The Lost Heir"; "The Resurrection Men"; "Milady Bigamy."

4. *The Exploits of Dr. Sam Johnson, Detector: Told as If by James Boswell.* New York: International Polygonics, 1987, 224 p.

ENGLAND, 1770s. The fourth collection of Sam Johnson tales. CONTENTS: "The Kidnapp'd Earl"; "The Westcombe Witch"; "The Banquo Trap"; "The Spirit of the '76"; "The Virtuosi Venus"; "The Aerostatick Globe"; "Coronation Story."

5. "The Earl's Nightingale," in *Once upon a Crime*, ed. by Janet Hutchings. New York: St. Martin's Press, 1994, p. 120–133.

Based upon a real crime that happened in 1779, in which the real-life James Boswell visited a killer in his cell, this story fictionalizes the detection of the villain in that murder. Historical Figures: David Garrick, Earl [of Sandwich]; Omiah.

6. "The Highwayman's Hostage," in *Mystery Cats.* New York: Signet, 1991, p. 184–194.

Dr. Sam: Johnson's cat, Hodge, solves a crime, and Dr. Sam resolves to have a sign made: Johnson and Hodge, Detectors.

7. de la Torre-Bueno, Theodore "Abduction into the Seraglio" in *Ellery Queen's Mystery Magazine* (February 1983): 90–107.

Wolfgang Amadeus, as a young child, is banished from a musical recital for his presumption. When he is next sent for, it is found that he has vanished, presumed kidnapped by gypsies. Historical Figures: Wolfgang Amadeus Mozart; George Handel; Antonio Salieri.

DOHERTY, Paul C(harles) (1946–). British.

AMEROTKE SERIES

Scene of the Crime: Ancient Egypt, beginning in 1479 BC.

Detective: Lord Amerotke, Chief Judge in Thebes, capital of Ancient Egypt.

Known Associates: Prenhoe, Amerotke's kinsman and a scribe in the Hall of Two Truths; Norfret, Amerotke's wife; Hatshepsut, more familiarly known as Hatusu, widow of Egyptian Pharoah Tuthmosis II (who dies in *The Mask of Ra*); Senenmut, Hatusu's lover and First Minister in her government; Valu, the royal prosecutor; Shufoy, servant to Amerotke.

Premise: A judge solves crimes in the ancient Egyptian capital of Thebes.

Comment: This series is set against the background of Egypt's Eighteenth Dynasty, a time of great change. Warlike Pharoahs fought not only to control the tribes on their western and southern borders, but also to bring their own subjects firmly under their rule. Queen Hatusu, the first of a number of resolute and astute female rulers, is swept into power after the death of her husband leaves a power void. With the assistance of Chief Judge Amerotke, she investigates and solves a number of politically inspired murders that threaten the peace and stability of her kingdom. Doherty studied history at Liverpool and Oxford, where he obtained a doctorate for his thesis on Edward II and Queen Isabella. He is not the only scholar to wander outside his major area of expertise: witness the efforts of such writers as Elizabeth Peters, with her nineteenth-century heroine, Amelia Peabody, and also of Lauren Haney and her ancient Egyptian mystery series. Doherty's extraordinary attention to historic detail brings Amerotke's world to life, with descriptions of daily life and characters drawn from every caste.

Literary Crimes & Chimes: Doherty's knowledge and intimate feel for ancient Egypt makes this mystery series a rare example of historical crime fiction that doesn't sacrifice suspense at the altar of trivial detail. Strong plotlines and bold characterizations strongly evoke the old Egyptian civilization and make the reader believe that he or she is really there. The mysteries aptly fit the situation of the times. One of the author's better literary creations.

THE CASES

1. *The Mask of Ra*. London: Headline, 1998, 276 p.

EGYPT, 1479 BC. His great battles against the sea raiders in the Nile Delta have left Pharaoh Tuthmosis II weak and frail, but he finds solace in his victory and in the welcome he is sure to receive on his return to Thebes. Across the river from Thebes, however, there are those who do not relish his homecoming, and assassins have induced a witch to pollute the Pharaoh's unfinished tomb. At last Tuthmosis is reunited with his beloved wife and half sister, Hatusu; he stands before the statue of Amun-Ra, with the roar of the crowd and the fanfare of trumpets ringing in his ears. But suddenly the Pharaoh falls dead, gasping, "It's only a mask!" and the people of Thebes are stunned by the sinister omen of wounded doves flying overhead, dropping blood specks on the scene of their ruler's death Rumor runs rife, speculation sweeps the royal city, and Hatusu vows to uncover the truth. With the aid of Amerotke, a respected judge of Thebes, she embarks on a path destined to reveal the great secrets of Egypt. Associates: Norfret; Prenhoe; Shufoy. Historical Figures: Egyptian Pharaoh Tuthmosis II; Egyptian Queen Hatusu; Minister Senenmut.

2. *The Horus Killings*. London: Headline, 1999, 276 p.

EGYPT, 1479 BC. Following the death of her husband, Pharaoh Tuthmosis II, under mysterious circumstances, his widow, Hatusu, emerges as ruler after a bitter struggle in which she is assisted by her lover, the wily Senenmut. She carries her people to victory in war, determined that all Egypt should accept her as its Pharaoh-Queen. But her ambition is threatened by a spate of killings in the Divine Temple of the House of Horus, crimes that the priests are swift to interpret as a sign of divine disapproval of a female Pharaoh. The capital becomes paralyzed as confusion and rumor abound. Only one man, Amerotke, a respected judge, can be trusted to find the truth among the intrigue surrounding the deaths and to bring the killers to justice—before rumor of the gods' displeasure with Hatusu consumes the whole of Egypt. Associates: Norfret; Prenhoe; Shufoy; Valu. Historical Figures: Egyptian Pharaoh Hatusu; Minister Senenmut.

3. *The Anubis Slayings*. London: Headline, 2000, 204 p.

EGYPT, 1479–1478 BC. Hatusu, the remarkable young widow of Pharaoh Tuthmosis II, has forced Egyptian society to acknowledge her as Pharaoh, and her success in battle is spreading Egypt's glory well beyond its frontiers. A rejoicing Egypt has just won a major victory over the Mitanni tribes in the north, and Queen Hatusu begins delicate peace negotiations with her humbled enemy, King Tushratta, in the Temple of Anubis. But in one night, two hideous murders in the temple and the sacrilegious theft of the sacred amethyst, the Glory of Anubis, threaten the tentative truce. The respected judge Amerotke must find the truth or Egypt's fragile peace could be destroyed. But after a slew of killings, each without leaving a single mark on the victim, rumor spreads that the slayer may have been the angry deity Anubis, the God of the Dead who takes no prisoners. Associates: Norfret; Prenhoe; Shufoy. Historical Figures: Egyptian Pharaoh Hatusu; Minister Senenmut.

4. *The Slayers of Seth*. London: Headline, 2001, 306 p.

EGYPT, 1478 BC. Lord Amerotke, Pharaoh's chief judge, is in the middle of a murder case. A young, ambitious scribe, Ipumer, allegedly in love with the daughter of a powerful general, had hoped to become betrothed to her. Instead, he has been poisoned, and the prosecution has accused Lady Neshratta—apparently tired of the dalliance—of the crime. Lady Neshratta, if she is found guilty, will be buried alive in the desert sands of the Red Lands. But when Amerotke is summoned to the Temple of Seth by Queen Hatusu's First Minister, Lord Senenmut, it seems that there is yet another murder to investigate. One of Egypt's greatest heroes, General Balet, has been brutally killed, and the Pharaoh-Queen herself has decided to intervene. She believes that Balet's murder is only the beginning of more evil to come, and she calls on the trusted Judge for help. There is more to link the deaths than originally meets the eye, but can Amerotke track down the killer before he—or she—strikes again? Associates: Norfret; Prenhoe; Shufoy; Valu. Historical Figures: Egyptian Pharaoh Hatusu; Minister Senenmut.

5. *The Assassins of Isis*. London: Headline, 2004, 306 p.

EGYPT, SUMMER 1478 BC. Rahimere's Tomb is a House of Eternity whose owner had gone across the horizon into the Far West. Somewhere deep in the desert and rich with treasures of the ages, its location has long been kept a closely guarded secret. But now, the Sebaus—a sect that takes its name from demons—has plundered and pillaged the sepulcher for its most powerful secret. This time the wrath of the fiery Pharaoh-Queen Hatusu will know no bounds. She must fight to protect the tombs of her kin and tighten her grip on the collar of Egypt, in the midst of its most sweltering season. But when Egypt's great military hero, General Suten, is bitten to death by a swarm of venomous vipers, it appears that events have spiraled out of control. Meanwhile, a dark shadow lies across the Temple of Isis. The peace of this holy place, renowned as an oasis of calm and healing, has been disturbed. Four of the Hesets, the temple handmaidens, have vanished without a trace. Lord Amerotke, the Queen's Chief Judge, is asked to unravel the mysteries before further violence erupts. Will he find the perpetrators are in league with forces beyond his jurisdiction? Associates: Norfret; Prenhoe; Shufoy; Valu. Historical Figures: Egyptian Pharaoh Hatusu; Minister Senenmut.

HUGH CORBETT SERIES

Scene of the Crime: England, beginning in 1284.

Detective: Sir Hugh Corbett, a former chancery clerk who becomes a master spy in the court of England's King Edward I. He is knighted by Edward in recognition of his services to the Crown, and eventually becomes master of the Essex estate known as Leighton.

Known Associates: Ranulf-atte-Newgate, Corbett's devious young henchman and chief steward; Ralph Maltote, his messenger (dead by 1303); Chanson, his faithful manservant; Lady Maeve-app-Llewellyn, his wife and the mother of their daughter, Eleanor; King Edward I of England (1272–1307); the King's wife, Queen Eleanor of Castile (died 1290); Amaury de Craon, a spy in the service of King Philip IV of France, and a constant irritant to, and rival of, Corbett; Bishop Robert Burnell, King Edward I's Lord Chancellor and chief adviser (died 1292).

Premise: A chancery clerk becomes a spy for King Edward I in thirteenth-century England, solving mysteries along the way.

Comment: Corbett, originally the hero of a Welsh expedition during which he helped save the life of England's King Edward I, is rewarded with a cushy clerk's job in London. But when the King calls on him to help foil an assassination plot, he begins to realize his position is no longer quite so secure as he thought. The Author's Note for the first book in the series, *Satan in St Mary's*, quotes from his source material, a London chronicle written in Latin: "London at that time was in the middle of political change and tumult, and the crime may well have been something to do with the murky politics of the time." Thus does Doherty take inspiration from actual events and known historic personages to create a believable and interesting backdrop for his thirteenth-century Sherlock, setting up high expectations indeed for his medieval PI.

Literary Crimes & Chimes: In the Author's Note for *Murder Wears a Cowl*, Doherty notes:

> Many people have written and asked me whether Hugh Corbett is based on an actual historical person and, perhaps, now it is time I confessed to the truth. He is; and this real clerk was a principal agent in discovering the crime and bringing Puddlicott to justice and the treasure back to the King. His name was John de Droxford and if anyone wants to look at the real Corbett's handwriting, then look at Cole's Records (Record Commission 1844), which prints the indenture in which de Droxford specifies the jewels lost and recovered. John de Droxford was also commissioned

to empanel the juries to try Puddlicott and was instrumental in resolving this and many other mysterious incidents. Perhaps it is only right and time to give credit where credit is due.

Corbett is depicted as bright, assertive, and bold. One wonders, however, how realistic it is to portray his character so openly defying the king on so many occasions, particularly a monarch with the irrascible reputation of King Edward I. Indeed, at one point he turns his back on the King and starts to walk out the door. Edward draws his sword, but instead of running his feisty retainer through, he knights him! Somehow we doubt that this would have happened in real life. A slight "plot-hole" on the road to verisimilitude?

THE CASES

1. *Satan in St Mary's.* London: Robert Hale, 1986, 186 p.

LONDON, ENGLAND, JANUARY 1284. Though the bloody Battle of Evesham in 1258 crushed Simon de Montfort's rebellion and cost him his life, the traitorous movement he founded was never completely eradicated. Decades later, when Edward I became king, he faced considerable opposition, with Simon's followers gathering in London's teeming warrens and ghettos to foster murder, treason, and revolt. In 1284 Edward's interest is aroused by the Cheapside murder of Ralph Crepyn by Lawrence Duket, who then flees to the Church of St. Mary le Bow for sanctuary and soon after apparently commits suicide. The King, deeply suspicious of the affair and fearing that it might be linked with the rebels and their powerful underground society, the Pentangle, a group practicing the black arts, orders his wily Chancellor Burnell to look into the matter. Burnell chooses Corbett, a sharp and clever clerk from the Court of King's Bench, to conduct the investigation. Together with his manservant Ranulf, a felon late of Newgate, Hugh is swiftly drawn into the tangled politics and dangerous underworld of medieval England. His search takes him on a macabre journey through the mean, disease-infested streets of thirteenth-century London, where he eventually uncovers a ghastly demonic cult whose god is Satan and whose goal is the overthrowing of the throne. Its members will let no man stand in their way. Associate: Ranulf. Historical Figures: British King Edward I; Bishop Burnell; Queen Eleanor.

2. *The Crown in Darkness.* London: Robert Hale, 1988, 187 p.

SCOTLAND AND ENGLAND, MARCH 1286. King Alexander III of Scotland is riding to meet his beautiful new French bride, Yolande, one dark and stormy night when he falls to his death in an apparent accident. The Scottish throne is left vacant of any heir save an infant granddaughter, Queen

Margaret, although the powerful nobles of his own kingdom, as well as the great European princes, immediately began jockeying to fill the power vacuum. Hugh Corbett, a clerk in the English Chancery, is sent to Scotland by his old master, Chancellor Bishop Burnell, to uncover the truth behind Alexander's death and report on the chaotic situation at the Scottish court. Corbett is drawn into malevolent intrigue, suspicion, and danger, before truth and lies can be separated and the mystery finally solved. Associate: Ranulf. Historic Figures: British King Edward I; Bishop Burnell; Scottish King Alexander III; Scottish Queen Yolande.

3. *Spy in Chancery.* London: Robert Hale, 1988, 176 p.

ENGLAND, PARIS, FRANCE, AND WALES, OCTOBER 1296. Edward I of England and Philip IV of France are at war. By devious means, Philip has seized control of the English Duchy of Aquitaine in France and is now determined to crush his rival, King Edward. The British King suspects that his enemy is being aided by a spy in the English court and commissions his chancery clerk, Hugh Corbett, to trace and, if possible, destroy the traitor. Corbett's mission brings him into danger both on land and at sea and takes him to Paris and its dangerous underworld and then to hostile Wales. Unwillingly, he is drawn into the murky undercurrents of international politics in the last decade of the thirteenth century. The spy will stop at nothing, not even murder, to keep his identity secret. Hugh meets his future wife, Maeve, in this entry in the series. Associates: Ranulf; Maeve. Historical Figures: British King Edward I; French King Philip IV; Robert de Winchelsea, Archbishop of Canterbury.

4. *The Angel of Death.* London: Robert Hale, 1989, 159 p.

LONDON, ENGLAND, WINTER 1299. Edward I of England has invaded Scotland and brutally sacked the town of Berwick, razing to the ground the Red House of the Flemings who had permission to trade there. He little thinks that his actions will have far-reaching repercussions. A year later, Edward convokes a great assembly of the realm in St. Paul's Cathedral. The main celebrant of the mass, Walter de Montfort, has been delegated to lecture the King on not taxing the church. During the ceremony Montfort dies a sudden and violent death, leaving men to wonder whether God was punishing Edward of England or vindicating his royal rights. Hugh Corbett, the King's clerk, is given the task of solving the mystery and tracking down the murderer. Against the background of Edward's struggle to maintain himself, both at home and abroad, Corbett's investigations become tortuous and laced with danger before he can uncover the truth of how a man can be murdered in full view of the King and most of the notables of the country. Hugh becomes engaged to Maeve in this novel. Associates: Ranulf;

Maeve. Historical Figures: British King Edward I; Walter de Montfort; Robert de Winchelsea, Archbishop of Canterbury.

5. *The Prince of Darkness.* London: Headline, 1992, 247 p.

LONDON, ENGLAND, AND PARIS, FRANCE, AUGUST 1300. A fragile peace now exists between Edward I of England and Philip IV of France. But in the fetid alleys and slums of medieval London and Paris, the secret agents of both countries still fight their own silent, deadly battle. Edward, the bisexual Prince of Wales, wallows in luxury under the sinister influence of his favorite, Piers Gaveston. The latter dabbles in the black arts and has secret political ambitions to dominate the young prince and the English Crown. These scandals are threatened with exposure by the mysterious death of Lady Eleanor Belmont, a former mistress of the prince, who is found dead at the foot of the nunnery steps, her neck broken. Is this suicide or an accident, or has a malicious murder been committed? Edward turns for help to his master spy, Hugh Corbett, whose task is to resolve not only Belmont's death but several other grisly murders. In doing so, he faces the deadly rivalry of his French counterpart, Amaury de Craon, the murderous rage of Gaveston, and the silent threats of assassins, as well as the lies and silken deceits of his own master. In the course of this novel, Hugh receives Leighton Manor from the King in recognition of his many services to the Crown. Associates: Amaury; Maeve; Ranulf; Maltote. Historical Figures: British King Edward I; French King Philip IV; Edward, Prince of Wales; Piers Gaveston, Earl of Cornwall.

6. *Murder Wears a Cowl.* London: Headline, 1992, 249 p.

LONDON, ENGLAND, MAY 1302. A violent serial killer lurks in the city of London, slitting the throats of prostitutes. Little notice is taken until Lady Catherine Somerville, one of the Sisters of St. Martha, a lay-guild under the King's protection, is murdered in the same barbaric fashion. When her death is closely followed by that of the order's chaplain, Father Benedict, under equally suspicious circumstances, Edward of England turns once more to his trusted clerk, Hugh Corbett, to seek out the identity of the bloodthirsty assassin. Corbett, who has been promised a two-month holiday in Wales with his wife and daughter, demurs, but he cannot deny the crafty monarch's request, especially when Edward suddenly draws his sword—and knights Sir Hugh! Joining Corbett in his mission is his devious manservant, Ranulf, and his faithful horseman, Maltote. In the dark, fetid streets of the capital and in the abbey's desolate grounds, they encounter danger and deceit at every turn. Only Ragwort, the mad beggar who sleeps beneath the scaffold, has seen the killer strike, and the one clue that Corbett has to help him is Lady Somerville's cryptic message: "*Calcullus non facit monachum*"—"the cowl does not make the monk." Associates: Ranulf; Maltote; Maeve; Amaury. Historical Figure: British King Edward I.

7. *The Assassin in the Greenwood*. London: Headline, 1993, 217 p.

NOTTINGHAM, ENGLAND, AND PARIS, FRANCE, JUNE–JULY 1302. Edward I of England and Philip IV of France continue to observe diplomatic niceties while their agents wage a secret bloody war in the filthy streets of Paris. Edward and his chief clerk and Keeper of the Secret Seal, Sir Hugh Corbett, are desperate to discover Philip's secret plans for the invasion of Flanders. They manage by seduction and murder to obtain this information, only to discover that it is hidden in a secret cipher that Corbett is unable to break. Edward has other problems; a few years previously, he had issued a pardon to the notorious outlaw Robin of Locksley, popularly known as "Robin Hood." Robin, however, has now returned to his outlaw ways in Sherwood Forest, where he continues to battle royal authority, culminating in the barbarous massacre of the royal tax collectors, as well as Sir Eustace Vechey, Sheriff of the Nottingham District. Corbett and his two faithful servants, Ranulf and Maltote, are sent to Nottingham to investigate the mysterious murders and are all the more perplexed on their arrival to find fresh mysteries awaiting them. Why have three fire arrows been shot into the air above Nottingham? Who is the traitor in Nottingham Castle? Corbett's peace of mind is further shattered by the news that the French have dispatched an agent to assassinate him. *Assassin in the Greenwood* is based on the theory that Robin Hood actually lived during the reign of Edward I and, according to various extant documents, was pardoned by that King. The author notes that "the Robin Hood story is an amalgam of many legends, and this novel must be viewed as just one interpretation of them." Associates: Ranulf; Maltote; Amaury. Historical Figures: British King Edward I; Robin of Locksley, or "Robin Hood"; French King Philip IV.

8. *The Song of a Dark Angel*. London: Headline, 1993, 249 p.

NORFOLK, ENGLAND, NOVEMBER 1302. A cold, cruel wind sweeps across the Norfolk coast and chills those who live in its small villages. But the wind, called the Dark Angel because of its treacherous effect on both sea and land, is nothing compared to the evil plotted in the human heart. Sir Hugh Corbett, King Edward's Keeper of the Secret Seal, together with his manservant, Ranulf, and messenger, Maltote, are sent to Mortlake Manor to confront the evil therein. A man's headless corpse has been found on the beach, the head impaled on a pole; at the same time, the pretty young wife of a local baker is found hanging from a gallows; and the scene is set for more gruesome deaths. Corbett soon realizes that the icy wastes of Norfolk, where the eerie song of the Dark Angel can still be heard, are just as treacherous as the silken intrigue at the royal court or the violence of London's fetid alleyways. Associates: Ranulf; Maltote; Maeve. Historical Figure: British King Edward I.

9. *Satan's Fire*. London: Headline, 1995, 250 p.

YORK, ENGLAND, MARCH 1303. The Old Man of the Mountain remembers when he nearly killed Edward I of England almost thirty years before. He never forgets his prey and now decides to release an imprisoned leper knight to avenge his old grievances. One windswept evening a few months later, two nuns are hurrying to their mother house in York when they smell the sickly odor of burning human flesh. Rounding the corner, they confront the macabre sight of a man being consumed by a roaring fire. News of this grisly death meets Edward as he arrives in York for secret negotiations with the leaders of the military Order of the Temple. His unease deepens for, as he enters the city, a would-be regicide attempts to murder him. When the assassin, wearing the livery of the Templar Order, is found dead—having been engulfed by a mysterious fire—Edward immediately enlists the help of his Keeper of the Secret Seal, Sir Hugh Corbett, to investigate. Associates: Ranulf (now a clerk in the Chancery of the Green Seal); Maeve; Maltote. Historical Figures: British King Edward I; Jacques de Molay, Grand Master of the Templars.

10. *The Devil's Hunt*. London: Headline, 1996, 249 p.

OXFORD, ENGLAND, SUMMER 1303. Murder makes its presence felt in the King's university city of Oxford. The severed heads of several beggars (their bleeding torsos hidden in undergrowth nearby) are found tied by the hair to the trees in the woods outside Oxford. In the city itself, all is not well at one of the colleges, Sparrow Hall; its Regent, John Copsale, has been found dead in his bed. Some claim that he died in his sleep, while others whisper that he was murdered by the eerie "Bell Man," a mysterious writer posting anonymous, treasonous bills and letters on church doors all over the city. Then the college librarian and archivist, Robert Ascham, is discovered in the locked and sealed library, a crossbow bolt sticking in his chest, and a piece of manuscript lying beside him. Are the Regent's death and Ascham's murder connected? King Edward hears of the unrest and arrives unannounced at Sir Hugh Corbett's country manor at Leighton to insist that his chief clerk go to Oxford to resolve the murders. Corbett reluctantly agrees, for when the King commands, few can resist, even if it means knowingly entering a dangerous and violent world. Associates: Ranulf (now Corbett's bailiff and chief steward); Maltote (now Corbett's master of horse); Maeve. Historical Figure: British King Edward I.

11. *The Demon Archer*. London: Headline, 1999, 250 p.

OXFORD, ENGLAND, SEPTEMBER 1303. The death of Lord Henry Fitzalan on the feast of St. Matthew is a matter widely reported but little mourned.

Infamous for his lecherous tendencies, his midnight trysts with a coven of witches, and his boundless self-interest, he was a man of few friends. So when Hugh Corbett is asked to bring his murderer to justice, it is not a matter of finding a single suspect, but of choosing among a great many. Immediate suspicion falls on Lord Henry's chief verderer, Robert Verlian. His daughter had been the focus of Lord Henry's roving eye in the weeks before his death, and Henry was not a man to take no for an answer. But the culprit could just as easily be Sir William, the dead man's younger brother. It's no secret that Sir William covets the Fitzalan estate, but would he kill to inherit? Then Hugh himself is attacked and nearly dies. The possibilities are endless, but the truth is more terrible than anyone could ever have imagined. Associates: Amaury; Ranulf; Maeve. Historical Figure: British King Edward I.

12. *The Treason of the Ghosts.* London: Headline, 2000, 249 p.

MELFORD, ENGLAND, OCTOBER 1303. Five years earlier in the village of Melford, a local lord had been executed for a spate of vicious murders. But now several other young women have been found violated and garroted, and the dead lord's son, Maurice Chapeleys, insists that a miscarriage of justice has taken place. Meanwhile, someone who apparently believes in Sir Roger Chapeleys's innocence is exacting his own kind of vengeance as, one by one, the members of the jury that had sent the lord to the gibbet are brutally murdered. Maurice's appeal to the royal council is answered when Edward I of England sends his chief clerk to Melford to discover the truth. Hugh Corbett, with his faithful servants Ranulf and Chanson, faces the difficult task of unraveling the secrets of a distrustful community tormented by murder. Seeking connections between the deaths, Corbett realizes that a serial killer is terrorizing the villagers. But Corbett believes there could now be two killers, one preying on the corrupt jurors, the other on vulnerable women and on anyone else who might stumble across his true identity. Associates: Ranulf (now principal clerk in the Chancery of the Green Wax); Chanson. Historical Figure: British King Edward I.

13. *Corpse Candle.* London: Headline, 2001, 310 p.

LINCOLNSHIRE, ENGLAND, NOVEMBER 1303. The Benedictine monks of the Abbey of St. Martin's-in-the-Marsh are accustomed to a comfortable existence inside their sprawling, peaceful estate. But that begins to change when Abbot Stephen, a well-respected leader and a personal friend of King Edward I, is found brutally murdered in his chamber, with the door and windows locked from the inside. Soon Sir Hugh Corbett, Keeper of the King's Seal, arrives with his two henchmen to investigate. Up to now, the brothers at St. Martin's have paid little heed to local rumors that circulate about the ghost of a robber baron, Sir Geoffrey Mandeville, who gallops through the Lincolnshire fens with a retinue of ghostly horsemen. They may hear the shrill blast of a phantom hunting horn or see the corpse candles glowing in the dark, but none really accept the peasants' belief that these flickering lights can forewarn men of their own deaths. Corbett disregards these tales, suspecting that someone much more alive is responsible for the bloody acts. As the death toll mounts, he sets about to unearth the dark secrets that the abbey and its inhabitants have been concealing for so long. Associates: Ranulf; Chanson.

MATTHEW JANKYN SERIES

Scene of the Crime: England, beginning in 1404.

Detective: Matthew Jankyn, "ex-scholar, liar, mercenary soldier, and thief."

Known Associates: Bishop Henry Beaufort (died 1477), Bishop of Winchester, King's Chancellor, illegitimate grandson of "The Black Prince," and half brother to British King Henry V.

Premise: A British official investigates the deaths of prominent political personages in fifteenth-century Europe.

Comment: Matthew Jankyn, the ninety-year-old Lord of the Manor of Newport in Shropshire, is dictating his life's story to his clerk. He recounts how in 1404 Bishop Beaufort, the King's Chancellor, rescued the thief Matthew Jankyn from Newgate prison and appointed him to investigate the death of Richard II and to track the suspected assassins, led by the evil Sir John Oldcastle. Matthew fulfills this task in *The Whyte Harte* but then is dispatched by Beaufort to France to fight for King Henry V in the Battle of Agincourt. Matthew continues his life story in *The Serpent amongst the Lilies,* where he recalls the details of King Henry's untimely death in 1422 and the events leading up to the execution of Jeanne d'Arc and some supposed sightings of her years later.

Literary Crimes & Chimes: Welladay, it's all rather improbable, isn't it? Doherty typically weaves together several supposed real-life mysteries into a story that sounds plausible enough on the surface but falls apart immediately upon inspection. The writer's later books do a much better job with such scenarios.

THE CASES

1. *The Whyte Harte.* London: Robert Hale, 1988, 256 p.
   ENGLAND, JANUARY 1404. Jankyn tells the tale of the murder of Richard II, the events leading up to that death, and the mystery enshrouding it. Of course, Jankyn is a liar, but perhaps "not so much of a liar." Jankyn's

narrative relates his own past spent unwillingly under the tutelage of priests and friars in an Augustinian monastery; his rebellious flirtation with the heresy of Lollardism; and finally his becoming a thief, an accused traitor, and ultimately a yeoman to Henry Beaufort, Bishop of Winchester and the King's Chancellor. It is Beaufort who "rescues" Jankyn from Newgate Prison. Rumors abound that King Richard II was not actually murdered in the year 1400 but continues to thrive in Scotland, where he is encouraging the small rebellion taking place under the sign of the Whyte Harte. Ultimately, Jankyn breaks the back of the rebellion and is rewarded with the restoration of his father's estates. Historical Figure: Bishop Beaufort.

2. *The Serpent amongst the Lilies.* London: Robert Hale, 1990, 189 p.

ENGLAND, 1429. Jankyn (the "serpent") is set among the followers of Jeanne d'Arc (the so-called Lilies) at the behest of Beaufort. Beaufort wants to know if Jeanne is really a saint or a witch and how to use her so that the war by the French against the British can be foiled. Jankyn, despite his criminal background, comes to like Jeanne and to resent being pitted against her. At the same time, Jeanne acts as if she knows that Jankyn is a spy. A twist in the story of the trial and execution of Jeanne finishes this book off nicely. Historical Figures: Bishop Beaufort; Joan of Arc.

CANTERBURY TALES SERIES

Scene of the Crime: Medieval England, beginning in 1350.

Detective: Various.

Known Associates: Master Harry, the taverner; Sir Godfrey, the knight; Nicholas Chirke, the man of law; Barleycorn, the franklin; the poor priest; the carpenter; Alice, the wife of Bath; Eglantine, the prioress; the miller; the pardoner; the clerk; Geoffrey Chaucer, the author of these tales; the summoner.

Premise: Pilgrims to Canterbury gather in the Tabard, a tavern in Southwark owned by Master Harry. At their host's suggestion, they agree to amuse themselves with tales of "terror and of mystery." Each book in the series constitutes one of the pilgrims' tales.

Comment: This time Doherty takes his cue from the *Canterbury Tales* of Geoffrey Chaucer, a frequent source of inspiration, but it's not all that much of an inspiration in the end. The stories are told as "tales within tales," and surprise of surprises, each one just happens to feature a murder mystery! The stories, however, are jumbled together, with chapters of commentary by the pilgrims interspersed with the tales themselves. The books are hard to follow and rather poorly assembled, filled with overly stilted language and improbable situations. The true identity of the teller of each tale is revealed at the end of each novel as one of the main characters in the tale. *Mirabile dictu!*

Literary Crimes & Chimes: The poor scribe's tale goes something like this: "I tried to read these books, gentle people, really I did, but I promptly entered a state of profound somnolence." Or, "my pen runneth over with verbiage." Doherty's poorest excuse for a historical mystery series, to be avoided like the proverbial plague.

THE CASES

1. *An Ancient Evil: The Knight's Tale of Mystery and Murder as He Goes on Pilgrimage from London to Canterbury.* London: Headline, 1994, 248 p.

SOUTHWORK, AND OXFORD, ENGLAND, APRIL 1350. As the travelers gather in the Tabard Inn at the start of a pilgrimage to pray before the blessed bones of St. Thomas à Becket in Canterbury, they agree to mine host Harry's suggestion of amusing themselves on each day of their journey with one tale, and on each evening with another, with the latter being stories of mystery, terror, and murder. Sir Godfrey, the knight, begins the cycle on the first evening. He tells of the destruction of a sinister cult at its stronghold in the wilds of Oxfordshire by Sir Hugo Mortimer during the reign of William the Conqueror and then moves to Oxford some 200 years later, where strange crimes and terrible murders are again being committed. The authorities seem powerless, but Lady Constance, Abbess of the Convent of St. Anne's, believes that the murders are connected with the legends of the cult, and she petitions the King for help. As the murders continue unabated, special commissioner Sir Godfrey Evesden and royal clerk Alexander McBain uncover clues that lead to a macabre sect that worships the dark lord. But they can find no solution to a series of increasingly baffling questions, and matters are not helped by the growing rift between Sir Godfrey and McBain for the hand and favor of the fair Lady Emily.

2. *A Tapestry of Murders: The Man of Law's Tale of Mystery and Murder as He Goes on Pilgrimage from London to Canterbury.* London: Headline, 1994, 247 p.

LONDON, AND KENT, ENGLAND, AUGUST 1358. Chaucer's pilgrims, quarreling among themselves, are traveling through open countryside and enjoying the fresh spring weather as they progress slowly toward Canterbury. A motley collection of travelers, they each have their dark secrets, hidden passions, and complex lives. As they shelter in a tavern from a sudden April shower, they choose the Man of Law to narrate the next tale of fear and sinister dealings. In August 1358 the Dowager Queen Isabella, mother of King Edward III, the "She Wolf of France," who betrayed and destroyed her husband because of her adulterous infatuation for Roger Mortimer, lies dying of the pestilence in the somber fortress of Castle Rising, where her "loving" son has kept her incarcerated. According to the Man of Law, Isabella dies, and her body is taken along the Mile End Road and laid to rest in Greyfriars next to the mangled remains of her lover, who has paid dearly for his presumption in loving a queen. Nevertheless, as in life so in death, Isabella causes intrigue, violence, and murder. Nicholas Chirke, an honest young lawyer, is brought in to investigate the strange events following her death and quickly finds himself at wit's end trying to resolve the mysteries before a great scandal unfolds. Historical Figure: Geoffrey Chaucer.

3. *A Tournament of Murders: The Franklin's Tale of Mystery and Murder as He Goes on Pilgrimage from London to Canterbury.* London: Headline, 1996, 249 p.

SINGLEWELL, AND COLCHESTER, ENGLAND, 1356. Chaucer's pilgrims are sheltering in a friary as they slowly wind their way toward Canterbury. As they settle for the night, the Franklin narrates a mysterious, bloody tale, a true story, he suggests, which affects not only his own life but the lives of some of his fellow pilgrims. In 1356 the Black Prince has won his resounding victory at Poitiers. However, in that bloody fight the impoverished knight Gilbert Savage received his death wound. As Gilbert lies dying in a ditch, he tells his squire, Richard Greenlee, that the story of his parents perishing during the plague is untrue. Richard, if he wishes to uncover what really happened, must travel to Colchester and seek out the lawyer Hugo Coticol, who holds a sealed letter telling the truth of Richard's parentage and the dreadful secrets surrounding his father's disgraceful death. This document contains a most macabre confession, and Richard finds himself a small step closer to discovering the truth, a bloody and heinous tale of duplicity and murder, one that compels him to avenge his father's name. Historical Figure: Geoffrey Chaucer.

4. *Ghostly Murders: The Poor Priest's Tale of Mystery and Murder as He Goes on Pilgrimage from London to Canterbury.* London: Headline, 1997, 250 p.

KENT, ENGLAND, 1389. Chaucer's Canterbury pilgrims have been caught by a sudden spring shower just as they're passing a deserted village. The sight of its decaying church and derelict cemetery provokes the poor Priest to tears, so when they get lost and have to take shelter in its ruins, it is he who tells the next mysterious tale of ancient evil, greed, devilish murder, and chilling haunting. There was once a young man, Philip Trumpington, who was appointed parish priest of Scawsby in Kent, a pleasant, prosperous village with a church built many centuries earlier. Philip is accompanied there by his brother Edmund and their close friend, stonemason Stephen Merkle. They secure permission to pull down the old church and build a new one outside the village at a place called High Mount. Years earlier a group of Templars had been brutally massacred on the marshes near Scawsby. Their attackers were led by a former vicar of Scawsby, Romenal, a warlock and a sorcerer. Philip soon discovers that the church and presbytery are haunted by "The Watchers" and by the ghost of the former wicked priest. The church holds other secrets: buried treasure, the identity of the old "Corpse Woman" who lives in the cemetery, and a terrible curse that scars the lives of the villagers. Philip realizes that the great and ancient evil that pervades the church must be brought into the light, resolved, and reparations made. But the price is great, taking the poor Priest and his brother, the Ploughman, to Canterbury to pray before the "blissful bones" of St. Thomas à Becket. Historical Figure: Geoffrey Chaucer.

5. *The Hangman's Hymn: The Carpenter's Tale of Mystery and Murder as He Goes on Pilgrimage from London to Canterbury.* London: Headline, 2001, 213 p.

ENGLAND, 13–? Stumbling upon a roadside execution, Chaucer's pilgrims witness a hanging that leaves the carpenter in a dead faint. That evening, as the travelers rest in a priory, he narrates a Gloucester hangman's tale of supernatural murder. When Simon Cotterill, a carpenter, follows his sweetheart to Gloucester, he is beaten by her father's thugs. Homeless and with no family to help him, he accepts the only job he can find and joins the local hangman's crew, replacing a man who was himself sent to the gibbet. But Simon feels rejected even by the desperate men with whom he now works, until he learns the secret of how a hanged man can walk away from his grave. Meanwhile, from the forest paths around Gloucester young women are disappearing. When a disfigured corpse is found, the mayor suspects a coven of witches is preying on vulnerable souls and arrests three hideous hags. Afraid the town's prosperity might suffer from a reputation for witchcraft, he calls the hangmen and Gloucester's chief aldermen to a midnight trial that condemns the women. They are taken to the scene of their crimes, the Forest of Dean, to be hanged for three days. But the unearthly sound of the forest at night frightens even the hangmen, and a violent storm drives them to seek shelter, leaving the witches swinging from the gibbet tree. The next morning, their bodies are gone. Back in Gloucester, the witches' *dominus*, the leader of their coven, wants revenge on every man involved in the secretive punishment of three witches. One by one, they are found dead, and Simon is forced into hiding as he attempts to destroy the coven and save his own life.

TELAMON SERIES

Scene of the Crime: Ancient Macedon.

Detective: Telamon, a Macedonian physician and friend of King Alexander the Great.

Known Associates: Macedonian King Alexander III the Great; Aristander, Master of Secrets and a magus; Queen Mother Olympias; Queen Eurydice.

Premise: A friend and colleague of Macedonian King Alexander the Great solves crimes on behalf of his master.

Comment: As with the earlier Doherty novels published under the pen name "Anna Apostolou," this series focuses on ancient Macedon and the character of its dynamic fourth-century BC monarch, Alexander the Great. Here the detective is the Greek physician Telamon, another friend of the King (the two Jewish detectives of the earlier series are not mentioned—did they even exist?!). Again, the crimes here are mostly political in nature, based on the intricate court battles that filled the Macedonian state. One is left wondering whether one reason that Alexander spent so much time away from home is to avoid his Macedonian relatives.

Literary Crimes & Chimes: Telamon is an engaging character, and the crimes themselves fit well within the *milieu* of the period. There is the usual somewhat supernatural character hovering around in the background, mumbling mysterious meanderings that don't mean much of anything. As Doherty series go, that's about par for the course.

THE CASES

1. *The House of Death: A Mystery of Alexander the Great.* London: Constable, 2001, 276 p.

MACEDONIA AND PERSIA, SPRING 334 BC. Alexander has led his troops to the banks of the Hellespont, poised to make his invasion into the empire of the great Persian King Darius III. He knows he must win the approval of the gods for his enterprise and makes sacrifice after sacrifice, yet the smoke does not rise; the sacrifices are tainted. Worse, the guide he has hired to lead him through Persian territory is brutally murdered. Persian spies are active in the camp, the men are becoming demoralized, and Alexander's own generals have their secret ambitions. Into this whirlpool of mistrust comes Telamon, an old friend of Alexander's boyhood, who has been sought out and cajoled into joining the Macedonian king by Queen Olympias, Alexander's mother. She charges him with protecting her son from the dangers that surround him. Events move swiftly. More murders occur and a party of assassins enters the camp. Alexander himself is threatened with mysterious messages, quotations from his favorite works, including *The Iliad*, which depicts him as a patricide, the murderer of his own father, Philip II. As the climax builds, Alexander displays his true heroic stature, throwing off the fears and nervous panics he is prey to, as he achieves a brilliant and bloody triumph over the Persian king. Telamon at last succeeds in revealing the secret enemies within the camp. Associate: Aristander. Historical Figures: Queen Mother Olympias; Queen Eurydice; Macedonian King Alexander the Great; Persian King Darius III.

2. *The Godless Man: A Mystery of Alexander the Great.* London: Constable, 2002, 303 p.

MACEDONIA, PERSIA, AND EPHESUS, SUMMER 334 BC. Alexander has smashed the armies of the great king Darius III at the Battle of Granicus and is roaming the Western Persian Empire, picking off the cities one by one like a hungry predator, living up to his nickname of "the Wolf of Macedon." Arriving at one of his prizes, the great town of Ephesus, Alexander and his successful campaign are threatened by a series of violent murders instigated by a high-ranking Persian spy known only as "the Centaur." Worse, one of Alexander's old tutors, Leonidas, is found floating facedown in a stagnant pool at the House of Medusa. Alexander, meanwhile, on the one hand, is preoccupied with finding a deepwater port for his ships and, on the other, is equally concerned to have the famous artist Appelles design a breathtaking portrait of himself to be placed in the Temple of Artemis, patron deity of Ephesus. Once again Alexander's friend and physician, the level-headed Telamon, must take it upon himself to unravel this swirling mass of bloodstrewn mysteries, this time working hand in hand with the king's eerie Master of Secrets, Aristander. As always, one of the biggest obstacles is the volatile and unpredictable nature of Alexander himself, a consummate actor whose lust for power and glory matches the carnage and intrigue that dog his footsteps like the furies themselves. Associate: Aristander. Historical Figures: Macedonian King Alexander the Great; Persian King Darius III.

3. *The Gates of Hell: A Mystery of Alexander the Great.* London: Constable, 2003, 292 p.

MACEDONIA AND PERSIA, LATE SUMMER 334 BC. King Alexander is besieging the city of Halicarnassus. A series of brutal killings seem to indicate that the Persians have infiltrated the nearby Macedonian court. While his lord prepares for the fight of his life, Telamon enters a maelstrom of murder and intrigue. He must go through the gates of Hell to find the traitors and protect King Alexander, but all the while the ever-cunning monarch keeps his own counsel and pursues his own plans to foil his enemies. Associate: Aristander. Historical Figures: Macedonian King Alexander the Great; Queen Mother Olympias; Queen Eurydice; Persian King Darius III.

MISCELLANEOUS SERIES

(As "Vanessa Alexander")

Scene of the Crime: England, various dates.

Detective: Henry Trokelowe, a clerk in the court of King Edward I (*The Love Knot*); Maria Eleanora, a beautiful young woman from the court of King Charles II and Queen Catherine (*The Loving Cup*).

Known Associates: Various.

Premise: Doherty fuses the romance and historical mystery genre in these two nonseries productions.

Comment: Both of these books deal with real-life historical situations and merge together actual figures from history with invented characters. The first novel features a series of supposed letters written from the principals to each other, but of course, the language and themes feature mostly present-day concerns, and are per se anachronistic in many respects. In the second book, *The Loving Cup*, Doherty chooses to tell a more conventional story based around the Great Plot against the British throne of 1678–1680. Interposed is a conventional romance between insider and outsider.

Literary Crimes & Chimes: These two novels are middle-of-the-road for Paul Doherty's fiction: both contain some worthwhile moments, but neither offers much of anything to write home about. So much of the author's fiction begins sounding alike after one has read just a few of them. Trokelowe could easily have been Hugh Corbett, the agent for King Edward I in the series of that name. And so forth. There's just nothing original here, not even the titles.

1. *The Love Knot.* London: Headline, 1999, 183 p.

ENGLAND, APRIL–JULY 1297. Joanna of Acre, the recently widowed daughter of King Edward I, is pleased at her father's unexpected visit. But Edward has heard a rumor of an inappropriate friendship between Joanna, still officially in mourning, and a penniless commoner, Ralph Monthermer. Edward, believing he has proof of a clandestine affair, whisks Joanna off to a nunnery and imprisons Ralph in Bristol Castle. Henry Trokelowe, Edward's clerk, convinces the King not to execute Ralph, who is spared while the cold, dispassionate Henry investigates the source of the rumors. Ralph and Joanna's only chance of survival now lies in the hands of a confirmed bachelor who cannot even begin to understand the emotions that bind them. One wonders if this story began as one of the novels in the Hugh Corbett series. Historical Figures: British King Edward I; Princess Joanna of Acre, Countess of Gloucester.

2. *The Loving Cup.* London: Headline, 2001, 244 p.

ENGLAND, OCTOBER 1678. Samuel Atkins is deeply in love with Maria Eleanora, a beautiful young woman from the court of Queen Catherine, consort of King Charles II. But Atkins is a poor clerk and Maria Eleanora a foreigner, so their love must remain a secret. When an important judge is found murdered, Samuel Pepys' followers are suspected, and Atkins is arrested. Suddenly, Maria Eleanora realizes that to save her love and discover the hideous truth behind the crime, she must thread her way through both the treacherous alleys of London and the murky and murderous politics of those seeking to destroy the king. Historical Figures: British King Charles II; British Queen Catherine; journalist Samuel Pepys, Secretary to the Navy.

MIRIAM AND SIMEON BARTIMAEUS SERIES

(As "Anna Apostolou")

Scene of the Crime: Ancient Macedon, beginning in 336 BC.

Detective: Miriam and Simeon Bartimaeus, brother and sister, Jewish clerks to Macedonian King Alexander III the Great.

Known Associates: Queen Olympias, Alexander's mother and King Philip II's first wife; Queen Eurydice, King Philip II's second wife; Macedonian King Philip II.

Premise: Two Jewish clerks to King Alexander the Great investigate crimes on behalf of their master.

Comment: The placement of two Jewish characters in a Macedonian setting is a stroke of genius. The twin detectives Miriam and Simeon had been born joined at the elbow; Olympias' physician cut them apart as infants, and they were raised with Prince Alexander in the Macedonian court, Simeon becoming one of Alexander's principal scribes. Their joint perspective as both outsiders and insiders in the midst of a seething political cauldron makes them perfect observers and detectives in an ancient world setting.

Literary Crimes & Chimes: This series works better than most of Doherty's fiction and is quite entertaining. The Old World setting, the use of very unusual detectives, and the insertion of real-life political killings, together with the author's usual extensive research into the period, make his picture of Macedonia come alive in the reader's mind. Well worth seeking out.

THE CASES

1. *A Murder in Macedon: A Mystery of Alexander the Great.* New York: St. Martin's Press, 1997, 243 p.

AGAEA, MACEDONIA, GREECE, AND PERSEPOLIS, PERSIA, JUNE 336 BC. The assassination of King Philip II of Macedon sets off tremors throughout Greece. Rumors abound: some say one of his wives did it, others say that it must have been the action of his ambitious son and successor, King Alexander III, and still others claim the murder must have been part of a Persian conspiracy. To quell the gossip and to clear his name, Alexander appoints two Jewish clerks, Miriam and Simeon Bartimaeus, to seek out the killer and clear the new King's name. Historical Figures: Macedonian King Alexander the Great; Persian King Darius III; Queen Mother Olympias; Queen Eurydice; Macedonian King Philip II.

2. *A Murder in Thebes: A Mystery of Alexander the Great.* New York: St. Martin's Press, 1998, 226 p.

THEBES, GREECE, FALL 332 BC. Just as Alexander the Great is set to capture Thebes, where Oedipus had, according to myth, killed his father and married his own mother, two of the King's favorite officers, Lysander and Mamnon, are discovered murdered. His sleuthing clerks, Miriam and Simeon Bartimaeus, are assigned to investigate the case and uncover the truth behind the killings and to solve the riddle of Oedipus' crown. Alexander is determined to seize the historic artifact as a vindication of his own assumption of power. Historical Figures: Macedonian King Alexander the Great; Persian King Darius III; Queen Olympias.

KATHRYN SWINBROOKE SERIES

(As "C. L. Grace")

Scene of the Crime: Canterbury, England, beginning in 1471.

Detective: Kathryn Swinbrooke, physician and apothecary.

Known Associates: Edward IV, real-life King of Great Britain (1460–1470, 1471–1483); Colum Murtagh, custodian of King Edward's horses, later the King's Commissioner in Canterbury, paramour of Kathryn, to whom he is betrothed in *Saintly Murders* and married in *A Feast of Poisons*; Thomasina, servant to Kathryn; Holbech, servant to Colum; Agnes, Kathryn's maid; Wuf, a foundling Kathryn takes in; Rawnose, a beggar Kathryn befriends.

Premise: An English apothecary solves crimes and heals the sick in fifteenth-century Britain.

Comment: Mistress Swinbrooke's profession as an apothecary and physician is, according to Doherty, historically accurate, and it certainly becomes a major factor in this series of mysteries. Women physicians were often hired by the British royal family to heal their sick relatives, which explains Kathryn's frequent encounters with King Edward IV and his minions. Also, many of the crimes revolve around the use of obscure poisons or potions, which Kathryn proves adept at deciphering. Kathryn is strongly assisted by an Irish mercenary, Colum, who chooses the right side in the War of the Roses and is rewarded by the king with the title of Master of Horse and later is given the commissionership of Canterbury. Colum's standing with the civil government lends *gravitas* to Kathryn's investigations. Kathyrn's sometime cook, Thomasina, notable for her colorful oaths, is another beloved companion.

Literary Crimes & Chimes: As with all of Doherty's historical fictions, the Swinbrooke series includes a number of questionable anachronisms and a concentration on themes that simply would not have been of contemporary importance to Kathryn and her friends. The author is at his strongest in depicting the political issues of the day and in establishing the historical background to his stories; but his characters are no more than skin-deep, even when they prove attractive to a modern audience. The Swinbrooke series is one of his better creations, however, revolving around the seemingly strange idea of a woman physician practicing in medieval times. Kathryn's freedom of movement in these books is probably an unlikely happenstance at best, but Doherty makes us want to believe in his scenario. Of all of his many series, this one does perhaps the best job of deromanticizing the Middle Ages and bringing the reader down to the nitty-gritty of everyday life. A remedy for *ennui* well worth pursuing.

THE CASES

1. *A Shrine of Murders: Being the First of the Canterbury Tales of Kathryn Swinbrooke, Leech and Physician.* New York: St. Martin's Press, 1993, 195 p.
   CANTERBURY, ENGLAND, MAY 1471. In the immediate aftermath of King Edward's defeat of the forces of King Henry VI, a demented serial killer is targeting pilgrims on their way to the renowned shrine in Canterbury, using Geoffrey Chaucer's *Canterbury Tales* as a guide to choosing his next victim. Kathryn is the first person to recognize the pattern of murders and with her friends, Colum Murtagh and Thomasina, tracks down the killer and puts an end to his vicious rampage. Associates: Colum; Thomasina; Holbech. Historical Figures: British King Edward IV; Queen Elizabeth; George, Duke of Clarence; Richard, Duke of Gloucester.

2. *The Eye of God.* New York: St. Martin's Press, 1994, 198 p.

CANTERBURY, ENGLAND, SUMMER 1471 (the Prologue is dated April 1471). As the bloody confusion of the War of the Roses rages around him, Richard Neville, Earl of Warwick, entrusts the precious relic, the Eye of God (a pendant with a large sapphire, inscribed in Latin on the front and with a scene of the Nativity engraved on the reverse), to his faithful soldier Brandon, just before Neville is killed at Barnet. Ordered to take the priceless artifact to the monks at Canterbury, Brandon is captured and held prisoner in the city. When Brandon dies under mysterious circumstances and the Eye of God is nowhere to be found, soldier Colum Murtagh is summoned by King Edward IV to find the relic, and physician Kathryn Swinbrooke is called in to assess Brandon's death. Resuming their unlikely partnership, the two find themselves in an increasingly dangerous situation. A corpse is pulled from a river and another murder takes place in Canterbury, while Colum is tracked by threatening pursuers. All signs point to an intrigue involving enemies of Edward IV, and Colum and Katherine must rely on each other's wits for protection. Associates: Colum; Thomasina. Historical Figures: Richard Neville, Earl of Warwick; British King Edward IV; George, Duke of Clarence; Richard, Duke of Gloucester.

3. *The Merchant of Death.* New York: St. Martin's Press, 1994, 182 p.

CANTERBURY, ENGLAND, CHRISTMAS 1471. Kathryn and her cook, Thomasina, are busily preparing for the holiday when terrible news arrives: the painter, Richard Blunt, has confessed to killing his young wife, along with the two men who were dallying with her. Then another death captures the apothecary's attention: a tax collector, Sir Reginald Erpingham, has been found poisoned in his room at the Wicker Man Tavern, and the king's revenues have been stolen from his purse. Kathryn's inquiry dovetails with the official investigation of Colum Murtagh regarding the missing tax moneys. Then the prime suspect, the tax man's clerk, Vavasour, suddenly vanishes. Associates: Thomasina; Colum.

4. *The Book of Shadows.* New York: St. Martin's Press, 1996, 195 p.

CANTERBURY, ENGLAND, 1471. Shortly after the murderous takeover of the throne by Edward IV and his Queen, Elizabeth Woodville, in 1471, blackmailers thrived by threatening detractors of the new King. The ugliest threat to the decent people of Canterbury is the Queen's necromancer, the magus known to his followers as Tenebrae. He controls his acolytes through the *Book of Shadows*, a *grimoire* of supposed magical spells that also holds the written secrets of Queen Elizabeth and other prominent members of the court. Elizabeth has begun to fear the magician's knowledge and power. When Tenebrae is murdered and his book disappears, Kathryn, locked in a loveless marriage to the missing rebel, Alexander Wyville, is called in to investigate the cause of death and, with the assistance of her special "friend," King's Commissioner Colum Murtagh, to restore the dangerous collection of secrets to the court. The price of failure is the threatened transfer of Colum to far-off London. Everyone is suspect, especially Tenebrae's last visitors, a group of goldsmiths from London, and the strange pilgrim lying near death whom Father Cuthbert is tending at St. Mary's Hospital. All the usual suspects begin falling victim, and Swinbrooke must move quickly to solve the puzzle or risk the potential removal of the man she has grown to love. Associates: Colum; Thomasina; Agnes; Wuf; Simon Luberon, the Canterbury city clerk; Father Cuthbert, supervisor of Saint Mary's Hospital; Rawnose. Historical Figures: British King Edward IV; Queen Elizabeth.

5. ***Saintly Murders: A Medieval Mystery Featuring Kathryn Swinbrooke.*** New York: St. Martin's Minotaur, 2001, 241 p.

CANTERBURY, ENGLAND, LATE SUMMER 1472. Kathryn is summoned to investigate another puzzling murder. She is appointed by the Archbishop of Canterbury as "*Advocatus Diaboli*" (Devil's Advocate) to argue against the beatification of Roger Atworth, a friar in the Order of the Sack and the confessor of Dame Cecily of York, King Edward IV's mother. Atworth has perished under mysterious circumstances, and there are rumors afloat of miraculous happenings surrounding his body. At the same time, an infestation of rats has begun to afflict the city. When Kathryn begins asking questions about Atworth's death, she discovers that the logical explanation is murder, not miracles. His involvement with Cecily may actually have brought about his demise. Associates: Luberon, clerk to the Canterbury City Council; Colum; Thomasina; Holbech. Historical Figures: Thomas Bourchier, Archbishop of Canterbury; British King Edward IV; British Queen Mother Cecily.

6. ***A Maze of Murders.*** New York: St. Martin's Minotaur, 2003, 239 p.

CANTERBURY, ENGLAND, AUGUST 1473. A violent past haunts Sir Walter Maltravers, the wealthy lord of Ingoldby Hall. As a commander during the War of the Roses, he fought alongside King Edward IV at the bloody Battle of Towton. Decades earlier and thousands of miles away, he also served in the bodyguard of the last Byzantine Emperor, Constantine XI Palaiologos. As Turkish janissaries breached Constantinople's walls and set the city aflame in 1453, Sir Walter committed an unforgivable sin: instead of defending the Emperor with his last drop of blood, Maltravers fled, but not before scooping up all the treasure he could carry, including the *Lacrima Christi*, a giant ruby relic of incalculable value. When the jewel disappears from the Canterbury Franciscan monastery, Sir Walter fears that the Emperor's vengeful loyalists, the *Athanatoi*, have tracked him to his estate. In the shrine at the center of his enormous private hedge-maze, Sir Walter encounters his ax-wielding killer. His head turns up days later impaled on a pole. Then Kathryn is called in to investigate, and her Irish *fiancé*, Colum Murtagh, the King's Commissioner in Canterbury, is summoned to assist her. Associates: Colum; Luberon.

7. *A Feast of Poisons*. New York: St. Martin's Minotaur, 2004, 240 p.

WALMER, ENGLAND, SEPTEMBER 1473. In the village of Walmer, the blacksmith Elias and his wife, Isabella, are murdered, but with two entirely different poisons. The village's medicine woman, Mother Croul, does not believe that the two killed each other, and neither do Kathryn and her new husband, Colum, who are visiting the region on state business. There Lord Henry Beauchamp, keeper of the Secret Seal, will receive the shadowy emissaries of King Louis XI on behalf of his own master, King Edward IV, with Colum looking on. Kathryn offers to help Croul solve the mystery surrounding the deaths of Elias and Isabella. Associate: Colum. Historical Figure: French King Louis XI.

SIR ROGER SHALLOT SERIES

(As "Michael Clynes")

Scene of the Crime: England, beginning in 1517.

Detective: Sir Roger Shallot (born 1502), a spy for Cardinal Wolsey in the time of Henry VIII of England.

Known Associates: Benjamin Daunbey, a nephew to Cardinal Wolsey and Shallot's mentor and friend; Cardinal Thomas Wolsey, the King's Minister; Doctor Agrippa, Wolsey's adviser and magician, who may be immortal; Margot and Phoebe, Shallot's servants as an old man; William Shakespeare, Shallot's friend as an old man.

Premise: Shallot, a Justice of the Peace under Cardinal Wolsey, is called upon by the King's adviser to investigate various crimes and misdemeanors and to assist with resolving various delicate matters of concern to King Henry's realm.

Comment: The series is presented, as is typical of Doherty's many mysteries, as the personal memoirs of the narrator, Sir Roger, dictated during his advanced old age in the 1590s. Shallot is subsumed into the Cardinal's service as a teenager, together with his close friend and compatriot Benjamin Daunbey. The author states: "We must remember Shallot is, by his own confession, a great teller of tall tales, but he may not be a liar. Indeed many of his claims can be corroborated by historical fact . . . Bluff King Hal and Cardinal Thomas Wolsey are accurately described in Shallot's memoirs."

Literary Crimes & Chimes: There's often a problem in Doherty's mysteries with the reader's willing suspension of disbelief. His characters encounter so many historical figures, are involved in so many key events of the reigns in question, that one wonders how such interactions could ever have been possible in real life. Roger is certainly a larger-than-life character, a kind of Falstaff-*cum*-spy-*cum*-rogue, and can be entertaining in small dabs, but his posturings too often just become tiresome. The setup here is very similar to that of the equally undistinguished Matthew Jankyn series. Ho hum, ho hum.

THE CASES

1. *The White Rose Murders: Being the First Journal of Sir Roger Shallot Concerning Certain Wicked Conspiracies and Horrible Murders Perpetrated in the Reign of King Henry VIII.* London: Headline, 1991, 244 p.

LONDON, ENGLAND, OCTOBER 1517. English armies have defeated and killed King James IV of Scotland at Flodden Field, and James' widow, Queen Margaret, a sister to King Henry VIII, has fled to England, leaving Scotland under a Council of Regency for her young son, King James V. Roger Shallot is drawn into a web of mystery and murder by his close friendship with Benjamin Daunbey, the nephew of Cardinal Wolsey, first minister of Henry VIII. Benjamin and Roger are ordered into Margaret's household to resolve certain mysteries as well as to bring about her restoration to Scotland. They begin by questioning Selkirk, a half-mad physician imprisoned in the Tower. He is subsequently found poisoned in a locked chamber guarded by soldiers. The only clue is a poem full of riddles. However, the verse also contains the seeds for other gruesome murders. The faceless assassin always leaves a white rose, the mark of *Les Blancs Sangliers*, a secret society plotting the overthrow of the Tudor monarchy. Roger and Benjamin passed the test set for them by Wolsey by solving the mystery, thereby becoming a permanent part of the Cardinal's entourage. Associates: Benjamin; Doctor Agrippa; Margot; Phoebe. Historical Figures: British King Henry VIII; Cardinal Wolsey; Scottish Queen Margaret.

2. *The Poisoned Chalice: Being the Second Journal of Sir Roger Shallot Concerning Certain Wicked Conspiracies and Horrible Murders Perpetrated in the Reign of King Henry VIII.* London: Headline, 1992, 280 p.

PARIS, FRANCE, SPRING 1520. England is at peace under the magnificent Cardinal Wolsey, who rules the country while Henry VIII spends his time in masques, banquets, and hunting, whether it is chasing the fleet-footed deer or the even more delicious quarry of the silken-garbed ladies of the court. But Richard Falconer, Chief Secretary of the English Embassy in Paris, has been found mysteriously murdered. Wolsey believes that Falconer's death is connected with the disturbing news that there is a spy in the English court or in its embassy in Paris, passing information to King François I of France. He summons his nephew, Benjamin Daunbey, and the wayward Roger Shallot to investigate. The only clue is the spy's code name, "Raphael." King Henry has secret instructions of his own before the pair journey to Paris: to retrieve a precious ring, the subject of a wager, and a certain book that the King does not want to fall into enemy hands. The pair is not to return to England without them. Naturally, Shallot objects to this assignment—he places a high value on his own skin, and the games of princes invariably include violent death, danger, treachery, and little thanks. On this occasion, as always, he is not disappointed! Associates: Benjamin; Doctor Agrippa; Margot; Phoebe. Historical Figures: British King Henry VIII; Cardinal Wolsey; William Shakespeare.

3. *The Grail Murders: Being the Third Journal of Sir Roger Shallot Concerning Certain Wicked Conspiracies and Horrible Murders Perpetrated in the Reign of King Henry VIII.* London: Headline, 1993, 244 p.

ENGLAND, SUMMER 1522. The rogue Roger Shallot and his sober-sided master Benjamin Daunbey are summoned by Cardinal Wolsey. Stafford, Duke of Buckingham, has been arrested for treason, and Benjamin and Roger are made to witness his bloody execution. The true reason for Buckingham's downfall soon becomes apparent; he was searching at Templecombe Manor and Glastonbury Abbey in Somerset for two precious relics: the Holy Grail and Excalibur, the sword of King Arthur. Benjamin and Shallot are ordered to Templecombe, accompanied by the leaders of King Henry VIII's dreaded secret service, the Agentes in Rebus, to find these relics for the monarch. They must pit their wits against the Templars, a secret organization plotting against the Tudors. Buckingham may have been a part of this group, and the Templars may still have a member of their society close to the Crown. The difficulties that wily Shallot—running true to his boast of possessing the fastest legs and quickest wits in Christendom—has to face include a duel, blackmail, the curses of a witch, the grisly hand of glory, decapitated heads, mysterious fires, and silent murder in the eerie Templar chapel. Associates: Benjamin; Doctor Agrippa; Margot; Phoebe. Historical Figures: British King Henry VIII; Cardinal Wolsey; Cuthbert Tunstall, Bishop of London.

4. *A Brood of Vipers: Being the Fourth Journal of Sir Roger Shallot Concerning Certain Wicked Conspiracies and Horrible Murders Perpetrated in the Reign of King Henry VIII.* London: Headline, 1994, 247 p.

FLORENCE, ITALY, SPRING 1523. Cardinal Wolsey's "beloved" nephew, Benjamin Daunbey, and the latter's rapscallion servant, Roger Shallot, are summoned to London. A Florentine envoy, Lord Francesco Abrizzi, has been foully murdered in Cheapside. He has been shot in the head by a new-fangled hand cannon, and King Henry is determined to unmask the perpetrators of this outrage. En route to court, Benjamin and Shallot are to collect an old court physician, Sir Edward Throckle. However, upon arriving at the lonely manor house, they find Throckle's corpse floating in a bath of blood—he has apparently committed suicide. In London, Shallot experiences King Henry's rage and spite, the insults of the Abrizzis, and a murderous attack on his own life. Shallot, a born coward with the fastest legs in Christendom, just wants to crawl away and hide, but the King and Wolsey are most insistent: Shallot and Benjamin are to journey to Florence, discover the identity of Lord Francesco's assassin, deliver a secret message to the Medici ruler of the city, and inveigle back to England a Florentine painter. It sounds simple enough, but the reality is murderously different, and the result may change England and Europe forever. Associates: Benjamin; Doctor Agrippa; Margot; Phoebe. Historical Figures: British King Henry VIII; Cardinal Wolsey.

5. *The Gallows Murders: Being the Fifth Journal of Sir Roger Shallot Concerning Certain Wicked Conspiracies and Horrible Murders Perpetrated in the Reign of King Henry VIII.* New York: Headline, 1995, 247 p.

LONDON, ENGLAND, SUMMER 1523. The hot weather and the sweating sickness provide a fertile breeding ground for terrible murders and the most treasonable conspiracies. King Henry VIII has moved the court to Windsor, where he slakes his lusts while the kingdom is governed by his first minister, Cardinal Wolsey. Wolsey, however, is not having an easy time. Someone is sending the King threatening letters from the Tower, under the name and seal of Edward, one of the princes supposedly murdered there, demanding that great amounts of gold be left in different parts of London. If the orders are not carried out, proclamations will be published throughout the capital that, coinciding with the outbreak of plague, may make it look as though the hand of God has turned against the Tudors for usurping the throne. Henry is truly terrified and also intrigued by the mysterious and grisly murders occurring among the hangmen of London, whose guild also happens to meet in the tower. Wolsey has only two people to turn to, his beloved nephew, Benjamin Daunbey, and Daunbey's faithful servant, Roger Shallot, who reluctantly agree to go to London to unmask the blackmailer and end the macabre murders among the hangmen. Benjamin and Roger become embroiled in the murky Tudor underworld. They also become immersed in the ghastly world of the Gallows men, the royal executioners, many of whom are dying the same hideous deaths that they have meted out to others. At the same time they must also confront the mystery surrounding the princes in the tower, an ancient murder that still haunts the English throne. When King Henry threatens that Shallot will hang from the highest scaffold in the kingdom unless the mysteries are resolved, the pressure mounts for Benjamin and Roger to find the answers. Associates: Benjamin; Doctor Agrippa; Margot; Phoebe. Historical Figures: British King Henry VIII; Cardinal Wolsey.

6. *The Relic Murders: Being the Sixth Journal of Sir Roger Shallot Concerning Certain Wicked Conspiracies and Horrible Murders Perpetrated in the Reign of King Henry VIII.* London: Headline, 1996, 246 p. As by "Paul Doherty." London: Headline, 1997, 246 p.

LONDON, ENGLAND, FALL 1523. Roger Shallot, self-proclaimed physician, rogue, charlatan, and secret emissary of King Henry VIII, suddenly has nothing to do. His master, Benjamin Daunbey, has been sent to Italy on a diplomatic mission, leaving him in charge of their manor outside Ipswich. Shallot, forbidden both to practice the art of medicine and to approach the beautiful Miranda, takes to reading. Discovering the potential wealth that can be accrued by the finding and selling of true relics, he goes in search of his own. Almost immediately he is in trouble—and in prison. Rescued by the return of his master and the influence of Cardinal Wolsey, Shallot finds himself at court, where he is ordered by both the King and the Cardinal to break the law by stealing back for the Crown the Orb of Charlemagne, now under close guard at the priory at Clerkenwell. Benjamin and Roger have no choice but to agree to the task. Before long they are drawn not only into the shadowy underworld of Tudor London and the illegal trade of relics but also into murder and blackmail, as they race against time to find the Orb of Charlemagne and save their own necks. Associates: Benjamin; Doctor Agrippa; Margot; Phoebe. Historical Figures: British King Henry VIII; Cardinal Wolsey.

BROTHER ATHELSTAN SERIES

(As "Paul Harding" or "Paul Doherty")

Scene of the Crime: London, England, beginning in 1377.

Detective: Brother Athelstan, a Dominican monk.

Known Associates: Sir John Cranston, Coroner of the City of London; Lady Maude, Sir John's beloved wife and mother of his twin sons; Father Prior, Athelstan's Abbot; John of Gaunt, Duke of Lancaster and Regent to his young nephew, King Richard II; Athelstan's one-eyed tomcat, Bonaventure; the widow Benedicta; the courteson Cecily; other denizens of Athelstan's parish at St. Erconwald's.

Premise: A Dominican cleric solves crimes in fourteenth-century England, with the assistance of the Coroner of London.

Comment: Brother Athelstan is a Dominican monk with two callings. He has been given a penance for his sins by his Father Prior and ordered to work as a parish priest at St. Erconwald's Church in Southwark, deep in the slums of the city of London, where he ministers chiefly to prostitutes, thieves, and beggars. He also has been retained as *secretarius* or clerk to Sir John Cranston, the larger-than-life coroner of the City of London. Cranston quickly discovers, to his delight, that Athelstan is of a like nature, curious and quick-witted, but with a subtle sense of humor. The two make a formidable team as they set about with great gusto to get to the bottom of things sinister in London. Doherty successfully contrasts the rollicking Falstaffian, Cranston, who loves his creature comforts a bit too well, especially rich food and fine wine, with the quieter, more introspective Athelstan, who is hard put to keep up with Cranston and prevent him from crashing off the tracks completely. For his own part, Brother "A." must also keep his own feet firmly on the path of righteousness, for he finds himself at times just a little too easily lured by Sir John into the local tavern for some well-earned "refreshment" after one of their ordeals. To Athelstan's credit, when released from his penance by his Prior (*The Nightingale Gallery, Murder Most Holy*), he chooses to remain with his poor parishioners and to continue, to Sir John's great delight, as the coroner's able assistant, rather than return to the relative comfort and obscurity of the abbey.

Literary Crimes & Chimes: After a time, after a remarkably short time, all of Doherty's books and titles begin sounding and reading alike, so that they seem almost interchangeable with each other. Alas and alack, however, that they work well neither as mystery nor as history. In the consistory of blustery investigation, the gist of our sagacious adjudication is that Brother "A." rates no better than a "D.," being the poor man's version of "Brother Cadfael." Prefer Ellis Peters.

THE CASES

1. *The Nightingale Gallery.* London: Headline, 1991, 248 p.
LONDON, ENGLAND, SUMMER 1377. In 1376 the famed Black Prince had perished of a terrible rotting sickness, closely followed by his father, King Edward III, who ended his life a bitter old man, his former glories forgotten. The Crown of England is left in the hands of a mere boy, King Richard II. The great nobles, led by Richard's uncle and Regent, John of Gaunt, Duke of Lancaster, gather like hungry wolves around the empty throne. A terrible power struggle threatens the country, and the prelates of the church and the powerful merchant princes of London are soon drawn in. One of these, Sir Thomas Springall, is foully murdered within a few days of the old king's death. Sir John Cranston, the fat Coroner of the City of London, is ordered to investigate. He is assisted by Brother Athelstan, a Dominican monk working in the slums of Southwark as a penance. Their investigations

take them from the sinister secrets of Nightshade House in the slums of Whitefriars to the barbaric splendor of the English Court. As others associated with Springall are found murdered, Cranston and Athelstan are drawn ever deeper into a dark web of intrigue. Associates: Cranston; Father Prior; the cat Bonaventure; Benedicta. Historic Figures: British King Edward III; John of Gaunt; British King Richard II.

2. *The House of the Red Slayer.* London: Headline, 1992, 280 p. As: *The Red Slayer: Being the Second of the Sorrowful Mysteries of Brother Athelstan.* New York: William Morrow, 1992, 283 p.

LONDON, ENGLAND, DECEMBER 1377. As London prepares for Christmas, a great frost has the city in its icy grip; even the Thames is frozen from bank to bank. Murder, revenge, and treachery also make their presence felt, for an ancient grudge is about to be settled in a city seething with discontent. The Constable of the Tower of London, Sir Ralph Whitton, is found murdered in a cold bleak chamber in the North Bastion. The door is still locked from the inside and guarded by trusted retainers, so how did the assassins slip across a frozen moat and climb the sheer wall of the fortress to commit such a dreadful crime? And why was Sir Ralph so terrified of the message he received a few days before his death—a crude drawing of a ship and a flat sesame seed cake? The Dominican friar, Athelstan, and Sir John Cranston, the fat, wine-loving Coroner of the City of London, are appointed to investigate these mysteries. They soon discover Sir Ralph's murder is only the first in a series of macabre killings that have their roots in a terrible act of betrayal committed many years previously. Associates: Cranston; the cat Bonaventure; Maude; Benedicta; Father Prior; Cecily.

3. *Murder Most Holy.* London: Headline, 1992, 243 p.

LONDON, ENGLAND, SUMMER 1379. Sir John Cranston, the corpulent Coroner of the City of London, is invited to the opulent Palace of Savoy on the Thames to attend a magnificent banquet hosted by John of Gaunt, the Duke of Lancaster, Regent to his nephew, young King Richard II. There the wily Gaunt traps Cranston into a wager of 1,000 gold crowns with Signor Gian Galeazzo, the wealthy Lord of Cremona, who challenges him to solve a certain old murder mystery within two weeks. Cranston is in a predicament: if he loses the wager, it will impoverish him, and if he refuses, he will be branded a coward and incur the further enmity of Gaunt, a man of great power who is not overly fond of Cranston. He accepts with a great show of confidence and then listens carefully as Galeazzo outlines the details of the case to Gaunt's guests. Several men have been found dead after spending the night in a scarlet chamber, reputed to be haunted by ghosts, in a Cremona family manor house located near the Alps. They have no mark upon them; they have neither drunk nor eaten poison; there are no secret passageways or entrances to the room. And they all have awful expressions of terror upon their faces. Gaunt is given a sealed envelope containing the answer to the riddle, and Cranston is given two weeks to come up with the correct solution. Realizing that his reputation and future wealth now rest upon the solving of this mystery, Cranston once more seeks the help of his faithful *secretarius*, Brother Athelstan. However, Athelstan has more immediate problems of his own. During renovation of the sanctuary at St. Erconwald's, a skeleton has been unearthed. Religious hysteria ensues when a man is miraculously healed while praying at the skeleton's coffin. Athelstan watches helplessly as his parish church attracts not only well-meaning pilgrims but all the religious hucksters and swindlers in London's underworld. Meanwhile, even more sinister influences are at work within the coterie of Dominican Friars conducting meetings at Blackfriars. One by one, the monks are dying in mysterious circumstances. Sir John Cranston and Athelstan, in the midst of their riddle-solving, are called in to investigate the suspicious deaths. A simple observation is all that is needed to provide the correct answer to the riddle; an ancient manuscript provides the key to the murders. Associates: Cranston; the cat Bonaventure; Father Prior; Maude; Benedicta; Cecily. Historical Figures: John of Gaunt; British King Richard II.

4. *The Anger of God*. London: Headline, 1993, 247 p.

LONDON, ENGLAND, FALL 1379. The power of the Crown is invested in John of Gaunt, Duke of Lancaster, and the kingdom is seething with discontent. The French are attacking the southern ports, and there is economic hardship in the countryside, where the peasants are planning a revolt organized by the mysterious leader of the Great Community of the Realm, who proclaims himself as "*Ira Dei*," the anger of God. Gaunt is involved in winning over the great merchant princes of the capital when his plans are plunged into chaos by a series of bloody and mysterious murders. In desperation, Gaunt turns to Sir John Cranston, the portly Coroner of the City, to bring the assassin to heel and to recover a king's ransom in gold that has disappeared. Cranston naturally calls on his ally, the Dominican monk, Brother Athelstan. They face threats and attack from the powerful as well as from the seedy underworld of medieval London, not to mention a chilling exorcism, as they try to bring order to their own lives and a subtle murderer to justice. Associates: Cranston; Maude; the cat Bonaventure; Benedicta; Cecily. Historical Figure: John of Gaunt.

5. *By Murder's Bright Light*. London: Headline, 1994, 279 p.

LONDON, ENGLAND, WINTER 1379. A sea of troubles besets England. French privateers are attacking the southern coast and threaten London itself. Sir John Cranston, the portly, wine-loving Coroner of the City, also has problems. Not only does he have to sit in court and listen to allegations of witchcraft, but he is also puzzled by the crimes of a skillful felon. Cranston's clerk, the Dominican monk Brother Athelstan, is preparing a mystery play and trying to placate the members of his church council, all of whom want to play God. But these mundane concerns pale into insignificance when an English flotilla of warships, with *God's Bright Light* in its number, drops anchor in the Thames; during the first night the entire watch of the ship disappears without a trace. The series of murderous and strange incidents leads to Sir John and Brother Athelstan being summoned to resolve the mysteries on board the ill-omened warship. In particular, they must search out the truth behind the death of Sir Henry Ospring, who was viciously stabbed in a tavern chamber. Their investigations uncover scandal, sexual misdemeanors, murder, and even treason, and they find themselves in the thick of a bloody battle on the Thames. Associates: Cranston; Benedicta; the cat Bonaventure; Father Prior. Historical Figure: John of Gaunt.

6. *The House of Crows.* London: Headline, 1995, 280 p.

LONDON, ENGLAND, SPRING 1380. British Regent John of Gaunt needs money and supplies for his war against the French. Unfortunately, the members of Parliament at Westminster are proving especially stubborn, and the Regent's cause is not aided when some representatives from the shire of Shrewsbury are foully murdered. John of Gaunt orders Cranston to find the assassin before he loses every chance of obtaining the taxes he requires. But Sir John and Brother Athelstan have their own problems. Someone is stealing cats from the streets and alleyways of Cheapside, and terrified parishioners are insisting that a devil incarnate is prowling around the parish of St. Erconwald's, claiming innocent lives. It takes all of the pair's skills to solve the mysteries. Associates: Cranston; Maude; the cat Bonaventure; Ranulf; Benedicta; Father Prior. Historical Figure: John of Gaunt.

7. *Assassin's Riddle.* London: Headline, 1996, 280 p.

LONDON, ENGLAND, SUMMER 1380. The corpse of Edwin Chapler, clerk of the Office of the Green Wax of the Chancery, has been pulled from the Thames; Chapler has drowned, but not before receiving a vicious blow to the back of the head. Then Bartholomew Drayton, a usurer and moneylender, is found dead in his strong room, a crossbow bolt firmly embedded in his chest; the windowless strong room was locked and barred from the inside. So who killed these men, and how? Are the two deaths connected? Sir John Cranston, the Coroner of the City of London, surveys the scene. When other clerks are murdered, each with a riddle pinned to his corpse, Cranston enlists the help of his *secretarius,* Brother Athelstan; together they must pit their wits against a deadly adversary bent on murder and mayhem. Associates: Cranston; the cat Bonaventure; Father Prior; Maude. Historical Figure: John of Gaunt.

8. *The Devil's Domain: Sorrowful Mystery of Brother Athelstan,* as "Paul Doherty." London: Headline, 1998, 245 p.

ENGLAND, SUMMER 1380. "A time of bloody tribulation! Of horrid sights! The season of murder and subtle trickery!" Thus proclaims the chronicler of Westminster, as the British and the French wage war on the Narrow Seas. In Hawkmere Manor, a lonely, gloomy dwelling place known as the "Devil's Domain," a Frenchman lies dying, poisoned by an unknown hand. He is one of five prisoners held for ransom by the Regent John of Gaunt. Sir John Cranston and his secretaries, Brother Athelstan, are summoned to investigate the mysterious death in the hope of averting French retaliation, but their path is riddled with obstacles. How could the murderer have entered the Frenchman's chamber when the room was locked from within and the window nothing but a narrow aperture? Their aide, Sir Maurice Maltravers, is more of a hindrance than a help, as he faces the misery of heartbreak. Lady Angelica, the woman he intended to marry, has been whisked away to a convent by her tyrannical and disapproving father. It soon becomes apparent that only when the lovers have been reunited will any progress be made in the investigation. Associates: Cranston; Sir Maurice Maltravers; Maude; Cecily; the cat Bonaventure; Benedicta. Historical Figure: John of Gaunt.

9. *The Field of Blood,* as "Paul Doherty." London: Headline, 1999, 256 p.

LONDON, ENGLAND, FALL 1380. Brother Athelstan, priest of St. Erconwald in medieval Southwark, is praying for a quiet week when he is interrupted by the cry of murder. Hurrying outside, he is confronted by the horrific sight of three mutilated corpses lying on the church step. Law dictates that if the killer is not found, the entire parish must be punished. Before he has time to investigate, Athelstan is called to the Assizes on urgent business in his capacity as *secretarius* to Sir John Cranston, Coroner of the City of London. Here, in a bizarre twist of fate, one of Athelstan's parishioners, a respectable widow, stands accused of committing multiple murder and of burying her victims in the "field of blood." Certain of the widow's innocence, yet convinced that the two incidents somehow must be related, Athelstan embarks on his most perplexing case yet. The consequences, should the cases not be solved, are unthinkable. Associates: Cranston; the cat Bonaventure; Cecily; Benedicta.

MISCELLANEOUS SERIES

Scene of the Crime: Various eras.

Detective: Various.

Known Associates: Various.

Premise: Various.

Comment: The latter three of these books are historical mysteries based around real-life crimes known to history. The first trio of books are historical novels in which the mystery elements are almost secondary to the main story lines. The later books tend to be better plotted and more vivid in realization.

Literary Crimes & Chimes: Doherty grinds them out like hotcakes, with plots that are fairly predictable and characters mostly cut from the same slice of pabulum. Pretty routine stuff, for the most part.

THE CASES

1. *Domina*. London: Headline, 2002, 288 p.

ROME, AD 54? Agrippina, wife of Claudius, mother of Nero, was a beautiful and talented woman who saw her father murdered, was banished by her brother, and was killed on the orders of her son. Her freed man, a one-eyed former gladiator named Parmenon, tells the story of Agrippina's battle to survive in, and control, the depraved and violent Imperial Roman court and the crumbling relationship between mother and son. Historical Figure: Roman Empress Agrippina.

2. *Murder Imperial*. London: Headline, 2003, 242 p.

ROME, 313. Under the rule of Emperor Constantine I the Great, Rome finally appears to be emerging from its turbulent past. In order to consolidate his control and under the guidance of his mother, Helena, Constantine plans to harness the power of the increasingly influential Christian Church. But his loyalties are brought into question when three courtesans from the Guild of Aphrodite—a guild Constantine himself frequents—are found dead. All three bodies have crosses etched on their foreheads and each cheek. Aiming at protecting her son's future, Helena calls upon the service of an "*agente in rebus politicus*." This spy, Claudia, the niece of a tavern-owner, is placed as a wine-server in Constantine's household. But Claudia has secret motives of her own! Historical Figures: Roman Emperor Constantine I; Empress Helena.

3. *The Plague Lord*. London: Headline, 2002, 280 p.

CHINA, 1200s. The legendary Kublai Khan rules over Cathay and the Middle Kingdom. Of his many ministers and advisers, his favorite is a foreigner, the Venetian Marco Polo, whose understanding of the language and etiquette of the court is exemplary and whose advice is widely sought. So when a flood of portents, strange visions, and ghastly murders occurs throughout the kingdom and even across the oceans, Marco's wisdom is once more needed. The leaders of a demonic sect have disappeared from the desert to which they were banished, and Kublai Khan believes that they will attempt to release the Plague Lord himself and open the gates of Hell. Historical Figure: Kublai Khan.

4. *The Death of a King.* London: Robert Hale, 1985, 176 p.

ENGLAND, 1327–1344. A horrifying murder has taken place, the killing of homosexual British King Edward II. But the crime has remained shrouded in secrecy for seventeen years, until Edmund Beche, a royal clerk, is ordered to investigate. The unsuspecting Beche finds his investigation leading to Berkeley Castle and to the court of King Edward III himself. Who conspired to kill King Edward II? Why did the dead king's son wait so many years to search for the truth? And why does the dreadful Queen Isabella keep her late husband's bloody heart encased in glass? Most of all, why was Beche, of all people, chosen to uncover these ugly secrets? The answers come from unlikely sources—the royal archives and ancient tombs—and from the mouths of liars and assassins. But for Edmund, with his life dangling over a pit of treachery, the truth may be the most shocking revelation of them all. Historical Figures: British King Edward II; British Queen Isabella; British King Edward III.

5. *The Fate of Princes.* London: Robert Hale, 1990, 192 p.

ENGLAND, AUGUST–DECEMBER 1483. Francis, Viscount Lovell, Chief Butler and Chamberlain of England, is asked by King Richard III to solve the mystery of the disappearance from the Tower of the two young sons of King Edward IV, King Edward V and his brother, Prince Richard. Were they murdered, or did they escape? As Francis comes closer to the truth, he fears that it may implicate the very monarch who initiated the investigation. Doherty offers an original amalgamation of documentary and archeological evidence that unravels a real-life historical mystery. Historical Figure: British King Richard III.

6. *The Masked Man.* London: Robert Hale, 1991, 174 p.

FRANCE, 1715? During the reign of Louis XIV, the Sun King of France, a very important prisoner was jailed in various fortresses from 1669 to 1703 under conditions of absolute secrecy. The prisoner always wore a mask and was not permitted to speak. His jailers were never changed, and each one came to mysterious ends. English rogue Ralph Croft, forger, smuggler, outlaw, and incurable liar, is plucked by the Duke of Orléans from the dungeon of the Bastille to search out the identity of the Man in the Iron Mask. Croft is assigned to work with the mysterious archivist Maurepas, his beautiful enigmatic daughter, Marie, and the cold killer Captain D'Estibet. Croft's quest takes him from the slums of eighteenth-century Paris to the opulent luxuries of the Louvre Palace, skirting threats and dangers from every side as he seeks the truth. Doherty here extrapolates from extant historical records to solve this real-life mystery, previously the subject of a well-known novel by Alexandre Dumas. Historical Figures: French King Louis XIV; Duke of Orléans, Regent of France under King Louis XV.

DOUGLAS, Carole Nelson (1944–). American.

IRENE ADLER SERIES

Scene of the Crime: England, Bohemia, France, and America, beginning in 1881 with the incident that led to the 1891 publication of Sir Arthur Conan Doyle's *A Scandal in Bohemia*, retold in this series from a different point of view in *Good Night, Mr. Holmes.* The events of *Good Night, Mr. Holmes* cover the better part of a decade.

Detective: Irene Adler, half-Irish, born in America in 1858. Her precise origins remain mysterious. Adler trained as an opera singer; during the days when she auditioned for parts in the chorus, and she supplemented her income through work as a private inquiry agent, first as a Pinkerton operative in America, later on her own in England. She stopped taking such jobs when she became established in her operatic career. She rose in that profession from the chorus to the position of a diva in *Good Night, Mr. Holmes.* While performing in the Imperial Opera of Warsaw, she came to the attention of the King of Bohemia. The events describing their liaison and separation from the King's perspective are recounted in the first Sherlock Holmes story, *A Scandal in Bohemia* (published in July 1891 in *The Strand*), and from the perspective of Irene's friend Miss Huxleigh in *Good Night, Mr. Holmes.* Irene is impetuous, clever, and easily bored. Her early retirement from the stage leaves her with ample time to pursue her investigations, which she does regularly to satisfy her own curiosity, to aid her friends, and for money.

Known Associates: Penelope Huxleigh, a Shropshire parson's daughter, came to London as a governess. When the war began and with positions few and far between, Penelope took a post as a shop assistant at Whiteley's, where they had 176 house rules for employees, all of which Penelope carefully observed. She lived in impoverished respectability until a coworker framed her for theft. At the outset of the series Penelope has been turned out on the street, fired by Whiteley's, with no prospects and no recommendation to help her gain another job. Penelope is rescued (and, better than that, avenged) by Irene. They become devoted friends and share a flat in the Saffron Hill district of London. Penelope gains a marketable skill by learning to work the newfangled typewriters and is able to set herself up as a "type-writer girl." Irene pursues her career on the stage. When Irene finds trouble in Bohemia, Penelope travels to her side, and together they escape the country. Penelope requests aid from her employer Godfrey Norton, of whom she has become quite fond, and he and Irene develop a passion for each other, marry, and flee the country. Lonely for Penelope, they convince her to come to France and join their household. Scenes from the viewpoint of Dr. Watson, describing Holmes' reactions to Irene's escapades, pepper the early books. Holmes and Watson enter the action of several of these stories; Holmes cannot resist the opportunity for a rematch against the only woman who ever bested him. Irene and Holmes begin as opponents, continue as rivals, and in the later books are allies (albeit competitive allies).

Premise: An opera diva pursues an alternative career as a private investigator in nineteenth-century Europe and America.

Comment: The only woman who ever bested Sherlock Holmes, one of only four individuals who ever got the better of him, Irene Adler is a force to be reckoned with. She began her career as an investigator to pay the rent when she was a struggling opera singer. She gains the means to give up her investigative career but finds that the skills she learned cannot be unlearned and, moreover, that her curiosity cannot be set aside. She is well known to the rich and famous, who trust her discretion. She can move freely among the wealthy and investigate and be regarded as a brilliant adventuress, where a commonplace investigator would be viewed as sordid. A diva born, always in the spotlight, she is wary of others' admiration and determined to remain her own woman. She resists the blandishments of rich men and eschews the role of dutiful wife. Penelope Huxleigh is simply respectable; she shuns the limelight and is flustered by a man's regard. In several of the books Penelope's voice is tinged with bitterness, but by the later works the character has grown and is once more a pleasant companion as a narrator.

Literary Crimes & Chimes: These are light, amusing reads, intentionally written in a "had I but known" style to great effect. The "editor's" notes at the beginning of *Irene at Large*, *Chapel Noir*, and *Castle Rouge* (by Fiona Witherspoon, of Friends or Advocates of Irene Adler) describe how the editor took several disparate sources (the diaries of Penelope Huxleigh, the "supposedly fictional" accounts of John H. Watson, M.D., and in one case a sheaf of mysterious yellow notepaper) and wove these into the narrative. The result is that different chapters offer perspectives from different narrators. Throughout the novels runs the theme of Victorian expectations of women, the inherent unfairness of that society, and how women were forced into roles with little regard for their wishes or talents. The addition of Sherlock Holmes to the investigations is carefully done; he does not lead

Irene but rather competes with her in his own separate but parallel investigations.

THE CASES

1. *Good Night, Mr. Holmes.* New York: Tor, 1990, 408 p.

LONDON, ENGLAND, 1881–1888. Irene, Holmes, and possibly others are hired by Mr. Charles Lewis Tiffany to find the "Zone of Diamonds," a belt of gems originally owned by French Queen Marie Antoinette. It vanished from the Paris Tuilleries in 1848 as the Paris mobs rioted against King Louis Philippe. Irene's search is stymied by a death, and she sends Nell in to spy on the dead man's son. Her operatic career distracts her for a time; but she returns to England to try to outwit Sherlock Holmes. Associates: Godfrey Norton; King of Bohemia. Historical Figures: Oscar Wilde; Bram Stoker.

2. **"Mesmerizing Bertie,"** in *Crime through Time II*, ed. by Miriam Grace Monfredo and Sharan Newman. New York: Berkley Prime Crime, 1998, p. 272–286.

LONDON, ENGLAND, 1882. (The tale is related by Irene to Penelope in 1901 in France.) Mr. William Gilbert has invited all the handsome young women in the chorus of his new operetta, *Iolanthe*, to dinner with Bertie, Prince of Wales. Gilbert shows off his newfangled telephone by calling the theater and giving the Prince the receiver so that he can hear the rehearsal; instead, Bertie hears the prelude to a murder. Irene must use her special skills to gain enough information so that the killer can be captured. Historical Figures: William Gilbert; Bertie, Prince of Wales.

3. **"The Thief of Twelfth Night,"** in *Holmes for the Holidays*, ed. by Martin Greenberg, Jon L. Lellenberg, and Carol-Lynn Waugh. New York: Berkley Prime Crime, 1996, p. 211–229.

ENGLAND, 1883. (The story is related by Holmes to Watson on January 5, 1903.) Both Holmes and a Pinkerton agent stationed in England are asked to help find a family heirloom that went missing some time during the Christmas season. Matters come to a head during the Twelfth Night feast, where they compete to be the first to solve the mystery. Holmes is later mortified to recall that he found the bean in the Twelfth Night cake, thereby being crowned "King of the Bean"; his only recompense was that it allowed him to choose a "Queen of the Pea."

4. **"Parris Green,"** in *Malice Domestic 2: An Anthology of Original Traditional Mystery Stories*, ed. by Mary Higgins Clark. New York: Pocket Books, 1993, p. 171–202.

LONDON, ENGLAND, 1886. Lysander Parris has been closeted, painting a portrait of his housemaid, for several days. The family is becoming concerned. When a friend of the family peers through the keyhole and sees the maid looking strangely corpselike, he calls on Irene for help. Historical Figure: Oscar Wilde.

5. *Good Morning, Irene.* New York: Tor, 1991, 374 p.

FRANCE, 1888. In London in 1882 Irene had viewed the corpse of a man that Bram Stoker had pulled from the water. Six years later and several hundred miles away, she sees a suspiciously similar corpse and resolves to discover the threat that links these deaths. Associates: Louise; Inspector François le Villard. Historical Figure: Sarah Bernhardt.

6. *Irene at Large.* New York: Tor, 1992, 381 p. As: *An Adventuress: An Irene Adler Novel.* New York: Forge, 2003, 402 p.

FRANCE, 1889. A villainous-looking man collapses at Nell's feet on the cobblestones of Notre Dame. He is revealed to be an old acquaintance lost in the war who has determined to return to his homeland to protect the man who saved his life, one Doctor Watson. Nell (and of course, Irene) work to preserve him from an assassin long enough to complete his self-imposed mission. Associates: Cobra (Mr. Emerson Quentin Stanhope); Tiger (Captain Sylvester Morgan, Colonel Sebastian Moran); Dr. Watson; Sherlock Holmes. Historical Figures: Sarah Bernhardt; Empress of All the Russias.

7. *Irene's Last Waltz.* New York: Forge, 1994, 480 p. As: *Another Scandal in Bohemia: An Irene Adler Novel.* New York: Forge, 2002, 465 p.

FRANCE, 1889. Irene is inundated with requests that she use her talents to investigate very different sorts of mysteries. The Queen of Bohemia has a domestic concern; she would like to understand the reason behind her husband's actions (or rather, inactions); the couturier Monsieur Worth would like Irene to investigate the murder of one of his workers; and Baron Rothschild offers riches if Irene, Godfrey, and Penelope will investigate a mythological creature and a political situation. Irene could never resist a challenge. Associates: Allegra; King of Bohemia; Queen Clotilde; Tatyana; Quentin. Historical Figures: Monsieur and Madame Worth; Baron Alphonse de Rothschild.

8. *Chapel Noir: An Irene Adler Novel.* New York: Forge, 2001, 494 p.

FRANCE, 1889. The police request Irene's assistance (at the command of a very eminent person) in investigating the murders and mutilation of two ladies of the evening. The case is disturbingly reminiscent of the Whitechapel horrors perpetrated by the villainous fiend called "Jack the Ripper"; the fear that this perversion has infected France brings not only Irene but also Sherlock Holmes to the investigation. This is the first-half of the story, which is completed in *Castle Rouge.* Associate: Inspector François le Villard. Historical Figures: Bram Stoker; Bertie, Prince of Wales; Baron Alphonse de Rothschild; Buffalo Bill Cody; Red Tomahawk; Nellie Bly.

9. *Castle Rouge: An Irene Adler Novel.* New York: Forge, 2002, 540 p.

FRANCE, 1889. Nell has been kidnapped, if not by Jack the Ripper, then by a cult that has exalted his crimes to the level of religious observance. Godfrey has been kidnapped as well. Irene knows that the fate of those she loves hangs in the balance as she continues her investigations into murder and madness. This is the second-half of the story begun in *Castle Noir.* Associates: King of Bohemia; Queen Clotilde; Tatyana; Quentin. Historical Figures: Bram Stoker; Bertie, Prince of Wales; Baron Alphonse de Rothschild; Nellie Bly.

10. *Femme Fatale: An Irene Adler Novel.* New York: Forge, 2003, 492 p.

NEW YORK, NEW YORK, 1889. A murder takes place before the very eyes of Nellie Bly; a medium is strangled by ectoplasm! Nellie's investigations uncover a plot against a woman she believes related to Irene; her transatlantic cable brings Irene to America to face the mysteries and dangers of her past. Unbeknownst to Irene, a second cable has been sent to Irene's sometime ally, Sherlock Holmes. Associates: Nellie Bly; Tiny Tim; Salamandra; Professor Marvel; Phoebe; Quentin.

11. *Spider Dance.* New York: Forge, 2004, 384 p.

NEW YORK, NEW YORK, AUGUST 1889. Reporter Nellie Bly has found information about Irene's parents, and Irene and her friend Nell are lured to a New York cemetery, where Sherlock Holmes also suddenly appears. Holmes believes that the grave actually contains the body of Lola Montez, the mistress of deceased King Ludwig II of Bavaria. Their quest ultimately takes them to California, where they encounter treachery, conspiracies, and treasure, dating back to the time of the California gold rush thirty years before. Associate: Nell. Historical Figures: Nellie Bly; Lola Montez.

DUNN, Carola (1946–). British.

DAISY DALRYMPLE SERIES

Scene of the Crime: England, beginning in 1923.

Detective: The Honourable Daisy Dalrymple, a British free spirit, is disapprovingly referred to by some as "one of those modern young women," because of her determination to make her own way in a society decimated by World War I.

Known Associates: The Honourable Phillip Petrie was Daisy's brother's best friend, and, with Gervaise Dalrymple now dead, feels some responsibility for her. Daisy meets Detective Chief Inspector Alec Fletcher of the Criminal Investigation Department (CID) and his subordinates, Detective Sergeant Tom Tring and Detective Constable Ernie Piper, when they are assigned to investigate in *Death at Wentwater Court*. After working together through a few successful investigations, Fletcher's superiors simply assign him to any case in which Daisy is involved. Daisy's best friend (and flatmate) is Miss Lucy Fotheringay, who is working as a photographer. Daisy's mother is the Dowager Lady Dalrymple. Alec's family includes his daughter, Belinda Fletcher, and his mother, Mrs. Enid Fletcher.

Premise: A British woman writer in the aftermath of World War I becomes involved in solving crimes in high society.

Comment: After the war the Honourable Daisy Dalrymple decided that she preferred independence to being smothered by her mother, the Dowager Lady Dalrymple. A courtesy title doesn't bring her any income, so she sets to work writing articles about the estates of the landed gentry. Her title gets her invited to the homes of the upper crust; her curiosity, sympathetic nature, and guileless countenance lead to revelations that are not fit for print in *Town and Country*! At first reading, these books seems like frothy period pieces, but they are much more than that. Dunn paints a compelling picture of a society whose world has been irretrievably altered by war. Daisy's adventures expose the reader to a microcosm of that altered world. Daisy had planned a stereotypical future: she was engaged to a young man of her social class, her brother was going to inherit a title, her life and her world were both stable and predictable. But Daisy's *fiancé* and her brother were both killed in the war, leaving her devastated and destroying the future she expected; so she mapped a new course for her life and in the process broke many of the rules of the "old society." In these novels you see all the different ways people coped with loss and societal change. Some mourn, some rail against their misfortunes, some retreat, some move forward; but no one is left unaffected.

Literary Crimes & Chimes: Many of the characters turn out to be more complex than the reader would guess at the beginning. Some start out as mere stereotypes (albeit stereotypes that are of a piece with the settings of the books) but then surprise the reader with their increasing depth as the series develops. The "supporting cast" of characters and the societal settings of the books quite logically change as Daisy's life changes. If you prefer mysteries set among the upper crust, you will most enjoy the early books in the series.

THE CASES

1. ***Death at Wentwater Court: A Daisy Dalrymple Mystery.*** New York: St. Martin's Press, 1994, 216 p.

ENGLAND, JANUARY 1923. The Honourable Daisy Dalrymple is both nervous and excited as she starts her first assignment for *Town and Coun-*

try. She's to be a guest at Wentwater Court while gathering material for her article. Another guest, the loathsome Stephen Astwick, has blackmailed his way into an invitation and then dies in a fatal skating accident. Rather, an *apparent* skating accident. Associates: Fenella; Sir Hugh Menton; Lady Josephine; Lord Wentwater and wife Annabel; Geoffrey Beddowe.

2. *The Winter Garden Mystery: A Daisy Dalrymple Mystery.* New York: St. Martin's Press, 1995, 226 p.

ENGLAND, JANUARY, 1923. While researching an article on Occles Hall, Daisy unearths the body of one of the Occles' maids from beneath a dying shrub in the Winter Garden. The overbearing Lady Valeria decides to fix the blame on Occles Hall's Welsh undergardener. Daisy soon realizes that the local police would rather condemn an innocent foreigner than antagonize Lady Valeria, so Daisy calls in Detective Fletcher to assist her investigation. Associates: Roberta (Bobby) Parslow; Owen Morgan; Fletcher.

3. *Requiem for a Mezzo: A Daisy Dalrymple Mystery.* New York: St. Martin's Press, 1996, 212 p.

ENGLAND, MARCH 1923. Daisy invites Detective Fletcher to accompany her to a concert of Verdi's *Requiem*, and they spend a pleasant afternoon until the mezzo soloist falls dead onstage in front of them. The case is complicated not only by foreign floozies, foreign singers, and foreign spies but also by the mixture of interest, suspicion, and contempt with which the foreigners are treated by many of the English snobs. Associates: Yakov (Yasha) Levich; Muriel Westlea; Fletcher.

4. "Unhappy Medium," in *Malice Domestic 7*, ed. by Sharyn McCrumb. New York: Avon Twilight, 1998, p. 77–94.

ENGLAND, SPRING 1923. So many young men of England have died in the war that fraudulent spiritualists have a ready clientele. Lord Ormerod enlists the help of the Society for Psychical Research to unmask the medium who is playing on Lady Ormerod's grief. Lucy and Daisy go along to help, knowing that she will be devastated when the truth comes out. Associate: Lucy.

5. *Murder on the Flying Scotsman: A Daisy Dalrymple Mystery.* New York: St. Martin's Press, 1997, 213 p.

ENGLAND, APRIL 1923. The express train *The Flying Scotsman* is filled with the presumptive heirs of Alistair McGowan, racing to his side to try to get him to change his will before he draws his last breath. They're also lobbying "dear Uncle Albert," whom they feel has lived an indecently long time and who will inherit the bulk of the entailed estate. Then "dear Uncle Albert" is himself found dead in his train coach, and Daisy is worried that a young man suffering from shell shock will become a scapegoat for the crime. Associates: Anne Bretton (née Smythe-Pike); Judith Smythe-Pike; Raymond Gillespie; Dr. Chandra Jagai.

6. **Damsel in Distress: A Daisy Dalrymple Mystery.** New York: St. Martin's Press, 1997, 234 p.

ENGLAND, APRIL 1923. The Honourable Phillip Petrie finds his own true love, only to see her kidnapped. Frantic, he enlists Daisy's help in tracking down the villains so that he can rescue his Gloria. The kidnappers' threat to kill Gloria if the police are brought into the matter leaves Daisy coordinating the investigation and her aristocratic friends doing the legwork. Associates: Cousin Edgar; Geraldine; Gloria Arbuckle; Caleb P. Arbuckle; Tom and Madge Pearson; Gerald "Binkie" Bincombe; Owen Morgan.

7. **Dead in the Water: A Daisy Dalrymple Mystery.** New York: St. Martin's Press, 1998, 249 p.

ENGLAND, SUMMER 1923. Daisy visits her Aunt Cynthia (Lady Cheringham) to do research for an article on the Thames Regatta. Lady Cheringham is also hosting her nephew's university rowing team. Basil Delancy, a member of that team, torments every one of his teammates; when he meets an unnatural end, Daisy is afraid that the police will not have to look far for the culprit. Associates: Cynthia, Lady Cheringham; Patricia; Tish; Roland "Rollo" Frieth; Erasmus "Cherry" Cheringham; Dottie Carrick; Horace Bott; Susan Hopgood.

8. **Styx and Stones: A Daisy Dalrymple Mystery.** New York: St. Martin's Press, 1999, 231 p.

ENGLAND, AUGUST 1923. Lord John, Daisy's brother-in-law, is receiving poison pen letters. He asks Daisy to investigate. Soon after she arrives, the Reverend Osborne's brother is murdered, and it is possible that the intended victim was the Reverend himself. Associates: Violet; Lord John; Derek; Peter; Wanda LeBeau.

9. **Rattle His Bones: A Daisy Dalrymple Mystery.** New York: St. Martin's Minotaur, 2000, 243 p.

ENGLAND, AUGUST? 1923. Daisy is writing two articles on the British Museum; she is there researching the piece when the overbearing Dr. Pettigrew is murdered. Then it is discovered that the gems in the museum collection have been replaced by paste copies! In order to find the crook, Daisy must first locate the murderer! Associates: Derek; Grand Duke Rudolf Maximilian.

10. **"Storm in a Tea Shoppe,"** in *Crime through Time*, ed. by Miriam Grace Monfredo and Sharan Newman. New York: Berkley Prime Crime, 1997, p. 339–348.

ENGLAND, SUMMER 1923. Lucy has volunteered to take the photographs for Daisy's article on the Natural History Museum. Daisy takes her to the Bluebell Tea Room for a spot of tea. She's been there before, and she partly knows the waitress' life story. Events that afternoon ensure that she'll never eat there again. Associate: Lucy.

11. *To Davy Jones Below: A Daisy Dalrymple Mystery.* New York: St. Martin's Minotaur, 2001, 248 p.

ENGLAND, AND AT SEA ON THE S.S. *TALAVERA*, OCTOBER 1923. Mr. Caleb P. Arbuckle has arranged a lovely post-honeymoon cruise to America for Daisy and Alec, but plans go awry. Shipboard intrigues lead to a series of suspicious accidents, and then to murder. With Alec laid up with seasickness, Daisy takes the lead in investigating the case. Associates: Alec; Gloria Arbuckle; Caleb P. Arbuckle; Jethro Gotobed; Miss Oliphant.

12. *The Case of the Murdered Muckraker: A Daisy Dalrymple Mystery.* New York: St. Martin's Minotaur, 2002, 262 p.

NEW YORK, NEW YORK, OCTOBER 1923. A meeting with Daisy's editor is interrupted by the shooting of a man whose articles had been exploring the underbelly of Tammany Hall. Daisy is out of her element: the local police are in the pay of the politicians, and a federal agent is lurking in the background. Daisy just can't stay away from a mystery. The real-life aviator, Bessie Coleman, helps chase down the culprit. Associates: Kevin; Genevieve Cabot; Ernestine Cabot; Agent Lambert; Mr. Thorwald; Sir Roland "Dipper" Amboyne. Historical Figure: Bessie Coleman.

13. *Mistletoe and Murder: A Daisy Dalrymple Mystery.* New York: St. Martin's Minotaur, 2002, 260 p.

ENGLAND, DECEMBER 1923. The Dowager Lady Dalrymple backs the Earl of Westmoor into issuing her family an invitation to celebrate Christmas at Brockdene. He conceals the fact that he won't be there; instead, the Dalrymples will be hosted by some illegitimate cousins. Amid odd and difficult circumstances they manage to celebrate Christmas, but there is a pall cast over the celebration when one of the house party is found murdered. Associates: Derek; Captain Victor Norville; Miles Norville; James Tremayne.

14. *Die Laughing: A Daisy Dalrymple Mystery.* New York: St. Martin's Minotaur, 2003, 276 p.

ENGLAND, SPRING 1924. Daisy has been impressed at the lovely manners of her middle-class neighbors. When the neighborhood dentist is murdered, she finds that her neighbors are just as prone to vicious gossip as are the aristocrats. Daisy must pick her way through all the backstabbing reports to find the truth concerning the crime. Associates: Mrs. Sakari Prasad; Deva; Melanie Germond; Lizzie; Daphne Talmadge; Lord Henry Creighton.

12. *A Mourning Wedding: A Daisy Dalrymple Mystery.* New York: St. Martin's Minotaur, 2004, 280 p.

ENGLAND, JUNE 1924. Lucy's great-aunt, Lady Eva Devenish, has spent her life collecting and keeping secrets. When she is murdered during the preparations for Lucy's wedding, Daisy wonders if one of those secrets had finally proven fatal. Associate: Gerald "Binkie" Bincombe.

ECO, Umberto (1932–). Italian.

Scene of the Crime: Northern Italy in 1327.

Detective: William of Baskerville, a Franciscan monk.

Known Associates: Adso of Melk, his German apprentice, a Benedictine monk, and the narrator of the tale.

Premise: A British monk demonstrates the power of his intellect in solving several murders in medieval Italy.

Comment: It is a time of chaos in the Catholic Church. The Franciscans are fighting with the Pope and his cardinals over the future of the church, basing their struggle on the interpretation of a passage in the Bible in which Christ seems to mandate the necessity of poverty for the clergy. The two factions decide to meet in a northern Italian abbey to seek some common ground by which the church may avoid a schism. But as soon as William and his assistant Adso arrive, the monks who are their hosts begin to die, murdered in particularly vile and vicious ways. Baskerville undertakes the solution of the crimes, but as the bodies continue to pile up, and tensions mount between the two competing factions of clergy, a solution seems no closer than before. The great library maze housed in an annex to the abbey seems to lie at the very heart of the problem. There, finally, William and Adso confront the murderer, and the ultimate cutting of the Gordian knot is both shocking and shivery. Eco's best seller was one of the key books that helped popularize the historical mystery genre.

Literary Crimes & Chimes: This is the big kahuna, the top of the heap, the king of the hill, the book by which all other medieval mysteries must be measured. Baskerville is obviously patterned after both Sherlock Holmes and William of Occam, and Adso, the narrator, is the innocent observer of it all, writing from a perspective years after the events have taken place. That any writer could actually base a series of brutal murders on a philosophical discussion—and bring it off, while simultaneously making the setting and the ongoing debate an integral and interesting part of the story—is beyond belief and certainly beyond the ability of most of the writers covered in *Murder in Retrospect*. Everything here works. Everything works here very well indeed. Baskerville and his protégé are believable and sympathetic characters, the monastery itself is a self-contained world in the grand tradition of closed mysteries, the inhabitants thereof seem almost as bizarre as the inhabitants of the outside, "real" world, and the killings, well, the killings are vicious and puzzling and troubling. Eco makes it all seem effortless. Here is the perfect amalgamation of historical fiction and the mystery novel. No sequel is necessary or even possible. Would-be writers take note: this is how it's done when it's done properly. Readers will not need any further urging to enjoy this novel over and over again. The movie adaptation, while certainly interesting and perfectly cast, does not come close to capturing the nuances of Eco's original fiction, being quite properly labeled a palimpsest.

THE CASE

1. *The Name of the Rose,* trans. by William Weaver from *Il nome della rosa*. San Diego, CA: Harcourt Brace Jovanovich, 1983, 502 p.
   ITALY, NOVEMBER 1327. See commentary in this series.

ASSOCIATIONAL BOOK

Postscript to the Name of the Rose, trans. by William Weaver from *Postille a Il nome della rosa*. San Diego, CA: Harcourt Brace Jovanovich, 1984, 84 p.

This is Eco's *Apologia Pro Opere Meo*, indicating how he devised the notion for his novel, how he devised the world of his mystery, why it was placed when and where it was, and how it was ultimately realized, with much discussion of the philosophy of historical fiction and literature in general. Thus are revealed the innermost musings of a very thoughtful and introspective writer.

EMERSON, Kathy Lynn (Gorton) (1947–). American.

<u>LADY APPLETON SERIES</u>

Scene of the Crime: England, beginning in 1552.

Detective: Susanna Leigh (later Lady Appleton) was born in 1534, in a time divided by religion. Her father, Sir Amyas Leigh, believed strongly in the New Religion, and when he died in 1546, he had ensured that she would be brought up in the Protestant Duke of Northumberland's household. He arranged Susanna's marriage to Robert Appleton, and so, theoretically at least, Susanna subjugated her beliefs to Robert's. This subjugation was more theoretical than actual. Robert was Catholic, then Protestant, then briefly Catholic once more, then Protestant; in short, his only immutable and fervent beliefs involved his own political advancement. Susanna has been brought up as a Protestant; knowing her father's Protestant friends, she has worked to help them escape persecution as heretics under the reign of Bloody Mary. While Robert attended Court to climb in society, Susanna turned their home into a way station for fleeing Protestant leaders. Robert would have been the first to denounce her if he had known of her activities. He learned of them only later during Elizabeth's reign, and then, with Protestantism once more the preferred religion, he claimed the credit for Susanna's work. Queen Elizabeth, no doubt admiring his ability to have kept such activities secret while he was at Queen Mary's Court, made him one of her inquiry agents (i.e., a spy). His absences give Susanna the freedom to detect, her knowledge of herbs enables her to diagnose poisoning, her very nature makes her decisive and assertive, and her nose for intrigue and conspiracies, honed during her clandestine work to save Protestant Leaders, makes her a great detective.

Known Associates: Susanna Appleton (*née* Leigh) is accompanied on most of her investigations by her trusted maidservant, Jennet, a woman of some learning and much curiosity. In the first book, *Face Down in the Marrow-Bone Pie*, she gains a friend and companion in Catherine Denholm, who also assists her in *Face Down upon an Herbal*, but afterward leaves the country to marry Gilbert, Baron Glenelg. Catherine reappears to help Susanna in times of need, appearing in some of the subsequent books (notably in *Face Down beneath the Eleanor Cross*). Other characters frequenting many works in the series include Susanna's husband, Sir Robert Appleton, who leaves England at the end of *Face Down among the Winchester Geese* and who dies in *Face Down beneath the Eleanor Cross*; Sir Walter Pendennis, originally a friend of Susanna's husband, Robert, who soon becomes an ardent admirer of Susanna, and marries Eleanor (one of Robert's mistresses) after the events in *Face Down upon the Eleanor Cross*; Robert's illegitimate child by Eleanor, Rosamond, who comes into Susanna's household in the same book; Susanna treats Rosamond as an adopted daughter but gives custody of her back to Eleanor in *Face Down across the Western Sea*; Susanna's friend (and, after Robert's death, her lover), Nick Baldwin, who is met under adverse circumstances in "Lady Appleton and the London Man" and who appears in person or by letter in the subsequent novels.

Premise: An herbalist solves crimes and treats patients in twelfth-century England.

Comment: When they were young children, Joanna, Susanna's younger sister, mistook banewort berries for wild cherries and died of poisoning. Susanna's interest in warning others of the harmful properties of certain herbs stems from that tragedy. Her life's work is gathering information on poisonous plants and publishing that information in a cautionary herbal to warn mothers, cooks, and gardeners of the properties of dangerous plants. At the onset of the series the biggest obstacle to Susanna's investigations is Robert. He governs Susanna's activities with more regard for his convenience than for her preferences. His governance ends in *Face Down in the Marrow-Bone Pie*, when he realizes that it would be foolish for a man whose wife has an extensive knowledge of poisons to cause her to feel confined by his rule. Though it galls him, he legally gives Susanna the freedoms of a widow: the ability to use her own money, to travel without her husband's express orders, and to govern herself in small matters in his absence. Emerson also wrote *The Writer's Guide to Everyday Life in Renaissance England* (1996); her knowledge of the period is formidable, and she creates a likely and lively background for the stories. Susanna, Lady Appleton, is an interesting character, being intelligent but not introspective. Her feelings often come as a surprise to her and are most often manifest through that surprise or through her actions, not through acknowledgment of them by the character. She is uncompromising with herself while being forgiving with others. Her strong morality comes out as unflinching kindness, not as pious sentiment. In fact, her relationship with Nick at some points in the series causes society to regard her as a fallen woman; she would much rather be a fallen woman than a controlled wife.

Literary Crimes & Chimes: In the first few books, the point of view alternates between Susanna and Robert. Robert's thoughts provide a window into the prevailing attitudes and prejudices of his time. In fact, one of the humorous elements in the early books is watching Robert get hoodwinked by the women of the French Court. His opinion of women's intelligence and abilities is so low that he is unwittingly useful to those who would spy on England; and his arrogance is so great that he cannot accept that he is being used. One of the themes of the books is that, in a society in which women are powerless, some women will compete with others for any scrap of influence, while others will form friendships and alliances with each other.

THE CASES

1. **"The Body in the Dovecote,"** in *Murders and Other Confusions: The Chronicles of Susanna, Lady Appleton, 16th Century Gentlewoman, Herbalist, and Sleuth.* Norfolk, VA: Crippen & Landru Publishers, 2004, p. 17–32.

   OXFORD, ENGLAND, 1552. Seventeen-year-old Susanna Leigh's joyful contemplation of the handsome and charming Robert Appleton, to whom she has been betrothed, is interrupted by Lady Katherine's cry for help over a body she found in the dovecote. Before she is through, Susanna will have solved a case of poisoning and been given an awkward reward for her trouble. Associate: Robert. Historical Figures: John Dudley, Duke of Northumberland; Lady Ambrose Dudley; Lady Warwick.

2. **"Much Ado about Murder,"** in *Murders and Other Confusions: The Chronicles of Susanna, Lady Appleton, 16th Century Gentlewoman, Herbalist, and Sleuth.* Norfolk, VA: Crippen & Landru Publishers, 2004, p. 33–53.

   ENGLAND, 1556. Susanna is in grave danger when a Protestant fugitive whom she was hiding dies in her storeroom. She must move the corpse to avoid official interest in her property, determine if her clandestine operation has been compromised, and discover the murderer, all while hiding the entire affair from her husband, Robert, who would certainly denounce her to protect himself. Associates: Jennet; Sir Eustace Thornley; Robert.

3. **Face Down in the Marrow-Bone Pie.** New York: St. Martin's Press, 1997, 218 p.

   LANCASHIRE, ENGLAND, 1559. Susanna receives word that Appleton Manor has been deserted; its steward is dead, and the rest of the servants have fled the so-called ghosts inhabiting the place. Robert adamantly has refused to go anywhere near his manor, but he's in France, and Susanna has always been curious. Within a few days of her arrival, she realizes that she is battling more than a ghost. Associates: Catherine Denholm; Queen Catherine; Diane St. Cyr; Alys; Robert.

4. **Face Down upon an Herbal.** New York: St. Martin's Press, 1998, 295 p.

   GLOUCESTERSHIRE, ENGLAND, 1561. When word reaches Queen Elizabeth that Lord Glenelg has been found murdered in Lord Madderly's study, she suspects that this is a crime of politics, not of passion. She determines to get her agent (Robert) on the scene by recommending that he and Lady Appleton visit the Madderlys, ostensibly to allow Susanna to help ready the lady of the house's herbal for publication. Once there, Susanna proves herself a more able sleuth than Robert, finding not only murder but also blackmail, forgery, and treason. Associates: Catherine; Annabel; Gilbert; Robert. Historical Figure: British Queen Elizabeth I.

5. **"Lady Appleton and the London Man,"** in *Murders and Other Confusions: The Chronicles of Susanna, Lady Appleton, 16th Century Gentlewoman, Herbalist, and Sleuth.* Norfolk, VA: Crippen & Landru Publishers, 2004, p. 71–84.

KENT, ENGLAND, 1562. Susanna meets Nick Baldwin, her new neighbor, when he storms into her garden accusing Jennet of theft. A small jade figure, a gift from the King of Persia for the Queen of England, has been stolen from his keeping. Susanna must not only solve the theft but do so in a way that protects all involved.

6. *Face Down among the Winchester Geese.* New York: St. Martin's Press, 1999, 244 p.

LONDON, ENGLAND, 1563. A note with Robert's address is found in the pocket of a murdered woman, and Susanna, suspecting that there are aspects to this woman's relationship with Robert that won't bear scrutiny, claims the body to give it proper burial. The woman was killed on St. Mark's day, a feather being left near the body; Susanna begins to unravel the case of a serial killer while Robert seizes his chance to plot against Queen Elizabeth. Associates: Diane St. Cyr; Petronella; Eleanor; Rosamond; Robert. Historical Figure: Lady Mary Grey.

7. **"Lady Appleton and the Cautionary Herbal,"** in *Murders and Other Confusions: The Chronicles of Susanna, Lady Appleton, 16th Century Gentlewoman, Herbalist, and Sleuth.* Norfolk, VA: Crippen & Landru Publishers, 2004, p. 85–102.

LONDON, ENGLAND, 1564. When a defaced copy of her own herbal is delivered to Leigh Abbey, Susanna is convinced that it is either an accusation or a warning of a poisoning. Historical Figure: John Day.

8. *Face Down beneath the Eleanor Cross.* New York: St. Martin's Minotaur, 2000, 280 p.

LONDON AND LANCASHIRE, ENGLAND, 1565. Susanna, Lady Appleton ventures into Winchester to meet with Robert, who is a fugitive and is now demanding money. Robert is killed at the foot of the Eleanor Cross, and Susanna is accused of his murder. Associates: Robert; Sir Walter Pendennis; Catherine; Gilbert; Constance Crane; Alys and Leonard Putney; Widow Sparcheforde; Matthew Grimshaw; Eleanor Lowell; Rosamond; Annabel

MacReynolds (spy for French regent Catherine de Medici). Historical Figures: Leicester; Lady Mary Grey; Thomas Keyes.

9. *Face Down under the Wych Elm.* New York: St. Martin's Minotaur, 2000, 250 p.

KENT, ENGLAND, MAY–JULY 1567. Sensational charges of witchcraft are brought against two women, Lucy Milborne and Constance Crane. Constance was one of Robert Appleton's diversions long ago, but she knows that Lady Appleton successfully defended herself against charges of murder two years ago, and she writes to her for help. The excitement over the accusations has touched off a rash of witch-hunting, and the town has become a dangerous place indeed for an innocent herbalist. Associate: Constance Crane.

10. *Face Down before Rebel Hooves.* New York: St. Martin's Minotaur, 2001, 261 p.

HAMBURG, GERMANY, AND NORTHERN ENGLAND, 1569. Eleanor, believing she is on her deathbed, confesses treason to her husband, Sir Walter Pendennis. Lord Pendennis is one of Elizabeth's agents and must find out how much information Eleanor has passed on. He convinces Susanna to pose as Eleanor to infiltrate the conspiracies against England's crown. Associates: Sir Walter Pendennis; Eleanor. Historical Figures: Thomas Percy; Anne, Countess of Northumberland; Sir George Bowes; Charles Neville; Jane, Countess of Westmorland; Leonard Dacre.

11. *Face Down across the Western Sea.* New York: St. Martin's Minotaur, 2002, 227 p.

CORNWALL, ENGLAND, 1571. Susanna is asked by Walter Pendennis to work with researchers to gather and integrate the English explorers' accounts of their travels across the Western Sea, so as to establish England's claim to the New World. One explorer's account disappears, and the researcher who worked on it is murdered; then another researcher goes missing. Susanna steps forward to investigate and protect the individuals working on the project. Associates: Sir Walter Pendennis; Eleanor.

12. "Lady Appleton and the Cripplegate Chrisoms," in *Murders and Other Confusions: The Chronicles of Susanna, Lady Appleton, 16th Century Gentlewoman, Herbalist, and Sleuth.* Norfolk, VA: Crippen & Landru Publishers, 2004, p. 122–139.

ENGLAND, 1572. Nick's investigation of church records, undertaken to free Goodwife Billings by proving the death of her runaway husband, uncovers a disturbing pattern. A young woman has given birth to one child per year, without identifying the father; and every child has soon died. It's been a year since the last incident, and Susanna is frantic to find the mother before another infant is killed. Associate: Jane Johnson.

13. "Lady Appleton and the Bristol Crystals," in *Murders and Other Confusions: The Chronicles of Susanna, Lady Appleton, 16th Century Gentlewoman, Herbalist, and Sleuth*. Norfolk, VA: Crippen & Landru Publishers, 2004, p. 140–161.

ENGLAND, 1572. Lady Applegate is accosted by a "seer" whose visions save Rob Jaffrey's life. Susanna is still dubious of the woman's talents, but when she rushes into danger, Susanna follows. Associate: Rob Jaffrey.

14. "Encore for a Neck Verse," in *Murders and Other Confusions: The Chronicles of Susanna, Lady Appleton, 16th Century Gentlewoman, Herbalist, and Sleuth*. Norfolk, VA: Crippen & Landru Publishers, 2004, p. 162–181.

ENGLAND, 1576. Nick recognizes a dead man exiting a Dover cook shop and realizes that the execution of the man's murderer may have been premature; the question is, Was it also premeditated? Was the law used as an instrument of murder? Associates: Jane (and little Susanna) Johnson.

15. "Confusions Most Monstrous," in *Murders and Other Confusions: The Chronicles of Susanna, Lady Appleton, 16th Century Gentlewoman, Herbalist, and Sleuth*. Norfolk, VA: Crippen & Landru Publishers, 2004, p. 182–202.

ENGLAND, 1577. Susanna attends the wedding of a distant cousin but is dismayed when the wedding goes forward in the face of the bride's objections. She helps the bride escape, only to find, when the groom is attacked, that she may have delivered the bride from the marriage bed to the gallows. Associates: Jocasta Dodderidge; Henry Markland; Gawen Poole.

16. "Death by Devil's Turnips," in *Murders and Other Confusions: The Chronicles of Susanna, Lady Appleton, 16th Century Gentlewoman, Herbalist, and Sleuth*. Norfolk, VA: Crippen & Landru Publishers, 2004, p. 203–226.

ENGLAND, 1577. Three of Sir Edmund's mistresses recently met untimely ends. Sir Edmund asks Susanna to attend his wife to save the good woman from a similar fate. Although Susanna suspects that Sir Edmund is more interested in retaining his wife's property than her company, she feels she must act to protect her.

ASSOCIATED CASES

1. "Rubaiyat of Nicholas Baldwin," in *Murders and Other Confusions: The Chronicles of Susanna, Lady Appleton, 16th Century Gentlewoman, Herbalist, and Sleuth*. Norfolk, VA: Crippen & Landru Publishers, 2004, p. 54–70.

PERSIA, 1559. Twenty-seven-year-old Nick Baldwin is a stranger in a strange land, having traveled to Persia on a trade mission and found his efforts to meet with the King stymied by foreign protocol. He is working on strategies to see the King when he hears the distressed cries of a young woman; he arrives too late to rescue her and is found standing over her corpse. His meeting with the King may well include Nick's sentencing for her murder. Detective: Nick Baldwin.

2. "The Riddle of the Woolsack," in *Murders and Other Confusions: The Chronicles of Susanna, Lady Appleton, 16th Century Gentlewoman, Herbalist, and Sleuth.* Norfolk, VA: Crippen & Landru Publishers, 2004, p. 103–121.

ENGLAND, 1569. Alys Putney has been found murdered, and her mother asks Jennet to solve the murder in Lady Appleton's absence. Mother Sparcheforde once cursed Jennet, but compassion for a mother's grief, coupled with the promise of some excitement, moves Jennet to agree. Detectives: Jennet and Mark Jaffrey.

3. "The Curse of the Figure Flinger," in *Ellery Queen's Mystery Magazine* (December 2004): 76–93.

LONDON, ENGLAND, 1585. Griselda Ferrers has been telling fortunes under the name, Dame Starkey; when the predictions in the star chart that "Figure Flinger" Starkey sells Mistress Fitt do not come true, Flit threatens to take Starkey to court. In the course of a loud argument, Dame Starkey curses Mistress Flit; when the latter is found dead the next morning, the fortune-teller is arrested. Twelve years earlier, Starkey had done Nicholas Baldwin a great favor. Now she sends to him for help, and he gets her released temporarily from Tyburn Jail, so that she can investigate the murder, find the true culprit, and ultimately clear her name. Associates: Bates, the guard; Nicholas Baldwin.

DIANA SPAULDING SERIES

Scene of the Crime: The series begins in New York, New York, in March 1888 and continues on to Bangor, Maine. At the end of the first book there are indications that the second will take place in April 1888.

Detective: Diana Spaulding, widow of actor Evan Spaulding, writer of the "Today's Tidbits" column in the *Independent Intelligencer.* Diana's marriage was a horrible mistake; her fortune-hunter husband actually wooed her in the expectation that her family would buy him off. Imagine his surprise and dismay when they disowned Diana instead. He drank, chased women, and gambled. He had been employed by Todd's Touring Thespians but left to found his own acting company. The attempt ended in disaster and soon after Evan was killed, leaving Diana penniless. Her friend Rowena took her in, but Rowena's husband felt that an actor's widow was not a suitable companion for his wife. Rowena talked her brother, Horatio Foxe, editor of the *Independent Intelligencer*, into hiring Diana.

Known Associates: Evan was with Todd's Touring Thespians for years. He and Diana traveled with that company. Evan was an actor, and Diana worked with costuming, props, or whatever else was needed. The original members of that company (Nathan Todd, Jerusha, and Patsy) regard her as a relative and do their best to help and protect her when they can. The newer members of the company, stung by her negative reviews, do not regard her as a friend. Diana's best friend is Rowena; her unscrupulous editor, Horatio Foxe, is Rowena's brother. In the first book, *Deadlier than the Pen*, Diana becomes enamored of Ben Northcote and meets his mother, Maggie, and brother, Aaron.

Premise: An actor's widow pens articles for newspapers and solves crimes in nineteenth-century New York.

Comment: Among the five prominent newspapers in New York—the *Independent Intelligencer*, the *Times*, the *Sun*, the *Tribune*, and Joseph Pulitzer's *World*—there are four women writers, all known either for genteel book reviews or for "stunts" such as Nellie Bly's pretending insanity in order to get a story from the inside of an asylum. Diana is trying to write a column of entertainment reviews; but her editor, knowing that scandal sells, demands that she dig up sensational stories. If she does not, he will "spice up" her reviews by adding lies about the actors and writers, many of whom are Diana's friends. This threat goads Diana into becoming an investigative reporter. In Diana's initial foray, her unscrupulous editor, Horatio Foxe, who has already "spiced up" her column on several occasions, demands that she dig up the dirt on a popular gothic writer. Determined to find something that will save her job while satisfying her integrity and believing that there must be some scandal associated with anyone who writes gruesome horror stories for a living, Diana dives in. By the time Mr. Foxe discovers that the other women columnists who had panned the writer's dramatic readings were actually murdered, Diana is committed to thoroughly investigating the attractive and seductive Mr. Bathory.

Literary Crimes & Chimes: This is a light, romantic mystery with an edge, the latter provided through Diana's knowledge of the grimness of poverty and the perfidy of (at least some) men. As an investigator, her greatest asset is her stubbornness; she continues to follow a lead even when she believes it's dangerous. She does have some research and investigative experience, which is put to use partly to gather information for a story but mostly to learn more about a man in whom she has established a romantic interest. Diana's desperate determination to keep her job stems from her firsthand knowledge of what it is like to be hungry, something she learned during her husband's disastrous attempts to start an acting company, and that fact causes the reader to take her and her plight seriously. The first book in the series is almost a play on a gothic novel; but the "plucky heroine" is a real woman who has found a tenuous place for herself in society. At one point in the book, Diana reveals that she is descended from a sixteenth-century woman who wrote a cautionary herbal, a connection to Kathy Lynn Emerson's Susanna, Lady Appleton series.

THE CASE

1. *Deadlier than the Pen: A Diana Spaulding Mystery.* Corona del Mar, CA: Pemberley Press, 2004, 266 p.
   NEW YORK, NEW YORK, AND BANGOR, MAINE, MARCH 1888. See commentary in this series.

FRAZER, Margaret (originally the joint pseud. of Mary Monica Pulver [1943–] and Gail Frazer, currently the sole pseud. of Gail Frazer). American.

DAME FREVISSE SERIES

Scene of the Crime: England, beginning in 1431. Some of the ancillary stories (in which people known to Dame Frevisse in the books have their own adventures) occur earlier.

Detective: Dame Frevisse became a Benedictine nun after a childhood of traveling the world with her parents. After her parents died, she lived in the home of her uncle, Thomas Chaucer (Geoffrey Chaucer's son). She is drawn into investigating suspicious deaths by circumstance, by the incompetence and greed of the local crowner, and, in some books in the series, by the orders of her superiors.

Known Associates: The nuns of St. Frideswide's include Domina Edith, who serves as Prioress through *The Boy's Tale*; Sister Alys, who is raised to Prioress before the events in *The Murderer's Tale*; Domina Elisabeth, who is the Prioress in the books after *The Prioress' Tale*; Sister Thomasine, who is admired for the strength of her calling; and Dame Claire, who is Dame Frevisse's closest friend.

Premise: A Benedictine nun solves crimes in fifteenth-century England.

Comment: Dame Frevisse was not always cloistered; her travels with her parents showed her much of the world. This knowledge makes her a likely candidate when her Prioress must send one of the nuns outside the Priory. The Benedictine Rule allows nuns to travel into society, provided that they are always attended when doing so by another religious, and Frevisse often functions in this role. The Prioress also assigns the work within the Priory; at the outset of the series, Dame Frevisse is hosteler and so has the duty of seeing to the Priory's guests. When trouble knocks at St. Frideswide's Priory, Frevisse is likely the first person there who knows of it. The nun's sharp mind and the local crowner's preference for easy and profitable answers at inquests cause Frevisse to do a fair amount of detecting. The careful research by the authors provides a rich historical background to the stories; not only are the food, dress, work, and architecture of the period true to their era, but so are the concerns, the fears, and the beliefs of the characters. Frevisse thinks deeply on theological matters, such as the two or three correct occupations of man; she worries more for the souls of the guilty than she does for their punishment; yet she is completely human and uncompromisingly honest with herself, as when she acknowledges that she can't find any sadness in her for Master Morys Montfort's death but forces herself anyway to pray for his soul. Frevisse sins, makes mistakes (at least one of them fatal), and at times falls into depression. Her sharp observations are saved from shrewishness by her sense of humor; as when she wonders whether the saintly Sister Thomasine's good health was sent to try Frevisse in *The Servant's Tale*. It takes Frevisse a good part of the next six years to learn to value Thomasine's goodness, piety, and perspicacity. Nine years later, in *The Hunter's Tale*, Frevisse surprises herself when she refrains from chiding young Sister Johane for her failings and instead praises the good that she has done. In return she learns more of Sister Johane and learns to respect her. One of the joys of the series is seeing Frevisse, while retaining her edge, gain wisdom, (some) patience, and a respect for the beliefs and thoughts of others.

Literary Crimes & Chimes: The tales are told from two first-person viewpoints. One of these is that of Frevisse; the other is provided by the title character (the novice in *The Novice's Tale*, the servant in *The Servant's Tale*, etc.). The second point of view allows the writer to explore thoughts and feelings that might be foreign to Dame Frevisse, as well as providing an *entrée* into different levels of this hierarchical society. At the outset the series was written in collaboration between Mary Pulver and Gail Frazer, Mary outlining the first book and Gail adding knowledge of medieval England; both worked on the writing. Their collaboration lasted through *The Murderer's Tale*; they plotted *The Prioress' Tale* together, but Gail wrote it on her own and has been the sole author of the series since then.

THE CASES

1. **"The Midwife's Tale,"** in *The Mammoth Book of Historical Detectives*, ed. by Mike Ashley. London: Robinson Publishing; New York: Carroll & Graf, 1995, p. 192–216.

PRIORS BYFIELD, ENGLAND (during Father Clement's tenure). Dame Frevisse and Dame Claire are called to help a woman whose husband is on the verge of death. They suspect that some stranger bent on robbery attacked him in his home, but even during the hue and cry Frevisse looks further (and closer) for answers. Associates: Dame Claire; Ada Bychurch; Father Clement.

2. **The Novice's Tale.** New York: Jove Books, 1992, 229 p.

ST. FRIDESWIDE'S PRIORY, ENGLAND, 1431. Thomasine will take her final vows in two weeks, if her great-aunt Lady Ermantrude doesn't manage to pry her from the convent first. Ermantrude arrives at St. Frideswide's Priory for a short visit, gossips in a most unseemly way, and then continues on to visit Thomasine's sister. She soon returns in a fury, and when she dies, most are willing to believe her temper caused her death; but Dame Claire asserts that she was poisoned, and the crowner is willing to convict any powerless person. Associates: Thomasine; Mistress Maryon; Master Montfort; Sir Walter Fenner; Robert Fenner.

3. **The Servant's Tale.** New York: Jove Books, 1993, 234 p.

ST. FRIDESWIDE'S PRIORY, ENGLAND, 1433–1434. Traveling players find an injured man on the road and bring him to the convent out of charity. All too soon, they are suspected in his death. Dame Frevisse's fond memories of journeying with her traveling parents strengthen her determination to make sure that the inept Crowner Montfort does not pin the crimes on the players. Associates: Master Naylor; Master Montfort; Gilbey Dunn; the players: Thomas Bassett; Ellis; Joliffe; Rose; Piers.

4. **The Outlaw's Tale.** New York: Jove Books, 1994, 217 p.

ENGLAND, 1434. Frevisse's cousin Nicholas was declared outlaw years earlier; he seizes Dame Frevisse and Sister Emma on their way to the christening of Emma's niece, in order to force Frevisse to petition her uncle Thomas Chaucer on his behalf. Afraid that they will take sick in the woods, he houses them with an accomplice. At the house Frevisse discovers more than is safe for her to know about the activities of the outlaws, including crimes of extortion and murder. Associates: Sister Emma; Master Naylor. Historical Figure: Thomas Chaucer.

5. **The Bishop's Tale.** New York: Berkley Prime Crime, 1994, 198 p.

ENGLAND, NOVEMBER 1434. At the funeral feast for Dame Frevisse's uncle, Thomas Chaucer, the most unpleasant guest, Sir Clement, predictably picks a fight and attempts to prove his argument by saying, "But if I'm wrong in this matter, may God strike me down within the hour!" He promptly dies; and many are ready to credit the Lord as the instigator of his passing. Bishop Beaufort believes that there may be a more worldly hand involved and orders Dame Frevisse to investigate. Associates: Dame Perpetua; Sir Walter Fenner; Robert Fenner. Historical Figures: Matilda Chaucer; Alice; Earl of Suffolk; Cardinal Bishop Beaufort of Winchester.

6. **"The Witch's Tale,"** in *The Mammoth Book of Historical Whodunnits,* ed. by Mike Ashley. London: Robinson Publishing; New York: Carroll & Graf, 1993, p. 204–220.

PRIORS BYFIELD, ENGLAND, 1435? Frevisse is hosteler. Margery Wilkins was generally liked and pitied in the village, liked because she gave of her skills as herb woman freely and pitied because her choleric husband Jack beat her overmuch. When Jack tramples her herbs in one such attack, Margery curses him; he promptly clutches at his chest and falls down dead. Associates: Mistress Margery; Master Naylor; Dame Claire; Master Montfort.

7. *The Boy's Tale.* New York: Berkley Prime Crime, 1995, 233 p.

ST. FRIDESWIDE'S PRIORY, ENGLAND, 1436. The Dowager Queen has retired to the country and secretly married a common man of no account (Lord Owen Tidder or Tydor, sometimes spelled Tudor). When rumors of the marriage get out, she sends her young Tudor sons into hiding; before they can gain their refuge, their party is set upon by "bandits," and they flee to the nunnery for protection. Frevisse is the first to guess that the attack was more about politics than gold, and with her Prioress' blessing, she works to protect the children from further murderous attacks. Associates: Mistress Maryon; Lady Adela Warenne; Master Montfort. Historical Figures: Dowager Queen Katherine; Edmund; Jasper.

8. *The Murderer's Tale.* New York: Berkley Prime Crime, 1996, 230 p.

MINSTER LOVELL, ENGLAND, 1436. Dame Frevisse and Dame Claire, at Minster Lovell to petition for money to restone the priory well, are present when Lionel Knyvet is accused of murder. He had seemed such a pleasant man, but he was known to have had the falling sickness and therefore was believed to be possessed by demons. Frevisse does not think that demons would leave bloody shoeprints walking away from both the murderer and the victim, and so she looks to find a more earthly villain. Associates: Dame Claire; Father Henry; John Naylor; Edeyn. Historical Figure: Lady Lovell.

9. *The Prioress' Tale.* New York: Berkley Prime Crime, 1997, 246 p.

ST. FRIDESWIDE'S PRIORY, ENGLAND, 1439. Domina Alys' ambitions for the priory have outstripped their wealth, and her relatives, the Godfreys, have overtaxed the priory's provisions. The priory is already in trouble when the Godfreys determine to use St. Frideswide's as a hideout while they carry on their feud with the Fenners. They go beyond vandalism and theft to abduction, and then someone goes even further—to murder. Associates: Sister Thomasine; Joliffe.

10. *The Maiden's Tale*. New York: Berkley Prime Crime, 1998, 247 p.

LONDON, ENGLAND, 1439. Dame Frevisse and Dame Perpetua travel with Abbot Gilberd to escort their new prioress, Domina Elisabeth, to St. Frideswide's. They stay in London with Frevisse's cousin, Lady Alice, Countess of Suffolk. There they must contend with the plots and counterplots, assassination attempts and blackmail, that swirl around the charming captive Duke of Orléans. Associates: Dame Perpetua; Lady Adela Warenne; Jane Pole; Bishop Beaufort. Historical Figures: Duke of Orléans; Lady Alice; Earl of Suffolk; Edmund; Jasper.

11. *The Reeve's Tale*. New York: Berkley Prime Crime, 1999, 274 p.

PRIOR BYFIELD, ENGLAND, 144? Master Naylor, the Priory's agent, and Simon Perryn, Lord Lovell's Reeve, usually work together to decide small village disputes. Then Master Naylor is placed under house arrest until accusations about his past can be answered. Dame Frevisse is sent to Prior Byfield as his substitute. Frevisse works to see disputes clearly and decide them fairly; but matters go beyond simple property disputes when one of the litigants is found murdered. Associates: Sister Thomasine; Simon Perryn; Master Naylor; Dickon; Mistress Margery; Father Henry; Gilbey Dunn; Master Montfort; Christopher Montfort.

12. *The Squire's Tale*. New York: Berkley Prime Crime, 2000, 277 p.

BRINSKEP MANOR, ENGLAND, LENT 1442. Dame Claire and Dame Frevisse journey to Brinskep Manor with Lady Blaunche, in case she needs their help while bearing her child. They find that they've stumbled into a nasty land dispute, which Blaunche wants to fight, while her husband would prefer to settle the matter amicably. In the midst of the dispute, a murder unbalances Blaunche's mind; Frevisse works to find the culprit in the hope that justice can restore order. Associates: Dame Claire; Robert Fenner.

13. *The Clerk's Tale*. New York: Berkley Prime Crime, 2002, 312 p.

GORING, ENGLAND, JANUARY 1446. Master Montfort was known (and despised) by Sister Frevisse through his work as crowner. When he's found dead, she tries to feel regret at his passing but can't. She does pray for his damned soul and also for the soul of his murderer, whom she believes may have had an excellent reason to commit the crime. When other murders occur, she realizes that the crimes must be solved. Associates: Domina Elisabeth; Christopher Montfort.

14. *The Bastard's Tale*. New York: Berkley Prime Crime, 2003, 309 p.

ENGLAND, 1447. The cunning Bishop Beaufort arranges for Frevisse to be sent by her Prioress to visit her cousin Alice. He demands that Frevisse act as his agent to investigate rumors that the already powerful Suffolk is plotting to increase his power by destroying the Duke of Gloucester. Suffolk's treachery is well laid, and the plots are enacted so quickly that they cannot be stopped. Alice, Joliffe, and Frevisse work together to try to save the innocent. Associates: Joliffe; Dame Perpetua. Historical Figures: Marquis of Suffolk; FitzGloucester; Bishop Pecock of St. Asaph's; Bishop Beaufort.

15. *The Hunter's Tale*. New York: Berkley Prime Crime, 2004, 323 p.

WOODRIM ESTATE, ENGLAND, SUMMER 1448. When Sir Ralph dies, his family feels little but relief; but his death does not end their misery. He has constructed his will to control them even beyond the grave; his widow is determined to prevail so that she can protect the children. When she realizes that there is a plot against her, she asks for Frevisse's company, knowing that an impartial witness may be all that stands between her and her family's ruin. Associates: Sister Johane; Ursula.

ASSOCIATED STORIES

NOTE: These short stories involve minor characters from the Frevisse series. Frevisse does not actually appear in any of them. Margaret Frazer has also begun another series of novels based on Joliffe the Player as the main protagonist.

1. "Volo Te Habere," in *Unholy Orders: Mystery Stories with a Religious Twist*, ed. by Serita Stevens. Philadelphia: Intrigue Press, 2000, p. 47–73.

ENGLAND, 1405. Bishop Beaufort of Winchester is asked to determine the validity of the claims of Catherine Dauntsey, daughter of a well-landed knight, and Stephen Hameden, younger son of an even wealthier family, who have said the words to each other so that they are legally married. Their families had thought to make their marriages elsewhere and to better advantage. The families bring forth a witness who mysteriously dies. Detective: Bishop Beaufort.

2. "The Traveler's Tale," in *The Mammoth Book of Locked Room Mysteries and Impossible Crimes*, ed. by Mike Ashley. London: Robinson Publishing; New York: Carroll & Graf, 2000, p. 36–57.

ENGLAND, 1400s (before *The Bishop's Tale*). Thomas Chaucer encounters an impossible crime, in which an entire family is slain inside their carriage while it is moving. Detective: Thomas Chaucer.

3. "Heretical Murder," in *The Mammoth Book of More Historical Whodunnits*, ed. by Mike Ashley. London: Robinson Publishing; New York: Carroll & Graf, 2001, p. 331–358.

LONDON, ENGLAND, 1431. Master Furseney, an inoffensive scribe who's never been in a brawl in his life, is found dead in the street after a bar fight.

The Undercrowner chalks this up to the actions of "foreigners" (anyone not of London; in this case, Kentish men mustering to put down the Lollard heretic rebellion). Sire Pecock reasons otherwise. Detective: Sire Pecock (later Bishop Pecock), assisted by his student, Dick Colop.

4. "Lowly Death," in *Murder Most Catholic: Divine Tales of Profane Crimes*, ed. by Ralph McInerny. Nashville, TN: Cumberland House, 2002, p. 131–149.

LONDON, ENGLAND, FEBRUARY 1437. Dick Colop asks Master Pecock's help in finding the truth about the seemingly accidental death of his friend John's mother-in-law. Detectives: Master Pecock; Dick Colop.

5. "The Simple Logic of It," in *Murder Most Medieval: Noble Tales of Ig- noble Demises*, ed. by Martin H. Greenberg and John Helfers. Nashville, TN: Cumberland House, 2000, p. 87–115.

WESTMINSTER PALACE, LONDON, ENGLAND (probably before the events in *The Bastard's Tale*). A Welsh courier is found dead in the palace yard, with an incriminating note attached written to the Duke of York. York's enemies immediately take the rumor of his treachery to the King. It's difficult for an honest man to prove that he's honest. Detective: Bishop Pecock.

6. "The World's Eternity," in *Much Ado about Murder*, ed. by Anne Perry. New York: Berkley Prime Crime, 2002, p. 210–227.

ENGLAND, 1441–1447. This is a different view (based on Shakespeare's play) of the events leading to charges of witchcraft against Eleanor Cobham and to the Duke of Gloucester's death. Historical Figures: British King Henry VI; Queen Margaret; Cardinal Beaufort; Suffolk.

JOLIFFE THE PLAYER SERIES

Scene of the Crime: Joliffe's first appearance is in *The Servant's Tale* in the Dame Frevisse series at Christmastide 1433. The first book in the Jo- liffe series takes place in the following June, during the Corpus Christi fes- tival in Oxford, England.

Detective: Joliffe studied at Oxford University in his youth. He realized that he would not be able to curb his sense of humor or his tongue well enough to rise in the sadly political hierarchy of scholars and that he would likely be miserable as well. He left his friends and teachers a note and set off into the world, becoming a player with Thomas Basset's company. The company fell on hard times a little while before the events in the first story in the series. They had been Lord Warenne's players, but when the old Lord died, the new Lord ordered them to procure village women for him while they were on their travels. They refused and thus became itinerant players without a patron. Their company split apart, and the little remnant of Basset, Joliffe, Ellis, Rose, and Piers has been struggling along ever since.

Known Associates: Thomas Basset, leader of their company, a talented man who drives his tiny group to be the equal of the best companies of players; Rose, his daughter, who is the company's costumer and props mistress; Piers, her cherubic-looking son, a fine actor with quick wits and a penchant for cheating at games; Ellis, another player, who wishes to marry Rose, but since she doesn't know if her runaway husband is alive or dead, she cannot remarry; Joliffe, the fifth member (the fourth actor, since Rose as a woman cannot go onstage) of the company. Historical Figures: John Thamys; Doctor Gascoigne; Lord and Lady Lovell.

Premise: A British actor solves crimes in fifteenth-century England.

Comment: When a rich "Eden-child" (a young man with Down's syndrome) becomes fascinated with the traveling players of Joliffe's company, they find themselves invited to perform at the estate of the man who holds his wardship. The actors are treated well enough, but when a man is found dead at the door of the storage barn where they sleep, they know they will immediately be under suspicion. The dead man was a Lollard, and Joliffe finds that they must fear the taint of heresy as well as the accusation of murder. Joliffe's detecting skills are matched by his instinct for self-preservation, which provides strong motivation for him to prove his company innocent of the charges. Margaret Frazer uses her research well to paint the background of another time and place, very clearly showing how power and wealth were kept and passed on through the control of marriages, how marriages were not for love but were for the profit of those who had the legal right to arrange them and for the passing on of property in the manner that those in power determined best. In some ways, this is contrasted with the obvious care the players take with each other, almost like a family. The reader instantly understands that a threat to any of the players would be terrifying to all of them.

Literary Crimes & Chimes: One of the fun aspects of the first book was Joliffe's obvious pride in his company's performances, the plays, the props, and the costumes. He makes a very convincing "player." The prejudices against players are well depicted, as are other aspects of the inherent harshness of the time. Margaret Frazer does not sugarcoat the past. Tragedies happen, and while people grieve, they also try to find ways to salvage whatever it is possible to salvage. The people in her books are tough, strong, and compassionate. Between acquainting the reader with the players, their current employment, the town, and the situation, the initial crime in the first book does not take place until about a third of the way through the novel. One might hope that future books in the series will get off the ground a little more quickly.

THE CASE

1. *A Play of Isaac.* New York: Berkley Prime Crime, 2004, 312 p. OXFORD, ENGLAND, JUNE 1434. See commentary in this series.

GABALDON, Diana (Jean) (1952–). American.

LORD JOHN GREY SERIES

Scene of the Crime: London, beginning in 1757.

Detective: As a teenager Lord John William Grey worked with his brother's company of British soldiers, attempting to quell rebellion in Scotland. A decade later he rose to a position in charge of Ardsmuir Prison. This series takes place after Ardsmuir has been closed and the prisoners transported. Lord Grey has just returned to London.

Known Associates: Yet unmarried, Lord John lives with his mother, the Dowager Countess Melton, and his orphaned cousin (now his brother's ward), Olivia Pearsall. In 1757 his brother Hal is out of the country. Lord John's associates are men from his regiment; these include Colonel Harry Quarry and Lieutenant Malwin Stubbs. In *Lord John and the Private Matter*, Lord John hires a valet, Tom Byrd, and is saved by a man whom he lobbies to work with him, Stephan von Namtzen. Other prominent individuals in his social sphere include Lady Mumford, the mother of his lover, Hector, who died at Culloden; Lady Lucinda Joffrey, a woman who hopes to find Lord John a wife; and Sir Francis Dashwood, a notorious rake.

Premise: A homosexual nobleman solves crimes in eighteenth-century England.

Comment: Lord John William Grey's basic decency was evident from the time he was a teenager, when he revealed secrets to save a damsel in distress. His *naiveté* was also in evidence, since the damsel was not actually in any distress. He swore revenge on the man who had tricked him; and a decade later, when he had power over that man as his jailer at Ardsmuir, they became friends. Lord John lives in some fear that his "awful secret" (he's homosexual) will come to light. His sympathy for the underdog, his decency, and his bravery cause him to become embroiled in mysteries in a world in which murder is seen as more respectable than homosexuality. He is forced to constantly conceal his thoughts and feelings, living a double life. Lord John's knowledge of how his society regards homosexuality and the careful way he hides his secret add an emotional dimension to this series. His sensitivity to the condemnation he would face, his belief that casual murder would be more readily forgiven than homosexuality, will be shocking to readers living in the modern world.

Literary Crimes & Chimes: This series started with a short story penned for an anthology. Lord John William Grey is a minor, but pivotal, character in Gabaldon's historical time-travel series, *Outlanders*. Those books focus on the bloody conflicts between England and Scotland. Galaldon refers to the pieces listed below as "interpolations" in the *Outlander* sequence. *Lord John and the Private Matter* is the first in a proposed trilogy of Lord John Grey novels.

THE CASES

1. **"Hellfire,"** in *Past Poisons: An Ellis Peters Memorial Anthology of Historical Crime*, ed. by Maxim Jakubowski. London: Headline, 1998, p. 325–352.
   LONDON, ENGLAND, 1757. A young man asks Lord John for help but is brutally struck down before they can speak further. Investigating his murder, Lord John joins a house party of the most depraved nobles of his acquaintance and learns of their shocking vices. Associate: George Everett.

2. **Lord John and the Private Matter.** New York: Delacorte Press, 2003, 305 p.
   LONDON, ENGLAND, 1757. In the early days of the Seven Years War, Lord John Grey is back in England awaiting news on his regiment's next posting. He learns that his cousin's *fiancée* is poxed and struggles to find a way to break off her engagement without causing offense or scandal. Simultaneously, he is asked to lead an investigation into the disappearance of requisition forms that, if sold to the French, would reveal Britain's troop deployment and so cost countless lives in the conflict to come. Associates: Mr. Bowles; Nessie.

GELLIS, Roberta (Leah) (1927–). American.

MAGDALENE LA BÂTARDE OR MADAM OF THE OLD PRIORY GUESTHOUSE SERIES

Scene of the Crime: England, beginning in 1139.

Detective: Magdalene la Bâtarde is honest, intelligent, independent, and reasonably well-to-do. She had been horribly abused as a wife and committed illegal acts to leave the marriage and to survive. She was eventually aided by William of Ypres, who offered Magdalene the chance to become the madam of a whorehouse in medieval London. The whorehouse is called the "Old Priory Guesthouse" because at some point in its history that is what it was; now it is rented to Magdalene by the Bishop of Winchester.

Known Associates: Magdalene has used the opportunity provided by William of Ypres' patronage to rescue other unfortunate women, women who were already whores but who were being systematically abused and destroyed. The women of the Old Priory Guesthouse are Ella, who is developmentally arrested; Sabina, who is blind; Lettice, who is mute; and Hager, who does not speak English. In *A Personal Devil* Sabina has retired to become one man's mistress, and Diot joins the women of the guesthouse. Dulcie is their cook. In *A Mortal Bane* the Bishop of Winchester assigns one of his men, Sir Bellamy of Itchen (nicknamed Bell by the women of the guesthouse), to assist in Magdalene's investigations. He and Magdalene develop a working partnership that evolves into a romantic relationship by the third book in the series. The historical figures who play a part in the series are William of Ypres (Magdalene's patron), Waleran de Meulan (William's enemy), and British King Stephen.

Premise: The owner of a house of prostitution solves crimes and rights wrongs in twelfth-century London.

Comment: Magdalene la Bâtarde was saved from a life of common prostitution many years earlier by William of Ypres. He had realized that a whorehouse would provide a good cover for him if he wanted to arrange clandestine meetings with other men who wielded power; and he gave her the funds to start her own "house," with the understanding that he would also use it as his meeting place. Magdalene is loyal to him in the same way that a liegeman would be loyal, and in return his protection has given her a sort of independence that she could never have gained on her own. William has her absolute loyalty, and she is also loyal to the women who work in the whorehouse, as they are to her. Any threat to any of them will be investigated and resolved, without regard for personal cost. Gellis has a master's degree in medieval history; she has taken great pains to ground the series in the world of medieval London. The professions and the materials of everyday life "feel" totally accurate. The actions of the minor characters are usually plausible; however, there are moments when Magdalene's thoughts and attitudes seem anachronistically modern. In the third book (*Bone of Contention*) Magdalene's initiative and independence are explored and explained as stemming from her "fealty" to Lord William of Ypres, which, in retrospect, makes her actions throughout the series and the existence of such a safe and almost uplifting whorehouse more believable. Overall, the writing is smooth, the characters are engaging, and the "puzzle aspects" of the mysteries are excellent.

Literary Crimes & Chimes: The third book is the most interesting historically, suggesting a motive for King Stephen to hold this court in Oxford. The writing is excellent throughout the series. Foreshadowing is done so well that by the time matters come to a head, actions that should have been deemed rash seem almost inevitable. Characters repeat the same explanation or story at various points in the tale to different people; besides reminding the reader of what has happened, these individual vignettes change a little with each audience, in a way that beautifully delineates each of the characters. After finishing each book in the series most readers will want to buy the sequel, just to see what happens next in the characters' lives.

THE CASES

1. *A Mortal Bane.* New York: Forge, 1999, 350 p.
LONDON, ENGLAND, APRIL 1139. Papal messenger Baldassare De Firenze is found dead on the steps of St. Mary Overy Church. The women of the Old Priory Guesthouse are immediately suspected of the murder. Magdalene must work very hard indeed to exonerate her friends and ladies. Associates: Brother Paulinus; Master Mainard.

2. *A Personal Devil.* New York: Forge, 2001, 316 p.
LONDON, ENGLAND, 1139. Bertrild, wife of Mainard the saddler, took great joy in causing others pain. When she is found dead, the gentle Mainard immediately becomes the chief suspect. Magdalene la Bâtarde and Sir Bellamy must uncover all of the poisonous Bertrild's crimes to discover her murderer. Associates: Sir Bellamy; Master Mainard; Bertrild; Cody; Henry.

3. *Bone of Contention.* New York: Forge, 2002, 431 p.
LONDON AND OXFORD, ENGLAND, 1139. King Stephen has decided to hold court at Oxford. This is seemingly an odd choice, for there are not

enough rooms in the city to house all the men who will be arriving with their Lords. William of Ypres is concerned over undercurrents he feels in the court and sends word to Magdalene that she must come to Oxford and there set up some sort of front for William's meetings, a place where men can come and go without their activities being noticed. When one of Waleran de Meulan's men is found murdered, a retainer of William's is suspected, and Magdalene feels that she must investigate to find the truth and clear her patron. Associates: Florete; Diccon; Sir Niall Arvagh; Loveday of Otmoor; Master Hardel; Tirell; William. Historical Figure: British King Stephen.

LUCREZIA BORGIA SERIES

Scene of the Crime: Ferrara, Italy, in 1502.

Detective: Lucrezia Borgia, daughter of Pope Alexander VI, had one of the most frightening reputations in Rome. She was rumored to have engaged in an incestuous relationship with her brother and her father, to have been a serial murderess, with her weapon of choice being poison. People took delight in telling each other, whenever they were invited to dine at Lucrezia's table, that they should make out their wills before leaving their homes. Everywhere there were whispers. When Alfonso's family recommends a match between him and Lucrezia, she realizes that, since he is Ferrara's heir, her family cannot demand that he live in Rome. She expects neither love nor joy from this marriage; all she wants is a safe haven from the merciless whispers about her character. Then one of her ladies-in-waiting is found dead, and Alfonso, rather than just whispering that Lucrezia poisoned the woman, accuses her at the top of his lungs.

Known Associates: Alfonso d'Este, Lucrezia's new husband; Ercole d'Este, the Duke; Alfonso's father; Alfonso's brothers, Sigismundo, Ferrante, and Giulio; Nicola la Sienese and Angela Borgia (Lucrezia's cousin), Lucrezia's ladies-in-waiting; Teodora Angelini, chief of the ladies assigned to Lucrezia; Beatrice Tisio; Elizabetta Dossi; and Diana Altoviti, the other ladies assigned to her; Lucia, Lucrezia's maid, a spy for Isabella, who likes Lucrezia and hates Isabella; Ferraran courtiers: Ercole Strozzi, a gallant; the intelligent Niccolò da Correggio; and Don Bernadino Zambotto; Don Guido del Palagio to Lucrezia, an execrable Neapolitan poet, rumored to be a spy for the Aragonese.

Premise: An Italian noblewoman solves crimes in sixteenth-century Italy.

Comment: When the harmless and somewhat silly Bianca Tedaldo is found dead, rumors fly through the court. Although Lucrezia was away from court at the time of Bianca's death, she is accused of the murder. She knows that she must find the true villain in order to clear her name. Lucrezia has lived with rumors before in Rome and is determined not to let them proliferate again, being acutely aware of what her life will be like if she allows such gossip to spread in Ferrara. The character of Lucrezia Borgia is sympathetic without being sweet. She handles her interactions with others like moves in a chess game. For example, she thinks about what the Duke's ladies will expect from her (after her husband has loudly accused her of poisoning his mistress); she realizes how she can get them to spread gossip favorable to her reputation and then determines to give them something colorful and positive to gossip about. She loudly proclaims that she will find the killer to clear her own name and proceeds to do just that.

Literary Crimes & Chimes: Seamless writing and great dialogue fill this entry, but there are so many characters that it almost becomes necessary for the reader to keep a list! Additional offerings may provide easier going, since some of the characters will have become known by then to the readers. A cast list would have been welcome.

THE CASE

1. *Lucrezia Borgia and the Mother of Poisons.* New York: Forge, 2003, 333 p. FERRARA, ITALY, 1502. See commentary in this series.

GORDON, Alan R(ichard) (1959–). American.

THEOPHILOS THE FOOL SERIES

Scene of the Crime: Europe and the Middle East, during the late twelfth and early thirteenth centuries.

Detective: Theophilos the Fool, a member of the Fool's Guild. He takes a different alias (he refers to them as *noms de bouffon*) for each new adventure, but his Guild name is always Theophilos. While in Umbria, he is known as Balaam, in Pisa he is Forzo, in Illyria he is Feste (mentioned by William Shakespeare in *Twelfth Night*), in Venice and in Constantinople he becomes Feste again, in Tyre he is known as Droignon. Generally, each book centers upon a single adventure, so we encounter only one alias per book. In the past Theophilos has been a fool of legendary skill and wit, saving countless lives as he travels the world and works behind the scenes to prevent or end wars. Theophilos is haunted by the memories of the people that he could not save. At the beginning of the series, Theophilos has retired; or, more accurately, he has gone into decline. The only amazing feats that he is moved to perform involve imbibing large quantities of liquor. In fact, when

Theophilos finally decides that he must take action, he is forbidden to do so, his friends believing that he is no longer able to function well enough to survive.

Known Associates: The pillars of the Fool's Guild include Father Gerald, who runs the Guild; Sister Agatha, the Guild's Costumer; Brother Timothy, who teaches juggling; and Brother Dennis, who cares for the Guild's horses. In the course of the adventures related in these books Theophilos marries Claudia (also known as Viola, Aglaia, and the Duchess of Orsino), who becomes an apprentice fool in *Thirteenth Night* and a full member of the Fool's Guild in *Jester Leaps In*. They have a daughter, Portia, on January 6, 1204, at the conclusion of *A Death in the Venetian Quarter*.

Premise: A professional fool solves crimes and tries to end political and military conflicts in twelfth- and thirteenth-century Europe.

Comment: This series balances two sorts of historical mysteries. The "history" in most of these books is both detailed and vivid and closely follows the historical texts from the periods covered. Tribute is paid to one of Europe's first historians, Niketas Choniates, by including him as a character in two of the novels. However, in two of the books (*Thirteenth Night* and *An Antic Disposition*) and in the basic premise that underlies the ongoing actions of the main character, the books follow a more imaginative history, almost a "literary history," or history as it might be portrayed in the plays of the time. Thus, we occasionally encounter both imaginary places and fantastical characters. The tradition of the fool who displays more wisdom than his masters and who works behind the scenes to bring about happy endings lies at the center of these books.

Literary Crimes & Chimes: Gordon has created herein an entire Fools' Guild, which he portrays as a (somewhat) religious order that trains novitiates and then deploys them. Its overarching purpose is to increase the chance for everlasting peace in the world. These Fools act as spies, provocateurs, and sometimes even executioners; but, as a group, they prefer using their wits to using steel and generally work behind the scenes to influence those in power. On page 242 of the paperback edition of *Thirteenth Night*, Alan Gordon gives us his apologia: "There is scant historical evidence for the existence of the Fools' Guild. This is that rare secret society that actually succeeded in remaining secret. In *The Age of Faith*, Will Durant writes of a '*confrèrie* of minstrels and jongleurs like that which we know to have been held in Fécamp in Normandy about the year 1000; there they learned one another's tricks and airs, and the new tales or songs of the *trouvères* and troubadours' (p. 1054). Frustratingly, this is virtually the only un-footnoted line in the entire book, and I have yet to discover its source." The premise is certainly fun, and the careful attention to historical detail saves the series from becoming silly. These are mysteries with a little bit of humor and a lot of heart. Many of the supporting characters in the Fools' Guild are heroes, and the reader will want to save them all. The historical background is exceptionally portrayed, particularly in the books that cover the events leading up to the Fourth Crusade. The series opens with *Thirteenth Night*, which takes place in Shakespeare's Illyria, fifteen years after the events of Shakespeare's *Twelfth Night*—and is therefore peopled only with imaginary characters. Subsequent books depict historical events; central to these actions are intrigues in Europe and the Middle East during the eleventh and twelfth centuries. The most recent book in the series, *An Antic Disposition*, is based on a 1204 Danish history written by a historian of questionable reliability, Saxo Grammaticus. This same Danish history was used as the basis for Shakespeare's *Hamlet*; readers should not fear this retelling of the story, since it is both more and less bloody than the more familiar version. Most of the series is told from Theophilos' point of view, although the third novel alternates between his perspective and that of Claudia (his wife). This allows the reader to see the machinations of the female members of the Imperial Court firsthand.

THE CASES

1. **"The Jester and the Saint,"** in *Ellery Queen's Mystery Magazine* (December 1995): 142–156. Reprinted in *Once upon a Crime II*, ed. by Janet Hutchings. New York: St. Martin's Press, 1996, p. 114–127.

   UMBRIA, ASSISI, ITALY, 1198. Theophilos (under the *"nom de bouffon"* Balaam) encounters the fifteen-year-old Giovanni de Bernardone (who later becomes Saint Francis), and helps him solve a murder. Associate: Saint Francis of Assisi.

2. **"The Jester and the Mathematician,"** in *Ellery Queen's Mystery Magazine* (February 2000): 90–109.

   PISA, ITALY, 1198. A Saracen spy in the city of Pisa implicates the great mathematician Leonardo Fibonacci in a murder. It is up to Theophilos (called Forzo in Pisa) and his fellow fool, the Great Frenetto (aka Fazio), to clear Fibonacci's name and capture the spy. Associate: The Great Frenetto (Guild name, Fazio). Historical Figure: Leonardo Fibonacci.

3. ***Thirteenth Night: A Medieval Mystery.*** New York: St. Martin's Press, 1999, 243 p.

   ORSINO, ITALY, 1201. Several of Shakespeare's comedies provide a time of comic confusion crowned by a marriage, in order to reach the desired "happy ending." This book is set fifteen years after the events chronicled in

Twelfth Night, and the aftermath of Feste's actions has been mixed, for some a blessing, for others a curse. *Thirteenth Night* reveals that Feste engineered the alliances that kept the stability of Orsino intact and that thwarted the plans of Malvolio. When a message is left at the Guildhall for Feste the Fool, telling him only that Duke Orsino is dead, is it a call for help—or a trap? Associates: Mark; Celia.

4. *Jester Leaps In: A Medieval Mystery.* New York: St. Martin's Minotaur, 2000, 276 p.

CONSTANTINOPLE, BYZANTINE EMPIRE, 1202. Constantinople is poised on the brink of chaos. The current Emperor has neglected the defense of the city, and his nephew has been spotted in Germany, mustering support to seize the throne. In the midst of this all five of the Fools stationed in Constantinople have disappeared. Feste is sent to find some way to stabilize the situation and prevent a war. Associates: Fat Basil; Thalia; Zintziphitzes; Father Essias; Plossus; Alfonso; Rico. Historical Figures: Imperial family of Constantinople; Imperial Treasurer Philoxenites; Senator Niketas Choniates.

5. "The Jester and the Thieves," in *Ellery Queen's Mystery Magazine* (October 2004): 72–85.

CONSTANTINOPLE, BYZANTINE EMPIRE, 1202. This story is an interpolation into the events near the beginning of *Jester Leaps In*, while Feste is Head Fool of Constantinople, with only Claudia to assist him. Father Essias commissions Feste to discover which one of three of his thieves has stolen from the Thieves' Guild. Knowing that discovering the truth will condemn one man to death but that not discovering the truth will condemn all three (two of them being comparatively innocent), Feste reluctantly complies. Associate: Father Essias.

6. *A Death in the Venetian Quarter: A Medieval Mystery.* New York: St. Martin's Minotaur, 2002, 288 p.

CONSTANTINOPLE, BYZANTINE EMPIRE, 1203. In the shadow of the Fourth Crusade, Feste, Chief Fool of Constantinople, is commanded to investigate the death of an Imperial spy. This was no simple murder; Feste suspects that it is the one untidy thread of an intricate plot to deliver the city to the Crusaders. Associates: Rico; Plossus; Alfonso; Tantalo; Raimbaut; Father Essias; Sebastion, Viola's brother. Historical Figures: Byzantine Imperial family; Imperial Treasurer Philoxenites; Senator Niketas Choniates.

7. *Widow of Jerusalem.* New York: St. Martin's Minotaur, 2003, 276 p.

ITALY, 1204. Rome has begun to persecute the Fools, and the Guild has fled from the Guild Hall. Theophilos and Claudia "rescue" the sign of the Scarlet Dwarf and follow the Guild into hiding. As they travel, Theophilos tells the story of the dwarf, Scarlet, the Chief Fool of Jerusalem, and the summer of 1191: TYRE, LEBANON, SUMMER 1191. Jerusalem was captured by Saladin in 1187, and the refugees therefrom fled to Tyre. The Fools Scarlet and Droignon work to uphold the peace of the city and preserve the outlying tent city of refugees, while trying covertly to strengthen Queen Isabelle's claim to the throne of Jerusalem. Associates: Scarlet(t) the Dwarf; apprentices Ibrahim, Magdalena, Sara, and Peter. Historical Figures: Isabelle, Queen of Jerusalem; Conrad, Marquis of Montferrat, Isabelle's husband; Henry of Champagne; Bishop of Beauvais.

8. *An Antic Disposition.* New York: St. Martin's Minotaur, 2004, 337 p.

SWABIA, GERMANY, 1204. At the Fool's hideout in the Black Forest, Father Gerald tells the story of Theophilos' first adventure: SOUTH JUTLAND, DENMARK, 1157. Terrence the Fool is sent to deflate the ambitions of a man who would become the King of Denmark. He fails, but at least one good thing survives his posting to Jutland. The novel is based on the same story that inspired *Hamlet.* Associates: Terence (Yorick); Gerald; Horace; La Vache.

GORMAN, Ed(ward Joseph) (1941–). American.

BLUE AND GRAY ANTHOLOGY SERIES

Scene of the Crime: United States, between 1861 and 1865.

Detective: Various.

Known Associates: Various.

Premise: An anthology of mystery and spy stories set during the American Civil War.

Comment: An anthology of historical mysteries and espionage stories set during the American Civil War (1861–1865). CONTENTS: "Hobson's Choice," by John Lutz; "Measure," by Gary Phillips; "Counterfeit Copperhead," by Edward D. Hoch; "Dead Line," by Kristine Kathryn Rusch; "South Georgia Crossing," by Loren D. Estleman; "Invisible Spy," by Brendan DuBois; "Monica Van Telflin and the Proper Application of Pressure," by James H. Cobb; "Worth a Thousand Words," by Aileen Schumacher; "Belle Boyd, the Rebel Spy," by Bill Crider; "Knights of Liberty," by Robert J. Randisi; "Port Tobacco," by Jane Haddam; "Swan," by Ray Vukevich; "Courtship of Captain Swenk," by P. G. Nagle; "Road to Stony Creek," by Jane Lindskold; "Other—1," by Janet Berliner; "Turncoat," by Doug Allyn; "Small and Private War," by Ed Gorman; "Slither," by Marie Jakober.

Literary Crimes & Chimes: The focus here is more on espionage than detection, although enough uncovering of crimes does occur to qualify this volume. Fairly standard fair.

THE CASE

1. *Blue and Gray Undercover,* ed. by Ed Gorman. New York: Forge, 2001, 318 p.
   UNITED STATES, BETWEEN 1861 and 1865. See commentary in this series.

GREENBERG, Martin H(arry) (1941–). American.

MURDER MOST . . . ANTHOLOGY SERIES

Scene of the Crime: Various.

Detective: Various.

Known Associates: Various.

Premise: Greenberg compiles a series of historical anthologies based around specific themes.

Comment: Martin Greenberg has edited more fiction anthologies than any individual in history, numbering well over 500 volumes. Many of his books are coedited with guest writers or editors with expertise in the particular subject of the volume in question.

Literary Crimes & Chimes: Greenberg always produces a quality volume, but these books are fairly standard fare for their type. The stories include a mixture of reprints and original tales specially written for the anthology, with all of the standard authors represented. Both British and American writers are included in about equal numbers. This is good solid material, but nothing to write home about. Many of these stories have already been encountered in the other anthologies covered elsewhere in *Murder in Retrospect.*

THE CASES

1. *Murder Most Medieval: Noble Tales of Ignoble Demises,* ed. by Martin H. Greenberg and John Helfers. Nashville, TN: Cumberland House, 2000, 291 p.
   An anthology of historical detective stories set in medieval times. CONTENTS: "Introduction," by John Helfers; "Like a Dog Returning . . . A Sister Fidelma Mystery," by Peter Tremayne; "Cold as Fire," by Lillian Stewart

Carl; "A Horse for My Kingdom," by Gillian Linscott; "The Simple Logic of It," by Margaret Frazer; "Plucking a Mandrake," by Clayton Emery; "A Gift from God," by Edward Marston; "The Queen's Chastity," by Tony Geraghty; "The Reiving of Bonville Keep," by Kathy Lynn Emerson; "For the Love of Old Bones," by Michael Jecks; "The Wizard of Lindsay Woods," by Brendan DuBois; "Improvements," by Kristine Kathryn Rusch; "The Light on the Road to Woodstock," by Ellis Peters; "Authors' Biographies."

2. ***Murder Most Confederate: Tales of Crimes Quite Uncivil,*** ed. by Martin H. Greenberg. Nashville, TN: Cumberland House, 2000, 274 p.

An anthology of historical detective stories set during the American Civil War (1861–1865). CONTENTS: "Introduction," by John Helfers; "The Hessian," by Doug Allyn; "The Price of Coal," by Edward D. Hoch; "Last Hours in Richmond," by Brendan DuBois; "Veterans," by John Lutz; "The Cobblestones of Saratoga Street," by Avram Davidson; "A House Divided," by Marc Bilgrey; "Blossoms and Blood," by Janet Berliner; "Whistling Dixie," by Billie Sue Mosiman; "Behind Enemy Lines," by John Helfers and Carol Rondou; "The Unknown Soldier," by Kristine Kathryn Rusch; "A Woman's Touch," by Max Allan Collins and Matthew V. Clemens; "Ghost," by Bradley H. Sinor; "The Last Day of the War," by James Reasoner; "Valuables," by Kristine Scheid; "The Face," by Ed Gorman; "Matthew in the Morning," by Gary A. Braunbeck; "Contributors."

3. ***Murder Most Celtic: Tall Tales of Irish Mayhem,*** ed. by Martin H. Greenberg. Nashville, TN: Cumberland House, 2001, 291 p.

An anthology of modern and historical detective stories set in Ireland. CONTENTS: "Introduction," by John Helfers; "Scattered Thorns," by Peter Tremayne; "The Wearing of the Green," by Brendan DuBois; "The World Is Mine; or, Deeds That Make Heaven Weep," by P. M. Carlson; "Black Irish," by Doug Allyn; "Murder in Kilcurry," by Mary Ryan; "Great Day for the Irish," by Edward D. Hoch; "Stealing the Dark," by Jane Adams; "A Book of Kells," by Jeremiah Healy; "Skiv," by Wendi Lee; "So Where've You Buried the Missus Then, Paddy?" by Mat Coward; "Green Legs and Glam," by Robert J. Randisi; "One of Our Leprechauns Is Missing," by Bill Crider; "The Dublin Eye," by Clark Howard; "The Male and Female Hogan," by Jon L. Breen; "Celtic Noir," by Paul Bishop; "Fenian Ram," by Simon Clark; "Authors' Bios."

4. ***Murder Most Catholic: Divine Tales of Profane Crimes,*** ed. by Ralph McInterny. Nashville, TN: Cumberland House, 2002, 244 p.

An anthology of both historical and contemporary crime stories featuring Catholic clerics. CONTENTS: "Introduction," by Ralph McInerny; "Whispers of the Dead," by Peter Tremayne; "Bless Me Father for I Have Sinned," by Ed Gorman; "Death by Fire," by Anne Perry and Malachi Saxon; "The Arrow of Ice," by Edward D. Hoch; "The Rag and Bone Man," by Lillian Stewart Carl; "Divine Justice," by Chuck Meyer; "Cemetery of the Innocents," by Stephen Dentinger; "Veronica's Veil," by Monica Quill; "Lowly Death," by Margaret Frazer; "Ex Libris," by Kate Gallison; "A Clerical Error," by Michael Jecks; "Through a Glass, Darkly," by Kate Charles; "The Knight's Confession," by P. C. Doherty; "The Shorn Lamb," by Ralph McInerny; "Contributors."

GREENWOOD, Kerry (1954–). Australian.

PHRYNE FISHER SERIES

Scene of the Crime: Australia, beginning in 1928.

Detective: The Honourable Phryne Fisher grew up fishing scraps out of the pig bins in Melbourne to get a bite to eat. Then her father inherited a title and a fortune. She has a cynical view of the wealthy and powerful, now coupled with the money and title to gain entrance into their world.

Known Associates: Phryne is accompanied in her investigations by her maid, Dorothy (Dot), whom Phryne meets (and avenges) in *Cocaine Blues*. In that same book she meets and gains the trust of Bert (Albert Johnson) and Cec (Cecil Yates), taxi drivers with revolutionary leanings; along with a hardworking detective inspector Jack Robinson; and a female Scottish doctor, Dr. MacMillan. In *Flying Too High* Phryne hires a butler, Mr. Butler, who makes imaginative cocktails, and his wife, Mrs. Butler, who cooks wonderful meals. In *Murder on the Ballarat Train* Phryne rescues and adopts two girls, Jane and Ruth. Phryne goes through a long list of liaisons but forms a semipermanent attachment to Lin Chung in *Ruddy Gore*. Lin Chung is usually accompanied by Li Pen, a Shaolin monk, who acts as his bodyguard.

Premise: A socialite solves crimes in early twentieth-century Australia.

Comment: The Honourable Phryne Fisher possesses a love of adventure, the wealth and title that allow her to get away with outrageous behavior, and a strong social conscience. She grew up powerless and in abject poverty and now enjoys every privilege due to her position and every penny of her newfound wealth. At the opening of the series the only fly in the ointment is that she is bored. She finds her calling when frantic parents ask her to investigate their suspicion that their daughter is being poisoned by her husband. At the close of the first book, she decides to set herself up as an investigator; not only to solve crimes but also to avenge their victims. Most of the books cover the investigation of multiple crimes, some of which come together in each novel's dénouement. The novels so far have taken place in 1928; in some cases, it is possible to determine a month or season (and remember that in Australia the seasons run opposite to those in the United States). The chronology of the books at times seems confused, not that this matters much. The stories below are presented in the best possible order, based both on identified months and seasons and on the characters' entrances and exits into Phryne's busy life.

Literary Crimes & Chimes: This is a remarkable series, authentic in mood as well as in historical detail. The books echo the feel of the 1920s Simon Templar series by Leslie Charteris, providing great fun, decisive and direct action, justice spiked with a touch of vengeance, and a main character whose actions cut through the everyday concerns that slow down ordinary mortals and resonate through time to make Phryne a worthy successor to "The Saint." The historical detail in these books turns what could be simple romps into windows onto another time. Greenwood has immersed herself in the newspapers from the period. Every detail rings true, not only such things as fashion but also the interests of the day. For example, "Tut-mania" sweeps the country in 1928 with the news of the discovery of King Tut's tomb, capturing the public's imagination; even children's games are influenced by excitement over Ancient Egypt. Many of the stories depict the public's fascination with "aeroplanes," and most of the gentlemen and some of the ladies in the books greatly admire Phryne's Hispano-Suiza. Not only the background of the stories but the tone, the interests of even minor characters, and the gossip are all designed to give the reader *entrée* into 1920s Australia.

THE CASES

1. *Cocaine Blues: The First Phryne Fisher Mystery.* Victoria, Australia: McPhee Gribble, 1989, 195 p. As: *Death by Misadventure: A Roaring Twenties Mystery.* New York: Ballantine Books, 1991, 185 p.

   MELBOURNE, AUSTRALIA, MAY 1928. The frantic parents of Lydia Andrews ask Phryne to find out if their daughter is being slowly poisoned. She journeys to Australia and not only uncovers the truth about the poisoning but also breaks up a cocaine ring and ends the career of "Butcher George," an abortionist who has killed countless young women. Associates: Sasha; Woman Police Officer Jones; Dr. MacMillan.

2. *Flying Too High: A Phryne Fisher Mystery.* Victoria, Australia: McPhee
   Gribble, 1990, 173 p.

MELBOURNE, AUSTRALIA, AUGUST 1928. When Mrs. McNaughton hires
Phryne to persuade her son not to kill his father, Phryne speaks to the young
man. She is sure that the matter is resolved, until the body of Mr. Mc-
Naughton is found and his son is arrested. Phryne must divide her energies
between her case and a search for a kidnapped six-year-old girl, Candida
Maldon. Associates: Mark Fielding; Bunji Ross; Jack Leonard.

3. *Murder on the Ballarat Train: A Phryne Fisher Mystery.* Victoria, Australia: McPhee Gribble, 1991, 163 p.

BALLARAT, AUSTRALIA, AUGUST 1928. Phryne, recognizing the smell of
chloroform, breaks a window of her train compartment and sets about rescuing the other passengers. When the head count is taken, one elderly lady
is missing, and one extra young girl is found. Phryne sets out to solve the
mysteries and in the process uncovers a murder and a gang of white slavers.
Associates: Lindsay Herbert; Eunice Henderson.

4. **"The Voice Is Jacob's Voice,"** in *Murder at Home: Crimes for a Summer Christmas Anthology,* ed. by Stephen Knight. St. Leonards, NSW,
   Australia: Allen & Unwin, 1993, p. 151–161.

ST. KILDA'S, AUSTRALIA, WINTER SOLSTICE, 1928. The guest list at
Phryne's Winter Solstice costume party has been constructed to clear her
slate of social debts to people of whom she is not overly fond; and also leav-
ened with people whom she adores, so that she will have some fun in the
process. When two of her guests die almost simultaneously, Phryne suspects
that the wine has been mixed with cyanide. Associates: Dr. MacMillan; Lindsay Herbert.

5. *Death at Victoria Dock.* Victoria, Australia: McPhee Gribble, 1992, 186 p.

MELBOURNE, AUSTRALIA, SEPTEMBER 1928. A stray bullet smashes
through Phryne's windshield as she drives home from the Explorer's Club,
drawing her into an investigation within the Australian community of revolutionary ex-patriots. In a separate investigation, Phryne is hired to find a
missing sixteen-year-old girl who has been collecting other people's secrets.
Associates: Peter Smith; Hugh Collins.

6. *The Green Mill Murder.* Victoria, Australia: McPhee Gribble, 1993, 259 p.

MELBOURNE, AUSTRALIA, OCTOBER 1928. A man is stabbed at the Green
Mill (a jazzy nightclub), and Phryne must not locate only the perpetrator
but also uncover the motive, the murder weapon, and a man who was declared dead years ago. Associates: Victor Freeman; Josephine; Anne; Tin-
tagel; Nerine.

7. ***Blood and Circuses.*** Victoria, Australia: McPhee Gribble, 1994, 289 p.

FITZROY, AUSTRALIA, OCTOBER 1928. There have been so many attacks and accidents at Farrell's Circus and Wild Beast Show that some of the circus folk suspect a curse is involved; when they consult a gypsy for information, she tells them that a black-haired, green-eyed woman whose name starts with "F" will solve their problems. Since one of them used to be Phryne's lover, the detective agrees to take the case, going undercover at the circus, both to help and also to prove to herself that she can still survive without the assistance of her position or money. When Christine/Christopher (half-man, half-woman) is found murdered at Mrs. Witherspoon's house for paying gentlefolk, Phryne realizes that the circus saboteur may go as far as murder. Associates: Doreen; Alan Lee; Samson; Jo Jo; Matthias; Mr. Burton; Dulcie Fanshaw; Molly Younger; Lizard Elsie.

8. ***Ruddy Gore.*** Victoria, Australia: McPhee Gribble, 1995, 283 p.

MELBOURNE, AUSTRALIA, 1928. Poisonings on stage cap a series of strange events that have plagued the run of the Gilbert and Sullivan operetta *Ruddigore*. The stage manager asks Phryne to either unmask or exorcise the theater ghost! Associates: Bernard Tarrant; Herbert, Hu and Lin families.

9. ***Urn Burial.*** Victoria, Australia: Penguin Books Australia, 1996, 258 p.

GIPPSLAND, AUSTRALIA, 1928. When the Honourable Phryne Fisher is invited to a house party, she asks Lin Chung to join her. She expects to battle prejudice against Lin, but not to solve a case involving threats, assault, and murder! (Miss Mary Mead, a wonderful tribute to Miss Marple, is one of the other houseguests.) Associate: Tom Reynolds.

10. **"The Vanishing of Jock McHale's Hat,"** in *More Crimes for a Summer Christmas*, ed. by Stephen Knight. North Sydney, NSW, Australia: Allen & Unwin, 1991, p. 97–106.

AUSTRALIA, AUGUST 1928. The Archbishop asks Phryne to investigate a mysterious disappearance that takes place in his church.

11. ***Raisins and Almonds.*** St. Leonards, NSW, Australia: Allen & Unwin, 1997, 248 p.

AUSTRALIA, SEPTEMBER 1928. Phryne is asked to investigate the inexplicable murder of a young Jewish scholar. He was blamelessly perusing a rare book when he fell dead, and the bookstore's proprietress is the chief suspect. Phryne's investigations uncover a dangerous invention, offered for sale to raise money to support the Zionist cause. Associate: Simon Abrahams.

12. ***Death before Wicket.*** St. Leonards, NSW, Australia: Allen & Unwin, 1999, 228 p.

SYDNEY, AUSTRALIA, 1928. Phryne's sojourn to Sydney was planned for relaxation: a little dancing, a little sightseeing, and a lot of test cricket. Her plans must be changed when two beautiful young men beg her to clear a friend of a charge of theft, before he is dismissed from the university. Phryne has just begun to get her teeth into the case when Dot finds that her sister has disappeared from her home, abandoning her children. In the underworld of Sydney Phryne discovers the answers to more than one family tragedy, battles pimps and practitioners of black magic, and works to reunite mothers with their children. Associates: Joan; Professor Ayers.

13. **"Come Sable Night,"** in *Malice Domestic 6*, ed. by Anne Perry. New York: Pocket Books, 1997, p. 180–193.

ST. KILDA'S, AUSTRALIA, SUMMER 1928. Phryne invites the Madrigal Choir to her bijou residence to rehearse. She enjoys the joyful singing but is surprised by an engagement announcement and is then shocked by a death.

14. *Away with the Fairies.* Crows Nest, NSW, Australia: Allen & Unwin, 2001, 276 p.

MELBOURNE, AUSTRALIA, 1928. Miss Lavender writes children's stories that feature Hilda among the flower fairies, with bunnies pulling fairy chariots and the "beautifullest" fairy; but even that does not seem reason enough to murder the woman. Phryne agrees to help with the magazine's fashion column to get close enough to investigate the murder. When she receives a communication informing her that Lin Chung has been kidnapped, she harnesses her rage and hunts his captors. Associate: Madame Lin.

15. *Murder in Montparnasse.* Crows Nest, NSW, Australia: Allen & Unwin, 2002, 292 p.

ST. KILDA'S, AUSTRALIA, 1928. Phryne is beginning an investigation in the whereabouts of a missing girl when Bert and Cec ask her to find out who is killing, one by one, their mates from the war. Her investigations force her to remember her past and to come to terms with her own postwar experience in Paris. Phryne had been part of an ambulance company, saving wounded soldiers at the front; the armistice had left her fragile and numb. Now events have brought her back to her old life. Associates: Anatole Bertrand; Elizabeth, Toupie; Dolly Wilde; Hugh; René Dubois; Camellia.

16. *The Castlemaine Murders.* Crows Nest, NSW, Australia: Allen & Unwin, 2003, 272 p.

CASTLEMAINE, AUSTRALIA, 1928. The resolution of the Lin and Hu family feud allows Lin Chung and Great Grandfather Hu to settle old grievances; these include the Hu family's theft of Lin gold in 1857, a crime the Hu family denies. Lin travels to Castlemaine, the site of the 1857 goldfields, to investigate. Phryne, hoping for an opportunity for dalliance away from her family, follows him, and they find that gold is not all that can move men to murder. Associates: Eliza Fisher; Dr. Treasure; Professor Ayers; Mr. Burton; Lady Alice Harborough; Fuchsia.

17. ***Queen of the Flowers.*** Crows Nest, NSW, Australia: Allen & Unwin, 2004, 279 p.

St. Kilda's, Australia, 1928. St. Kilda's flower parade will include Phryne as Queen of the Flowers and four young women acting as her flower maidens. The young women vary in gifts, talent, intelligence, charm, beauty, and murderous viciousness. When one of the young women disappears, Phryne is asked to find her; she uncovers heinous crimes and fights to save the child before she is silenced forever. Associates: James Murray; Diane Pridham; Joannie Smythe; Rose Westin; Jessica Adams; Marie Bernhoff; Dulcie Fanshawe.

18. **"I Am Dying Egypt, Dying,"** in *Crosstown Traffic*, ed. by Stuart Coupe, Julie Ogden, and Robert Hood. Wollongong, NSW, Australia: Five Islands Press Associates in Association with Mean Streets Magazine, 1993, p. 196–212.

Australia, probably 1928. Phryne is enticed into attending a costume party dressed as an Egyptian Queen from the time of the Pharaohs. She suspects her host's motives, but his plans go far beyond anything she could have imagined.

19. **"Tamam Shud: A Phryne Fisher Mystery,"** in *Case Reopened*, ed. by Stuart Coupe and Julie Ogden. St. Leonards, NSW, Australia: Allen & Unwin, 1993, p. 135–161.

Australia, 1941. Phryne finds a body on the beach. Partly to quiet the haunting memories of her work with the French Resistance and partly to help a young policewoman, Phryne investigates the death.

GREGORY, Susanna (1958–). British.

Matthew Bartholomew Series

Scene of the Crime: Cambridge, England, beginning in 1348.

Detective: Doctor Matthew Bartholomew (born approximately 1315) was educated at the great Benedictine Abbey at Peterborough and had been expected to take his vows and become a monk. His brother-in-law, a cloth merchant, had instead planned an advantageous marriage to Francis de Belem, whose father is a dyer. Bartholomew confounded everyone by running away to Oxford, then to Paris to become a physician. There he was trained by Ibn Ibrahim, an Eastern doctor who believed that leeches were used by physicians too lazy and clumsy to discover the actual causes of each patient's illness. Thus, Bartholomew does not believe in the conventional medical wisdom of his time, instead trusting cleanliness, hydration, and herbal remedies more than bleeding or casting horoscopes. His methods are so suspect that he cannot gain rich patrons, even though his patients usually do well. He is, in any case, just as happy to tend the poor. At age twenty-nine, four years before the events recounted in *A Plague on Both Your Houses*, he was hired as Cambridge's Master of Medicine. He is a good man, pushing himself past exhaustion to ease the suffering of others; it is a joy to see him filled with wonder at the birth of a child after he's spent months tending those dying from plague.

Known Associates: Bartholomew's sister Edith lives in the town near the university, with her husband, Sir Oswald Stanmore, and their son, Richard. Members of the university community include Brother Michael, Cambridge's Benedictine Master of Theology; Franciscan Father William, who was dismissed from the Inquisition for overzealousness and who now teaches theology and the Trivium (grammar, rhetoric, and logic); Gilbertine Friar Master Thomas Kenyngham, who serves as Master of Michaelhouse throughout part of the series; Master of Philosophy Ralph de Langelee, who joins Michaelhouse before the events in *A Deadly Brew* and becomes its Master in *A Masterly Murder*; Fellow John Runham, first seen in *A Deadly Brew*, exiting in *A Masterly Murder*, who teaches law; Cluniac Fellow Roger Alcote, through *A Wicked Deed*; gentle blind Franciscan Brother Paul, who teaches theology and the Trivium; Carmelite Friar Master Thomas Suttone, who joins Michaelhouse to teach the Trivium in *A Masterly Murder*, as does the mad Dominican Master John Clippesby, who teaches astronomy and music; Cynric ap Huwydd, Batholomew's book-bearer; and Agatha, laundress and leader of the college staff. Historical Figures depicted in the books include Bishop Thomas de Lisle, Bishop of Ely; Richard Tulyet, who occupies the position of Sheriff in most of the novels; some of the names of the real-life Masters of Cambridge of the time are also used as character names for the series.

Premise: A physician tends the sick and examines the dead, while also solving crimes in fourteenth-century Cambridge, England.

Comment: When the books were first published in the United States, they were issued out of order, causing some confusion. The list below has been reordered according to the events within the books. These should be read as shown, since characters recur, and sometimes their histories are essential to the plots. Most books in the series end with a historical note, explaining which plot elements were based on fact and illuminating a little more of the society from a historical perspective.

Literary Crimes & Chimes: Intricate plots, schemes within intrigues, wrapped in nefarious strategies, and bound with rumors: there are so many constituencies here, not only town and gown, but covering the various factions within each, that the reader sometimes has problems keeping them straight. Within the college there are differences between those who have taken major and minor orders, and between those of different religious groups. Within the town we see different levels of society, and within those, the different guilds stand out. Rivalries, jealousies, remembered slights, and anticipated advantages form a potent, but unstable, brew. The year of the Great Death (the plague) greatly damages the foundations of society; in the following years the people are even more desperate to gain protection and even more ruthless in what they will do to gain prosperity. Bartholomew is an appealing character, a little self-consciously naïve, and surprisingly ahead of his time regarding medical practice. Both traits are explained by his convictions and education. Nicely done.

THE CASES

1. *A Plague on Both Your Houses.* London: Warner Books, 1996, 406 p.

CAMBRIDGE, ENGLAND, 1348. Bartholomew's friend, Sir John Babington, Master of Michaelhouse, has been found dead, and the death is determined to be a bizarre suicide, a verdict that Bartholomew simply cannot believe. The next death in Michaelhouse was an expected passing, involving an old man; but his body is stolen away soon after Bartholomew finds him dead. The new Master of Michaelhouse, intent on avoiding a scandal, decrees that no foul play has occurred. Bartholomew cannot abide the cover-up but knows that he's on his own for any investigation that he conducts. Then plague is visited upon Cambridge, some say in retribution for the town's sins; but the innocent as well as the guilty die. Associates: Master of Philosophy Giles Abigny; Philippa; Rachel Atkin; Samuel Gray.

2. *An Unholy Alliance.* London: Little, Brown, 1996, 310 p.

CAMBRIDGE, ENGLAND, 1350. Bartholomew is given two cases to solve: Chancellor de Wetherset orders the physician to investigate the attempted theft of a secret history of Cambridge University (and, incidentally, the murder of the man who tried to steal it); and a distraught father asks Bartholomew to bring a serial killer to justice. Cambridge has a Sheriff, but he has shown little interest in the killings, probably because most of the victims have been whores. The novel takes place in the aftermath of the plague and the social chaos still being caused by it. People who once placed their trust in God are angry he failed to save their loved ones and are turning to witchcraft. Abandoned buildings are being put to unorthodox uses, and commerce is being disrupted by shortages of everything from sheepherders to customers. To all these the Stourbridge Fair hot weather, cheap ale, and streets thronged with strangers makes for a combustible combination. Associates:

Samuel Gray; Thomas Bulbeck; Robert Deynman; Brother Boniface; Frances de Belem; Lady Matilde. Historical Figure: Richard de Wetherset.

3. *A Bone of Contention*. London: Little, Brown, 1997, 375 p.

CAMBRIDGE, ENGLAND, 1352. Feelings in Cambridge are running unusually high; the city is seething with discontent, and every incident between the students and the townspeople ratchets up the tension. It almost seems as if someone is working behind the scenes to foment a riot. The problems are exacerbated by the activities of Roger Thorpe, Master of the new Hall of Valence Marie. Thorpe has his people pouring over the refuse dredged out of the nearby King's Ditch, in the hope of finding the bones of a local martyr, so that his Hall can house the holy relics. Associates: Lady Matilde; Samuel Gray; Thomas Bulbeck; Robert Deynman; Eleanor Tyler; Master of Michaelhouse, Thomas Kenyngham; Junior Proctor, Guy Heppel; Master Thorpe (based on Robert de Thorpe). Historical Figure: Richard de Wetherset.

4. *A Deadly Brew*. London: Little, Brown, 1998, 360 p.

CAMBRIDGE, ENGLAND, 1353. Pilfered wine containing poison is being sold to unsuspecting students; Matthew Bartholomew is called to heal the afflicted but is too late to save the first victim. After that it's a race against time to uncover the tainted brew before the next bottle kills. As spring rains bring contagion to the town, and a new college brings an increase in infighting among the masters, Bartholomew tracks a thief and a murderer. Associates: Samuel Gray; Thomas Bulbeck; Robert Deynman; Rob Thorpe; Abbess of Denny, Dame Pelagia; Lady Matilde; Juliana; Chancellor Tynkell. Historical Figure: Mary de Pol, Countess of Pembroke.

5. *A Wicked Deed*. London: Little, Brown, 1999, 392 p.

SUFFOLK, ENGLAND, 1353. A small delegation travels to Suffolk to draw up a deed to transfer property from Sir Thomas Tuddenham to Michaelhouse. They travel through a town abandoned to the plague and later find that it is considered haunted by its neighbors. If so, there must one more soul walking with its dead: a man illegally hanged, his corpse having been supposedly spirited away. Associates: John de Horsey; Robert Deynham.

6. *A Masterly Murder*. London: Little, Brown, 2000, 406 p.

CAMBRIDGE, ENGLAND, 1353. Bartholomew's work of healing is increasingly interrupted by calls to determine causes of death; there seem to be an unusually large number of corpses surfacing in Cambridge. First Justus, bookbearer to Cambridge Fellow John Runham, seems to have committed suicide. Then a mother dies in childbirth, a man perishes of putrefication from a wound, and another dies in a building accident. Bartholomew receives private information that the latter victim did not fall but was pushed, and then Bartholomew's informant dies. Something is very wrong indeed, and the new Master of Michaelhouse is so concerned with his own comfort and importance that he is making any investigation close to impossible. Associates: Lady Matilde; Mayor Horwoode; Simekyn Simon; Robert Deynman; Samuel Gray; Rachel Atkin. Historical Figure: Duke of Lancaster.

7. *An Order for Death*. London: Little, Brown, 2001, 470 p.

CAMBRIDGE, ENGLAND, 1354. William of Occam resurrected the great philosophical debate of Nominalism vs. Realism. This argument has now been taken up by the religious orders. Each side considers the others to be heretics, claiming that the Great Pestilence (the plague) has been sent by the Lord to punish these transgressors. Students riot in defense of one side or the other, most not even understanding the essence of the debate but simply determined that the view held by leaders of their order should prevail. Into all of this Bartholomew attempts to save a mortally wounded Carmelite student. As the investigation of his death expands, it looks as if someone may have taken advantage of the college unrest to commit murder. Associates: Prioress Mabel Martyn; Eve Wasteneys; Tysilia de Apsley; Beadle Tom Meadowman.

8. *A Summer of Discontent*. London: Little, Brown, 2002, 520 p.

ELY, ENGLAND, 1354. Bishop Thomas de Lisle summons Brother Michael to prove the Bishop innocent of allegations that he murdered Lady Blanche de Wake's steward. The case is complicated by the fact that the Bishop had mused aloud about the benefit of burning out some of Lady Blanche's tenants, and his servant Ralph had taken these musings as an order. Bartholomew worries that Brother Michael's faith in his Bishop may be misplaced. Then his investigation leads the physician to believe that the steward was only the latest victim of a serial murderer. In the meantime, the murderer seems to be honing both his skills and his knife. Associates: Tysilia de Apsley; Eulalia. Historical Figures: Lady Blanche de Wake; Alan de Walsingham.

9. *A Killer in Winter*. London: Little, Brown, 2003, 488 p.

CAMBRIDGE, ENGLAND, CHRISTMAS 1354. The winter of 1354 is the hardest, the earliest, and the coldest in living memory. The bitter snow hides the victims of both accidental and purposeful deaths, so it takes some time for the law to realize that there is a killer loose in the town. Bartholomew works to help the poor survive the freezing cold, and save the careless from dangers of the cold weather; it is difficult to spare the time and energy also to track a killer. Associates: Giles Abigny; Philippa; Lady Matilde; Sheriff Morice; Robert Deynman; Samuel Gray.

10. *The Hand of Justice*. London: Little, Brown, 2004, 496 p.

CAMBRIDGE, ENGLAND, 1355. Problems resolved years ago stubbornly return to Cambridge. The "Hand of Valence Marie," mentioned in *A Bone of Contention*, was proven to be a false relic, yet townspeople are still paying to pray in its presence; more sinister is the return of Rob Thorpe (*A Deadly Brew*), a murderer who received a pardon from the King and who has now come back to Cambridge, where he is asking after Bartholomew's family. When corpses are found at the mill, Bartholomew must investigate. Associates: Rob Thorpe; Edward Mortimer; Dame Pelagia; Martyn Quenhyth; Redmeadow; Robert Deynman; Lady Matilde. Historical Figures: Richard de Pulham; William de Rougham.

GULIK, Robert (Hans) van (1910–1967). Dutch.

JUDGE DEE SERIES

Scene of the Crime: Various districts in the ancient China of the seventh century.

Detective: Judge Dee Jen-Djieh (Di Renjie in the modern Chinese transliteration), a real-life magistrate who lived 629–700 in China and who was later ennobled as the Duke of Liang for his services to the Chinese Emperor. The events in the stories focus on his early career as a magistrate and judge in various district towns in rural China.

Known Associates: Sergeant Hoong Liang, the elderly supervisor of the magistrate's three constable lieutenants and Dee's longtime trusted adviser; Ma Joong, Dee's first lieutenant; Tao Gan, Dee's second lieutenant; Chiao Tai, Dee's third lieutenant; Magistrate Lo Kwan-Choong, the judge of the district of Chin-Hwa, Judge Dee's friend and associate; Sheng Pa, Head of the Beggars in Poo-Yang; Han Yung-Han, a wealthy landowner of Han-Yuan; Mrs. Kuo, wife of a pharmacist in Pei-Chow and also matron of the women's jail there.

Premise: A magistrate uses his powers of observation and logic to solve seemingly intractable mysteries in seventh-century China.

Comment: The first book in the series is actually a translation by Gulik of an eighteenth-century Chinese detective novel, *Dee Goong An*, anonymously penned by a magistrate familiar with the Chinese system of law. He continued the series with his own novels, beginning with *The Chinese Bell Murders* and ending with *Poets and Murder*. Often the scenarios presented in these books are adapted from puzzles featured in various untranslated eighteenth-century Chinese detective stories. Many of the books include two or three different, but unconnected, cases on which Dee works simultaneously, being adapted after the pattern in *Dee Goong An*.

Literary Crimes & Chimes: The settings here are absolutely true-to-life. Gulik clearly knows his period inside and out, and one has the sense of being transported back in time to seventh-century China. However, we actually learn very little of Judge Dee himself or of his character, beyond his obvious desire to see justice done and the perpetrators punished. He comes across as rather stodgy or even unlikable at times, prizing his position of power above all else. Dee is not afraid to take chances with his deductive reasoning (a wrong guess could cost him his position or even his life), but sometimes his leaps of faith seem no more than that. There is also a strain of ghostly intervention in the books that reflects the tradition of Chinese mystery stories but may be offputting to contemporary readers of the detective tale.

THE CASES

1. *Dee Goong An: Three Murder Cases Solved by Judge Dee,* trans. by Robert van Gulik. Tokyo: Printed for the Author by Toppan Printing Co., 1949, 237 p. As: *Celebrated Cases of Judge Dee: Dee Goong An: An Authentic Eighteenth-Century Chinese Detective Novel.* New York: Dover Publications, 1976, 237 p.

   CHANG-PING, CHINA, SEVENTH CENTURY. Judge Dee, here serving as magistrate of the Chang-Ping District, investigates three killings: the murders of two traveling businessmen, the poisoning of a bride on her wedding night, and, most puzzling, the killing of a shopkeeper in a small neighboring town. This first book in the series is a translation by Gulik of an actual eighteenth-century Chinese detective story authored anonymously by a magistrate of that time. The events that take place in this novel cannot be fitted into the rest of the chronology of the life of Judge Dee and are not included in Gulik's own dating of the series in *Judge Dee at Work.* Associates: Hoong; Ma; Tao; Chiao.

2. *The Chinese Gold Murders: A Chinese Detective Story.* London: Michael Joseph, 1959, 221 p.

   PENG-LAI, CHINA, 663. The young Dee is tired of his position as Junior Secretary to the Metropolitan Court of Justice, where he spends his days filing reports and demands to be given a real assignment. But the only position available is the judgeship of the god-forsaken district of Peng-Lai, where his predecessor has been recently murdered. He accepts this difficult task and ultimately solves the mysteries of "The Murdered Magistrate," "The Bolting Bride," and "The Butchered Bully." This is our first meeting with Ma Joong and Chiao Tai, who become Dee's lieutenants and with the prophecy that Chiao will eventually be killed by the sword called Rain Dragon. Associates: Hoong; Ma; Chiao.

3. *The Lacquer Screen: A Chinese Detective Story.* New York: Charles Scribner's Sons, 1961, 180 p.

WEI-PING, CHINA, 663. While vacationing incognito for a few days with Lieutenant Chiao in the neighboring district of Wei-Ping, Judge Dee is asked by the local Magistrate, Teng Kan, to assist him with unraveling of a mystery: Teng's wife has just been murdered by the magistrate's own knife, and Teng can remember nothing of what had actually happened. Since he is the obvious suspect in the killing, someone else must conduct the investigation. Dee eventually solves the cases of "The Lacquer Screen," "The Credulous Merchant," and "The Faked Accounts." The book includes a second prophecy of Chiao's eventual death. Associate: Chiao.

4. *The Chinese Lake Murders: Three Cases Solved by Judge Dee.* London: Michael Joseph, 1960, 270 p.

HAN-YUAN, CHINA, 666. In the isolated town of Han-Yuan, known for its famous floating brothels ("flower boats"), Dee is confronted with a cruel murder. Just when his investigation of that crime has begun, he is faced with two new baffling mysteries, and he soon finds himself enmeshed in a maze of political intrigue, greed, and forbidden passion. The magistrate ultimately solves the cases of "The Drowned Courtesan," "The Vanished Bride," and "The Spendthrift Councillor." Tao Gan makes his first appearance in the series, with Dee saving him from a nasty situation. Associates: Hoong; Ma; Chiao; Tao; Han.

5. *The Monkey and the Tiger: Two Chinese Detective Stories.* London: Heinemann, 1965, 143 p.

HAN-YUAN, CHINA, 666; PEI-CHOW, CHINA, 676. Unlike most of the Dee novels, where three crime stories are normally interlinked, this volume includes two separate novellas: *The Morning of the Monkey* (Han-Yuan, 666), in which the murder of a tramp is solved by Dee and Tao, and the latter is finally taken formally into the magistrate's service; and *The Night of the Tiger* (Pei-Chow, 676), in which the murder of a young girl is solved by Judge Dee while traveling from Pei-Chow to take up his new position in the Imperial Capital. Associates: Tao; Mrs. Kuo; Han; King of the Beggars.

6. *The Haunted Monastery: A Chinese Detective Story.* Kuala Lumpur: Art Print. Works, 1961, 168 p. Collected together as *The Haunted Monastery and The Chinese Maze Murders.* New York: Dover Publications, 1977, 328 p.

MOUNTAINS OF HAN-YUAN, CHINA, 666. The Abbot Jade Mirror is murdered before his monks while giving a sermon at the Taoist Monastery of the Morning Cloud. Then three women are also killed at the same abbey. When Judge Dee and his wives seek the shelter of the monastery during a storm, the magistrate is thereupon enlisted to solve the three seemingly intractable mysteries: "The Embalmed Abbot," "The Pious Maid," and "The Morose Monk." Associate: Tao.

7. *The Chinese Bell Murders: Three Cases Solved by Judge Dee.* London: Michael Joseph, 1958, 287 p.

Poo-Yang, China, 668. The first of Judge Dee novels was written in English in 1950 but originally published in Japanese and Chinese translations, not appearing here in its original form until much later. Gulik adapted the work from plots featured in non-Dee Chinese detective stories published in the nineteenth century. Three interwoven stories are solved: "The Rape Murder in Half Moon Street," "The Secret of the Buddhist Temple," and "The Mysterious Skeleton." This novel and its immediate sequels form a transition in Gulik's writing between the straightforward translation of *Dee Goong An* and wholly original work that he published in the 1960s. Thus, the format followed here is very similar to that of its predecessor and shares some of its faults, seeming a little clunky by modern fiction standards. Associates: Hoong; Ma; Tao; Chiao; Magistrate Lo; Sheng.

8. *The Red Pavilion: A Chinese Detective Story.* Kuala Lumpur: Art Printing Works, 1961, 199 p.

Paradise Island, China, 668. While on a two-day visit to Paradise Island, a popular amusement resort, Judge Dee has a chance encounter with Autumn Moon, the most powerful courtesan there, and is led to investigate three suspicious deaths: "The Callous Courtesan," "The Amorous Academician," and "The Unlucky Lovers." Associates: Ma; Magistrate Lo.

9. *The Emperor's Pearl: A Chinese Detective Story.* London: Heinemann, 1963, 184 p.

Poo-Yang, China, 668. During the dragonboat races at Poo-Yang, an annual festival that draws large crowds to the region, Dee solves the cases of "The Dead Drummer," "The Murdered Slavemaid," and "The Emperor's Pearl." The beggar Sheng Pa again plays a role in the investigation of these crimes. Associates: Hoong; Magistrate Lo; Sheng.

10. *Necklace and Calabash: A Chinese Detective Story.* London: Heinemann, 1967, 144 p.

Riverton, China, 668. While returning to Poo-Yang, Judge Dee takes a fishing vacation at Riverton, not far from the Emperor's favorite daughter's Water Palace. There he meets a Taoist recluse and encounters strange guests at the Kingfisher Inn. But when a body is pulled out of the river, the magistrate is enlisted to solve the crime and faces one of the most baffling mysteries of his entire career. The usual associates are absent here.

11. *Poets and Murder: A Chinese Detective Story.* London: Heinemann, 1968, 174 p. As: *The Fox-Magic Murders: A Chinese Detective Story.* St Albans, Herts: Panther Books, 1973, 160 p.

POO-YANG, CHINA, MID-AUTUMN FESTIVAL 669. Judge Dee is visiting Lo Kwan-Choong, magistrate of the neighboring district of Chin-Hwa, when a student is found with his throat cut. When Dee investigates on his friend's behalf, he discovers that Soong's father was a general who had apparently supported the rebellion of the infamous "Ninth Prince" a generation earlier. Soong evidently believed his father innocent of the charge of treason. Is this why he was killed? Or does the murder have something to do with the local cult of "fox-magic"? Associate: Magistrate Lo.

12. *The Chinese Maze Murders: A Chinese Detective Story Suggested by Three Original Ancient Chinese Plots.* The Hague: W. Van Hoeve, 1956, 322 p. Collected together as *The Haunted Monastery and The Chinese Maze Murders.* New York: Dover Publications, 1977, 328 p.

LAO-FANG, CHINA, 670. Judge Dee must solve three different mysteries involving a garden maze ("The Murder in the Sealed Room"), a hidden message in a scroll painting ("The Hidden Testament"), and a murderer who targets women with his torture killings ("The Girl with the Severed Head"). To make matters even worse, a robber baron has decreed that Judge Dee, his mortal enemy, must die! Associates: Hoong; Ma; Tao; Chiao.

13. *The Phantom of the Temple: A Chinese Detective Story.* London: Heinemann, 1966, 206 p.

LAN-FANG, CHINA, 670. A phantom stalks the century-old Buddhist temple perched on a local hillside, and three mysteries unfold: the vanishing of a wealthy merchant's daughter, the disappearance of twenty bars of gold, and the discovery of a decapitated corpse. Judge Dee must piece together these strange occurrences to reveal one complex and gruesome crime. Associates: Hoong; Ma.

14. *The Chinese Nail Murders: Judge Dee's Last Three Cases.* London: Michael Joseph, 1961, 216 p.

PEI-CHAO, CHINA, 676. Judge Dee has recently been appointed magistrate of the far-western district of Pei-Chao, not far from the great northern deserts. The area is cold and sere, and the wind blows constantly. In this desolate environment Dee and his lieutenants must solve the cases of "The Headless Corpse," "The Paper Cat," and "The Murdered Merchant." Sergeant Hoong is killed during the course of the investigation, but Dee is promoted at the end of the novel to President of the Metropolitan Court in the Imperial Capital. Associates: Hoong; Ma; Chiao; Tao; Mrs. Kuo; King of the Beggars.

15. *The Willow Pattern: A Chinese Detective Story.* London: Heinemann, 1965, 183 p.

IMPERIAL CAPITAL, CHINA, 677. Judge Dee has been promoted to the rank of Lord Chief Justice in the Imperial Capital and is also acting as temporary Emergency Governor. His associates have shared in his success, Ma and Chiao becoming Colonels of the Imperial Guard and Tao being named Chief Secretary of the Metropolitan Court. But as plague infests the city, Dee must unravel three seemingly unconnected murders: "The Willow Pattern," "The Steep Staircase," and "The Murdered Bondmaid." Associates: Ma; Chiao; Tao.

16. *Murder in Canton: A Chinese Detective Story.* London: Heineimann, 1966, 208 p.

CANTON, CHINA, 681. Near the end of his career as magistrate, Judge Dee is sent incognito to Canton on special assignment to investigate the disappearance of a court censor. With the help of his trusted lieutenants and with that of a clever blind girl who collects crickets, Dee solves the three murders of "The Vanished Censor," "The Smaragdine Dancer," and "The Golden Bell." Chiao Tan is killed, as previously prophesied, by the sword Rain Dragon, but Tao Gan marries Lan-Lee, the girl who had helped them in their investigation. The last book chronologically in the series. Associates: Chiao, Tao; Lan-Lee.

17. *Judge Dee at Work: Eight Chinese Detective Stories.* London: Heinemann, 1967, 178 p.

CHINA, 663–674. A collection of short stories featuring Judge Dee. CONTENTS: "Five Auspicious Clouds" (Peng-Lai, 663); "The Red Tape Murder" (Peng-Lai, 663); "He Came with the Rain" (Peng-Lai, 663); "The Murder on the Lotus Pond" (Han-Yuan, 666); "The Two Beggars" (Poo-Yang, 668); "The Wrong Sword" (Poo-Yang, 668); "The Coffins of the Emperor" (Lan-Fang, 670); "Murder on New Year's Eve" (Lan-Fang, 670); "Colophon"; "Judge Dee Chronology." Associates: Hoong; Chiao; Magistrate Lo; Sheng.

ASSOCIATIONAL BOOK

Judge Dee Plays His Lute: A Play and Selected Mystery Stories, by Janwillem van de Wetering. Bar Harbor, ME: Wonderly Press, 1997, 190 p.

This collection includes nine unrelated stories by mystery writer van de Wetering, plus a play, "Judge Dee Plays His Lute," a tribute to the Dutch mystery writer that features both of the authors as characters at Gulik's funeral, as well as Gulik himself in the guise of his literary creation, Judge Dee. Rather bizarre for our tastes.

HAMBLY, Barbara (Joan) (1951–). American.

Scene of the Crime: New Orleans, beginning in 1833.

Detective: Benjamin January (born 1793), the son of two slaves, Jumah and Livia. A friend of their master's had purchased Livia and her children and had "placed" her, giving them a house so that he could keep Livia as his mistress, or "*plaçée.*" Her protector was a wealthy Creole named St. Denis Janvier, and Livia was of mixed race; this was the normal "custom of the country," one of its many forms of racism. Benjamin accepts this with some anger. He was able to laugh at these customs from a distance during the years he had spent in France. There Benjamin trained and worked as a surgeon at the Hôtel Dieu. However, he did not have the money to purchase his own practice, and so, when he decided to marry, he improved his income by returning to work as a musician. He married a Moroccan seamstress who owned her own business, Ayasha. She died of cholera six months before the events of the first book. At her death Benjamin returned to New Orleans, a city in which the "customs of the country" dictate that he accept blows without returning them, that he not raise his eyes to the eyes of a white person, that he support his sister and her friends in their efforts to become *plaçées.* He is forty years old, six feet, three inches tall, and a powerful man; strong, compassionate, and quick-witted, he is sickened by the role he must play. As a child he had learned to pretend a subservience that he does not feel, manipulating white men while presenting to them a mask that conformed to their expectations of a black man.

He finds that he remembers now how to play the same role but bitterly resents the need to do so.

Known Associates: For better or worse, Ben's closest associates are his family. His mother, Livia Levesque, was born a slave; when Ben was eight years old, she was purchased, along with her two children, Ben and Olympia (born 1795, nicknamed Olympe), and freed to be a St. Denis Janvier's *plaçée*. She had a daughter by him, Dominique (born 1813, nicknamed Minou). Janvier died in 1822, and Livia married a carpenter named Levesque. He died a few years before the events related in this series. Olympe ran away from home at age sixteen, married an upholsterer named Paul Corbier, and had four children: Zizi-Marie, Gabriel, Chouchou, and Ti-Paul. Olympe, an active *voodooienne*, works at times with the Queen of the Voodoos, Marie Laveau. Dominique is a *plaçée*; her protector is Henri Viellard. Ben works as a musician; his closest friend is Hannibal Sefton, an Irish fiddler. In *A Free Man of Color* Ben meets Lieutenant Abishag Shaw, a (mostly) honest policeman. In *Fever Season* he meets Rose Vitrac, a free woman of color who believes strongly in learning and who becomes a close friend. Rose and Ben marry in *Wet Grave*.

Premise: A former slave solves crimes and rights wrongs in nineteenth-century New Orleans.

Comment: Ben is part of many worlds but does not fit precisely into any of them. He is not a slave, but he was one once and still knows the rules of that society. He is a free man of color; but most of the people in that society are lighter-skinned than he. The darkness of Ben's skin is remarked on most often by other people of mixed race; thus, he is not treated as a full equal; even though he is one of them legally and by blood. Ben's own mother won't let him use the front entrance to her house. Ben also can attend gatherings of white people, since he is a musician and is hired to play music. Ben understands each of these cultures and act as an observer of each. If Ben had just accepted the abuse passively, as he would have had to do to be able to survive, readers would be too frustrated and angry on his behalf to become involved actively in his world. Ben's fury makes it possible for readers vicariously to stand by him, to root for him as he navigates this dangerous and massively unjust society.

Literary Crimes & Chimes: Hambly's novels are written beautifully and vividly; they are full of emotion. The author prefaces the first two books in the series with notes on how the terminology of the time was used and apologizes to anyone who might find it offensive. *Fever Season* includes a short Afterword on the factual basis for the story. Many of the books in the series include maps and family trees. *Graveyard Dust* contains a Foreword on the terminology of voodoo and an Afterword providing a historical note. *Sold Down the River* has a Foreword with a partial glossary of Creole and Afro-Creole words and Afterwords on work songs and spirituals and on masters and slaves. *Die upon a Kiss* includes an Afterword on opera in New Orleans. *Wet Grave* contains a historical note. There are Afterwords on Santa Anna, one on Mexico City, and one on anaphylactic shock in *Days of the Dead*. *Dead Water* includes an Afterword on steamboats and another on Jefferson Davis. First-rate in every respect.

THE CASES

1. *A Free Man of Color.* New York: Bantam Books, 1997, 311 p.

NEW ORLEANS, LOUISIANA, SPRING 1833. During Carnival season rich men escort their wives and relations to the subscription ball at the Théâtre, then duck down a passageway to the quadroon ball at the Salle d'Orléans to meet their *plaçées* or to choose from new young girls looking for protectors. The most beautiful woman at the ball is found murdered, and the manager is intent on concealing the crime long enough to avoid embarrassing the powerful men on the premises. Ben has other concerns, such as the little matter of justice. Associates: Mademoiselle Madeleine Trepagier (nee Dubonnet); Augustus Mayerling.

2. *Fever Season.* New York: Bantam Books, 1998, 321 p.

NEW ORLEANS, LOUISIANA, 1833–1834. The fever season has arrived in New Orleans, and most of the population has fled; Ben helps tend the sick during the cholera epidemic. People come searching the hospitals for missing loved ones, some being found, some not. When a young woman named Cora follows Ben home from the hospital to ask that he get a message to a slave in one of his piano student's homes, Ben is willing to risk "slave stealing" (helping a runaway slave); but when he is told that Cora attempted to murder both her master and her mistress, he must decide if he is willing to risk being an accessory after the fact. Associates: Cora Chouteau; Emily Redfern; Reverend Micajoh Dunk; Judge J. F. Canonge; Dr. Soublet; Dr. Sanchez; Dr. Ker.

3. *Graveyard Dust.* New York: Bantam Books, 1999, 315 p.

NEW ORLEANS, LOUISIANA, 1834. Ben's curiosity compels him to investigate the location of some distant drumming that he overheard. As expected, he finds evidence of a voodoo ceremony, one that included graveyard dust instead of salt. This is an indication that the rite was to invoke someone's death. When he finds that his sister Olympe has been charged with murder, he is afraid that there may be some connection. In any event, she cannot be left in the Cabildo jail, where the police are covering up an epidemic of yellow fever. Associates: Emily Redfern; Mr. Hubert Granville; Antoine; Isaak Jumon; Vachel Corcet; Dr. Ker; Augustus Mayerline; Judge J. F. Canonge.

4. *Sold Down the River.* New York: Bantam Books, 2000, 317 p.

NEW ORLEANS, LOUISIANA, 1835. The man who used to own Ben's family, Monsieur Simon Fourchet, offers (actually, demands) that Ben pose as a slave to spy upon slaves on his plantation, Mon Triomphe. Many years ago there had been a slave uprising on one of Fourchet's plantations; a recent attempt on Fourchet's life (his butler was poisoned) has convinced Fourchet to hire his own investigator. Ben initially refuses, unwilling to have any part in identifying the person or persons who are trying to end the life of the tyrant. But his sister Olympe points out that, if the poisoner is ultimately successful, every slave on the plantation will probably be put to death. Ben must take the job not to save one life but 1,000. Associates: Mohammed; Quashie; Jeanette.

5. *Die upon a Kiss.* New York: Bantam Books, 2001, 333 p.

NEW ORLEANS, LOUISIANA, FEBRUARY 15, 1835. Ben foils a murderous ambush aimed at the opera master Belaggio, who has turned Shakespeare's *Othello* into an opera for an opening-night performance. It's an amazingly complex and hauntingly beautiful work, but Ben knows that all the audience will see is a black man kissing a white woman. This means that there will be further attempts on the life of Belaggio, until the impresario is dead. Associates: Madame Bontemps; Lorenzo Belaggio; Madame Marguerite Scie; Consuela Montero; Drusilla d'Isola; Monsieur Vincent Marsan; Incantobelli; Emily Redfern; Isaak Jumon; Henri Viellard; Chloë St. Chinian.

6. *Wet Grave.* New York: Bantam Books, 2002, 288 p.

NEW ORLEANS, LOUISIANA, 1835. In 1812 Ben played at a party attended by Jean Lafitte, his captain, and by Lafitte's women, one of whom was Hesione LeGros. Twenty-three years later she is murdered. She had become a poor drunkard, living in a shanty at the edge of town, and Ben knows that the white City Guards will not search very hard for her killer. Associates: Madame Bontemps; Suzie; Cut-Nose Chighizola; Henri Viellard; Chloë St. Chinian.

7. *Days of the Dead.* New York: Bantam Books, 2003, 314 p.

MEXICO CITY, MÉXICO, 1835. Three years ago Hannibal's haunting music pulled Ben back from the brink of suicide; more recently, it tempted Don Prospero de Castellón into holding Hannibal prisoner forever in the Castellón hacienda to play for his family. Then Prospero's son, Fernando, is found dead of poison, soon after drinking with Hannibal. Hannibal's execution has been delayed over questions of jurisdiction, religion, and even methods of execution; with the uncertainty, Ben cannot be sure of how much time he has to uncover the true murderer. Associates: John Dillard;

Consuela Montero; Ylario; Valentina. Historical Figure: General and President Antonio de Santa Ana.

8. *Dead Water.* New York: Bantam Books, 2004, 297 p.

NEW ORLEANS, LOUISIANA, 1836. Ben, trying to save the life of one of Rose's students, crosses a voodoo priestess. She curses him. In short order Ben finds himself on the brink of ruin, his money embezzled. His investigation keeps coming to dead ends. In the course of pursuing the case he encounters treachery, murder, and the Underground Railroad. Associates: Mr. Hubert Granville; Cosette Gardinier; Queen Régine; Sophie; Julie; Bobby; Gleet; Jubal Cain (Mr. Judas Bredon). Historical Figure: Colonel Davis.

HANEY, Lauren (pseud. of Betty J. Winkelman) (1936–). American.

LIEUTENANT BAK SERIES

Scene of the Crime: Ancient Egypt, beginning about 1465 BC.

Detective: Lieutenant Bak, formerly a chariot officer in the regiment of Amon, now in charge of a company of Medjay police at the Fortress of Buhen.

Known Associates: Queen Maatkare Hatshepsut of Egypt, Regent for Pharaoh Thutmose III; Sergeant Imsiba, Bak's second in command at Medjay; Ptahhotep, Bak's father; Nofery, proprietess of a house of pleasure in Buhan who also serves as Bak's spy; Hori, a youthful police scribe; Commandant Thuty, in charge of the garrison at Buhan; Troop Captain Nebwa, Thuty's second in command; Amonked, the Queen's cousin and a friend from the past; Pashenuro, Imsiba's assistant.

Premise: An official solves crimes and acts as an agent for the Pharaoh in Ancient Egypt.

Comment: During the time of the eighteenth dynasty, Maatkare Hatshepsut, Queen Mother of a sun-seared realm she nominally corules with her young nephew and stepson, Menkheperre Thutmose III, works mightily to hold her realm together. Lieutenant Bak is a loyal servant of the royal house of Egypt, a man of honor and ability who was once a proud officer in the service of Queen Hatsepsut. It was his great misfortune to lead his charioteers in a raid on a house of pleasure frequented by Egyptian noblemen. Reassigned for daring to judge his betters, Bak has been exiled in disgrace to Buhen, a fortified city in the most desolate part of the Nile valley, where he takes up his duties as commander of the Medjay police. From the "Author's Note" in *The Right Hand of Amon*, Haney states:

> At the time of this novel, the commandant of Buhen loosely administered a chain of at least ten fortresses strung along the Belly of Stones. This was the most rugged, desolate, and arid portion of the Nile valley, and the river was filled with rapids and small islands, making it navigable only during the highest flood stage. Originally built several centuries earlier, these fortresses lay in various stages of ruin or repair. The garrison troops protected and controlled traffic through this natural corridor, collected tribute and tolls, and conducted punitive military expeditions. The Medjays were initally desert-dwelling people of Lower Nubia. By the Eighteenth Dynasty, they were men who served as law enforcement officers, maintaining order throughout Egypt and along the desert frontiers.

Helpful "Casts of Characters" and Maps of the region accompany all the volumes in the series.

Literary Crimes & Chimes: Once again Ancient Egypt is the setting for our historical detective (see P. C. Doherty's "Amerotke" series, a vastly superior creation, or Lynda Robinson's "Lord Meren" series for comparable stories in this time frame). Haney seems to have done her research, and there is no lack of factual detail, but her characters are rather wooden and her plots fairly predictable. The "prequel" setting up the premise for the series (*Flesh of the God*) appears as an afterthought midway through the sequence of books and should be read first in order to understand Bak's initial sense of isolation and anger at being exiled, as well as to get a better feel for his motivations further along in the tales. Middlin' entertainment.

THE CASES

1. *Flesh of the God: A Mystery of Ancient Egypt.* New York: Avon Books, 2002, 338 p.

   BUHEN, EGYPT, 1465–1464 BC? A proud officer in the service of Queen Hatshepsut, Lieutenant Bak has been reassigned for his transgressions to Buhen, a fortified city in the most desolate part of the southern Nile valley. Barely has he set foot in his new posting, when he is dismayed to discover its capable commandant, Nakht, slain with a dagger in his breast—and Nakht's beautiful young foreign-born wife, Azzia, cowering nearby—covered with fresh blood. Bak hesitates to condemn the frightened widow prematurely. Perhaps the man's death was divine retribution for recent offenses against the gods? Bak finds himself drawn into a conspiracy of greed and deceit, at the same time finding himself slowly falling in love with the dead man's widow. Discovering the truth in this terrible place will be nearly as difficult as finding water in the heartless desert that surrounds it, while death may be far easier to come by. This "prequel" sets up the initial premise of the series. Associates: Imsiba; Azzia, the dead man's widow, who is of special interest to Bak; Lupaki, Azzia's devoted servant; Lieutenant Nebwa, Nakht's second in command; Harmose, an archer friend of Azzia's; Nofery. Historical Figures: Queen Maatkare Hatshepsut; Commander Maiherperi, her Head of Guards; Pharaoh Menkhepperre Thutmose III.

2. *The Right Hand of Amon.* New York: Avon Books, 1997, 300 p.

Fortress of Buhen, and Fortress of Iken, Egypt, circa 1464–1463 BC. Lieutenant Bak, loyal servant of the royal house of Egypt and commander of the Medjay police in the frontier fortress city of Buhen, must oversee the corps assigned to accompany the golden idol, the god Amon, on its journey up the Nile to heal the ailing son of a powerful tribal king. But the mighty river has yielded up a sinister "treasure," the body of a brave soldier horrifically slain for unknown reasons, and only the drawings of a missing mute boy can aid in unraveling the mystery of the officer's foul death—before it leads to far greater crimes that could imperil the empire. Associates: Imsiba; Thuty; Nebwa; Nofery; Amon-Psaro, a powerful Kushite King who rewards Bak for his services. Historical Figures: Queen Maatkare Hatshepsut; Pharaoh Menkheperre Thutmose III.

3. *A Vile Justice: A Mystery of Ancient Egypt.* New York: Avon Books, 1999, 290 p.

Fortress of Buhen, and City of Abu, Kemet, Egypt, 1464–1463 BC? Evil runs rampant through the grand abode of Djehuty, the much despised Governor of Abu. Four deaths, each exactly ten days apart, have occurred in and around the powerful functionary's premises: an expert swimmer has drowned, a spearman has accidentally been impaled on his own weapon, a sergeant of the guard has been found with a dagger through his breast, and a young officer has been trampled to death by a horse gone mad. Lieutenant Bak of the Medjay police fears for his own life and for the safety of the men in his charge. But the vizier has requested that this deadly puzzle be investigated, and it is Bak's duty to serve. Could this rampant violence be the retribution of the gods for a long-past, yet still-remembered transgression? Bak is not sure who will ultimately be revealed as the slayer—be he human or divine—when the disturbing cache of previously well-protected secrets is opened at his feet. One thing is certain: if the killer is true to his pattern, another will die this day. Associates: Imsiba; Thuty; Nebwa; Nofery; Hori. Historical Figures: Queen Maatkare Hatshepsut; Pharaoh Menkhepperre Tuthmose III.

4. *A Face Turned Backward: A Mystery of Ancient Egypt*. New York: Avon Twilight, 1999, 286 p.

EGYPT, 1464–1463 BC? The many, mighty deities of Egypt must be given their due. All commerce is conducted under the watchful eyes of the functionaries of the great Queen Maatkare Hatshepsut. Death faces any and all who would rob the royal house of Kemet of its rightful share. Lieutenant Bak, commander of the Medjay police, willingly accepts an assignment to search all the Nile River traffic for contraband, for rumors are rife of valuable elephant tusks passing unlawfully from the south to the north. But greed has spawned death, hideous and unexpected, and someone who would become rich illegally is dealing in far more than precious ivory. Whoever threatens to expose a lethal cache of secrets will not live to see a new dawn, and the loyal Bak could be the next victim, as he heads relentlessly toward a grim confrontation, a shocking revelation, and very possible doom in the realm of the dead. Associates: Imsiba; Hori; Thuty; Nebwa; Nofery; Pashenuro. Historical Figures: Queen Maatkare Hatshepsut; Pharaoh Menkheperre Tuthmose III.

5. *A Curse of Silence*. New York: Avon Books, 2000, 304 p.

FORTRESS OF BUHEN, EGYPT, 1464–1463 BC? A vile rumor sweeps across the desert like a swiftly gathering sandstorm: Queen Hatshepsut plans to disband much of her frontier army and transform its fortresses into storehouses. The arrival of Amonked, the Queen's cousin and Storekeeper of Amon, at the city of Buhen convinces an uneasy Lieutenant Bak of the Medjay police that the whisperings that have alarmed the populace are true. Then, a day after Amonked inspects the local garrison and departs, a body is found stabbed in the house where he and his party had rested. The slain man was a local prince beloved by his people, so Bak travels upriver to join the caravan and investigate. Though nothing tangible seems to connect Amonked and his entourage to the heinous act, Bak's inquiry soon sheds a disturbing light on another inexplicable crime, for the clues suggest that twisted honor and vengeance lie at its root, plus a shocking secret that could itself silence the truth—and Bak—for all eternity. Associates: Imsiba; Thuty; Nebwa; Hori; Nofery; Amonked; Nefret, his concubine; Pashenuro. Historical Figures: Queen Maatkare Hatshepsut; Pharaoh Menkheperre Tuthmose III.

6. *A Place of Darkness*. New York: Avon Books, 2001, 285 p.

FORTRESS OF BUHEN, CITY OF WASET, EGYPT, 1464–1463 BC? Some transgressions may never be forgiven, and Lieutenant Bak seems destined to remain out of favor with the powers of Kemet. Bak is in transit from his exile in Buhen to a new posting. The disgraced policeman stops at the capital city of Waset in hopes of learning more about the troubling rumors of relics being plundered from ancient tombs and smuggled through the southern frontier. Instead, he is sent to Djeser Djeseru, the partially built memorial temple of the divine Queen Maatkare Hatshepsut, where a series of fatal accidents and whispers of a malign spirit are plaguing the construction effort. Can the thefts and these deaths somehow be connected? The clues lead the ever-loyal investigator to a magnificent tomb. But this realm of the dead threatens to become Bak's own place of burial when he must confront the source of the spectral malevolence. Associates: Imsiba; Thuty; Nebwa; Hori; Nofury; Ptahhotep; Amonkedt. Historical Figures: Queen Maatkare Hatshepsut; Pharaoh Menkheperre Thutmose III; Senenmut, the Queen's architect.

7. *A Cruel Deceit: A Mystery of Ancient Egypt.* New York: Avon Books, 2002, 290 p.

CITY OF WASET, EGYPT, 1464–1463 BC? From far and wide, visitors have traveled to the capital city of Waset to attend the opulent Feast of Opet; sovereigns and supplicants, the pious and proud, are all gathering for the eleven-day-long revelries. While greeting his friends and fellow Medjay officers at the bustling harbor, Lieutenant Bak is distracted by the puzzling discovery of the body of a Hittite horse trader whose throat has been savagely cut. Bak has no authority to investigate what could be a simple matter of Hittite politics, until similar murders begin to occur within the sacred precinct of Lord Amon. Although this city is not his, Bak eagerly agrees to aid in the investigation. But his determined search for connections embroils him in a terrifying conspiracy that points to the court of Queen Hatshepsut herself. Untold others may be joining the ranks of the dead before the villain is unmasked, with Lieutenant Bak numbered among them. Associates: Imsiba; Thuty; Nebwa; Hori; Amonked; Pashenuro. Historical Figures: Queen Maatkare Hatshepsut; Pharaoh Menkheperre Thutmose III.

8. *A Path of Shadows: A Mystery of Ancient Egypt.* New York: Avon Books, 2003, 302 p.

FORTRESS OF BUHEN, CITY OF KAINE, THE PORT AND MINES BEYOND THE EASTERN SEA, EGYPT, 1464–1463 BC? The gods have blessed Lieutenant Bak, head of the Medjay police, with a rare brilliance, which is why he is the one to whom his commander turns in a time of need. The explorer Minnakht has vanished into the vast and merciless Egyptian desert, or perhaps he has strayed perilously close to Queen Maatkare Hatshepsut's well-guarded turquoise mines; and before Bak sails north on a new assignment, he is asked to seek out the missing man. But evil is traveling with him and his Medjays in the caravan they accompany eastward. Someone—or something—is responsible for the strange rash of deaths that is rapidly thinning the ranks of their fellow travelers. A straightforward search for a missing adventurer becomes a twisted knot of treachery and blood that threatens to strangle the life from Bak and his men and leave them buried for all eternity beneath the blistering sands. Associates: Imsiba; Thuty; Nebwa; Amonmose, a merchant on the Eastern Sea. Historical Figures: Queen Maatkare Hatshepsut; Pharaoh Menkheperre Thutmose III.

HUTCHINGS, Janet. American.

Once upon a Crime Anthology Series

Scene of the Crime: Various.

Detective: Various.

Known Associates: Various.

Premise: Hutchings gathers together historical detective stories originally published in *Ellery Queen's Mystery Magazine* (*EQMM*).

Comment: *EQMM*, the longest-lasting of the American mystery magazines, always went to great lengths to provide its readers with as large a variety of short fare as possible, including historical mystery tales as well as stories with unusual themes and subjects. Hutchings here gathers together the best of the lot in these two reprint anthologies.

Literary Crimes & Chimes: Some of these tales seem a trifle creaky by today's literary standards, but many of these stories have also been reprinted by Mike Ashley in his "Mammoth Book" historical detective anthology series, demonstrating their long-term viability. The authors range from the long-deceased Theodore Dreiser to modern British writer Peter Tremayne and his Sister Fidelma tales. There is a clear bias evident toward American writers, reflecting the general content of the magazine itself. Overall, these two books are well worth acquiring—and keeping close to one's bedstand.

THE CASES

1. *Once upon a Crime: Historical Mysteries from Ellery Queen's Mystery Magazine.* New York: St. Martin's Press, 1994, 225 p.
   An anthology of general historical detective stories. CONTENTS: "Introduction," by Janet Hutchings; "The Lemures," by Steven Saylor; "The Prince Who Was a Thief," by Theodore Dreiser; "The Light on the Road to Woodstock," by Ellis Peters; "Witch Hunt," by Terry Mullins; "Gather Not Thy Rose," by Miriam Grace Monfredo; "Death of a Noverint," by William Bankier; "The William Shakespeare Murder Case," by George Baxt; "The Earl's Nightingale," by Lillian de la Torre; "Chinoiserie," by Helen McCloy; "The Notorious Snowman," by James Powell; "A Stateman's

Touch," by Robert Barnard; "Smiling Joe and the Twins," by Florence V. Mayberry; "The Problem of the Leather Man," by Edward D. Hoch.

2. ***Once upon a Crime II: Stories from Ellery Queen's Mystery Magazine.*** New York: St. Martin's Press, 1996, 262 p.

A second anthology of general historical detective stories. CONTENTS: "Introduction," by Janet Hutchings; "Socrates Solves a Murder," by Brèni James; "Alexander the Great, Detective," by Theodore Mathieson; "King Bee and Honey," by Steven Saylor; "The Hiccup Flask," by James Powell; "A Canticle for Wulfstan," by Peter Tremayne; "A Loaf of Quicksilver," by Clayton Emery; "The Jester and the Saint," by Alan Gordon; "Galileo, Detective," by Theodore Mathieson; "The Bedlam Bam," by Lillian de la Torre; "The Escape," by Anne Perry; "The Best Sort of Husband," by Susan B. Kelly; "Traveller from an Antique Land," by Avram Davidson; "Balmorality," by Robert Barnard; "The Passion of Lizzie B.," by Edward D. Hoch; "Miz Sammy's Honor," by Florence V. Mayberry; "The 1944 Bullet," by Jeffry Scott.

JAKUBOWSKI, Maxim (1944–). British.

Scene of the Crime: Various.

Detective: Various.

Known Associates: Various.

Premise: Jakubowski gathers together a series of anthologies of historical mystery stories taken from all eras of history.

Comment: Like Mike Ashley, Jakubowski is an experienced British editor and writer, with a large number of publications to his credit. These books feature mostly original stories by mostly British writers, including all of the major names in the field.

Literary Crimes & Chimes: Jakubowski's books include a number of high-profile writers not featured in the Ashley volumes, including Anne Perry. The story quality here is consistently high, comparable to that in Ashley's books. These volumes are "must" purchases for any aficionado.

THE CASES

1. *Past Poisons: An Ellis Peters Memorial Anthology of Historical Crime.*
London: Headline, 1998, 373 p.
An anthology of general historical detective stories. Contents: "Introduction: In Memory of Ellis Peters," by Maxim Jakubowski; "A Counter-Blast to Tobacco," by Paul C. Doherty; "Wheel in the Sky," by Edward D. Hoch; "Starstruck at San Simeon," by Janet Laurence; "Death by Eros," by

Steven Saylor; "Damned Spot," by Julian Rathbone; "Showmen," by Peter Lovesey; "The Padder's Lesson," by Molly Brown; "To Dispose of an Abbot," by Susanna Gregory; "The Mamur Zapt and the Catherine Wheel," by Michael Pearce; "The Great Brogonye," by David Howard; "The Unkindest Cut," by Kate Ross; "Girl Talk," by Marilyn Todd; "Invitation to a Poisoning," by Peter Tremayne; "The Last High Queen," by Anne Perry; "To Encourage the Others," by Martin Edwards; "Psalm for a Dead Disciple," by Edward Marston; "Handsel Monday," by Catherine Aird; "An Academic Question," by John Maddox Roberts; "Hellfire," by Diana Gabaldon; "The Party May Yet Be Living . . ." by Lindsey Davis.

2. *Chronicles of Crime: The Second Ellis Peters Memorial Anthology of Historical Crime.* London: Headline, 1999, 372 p.

A second anthology of general historical detective stories. CONTENTS: "Introduction," by Maxim Jakubowski; "The Musket Ball," by Paul C. Doherty; "The Coroner's Tale," by Michael Jecks; "Death at Strawberry Hill," by Deryn Lake; "Lord of Storms," by Anton Gill; "Line Engaged," by Basil Copper; "The Fatal Step," by H.R.F. Keating; "A Lock of Hair for Proserpine," by Mary Reed and Eric Mayer; "The Serpent's Back," by Ian Rankin; "Anna and the Players," by Ed Gorman; "Bloody Windsor," by Gwendoline Butler; "The Iron Fan," by Laura Joh Rowland; "For All the Saints," by Gillian Linscott; "The Virgin's Circlet," by Kate Ellis; "The Mind of the Master," by Martin Edwards; "The Choosing of Barabbas," by Jonathan Gash; "Miss Nightingale Sang in Berkeley Square," by M.J. Trow; "Disease-Demon," by Lynda S. Robinson; "Those Who Trespass," by Peter Tremayne; "Further Developments in the Strange Case of Dr Jekyll and Mr Hyde," by Kim Newman.

3. *Murder through the Ages: A Bumper Anthology of Historical Mysteries.* London: Headline, 2000, 368 p.

A third anthology of general historical detective stories. CONTENTS: "Introduction," by Maxim Jakubowski; "Who Killed Dido?" by Amy Myers; "Investigating the Silvius Boys," by Lindsey Davis; "Trunk Call," by Marilyn Todd; "Who Stole the Fish?" by Peter Tremayne; "The Fury of the Northmen," by Kate Ellis; "Raven Feeder," by Manda Scott; "The Shoulder-Blade of a Ram," by Edward Marston; "Flyting, Fighting," by Clayton Emery; "The Trebuchet Murder," by Susanna Gregory; "Id Quod Clarum . . ." by Paul Doherty; "Pie Powder," by John Hall; "Cold Comfort," by Catherine Aird; "A Gift to the Bridegroom," by Judith Cook; "A Matter of Flesh and Blood," by Gavin Newman; "Spellbound," by Carol Anne Davis; "But Poor Men Pay for All," by Mat Coward; "A Poisoned Chalice," by John Sherwood; "Miss Unwin's Mistake," by H.R.F. Keating; "The Case of the Abominable Wife," by June Thomson; "The Curzon Street

Conundrum," by David Stuart Davies; "Unsettled Scores," by Jürgen Ehlers; "A Right Royal Attempt," by Ian Morson; "The Playwrights," by Michael Hemmingson; "The Problem of Stateroom 10," by Peter Lovesey; "Dark Mirror," by Lauren Henderson.

4. *Royal Crimes,* ed. by Maxim Jakubowski and Martin H. Greenberg. New York: Signet Books, 1994, 254 p.

An anthology of contemporaneous and historical detective stories focusing on royal crimes. CONTENTS: "Introduction," by Maxim Jakubowski; "About the Authors"; "The Monster of Glamis," by Sharyn McCrumb; "A Statesman's Touch," by Robert Barnard; "A Black Death," by Edward Marston; "A Day at the Races," by Edward D. Hoch; "Bring Me the Head of Anne Boleyn," by Kristine Kathryn Rusch; "A Sort of Miss Marple?" by H.R.F. Keating; "The Reckoning," by Graham Joyce; "Victoria," by Mark Timlin; "The Lemon Juice Plot," by Molly Brown; "The Searcher," by Gwendoline Butler; "The Stranger," by Michael Z. Lewin; "Brotherly Love," by Mike Ripley; "Lex Talionis," by Jessica Palmer; "Queen Alienor's Favor," by Paul Dorrell; "Balmorality," by Robert Barnard; "Bertie and the Fire Brigade," by Peter Lovesey.

JECKS, Michael (1960–). British.

SIR BALDWIN FURNSHILL AND SIMON PUTTOCK SERIES

Scene of the Crime: Devonshire, England, beginning in 1314.

Detective: Sir Baldwin Furnshill (born 1273), Keeper of the King's Peace in Crediton, Devonshire, and a former Knight Templar who escaped when his order was destroyed by the Pope, an astute investigator of violent crimes; Simon Puttock, Bailiff to the Warden of the Stannaries at Lydford Castle, the mining areas of Dartmoor, and a friend to Sir Baldwin.

Known Associates: Lady Jeanne, widow of Ralph de Liddinstone, who abused her, and now Baldwin's wife, whom he met in Tavistock while investigating a crime there; Richalda, Baldwin and Jeanne's daughter; Edgar, Sir Baldwin's former man-at-arms and now his faithful servant; a trained fighter, he enjoys the quieter country existence; Margaret ("Meg"), Simon's wife, who is mourning the death of their only son and heir, eighteen-month-old "Peterkins"; Edith, Simon, and Margaret's daughter and their only surviving child; Hugh, Simon's devoted servant; Peter Clifford, Rector of Crediton, and a friend to both Simon and Baldwin; Walter Stapledon, Bishop of Exeter; Lord Hugh de Courtenay, head of the county's leading family and Simon's mentor; Sir Roger de Gidleigh, Exeter's coroner.

Premise: A former Knight Templar returns to England, where he acts in concert with the local magistrate in solving crimes and setting matters right.

Comment: Sir Baldwin, a former Knight Templar, has seen his order destroyed and his friends executed. He returns to the Devonshire countryside to take up his place as the master of Furnshill Manor, his older brother being recently deceased. He quickly makes the acquaintance of Simon Puttock, the thirty-five-year-old bailiff of Lydford Castle, currently in the service of the de Courtenay family, Lords of Devon and Cornwall. The two soon form a bond of friendship and mutual respect that leads to their collaboration in the investigation and solving of the various crimes and misdemeanors that take place in the Devonshire countryside.

Literary Crimes & Chimes: The history of the Knights Templar is a familiar one to buffs of the medieval scene, having been used frequently as a jumping-off point for various fictional tales. Here is yet another twist on the theme. Jecks prefaces the first novel in the series with a detailed account of the demise of the order in 1314, the starting date for the series. The executions of his comrades provide the motivation for Jecks' hero, Sir Baldwin, Lord of Furnshill Manor, to return to his roots in the English countryside and assume the obligations of his inheritance. All this is laid out succinctly in the first two chapters of *The Last Templar*, setting the stage for a series of mysteries involving the continuing characters of Sir Baldwin and his newfound friend, Simon Puttock. Jecks continues to provide miniessays in the prefaces to his novels that outline his research and provide historical notes relevant to the topics he covers in the novels. Beginning with *Squire Throwleigh's Heir*, a "Cast of Characters" is appended, as well as helpful glossaries and other documents that elucidate the background information accompanying each tale. The characters are well-rounded, and Jecks seems to make a genuine effort to provide the appropriate psychological motivation for their choices. The plots, too, are diverse and fresh enough to hold most readers' interest throughout the series, although the more recent books in the sequence seem to meander away from their original setting.

THE CASES

1. *The Last Templar.* London: Headline, 1995, 375 p.
PARIS, FRANCE, 1314, AND DEVON, ENGLAND, FALL 1316. In Paris in 1314 Pope Clement V has destroyed the last remnants of the Order of Knights Templar, wrongly persuaded of their corruption. Watching through a veil of tears as his friends and Grand Master die at the stake, a surviving knight, Sir Baldwin Furnshill, swears vengeance on their false accusers. Two

years later, when a spate of burnings begins to occur in a quiet Devonshire village, the newly appointed bailiff of Lydford Castle, Simon Puttock, is called to a village where a charred body has been found in a burned-out cottage. He assumes it to be an accidental death until Sir Baldwin Furnshill, the astute, yet strangely reticent, knight who has recently returned from abroad, convinces him that the victim had been murdered before the fire began. Then word comes of another killing, more horrible by far. Are the two incidents linked—and will the killer strike again? Can they find and destroy the outlaw band? Baldwin himself becomes a prime suspect in one of the murders before the matter is finally resolved. Associates: Margaret; Edgar; Hugh; Edith; Peter. Historical Figures: Pope Clement V; Jacques de Molay, last Grand Master of the Knights Templar.

2. *The Merchant's Partner.* London: Headline, 1995, 377 p.

WEFFORD, DEVON, ENGLAND, SPRING 1317. Midwife and healer Agatha Kyteler is regarded as a witch by the superstitious villagers of Wefford, yet she has no shortage of callers, from the humblest villein to the most elegant and wealthy in the area. But when Agatha's body is found frozen and mutilated in a hedge one wintry morning, there seems to be no clue as to who could be responsible, at least not until a local youth runs away, and a hue and cry is raised. Sir Baldwin Furnshill, Keeper of the King's Peace, is not convinced of the youth's guilt and soon persuades his close friend, Simon Puttock, Bailiff of Lydford Castle, to help him continue with the investigation. As they endeavor to find the true culprit, the darker side of the village, with its undercurrents of suspicion, jealousy, and disloyalty, emerges. And what is driving the young foreigner son of a nobleman, who has visited the normally sleepy area, last seen heading toward the moors? Associates: Peter; Margaret; Hugh; Edgar; Edith.

3. *A Moorland Hanging.* London: Headline, 1996, 375 p.

DEVON, ENGLAND, FALL 1318. In fourteenth-century Devonshire runaway villeins were brutally punished if apprehended by their masters. But when Peter Bruther flees the home of Sir William Beauscyr, he puts himself in the protection of the king by setting up as a tin miner on the moors. And the bailiff of Lydford, Simon Puttock, is forced to inform an irate Sir William that he has no legal claim on his wayward servant. When Bruther's body is found hanging from a tree, Simon, assisted by his friend Sir Baldwin Furnshill investigates a cold-blooded murder. There's no shortage of usual suspects, from Sir William himself, to his feuding sons, to Thomas Smyth, a wealthy tinner who runs a ruthlessly enforced protection racket funded by landowners. The pressure is on Simon and Baldwin to unravel the truth before further violence ensues. Associates: Margaret; Edith; Hugh; Edgar.

4. *The Crediton Killings.* London: Headline, 1997, 378 p.

CREDITON, DEVON, ENGLAND, AUGUST 1319. The Devonshire town of Crediton is awaiting an important guest, the Bishop of Exeter, Walter Stapledon. But a band of mercenary soldiers is already in residence, and though mercenaries are a common sight in the fourteenth century, these men are bent on havoc. They terrify travelers and show no respect toward anyone. There's a rumor that their captain, Sir Hector de Gorsone, has seduced a naïve local girl, Sarra. Bailiff Simon, who is mourning his recently deceased son, Peter, and his friend, Sir Baldwin Furnshill, reluctantly prepare for the Bishop's welcome dinner and are relieved when the local disturbance interrupts the meal. They are less pleased, though, when they discover there's been a robbery among the mercenaries. Then a young girl is discovered murdered, hidden in a chest. The Crediton killings have begun. As murder follows brutal murder, Simon and Baldwin must identify the killer before their own lives are put at risk. Associates: Peter Clifford; Peter, Simon's son; Margaret; Edgar; Hugh; Edith. Historical Figure: British King Edward II.

5. *The Abbot's Gibbet.* London: Headline, 1998, 336 p.

TAVISTOCK, DEVON, ENGLAND, LATE AUGUST 1319. Tavistock's fair has drawn merchants to Devonshire from all over England and beyond. Keeping the streets clean and the locals in order is no easy task, for the influx of visitors and their money puts temptation in the way of cut-purses and other villains. But no one expects a murder, and butcher Will Ruby is stunned to discover a corpse, and a headless one at that. Simon and Baldwin have just arrived in Tavistock as guests of Abbot Robert Champeaux when the body is found. When the Abbot asks them to investigate, they can hardly refuse their host. But with an unidentifiable victim, they're badly hampered in their inquiries. Can Simon and Baldwin unravel the complex web of intrigue that has brought death to Tavistock, as the undercurrents of anger and violence that lie beneath the bustling activity of the fair grow ever fiercer? Baldwin meets his future wife, Jeanne, in this novel. Associates: Margaret; Edith; Edgar; Hugh; Jeanne; Bishop Stapledon. Historical Figure: British King Edward II.

6. *The Leper's Return.* London: Headline, 1998, 340 p.

CREDITON, DEVON, ENGLAND, WINTER 1320. Civil war is looming as Ralph of Houndeslow rides into Crediton. Ralph faces a daunting task as master of St. Lawrence's, a leper hospital. Not only are his charges grievously ill, but they are also outcasts of society, shunned by all healthy folk. The citizens of Crediton have other concerns. The murder of Godfrey of London and the assault on his daughter Cecily are crimes all too easily attributed to the disreputable womanizer John of Irlaunde. But Sir Baldwin is not convinced that John is the culprit, and soon he is following other leads, assisted by his friend Simon. Only when they discover the identity of the man overheard talking to Cecily before the attack will the astounding truth begin to emerge. Meanwhile, animosity against the lepers is spreading, fed by deliberate rumors. Unless the burgers of Crediton can be made to see reason, Baldwin and Simon could have a full-scale slaughter on their hands. Associates: Peter Clifford; Bishop Stapledon; Hugh; Jeanne; Edgar; Margaret; Edith.

7. *Squire Throwleigh's Heir.* London: Headline, 1999, 320 p.

DEVON, ENGLAND, SPRING 1321. Sir Baldwin is preparing for his wedding to Lady Jeanne, whom he met in Tavistock the year before. He receives the news that one of his guests, Roger, the Squire of Throwleigh, has just died. The new master of Throwleigh is little Herbert, age five and isolated in his grief, for his distraught mother, Katherine, unfairly blames her young son for her husband's death. Baldwin feels deeply disturbed about the new heir's apparent lack of protection; having inherited a large estate and much wealth, the child will inevitably attract dangerous enemies. A horse and cart hit Herbert just a few days later, killing him, seemingly by accident. Baldwin and Simon immediately suspect foul play. As they begin to investigate the facts surrounding the case, they are increasingly convinced that young Herbert was killed deliberately, but little do they realize that their investigation will lead them to the most sinister and shocking murderer they have encountered yet. Associates: Jeanne; Edgar; Margaret; Hugh.

8. *Belladonna at Belstone.* London: Headline, 1999, 332 p.

BELSTON, DEVON, ENGLAND, SPRING 1321. Lady Elizabeth of Topsham, prioress of St. Mary's, Priory, Belstone, has been struggling to retain her position in the face of devastating opposition. Not only is St. Mary's in the worst possible state of disrepair due to lack of funds, but Sister Margherita, her treasurer, has accused her of lascivious disregard, claiming that, instead of paying for a new roof, Elizabeth has given money to the new vicar, a man she often sees alone—at night. Many of the nuns are convinced that Margherita would make a better prioress, especially after Moll, a young nun, is murdered as she lies ill in the infirmary at St. Mary's. Sir Baldwin Furnshill, together with his old friend Bailiff Simon Puttock, is summoned immediately by the Bishop of Stapledon to investigate. There is no doubt that the threefold vows of obedience, chastity, and poverty are being broken with alarming frequency at the priory. When a second nun is murdered, the pair faces their most difficult case yet. The path to the truth twists and turns with the sinister forces of forbidden passions and secret ambitions, finally leading them to a dangerous wolf in sheep's clothing. Baldwin marries Jeanne three weeks before the action of the book begins. Associates: Jeanne; Peter Clifford; Bishop Stapledon; Edgar; Hugh.

9. *The Traitor of St. Giles.* London: Headline, 2000, 335 p.

TIVERTON, DEVON, ENGLAND, JULY–AUGUST 1321. The folk of Tiverton are preparing for St. Giles' feast under the shadow of murder. Philip Dyne, a spicer, has confessed to the vicious rape and killing of his lover, Joan Carter. He has claimed sanctuary in St. Peter's church, but danger still lurks within the community. As Sir Baldwin and Simon arrive at Lord Hugh de Courtenay's castle for the feast, another body is found, that of Sir Gilbert of Carlisle, an important ambassador—and he is lying next to the decapitated figure of Dyne. The coroner, Harlewin le Poter, is satisfied that Dyne killed the knight and was then murdered in turn. Since Dyne was already an outlaw, his death does not merit the law's attention. But Sir Baldwin feels too many questions remain unanswered. How could an unarmed peasant, for instance, kill a trained warrior? And even if he did, what then happened to Sir Gilbert's horse and money? When Baldwin and Simon are themselves viciously attacked, they know that a more sinister enemy is at large. And then there are all those usual suspects. . . . Associates: Edgar; Jeanne; Hugh de Courtenay.

10. *The Boy-Bishop's Glovemaker.* London: Headline, 2000, 331 p.

EXETER, DEVON, ENGLAND, CHRISTMAS 1321. Sir Baldwin and his friend Simon are looking forward to the Christmas celebration, which promises to be a scene of great festivity. As a reward for their investigative services, they've been summoned to Exeter to receive the prestigious "gloves of honor" in an ancient and ritualistic ceremony led by the specially elected Boy-Bishop. But the dead man swinging on the gallows as they arrive is a portentous greeting. Within hours, they learn that Ralph—the cathedral's glove maker and the city's beloved philanthropist—has been robbed and stabbed to death. When Peter, a Secondary at the cathedral, collapses from poisoning in the middle of Mass, the finger of suspicion turns to him. Yet if he was Ralph's attacker, where have his missing riches gone? And did Peter commit suicide, or was he murdered, too? When Simon and Baldwin are asked to solve the riddles surrounding the deaths, they soon find that many of Exeter's leading citizens are not what—and who—they first seem to be, and that the city's Christmas bustle is concealing a ruthless murderer who is about to strike again. Associates: Jeanne; Edgar.

11. *The Tournament of Blood.* London: Headline, 2001, 362 p.

OAKHAMPTON, DEVON, ENGLAND, SPRING 1322. Lord Hugh de Courtenay's plan to host a tournament is a golden opportunity for the moneylenders of Oakhampton. When the defeated knights find themselves unable to pay the traditional ransoms to their captors, they will have only one avenue open to them, no matter how much they hate it—the moneylenders. But for Benjamin Dudenay, to whom so many of the knights of Devon are indebted, the tournament will yield no such riches. A month before the festivities, he is found beaten to death. For Sir Baldwin and Simon, the priority is to complete the preparations for the tournament in time for Lord Hugh's arrival. But when Wymond Carpenter, commissioned to build the viewing stands, is found dead, his injuries are identical to Benjamin's. And Baldwin and Simon are faced with an additional problem: whoever killed the moneylender is not simply a debtor desperate to gain financial freedom but a killer with a far greater and more sinister plan. Associates: Jeanne; Edgar; Margaret; Edith; Hugh; Hugh de Courtenay; Roger.

12. *The Sticklepath Strangler.* London: Headline, 2001, 366 p.

STICKLEPATH, DEVON, ENGLAND, SUMMER 1322. The summer brings welcome sunshine to the Devonshire countryside, but it seems that the small village of Sticklepath is destined to remain in the shadows. Two playmates discover the body of a young girl on the moors. She is Aline, the ten-year-old daughter of Swetricus, who went missing six years earlier. Sir Baldwin Furnshill and his friend Simon Puttock are summoned to the scene to investigate and soon learn that Aline is not the only young girl to have been found dead in recent years. It seems the villagers have been concealing not only a serial killer but, judging by the state of the girls' bodies, a possible case of cannibalism. Or, if local rumors are to be believed, a vampire is on the loose! That would certainly explain the haunted looks in the eyes of so many villagers, and the strange noises heard emanating late at night from the Sticklepath Cemetery! Associates: Jeanne; Edgar; Roger; Edith.

13. *The Devil's Acolyte.* London: Headline, 2001, 395 p.

TAVISTOCK, DEVON, ENGLAND, FALL 1322. Amid the myth and folklore of Tavistock, one tale above all others strikes fear into the hearts of the town's inhabitants, that of the murders on the Abbot's Way. One cold winter many years ago Milbrosa, a young acolyte eager for distraction, led a group of his fellow novices in the theft of their abbot's wine. Later, riddled with guilt and fear of discovery, Milbrosa was driven to commit still more crimes in a misguided effort to conceal his original sin. But his soul had been destroyed with that first sip of illicit wine, and, as legend has it, the devil himself appeared to mete out his punishment, leading the unwitting Milbrosa and his cohorts to their deaths on the treacherous moors. Now it looks as if history might be repeating itself. Abbot Robert finds his wine barrel empty, and a body has been discovered on the moors. Simon Puttock, in Tavistock for the coining, is called upon to investigate, but it soon becomes apparent that it's not just the wine that has gone missing from the abbey, and the body on the moor isn't the last. Sir Baldwin of Furnshill is called in to assist with the investigation, and the townspeople hope the mystery will finally be solved, but do the terrors of the past provide the key to their present turmoil? Associates: Hugh; Roger.

14. *The Mad Monk of Gidleigh.* London: Headline, 2002, 460 p.

DARTMOOR, DEVON, ENGLAND, WINTER 1323. As winter descends on Dartmoor, life has never seemed so bleak to the young priest Father Mark in his isolated, windswept chapel. It is a far cry from the cathedral cities of Europe of which he dreamed as a novice. So who could blame him for accepting some longed-for human contact and companionship when it is offered by the local miller's daughter, Mary? But when Mary and the unborn child she carries are found brutally murdered, the villagers are quick to point the finger of blame. The investigators assigned to the case, Sir Baldwin and Simon, soon begin to have their doubts. It becomes clear that Mary was far from the simple village girl she seemed. What exactly was her relationship with the Squire of Gidleigh, Sir Ralph, who is uncharacteristically grief-stricken at her death? Or perhaps Osbert, the mill-hand whose love she rejected time and again, could withstand his torment no longer? In their search for the truth, Baldwin and Simon unwittingly put themselves into grave danger. And by the time the investigation is over and the shocking crime uncovered, life for themselves and their families will never be the same. Roger dies in this book. Associates: Jeanne; Edgar; Margaret; Edith; Hugh; Roger.

15. *The Templar's Penance.* London: Headline, 2003, 364 p.

ON PILGRIMAGE IN SANTIAGO DE COMPOSTELA, PORTUGAL, SUMMER 1323. Sir Baldwin and his friend Simon Puttock have been granted leave from their posts to go on pilgrimage, both seeking solace from the recent traumatic events in Gidleigh. Together they travel across Europe to Santiago de Compostela in Portugal, but, as usual, danger is never far away. Foreign travel in 1323 is perilous: outlaws and robbers threaten at all times, not to mention the risks from political unrest and a recent spate of attacks on pilgrims. But it seems an even greater menace hangs over the sacred city of Santiago. A beautiful young girl is found raped and murdered on a hillside, her broken body leaving no doubt that she is the victim of the most brutal of killers. Baldin and Simon are among the first to arrive on the scene and offer their investigative skills to the local *pesquisidore*, Munio. With so many keen minds on the case, it can be only a matter of time before the culprit is found. But the two detectives are reckoning without the unexpected appearance of a face from Baldwin's past, an entity that threatens both the outcome of the investigation and Baldwin's very future. None of the usual suspects accompany our intrepid duo.

16. *The Outlaws of Ennor.* London: Headline, 2003, 320 p.

ENNOR AND ST. NICHOLAS, THE SCILLY ISLES, BRITAIN, LATE SUMMER 1323. Simon has been promoted to a new position in Dartmouth. On their return home from their pilgrimage to the Spanish Peninsula, Baldwin and Simon's ship is attacked off the coast of the Scilly Isles by the twin evils of pirates and a terrible storm. As Simon looks on in horror, Baldwin is swept overboard and disappears from sight. Washed ashore on the tiny island of Ennor, Simon is distraught to think that his closest friend is dead. But he is forced to put aside his grief when the master of the local castle, Ranulph de Blancminster, orders him to investigate the murder of Robert, the island's despised tax collector. Ranulph is convinced that one of the lawless inhabitants of the neighboring island of St. Nicholas is the culprit and prepares to attack the residents there. Meanwhile, Baldwin himself has been washed up on St. Nicholas and is being nursed back to health by the beautiful Tedia. He uncovers a different picture of the island as he, too, begins to investigate the murder at the Prior's insistance. Although there are plenty of suspects, Baldwin finds it impossible to penetrate the tight network of secrets and loyalties that bind the close-knit villagers in this isolated community. As Baldwin and Simon pursue parallel paths of investigation, they become embroiled in the bitter rivalry between the two island communities. Can they uncover the truth in time to prevent further bloodshed? None of the usual suspects accompany our intrepid duo.

17. *The Tolls of Death.* London: Headline, 2004, 392 p.

CARDINHAM, BODMIN MOOR, ENGLAND, SUMMER 1323. After their grueling journeys, Baldwin and Simon are at last back on English soil, unceremoniously dumped on the mainland when their shipmaster partakes of his liquid cargo and almost wrecks the ship. Eager to return home, the pair set off on horseback but get only as far as Cardinham on Bodmin Moor. Here, they are detained by the castellan, who requires their assistance to solve two murders on the estate. The first victim is a widow, found dead with her two children. The second is Serlo the Miller, who has recently been accused of embezzling the castle money he took in tolls. As Baldwin and Simon begin a double investigation, they must also look beneath the village friendships and family loyalties to discover an evil killer and secure Cardinham's safety. None of the usual suspects accompany our intrepid duo. Associates: Margaret; Simon's young son (mentioned without name at novel's end).

KING, Laurie R. (1952–). American.

MARY RUSSELL SERIES

Scene of the Crime: The series begins at Sussex Downs, England, in 1915, ranging thereafter from London to Jerusalem, but is usually set somewhere in the British Isles. The books cover different time spans, depending not only on cases covered but on the life-stage of the characters. For instance, the first book focuses on Mary's apprenticeship, which lasts about four years. The second novel delineates the changes in her perception of Sherlock Holmes and covers about two months. After that the time spans are case-driven.

Detective: Mary Russell, orphaned in a car accident, is now determined to study theology; she meets the retired detective Sherlock Holmes quite by accident. He recognizes in her a mind that is the equal of his own and begins to teach her the skills and methods of detection. Mary is a theologian and a feminist, strong, tall (almost six feet), with long, strawberry blonde hair (it is easier to care for long hair). When she first meets Holmes, she is only fifteen years old; by the second book, however, she has achieved her majority.

Known Associates: Mrs. Hudson, bored to distraction after Holmes retires, who sells her own house to move in as his housekeeper; Dr. Watson, who continues to consult in medical matters but whose talents in deception and subterfuge have not improved; Inspector Lestrade, who is not sure at the beginning of the series if Holmes' new partnership is simply a jest; Mycroft Holmes, who is both helpful and demanding; Patrick Mason, Mary's farm manager.

Premise: A young detective solves crimes, initially with the help of Sherlock Holmes, in early twentieth-century Britain.

Comment: Mary almost trips over Holmes as she walks the hills of Sussex Downs, reading (Holmes is sitting on the hillside watching the bees). Holmes is as arrogant and impatient as one would expect and is brought up short when Mary deduces his problem, interprets his plans, and jumps ahead of him to make a helpful recommendation. His stunned assessment—"It can think!"—is less than flattering but marks the moment when he finally realizes that, at age fifty-four and now retired, he has met a mind that's a match for his own. The pair begins a friendship that will evolve in time to a partnership, as Mary learns the strategies of deduction, and Holmes learns that she is not dependent on him for thinking, planning, or acting. It is extraordinarily difficult to do justice to another writer's character, but Laurie King has done well by Sherlock Holmes. He has both Holmes' faults and his humanity, with more of the latter exposed in these works than in those of Arthur Conan Doyle. The greatest complaint Holmes' fans have of these books is the obvious attachment between Holmes and Russell. King acknowledges that complaint in a passage in *A Letter of Mary*, in which Holmes states that he never thought to marry, that he had been convinced that "strong emotion interfered with rational thought, like grit in a sensitive instrument" [p.119]. However, if fans will allow that Holmes, while brilliant, was not always wise, and that it is possible that he could yet alter his views, after the events chronicled by Doyle, they will find in these books the same dedication to logic and passion for truth that marks the stories written at the turn of the previous century.

Literary Crimes & Chimes: The writing here is superb, being so emotionally evocative that it transports the reader not just to another time and place but to the mind and feelings of another person, Mary Russell, recounting her adventures in her old age. Her youthful voice is resonate with wisdom and passion, so brilliantly rendered that the reader finds Mary's thoughts and experiences merging with the echoes of memories and feelings of his or her own. As befits fictions dealing with Sherlock Holmes, these books also bestir the mind. Each of the books explores many different themes. *Beekeeper's Apprentice* examines the passage from novice to master and the changes entailed in those roles. *O Jerusalem* examines the themes of competence and trust. *A Monstrous Regiment of Women* blends a coming-of-age story with a look at how women can lose themselves and how their actions can be subverted through their relationships. *A Letter of Mary* and *The Moor* focus on aging, the loss of physical power, and the question of what remains of one's work. *Justice Hall* covers duty, the subversion of duty, and the question of what happens to a man when his duty conflicts with who he is at his core. *The Game* explores games, dangerous games (which Mary plays up to a point), and how to change the rules. All of these books discuss feminism, and all of them explore what it means to be and to have an equal partner. The reader will savor these books, turning over phrases and ideas through his or her mind long after finishing each novel. Read *Beekeeper's Apprentice* and *A Monstrous Regiment of Women* (in that order) before looking at any of the other books. Many readers who did not care for *A Monstrous Regiment of Women* became fans once again with *A Letter of Mary*.

1. *The Beekeeper's Apprentice; or, On the Segregation of the Queen.* New York: St. Martin's Press, 1994, 347 p.

SUSSEX DOWNS, LONDON, AND OXFORD, ENGLAND, 1915. Holmes and Russell meet, and Mary's apprenticeship begins and moves through its logical stages: basic skills, assisting with a case, solving her own (small) case, and then, while partnering with Holmes, altering her (and their) plans on the fly, without consultation, when she realizes that there is a better way to gain their ends. In the course of these events Holmes and Russell uncover a villain who toys with them, wanting nothing more and nothing less than a protracted, painful revenge. Associates: Ronnie; Dorothy Ruskin; Ali and Mahmoud Hazr.

2. "Mrs. Hudson's Case," in *Crime through Time*, ed. by Miriam Grace Monfredo and Sharan Newman. New York: Berkley Prime Crime, 1997, p. 218–230.

SUSSEX DOWNS, ENGLAND, 1918. This story is an interpolation into the events of *The Beekeeper's Apprentice*, taking place soon after the Jessica Simpson kidnapping. Holmes is called upon to solve another suspected kidnapping and has no time to help Mrs. Hudson with her worries about the small thefts that have been taking place in the neighborhood. While Holmes is away, Mrs. Hudson solves the mystery and determines upon a course of action. Associate: Mary Russell.

3. *O Jerusalem: A Mary Russell Novel.* New York: Bantam Books, 1999, 367 p.

PALESTINE, 1918 (an interpolation within events of *The Beekeeper's Apprentice*; the events taking place within the two months following the beehive bomb). Mycroft Holmes assists Holmes and Russell in fleeing to Palestine, asking, in return, that they investigate the suspiciously frequent deaths of his agents. Mycroft's men have difficulty accepting the fact that a green girl who does not even speak fluent Arabic and a man who does not know the country can be in any way useful. Associates: Ali; Mahmoud; Mycroft. Historical Figures: General Allenby; brief sighting of T. E. Lawrence.

4. *A Letter of Mary: A Mary Russell Novel.* New York: St. Martin's Press, 1997, 276 p.

ENGLAND, 1923. Archeologist Dorothy Ruskin gives Russell a letter that seems to have been written by Mary Magdalene, in which she refers to herself as an apostle of Jesus. That evening Dorothy is run down by a motorcar. When the Holmes' residence is sacked, Russell and Holmes realize that there is someone out there who will stop at nothing to get the artifact. Associate: Dorothy Ruskin; cameo by Lord Peter.

5. *The Moor: A Mary Russell Novel.* New York: St. Martin's Press, 1998, 307 p.

DARTMOOR, ENGLAND, 1921. On the moor near the Baskerville residence, a man is found murdered; and near him are the "footprints of a gigantic hound!" Actually, as Holmes points out, it's not possible to determine whether or not the dog is a hound from such prints. Notwithstanding, when rumors that the ghostly Hound has reappeared come to the attention of the Reverend Baring-Gould, he sends for Holmes (who then sends for Russell, compass, and maps) to solve the case. Historical Figure: Reverend Sabine Baring-Gould.

6. *A Monstrous Regiment of Women.* New York: St. Martin's Press, 1995, 326 p.

ENGLAND, 1921. This is a book of awakening, of becoming sensitive to another's feelings, of Mary's beginning to see Holmes not just as a mentor, but as a person. It is subtly written, tracing the narrator's feelings as she is just beginning to become aware of them herself. The novel is framed by proposals, beginning with Mary's to Holmes; she envisions a logical (and passionless) partnership that will be accepted by the world. Holmes' refutation of that idea is scathing. Mary's theological and sociological interests take her to the New Temple of God, a political force and a shelter for abused women. Her criminological interest is aroused when she suspects that another young woman involved with the Temple has been murdered. Associate: Ronnie.

7. *Justice Hall: A Mary Russell Novel.* New York: Bantam Books, 2002, 331 p.

ENGLAND, 1921. When Ali Hazr turns up at their door, covered with blood *and* wearing an English suit, it can mean only one thing: that his cousin Mahmoud is in desperate straits. Holmes and Russell's investigation uncovers the story of a young man whose strength, bravery, and decency were used against him by a villain during the Great War. The villain is ready to strike again and may employ the cover of a masked ball to commit murder. Associates: Ali; Mahmoud.

8. *The Game: A Mary Russell Novel.* New York: Bantam Books, 2004, 368 p.

INDIA, 1924. Holmes and Russell go to India in search of one of Mycroft's men, Kimball O'Hara, the same "Kim" of whom Rudyard Kipling wrote in his famous novel. Holmes and Russell don disguises and insinuate themselves into different communities, but when their possessions are stolen and they narrowly survive "accidents" that could have been fatal, they know they must discover who among their fellows is also in disguise. Associates: Bindra; Tom Goodheart; Jamalpandra; Geoffrey Nesbit; Kim.

KNIGHT, Bernard (Henry) (1931–). British.

CROWNER JOHN SERIES

Scene of the Crime: Exeter and Devon, England, beginning in 1194.

Detective: Sir John de Wolfe (called "Crowner John"), a county coroner.

Known Associates: John's bodyguard and chief officer, Gwyn of Polruan, a burly Cornishman; John's clerk, the disgraced ex-cleric Thomas de Peyne; John's shrewish wife, Matilda; Matilda's brother, the corrupt Sheriff Richard de Revelle; Nesta, a local tavern keeper and John's love interest on the side; Ralph Morin, the castle constable; Ralph's man, Gabriel, a former soldier; Bran, a massive grey stallion and John's noble steed from the wars, who dies on the tourney field (*The Awful Secret*); Odin, the black stallion who replaces Bran; Mary, John's maid; Lucille, Matilda's maid; Edwin, Nesta's man; John de Alençon, Archdeacon of Exeter; Brutus, John's great hound; British King Richard I, called the Lion-Hearted (1189–1199); Hubert Walter, Justiciar and Archbishop of Canterbury.

Premise: The first appointed coroner for the County of Devonshire solves crimes and conducts investigations into deaths from questionable causes in twelfth-century England.

Comment: After twenty years as a soldier with service in the Holy Land, Sir John de Wolfe (known affectionately among his fellow crusaders as "Black John") has been appointed by his mentor and good friend King Richard I as the first Coroner for the County of Devon. The office of coroner had been established by King Richard in September 1194. County coroners have been given many legal and fiscal duties, including the examination of dead bodies in general, and well as deaths occurring from accidental wrecks, fires, and assaults; they can also be awarded a special investigation on an ad hoc basis by means of a royal commission, charging them with a particular task on behalf of the King, as happens in many of these stories. Knight, by profession a modern-day forensic pathologist, was called to the Bar at Gray's Inn in 1966. He was made a Commander of the Order of the British Empire in 1993 for his services in the field, and he acted as the pathologist who recovered all twelve bodies in the infamous Fred West case in Gloucester in 1994. His extensive medical and legal expertise, in additional to his own research, makes his detective novels particularly faithful to their era in both scientific and historical detail. The author has noted that the Crowner John series features many adjunct characters who actually existed in fact. In addition to maps of medieval Exeter, the books usually contain a useful glossary of terms.

Literary Crimes & Chimes: The language and situations in these books have been criticized by some as sexist, or at the very least condescending toward women. Crowner John is definitely a "ladies' man," having several bawdy mistresses at his beck and call (with others suggested), and he is constantly at odds with his shrewish wife, whom he demeans as a "foolish, middle-aged woman." The settings of the novels, with their gritty portrayal of an area rife with poverty, corruption, and brutality, may not appeal to more sensitive natures. In comparing this series with Paul Doherty's "Brother Athelstan" series, which is set in London in 1377 and which features Athelstan's larger-than-life associate, the London City Coroner, Sir John Cranston, the reader can see immediately the influence of Knight's greater knowledge of historical pathology in the Crowner John series. These novels are tougher, grittier, and more graphic, and undoubtedly more true to life to the period. To be fair, however, Doherty's books focus more on his chief character, a medieval monk, which gives his series a completely different flavor. If one can stomach the antifeminist attitude so blatantly portrayed in these fictions, these are entertaining reads.

THE CASES

1. *The Sanctuary Seeker.* London: Pocket Books, 1998, 320 p.
EXETER, ENGLAND, NOVEMBER 1194. Appointed by Richard the Lionheart as the first coroner for the county of Devon, Sir John de Wolfe rides out to the lonely moorland village of Widecombe to hold an inquest on an unidentified body. On his return to Exeter, de Wolfe is incensed to discover that his own brother-in-law, Sheriff Richard de Revelle, is intent on thwarting the murder investigation, particularly when it emerges that the dead man is a Crusader, Hubert de Bonneville, and a member of one of Devon's finest families. John must face down the combined mights of Church and nobility to unmask

the killer. Associates: Gwyn; Thomas; Matilda; Mary; Nesta; Edwin; Ralph; Richard; Bran; Archdeacon John. Historical Figure: British King Richard I.

2. *The Poisoned Chalice.* London: Pocket Books, 1998, 355 p.

EXETER, ENGLAND, DECEMBER 1194. The well-born ladies of Exeter are not having a good week. First, Christina Rifford, the daughter of a rich Exeter businessman, is raped. Then, Lady Adele de Courcey is found dead in one of the city's poorest areas, apparently the victim of a botched abortion. The common factor in the two events is Godfrey Fitzosbern, a local silversmith, and his workmen, Garth and Arthur. It becomes the duty of the county coroner, Sir John de Wolfe, to protect Godfrey until he can find proof of his guilt. John slowly begins to put the pieces together. But a final, brutal act of violence brings a new twist to his investigation, and it will take all of John's abilities to keep the peace and uphold law and order in the face of the victims' incensed relatives and the mob of townspeople they incite. Associates: Gwyn; Thomas; Gabriel; Ralph; Richard; Matilda; Lucille; Nesta; Mary; Bran; Brutus the hound; Archdeacon John; Edwin. Historical Figure: Hubert Walter.

3. *Crowner's Quest: A Crowner John Mystery.* London: Pocket Books, 1999, 328 p.

DEVON, ENGLAND, CHRISTMAS EVE 1194. Crowner John is called from a celebration to examine the body of a canon who has apparently hanged himself. The death is believed to be suicide, but de Wolfe establishes that the old man could not have done the deed himself. Then a prominent local nobleman perishes, apparently as the result of falling from his horse. Again John decides that the accident is actually a murder, and he begins to suspect that the two cases are somehow linked. As usual, John's brother-in-law, the corrupt and vengeful Sheriff Richard de Revelle, erects numerous stumbling blocks to the investigation. The official may be part of a broader conspiracy to raise Prince John to the throne of England! When the crowner is tossed into prison on a rape charge, all seems lost. Associates: Gwyn; Thomas; Richard; Matilda; Nesta.

4. *The Awful Secret.* London: Simon & Schuster, 2000, 335 p.

DEVONSHIRE, ENGLAND, JANUARY–MARCH 1195. Crowner John has been unable to carry out his duties due to a broken leg he received on the tourney field at Bull Mead in January. But with the vigorous, if resentful, nursing of his wife, Matilda, he is finally able to mount his horse unaided, and just in time, because John is being stalked by a mysterious figure who seems to be watching his every move. John's man, Gwyn, finally catches up with the man and is surprised at the identity of the stalker: Gilbert de Rideford, a Knight of the Temple of Solomon and an acquaintance from John and Gwyn's crusading days. He claims to have come into possession of an "awful secret" that could shake Christendom to its very foundation. He desperately needs John's help to escape from the secretive order of warrior monks, an order so powerful that they are answerable only to the Pope. Skeptical but nevertheless intrigued, John agrees to help, and when three Knights Templar and an important Papal message arrive in Exeter, he begins to take Gilbert seriously. Suddenly, John is swept into a world of religious intrigue and dangerous politics that takes him on a life-threatening mission to the Island of Lundy, inhabited only by notorious pirates, and finally leads him to the revelation of Gilbert's secret (yet another tired take-off on the "Mary Magdalene, wife of Christ and mother of his children" theme) and a newfound belief in the terrible wrath of God. Associates: Gwyn; Thomas; Matilda; Lucille; Mary; Bran, his noble steed, who dies on the tourney field; his new horse, Odin, a black stallion; Gabriel; Ralph; Richard; Nesta; Archdeacon John. Historical Figure: Hubert Walter.

5. *The Tinner's Corpse.* London: Simon & Schuster, 2001, 352 p.

DEVON, ENGLAND, APRIL 1195. When Crowner John is summoned to the bleak Devonshire moors to investigate the murder of a tinner, he discovers that the victim works for Devon's most powerful and successful mine owner, Walter Knapman. One possible motive for the crime may be an effort to sabotage Knapman's business. But the tinners have their own laws, and they are not pleased at John's interference in their affairs. In the midst of the turmoil Walter Knapman turns up missing. A decapitated body, a missing tinner, a disgruntled band of miners, and a mad Saxon intent on destroying all things "Norman" are just a few of the issues the Exeter coroner must sort out. In the meanwhile, he is forced to deal with a few personal issues: his wife is threatening to leave him, his mistress has spurned him for a younger man, and his clerk is in the grip of a suicidal depression. Then Gwyn, John's indispensable "right-hand man," is arrested for murder and put on trial for his life! Crowner John must put other matters aside in order to solve the murder and save his friend. Associates: Gwyn; Thomas; Matilda; Lucille; Richard; Mary; Nesta; Edwin; Gabriel; Odin; Brutus, his hound; Archdeacon John. Historical Figures: British King Richard I; Hubert Walter.

6. *The Grim Reaper.* London: Simon & Schuster, 2002, 336 p.

EXETER, ENGLAND, MAY 1195. Sir John de Wolfe is faced with a strange series of serial murders, which begins with the strangulation of Aaron of Salisbury, a Jewish moneylender, and proceeds through the killing of a London harlot, a dissolute priest, and a burgess suspected of abusing young boys. The common factor is an appropriate biblical text left at each murder scene, the mode of which reflects the alleged sin of the victim. The murderer is obviously literate and knows his Bible, which, in an age where only a small percentage of the population can read or write, suggests a priest. There are at least twenty-five parish churches in Exeter, however, and the killer could be any one of more than 100 members of the various religious communities. Crowner John sets about to discover the identity of the homicidal maniac. Associates: Gwyn; Thomas; Matilda; Lucille; Richard; Mary; Nesta; Edwin; Gabriel; Ralph; Brutus, the hound.

7. *Fear in the Forest.* London: Simon & Schuster, 2003, 364 p.

EXETER, ENGLAND, JUNE 1195. Much of the Devonshire countryside lies under the iron rule of the Royal Forest, which is reserved exclusively to the hunting rights of the King. The penalty for killing a deer on the King's land is mutilation and death. These harsh laws are rigorously upheld by the King's foresters, a group notorious for their savagery and corruption. One summer's day, a tall, brown mare gallops into the sleepy village of Sigford, dragging a dead man by its stirrup, the broken shaft of an arrow protruding from his back. The badge on the dead man's tunic identifies him as a senior officer of the Royal Forest service. Plenty of money remains in the victim's purse, indicating that robbery was not a motive. When a second forester is violently attacked, Crowner John begins to suspect some sort of conspiracy is afoot. And why is his unscrupulous brother-in-law, Sheriff Richard de Revelle, taking such an interest in the case? At the end of the book, Nesta miscarries a child that John believes is his; Matilda knows the truth, however, but fails to inform her husband. Associates: Gwyn; Thomas; Matilda; Richard; Nesta; Edwin; Odin.

8. *The Witch Hunter.* London: Simon & Schuster, 2004, 320 p.

EXETER, ENGLAND, 1195. When a prominent mill-owner and guild-master falls dead across his horse, Crowner John declines to hold an inquest: the man had been severely overweight, had been complaining of chest pains, and showed no visible signs of injury. This is a clear-cut case of death from natural causes. Events take a sinister turn, however, when a "straw-dolly" is discovered hidden under the man's saddle, with a spike driven through its little heart. The victim's strident wife declares that her husband's death must have resulted from an evil spell cast at the behest of a rival mill-owner who wants to acquire the dead man's business. Enlisting the help of her cousin, Gilbert de Bosco, a cathedral canon with ambitions for ecclesiastical advancement, the widow begins a campaign in the name of the Church against witchcraft and the so-called cunning women who practice it. The ill-will escalates until Exeter is divided into two seething camps, and a climate of fear predominates. Still the coroner refuses to be dragged into the fray, until his own beloved mistress is accused of witchcraft! Can Crowner John unearth the real culprit behind the killing and save Nesta from the hangman's noose? Associate: Nesta.

LAWRENCE, Margaret K. (1945–). American.

Scene of the Crime: Maine, beginning in 1786; however, the events in *The Iceweaver* take place in New York in 1809.

Detective: Lucy Hannah Trevor turned thirty-eight in February 1786, the same month in which she received confirmation that her husband, James Trevor, had died of a fever in Québec. He had fled, abandoning her, when the townspeople began turning on British Loyalists. While the law had kept Hannah tied to her husband up until his flight, she had emotionally and spiritually left him long ago, when his selfishness cost the lives of their children. When her children died, Hannah began casting off society's conventions, striving simply to become herself and to hold some small kernel of her own integrity safe against the world. She feels constantly divided and battered, and when James leaves her, she rejoices and resolves to have another child, one that will be wholly hers and that no one can prevent her from protecting. She chooses Daniel Jossclyn to father the girl; one of his attractions is that he warns her at the outset that he is already married and so cannot wed again. Hannah gives birth to her adored daughter Jennet, who is born deaf, ten months after James leaves Rufford. She does not respond to gossips who claim that her daughter is illegitimate; she acts as she thinks appropriate, which at times involves standing against the powerful; and she wears her hair short and without a cap. (This last act has angered the neighboring women out of all proportion.) Hannah works with her Aunt Julia as a midwife, having taken over much of Julia's practice. They are the most sought-after midwives in the township, both for their abilities and for their disinclination to gossip.

Known Associates: Rufford is a relatively small place, and many characters appear in more than one book. The most prominent of the recurring characters are Jennet, Hannah's dearly beloved deaf daughter, who is mute through the Hannah Trevor stories but who finds her voice in *The Iceweaver*; Daniel Jossclyn, Jennet's father; Charlotte Jossclyn, Daniel's invalid wife, who was maimed by the ineptitude of Dr. Clinch years before the action in the books and who dies in *Blood Red Roses*. Other characters in the Hannah Trevor books include the Jossclyns' servants, John English and Arabella Twig; Hannah's Aunt Julia and Uncle Henry Markham; their youngest son, Jonathan; and Jonathan's wife, Sally. Their neighbors include Hamilton Siwall and his family (including his gossiping cook Mistress Kemp), and the barber surgeon Samuel Clinch.

Premise: A midwife solves crimes in eighteenth-century America.

Comment: In the six years since Hannah took over most of her Aunt's practice, she has helped bring 100 babies into the world and has lost only six; all of the mothers have survived. This is credited to her ability to piece together the information given her by the expectant mothers, her knowledge of herbal and other remedies, her study of anatomy, and her standards of cleanliness. Her work as a midwife extends to helping sick women and children; she has an entrée into the secret stifled world of those who have no power. She knows more than the idle gossips know of the scandals of Rufford and the follies and cruelties of its inhabitants. The qualities that make her an excellent midwife, along with her knowledge of the people of the township and allied with the unflinching honesty she brings to everything she views, make her a formidable detective. In the first novel, *Hearts and Bones*, she is present when a young woman's corpse is discovered and is able to read the note the woman left. Her concerns for the men accused of the crime cause her to take an active interest in the case. The books take place in the aftermath of the Revolutionary War; every person present has experienced the bloody viciousness that has been spread through the actions of "non-combatants" who set upon neighbors with suspect political views. When testimony is gleaned from average townspeople, their thoughts and emotions are still fully engaged in the conflict. Everyone has been wounded, if not physically, then emotionally and spiritually. Some wounds heal and some fester, some men and women come back to being themselves and find ways to live, maimed as they are; others are forever broken, overwhelmed at times with fear and a rage that may turn either inward or outward. The books take place at the beginning of Shay's Rebellion, so in some ways they bridge the two conflicts. The people of Rufford Township fought in the War for Independence with the belief that, if they won, they would gain freedom and would be able to earn their prosperity through hard work. By 1786 that hope has diminished. Poor men are taken advantage of by the wealthy, with loans offered at uxorious rates and records of repayment conveniently lost. Men work as hard as they are able and still find themselves in debtor's prison. The citizens gain the conviction that there are two sets of laws applied, one for the rich and another for the poor, and that they threw off the British only to be treated as chattel by their more prosperous countrymen. In *Hearts and Bones* a few of the disaffected are seen; in *Blood Red Roses* some of the main characters are found to be involved in the clandestine vigilante movement called the "Regulators"; in *The Burning Bride* the rebellion breaks out into the open.

Literary Crimes & Chimes: The Hannah Trevor books all begin with the thoughts of the killer, sometimes utterly mad thoughts that mix insane beliefs with reality. We see the killer at the moment when he or she breaks down and steps outside civilization. The books are beautifully written, filled with graceful language and interesting imagery. The theme of waste—wasted objects, wasted lives, wasted chances—and the theme of birth—its dangers and its inherent hope—work well to convey the harm and the possibilities in the beginning years of our nation. The waste left over from the war, the way in which men and women are used for profit or pleasure by the unscrupulous survivors, highlights the ways in which the maimed prevail and the ways in which they do not. Waste is fought in small positive actions taken by many of the people in the stories, including the making of quilts, where what is damaged is discarded, but what is still strong is used and can be pieced together with other bits to make a valuable and useful whole. The structure of each of the first three books is like a quilt itself, with bits of Hannah's diary, recipes, instruction on housewifery chores, letters, autopsy reports, transcripts from constable's interviews, trial transcripts, drawings of quilt blocks, and embroidery designs being patched together in a pleasing pattern to make an arresting whole. Another theme, that of the dangers and possibilities inherent in birth, is seen partly through the actions of Dr. Clinch, an incompetent surgeon, so sure of his own superiority that he cannot learn anything new. In what should have been the birth of Daniel and Charlotte Jossclyn's son, Clinch, not knowing how to turn the baby, accidentally dismembers it, killing the child and maiming the mother. This is mirrored in the actions taken at the birth of our nation, where entrenched incompetence maims freedom, and the danger that the budding country will die a-borning is very real. *The Iceweaver* stands apart from the other books, opening with the end of Hannah's story, and continuing with her daughter

Jennet's. This novel shines with the hopes of reclamation and redemption. Unusually, the book is written in the present tense, which gives the prose a strange immediacy.

THE CASES

1. ***Hearts and Bones.*** New York: Avon Books, 1996, 307 p.

RUFFORD TOWNSHIP, MAINE, FEBRUARY 1786. Nan Emory's chimney is not smoking, even though the winter is fierce, and Hannah hastens to bring some live coals to the young mother. She finds Nan's strangled corpse, along with a letter that the supposedly illiterate Nan left, accusing three men of the township of brutalizing and raping her. One of the accused men is Jennet's father, Daniel; partly on his behalf Hannah investigates this vicious crime, which has roots in the bloody past. Associates: Josh Lamb; Will Quaid; Daniel.

2. **"The Cat-Whipper's Apprentice,"** in *Murder They Wrote*, ed. by Martin H. Greenberg and Elizabeth Foxwell. New York: Boulevard Books, 1997, p. 241–264.

MAINE, JUNE 1786. Winnie Sprodge was beaten until she miscarried; her bully of a husband continues to beat her and anyone else within range, and it is generally believed that Winnie's only possible escape is death. But the death, when it comes, is of Winnie's husband, Gaffer Sprodge, and there is no shortage of suspects. Hannah feels that every motive is so reasonable that charging anyone with a crime would be most unjust! Associates: Martin Vise; Philemon Tucket; Josh Lamb.

3. ***Blood Red Roses.*** New York: Avon Books, 1997, 353 p.

RUFFORD TOWNSHIP, MAINE, JULY 1786. The Orphanmaster's Court summons Hannah, proposing to sell Jennet as an indentured servant if her widowed mother cannot prove that she is able to support her daughter. Hannah is fighting to keep Jennet, even contemplating remarriage, when a man who is new to the area is found dead. When the body is recognized as that of Hannah's missing husband, James Trevor, the midwife is suspected of murdering the spouse that she'd been convinced was already dead. Associates: Lady Sibylla; Andrew Tyrrell; James; Jennet.

4. ***The Burning Bride.*** New York: Avon Twilight, 1998, 387 p.

RUFFORD TOWNSHIP, MAINE, NOVEMBER 1786. Hannah moves with some trepidation towards a December marriage. The farmers and tradesmen are up in arms over laws that seem designed to beggar them, literally up in arms, taking a stand in a rebellion that will leave many of them branded traitors. In all of this Dr. Clinch is found dead; it was no secret that he and Hannah hated each other. Associates: Susannah Penny; Josh Lamb; Dr. Clinch.

5. *The Iceweaver.* New York: William Morrow, 2000, 403 p.

New Forge, New York, 1809. John Frayne returns to New York to reclaim property confiscated from his father. As he works to rebuild his estate, young Jennet, who was captured and offered for sale as an indentured servant, works with him. A jealous man, Herod Aldrich, plots to destroy them as Frayne makes his third attempt to build a family. Associates: Gabriel Hines; Marius Leclerc; Herod Aldrich; Jennet.

LINSCOTT, Gillian (1944–). British.

Nell Bray Series

Scene of the Crime: London, England, and elsewhere in Europe, beginning in 1910.

Detective: Nell Bray, born in Liverpool, England, in 1877.

Known Associates: Nell's brother, Stuart, three years her senior; her mother, Ida; various workers in the suffragette movement, including real-life suffragette Emmeline Pankhurst; Simon Frater (from *Crown Witness*).

Premise: A suffragette works to solve crimes and to implement the right of women to vote in early-twentieth-century Britain.

Comment: The death of her father, a radical eccentric, when she was seventeen, has sent Nell and her mother wandering the world in gentle impoverishment. When her mother eventually marries a German professor, Nell is free at last to continue her education at Oxford. She becomes a suffragette, convinced that success of the movement is necessary before she can advance her own career or personal ambitions. Nell herself states: "When I was growing up, we'd always assumed that by the time I reached voting age, the suffrage would have been extended to women. When it became obvious that this was not going to happen I knew that any career or personal ambitions must give way to this struggle. I set myself up as a freelance translator to get enough money to live on and joined the most militant and effective of the groups fighting for the Vote, the Women's Social and Political Union, soon after it was founded by Mrs. Emmeline Pankhurst in 1903." In the course of her activities both in the women's movement and as a translator, Nell finds herself frequently called upon to assist in the investigation of various crimes and misdemeanors.

Literary Crimes & Chimes: The odd way in which the series has been written and published makes it difficult for the average reader just coming into these books to make sense of them. A number of the books, including the first one published, have only vague dates attached to them. Since Nell experiences a progression of changes in her personal life, as well as in her attempt to secure voting rights for women (and simultaneously to solve whatever murders come her way!), the reader cares about such details and may find the release of novels "out of order" to be somewhat jarring. The best book in the series is also the final one chronologically—*Absent Friends*—which focuses both on the winding down of the war and the fulfillment of Nell's personal and professional dreams.

THE CASES

1. *Dead Man Riding*. London: Virago, 2002, 314 p.

LONDON; LAKE DISTRICT, ENGLAND, SUMMER 1900. After three years of traipsing across Europe with her lovesick widowed mother, Nell Bray has finally found her way to Oxford University. There she has befriended the beautiful Imogene and the charming Midge. When the three girls decide to accept an invitation by their male classmates to join a summer reading party in the country during vacation, accompanied by a dashing philosophy don with a reputation for stirring up trouble, they go against what is quickly becoming the obsolete conventions of the nineteenth century. Intellectual pursuits become secondary, however, when the group is greeted by the unpleasant fact that their host has been accused of murdering a local boy, a magistrate's son, who has gone missing. Rather than return home, however, the six students and their mentor decide to put down their books and put their intellectual prowess to the test by solving the mystery. Doubting the man's guilt, Nell begins her inquiries. But things take a more desperate turn when a silver stallion named Sid comes galloping out of the mist with yet another dead man on its back! The answers to the mystery are shocking, and what began as an idyllic summer vacation ends up as an unsettling loss of innocence. The novel takes place in the first summer of the twentieth century and the last summer of Queen Victoria's reign. Associates: Nell's friends and classmates, Imogene, Midge, Alan, Kit and Nathan; Alan's uncle, the "Old Man"; Michael Meredith, an Oxford don and the group's mentor.

2. *Sister beneath the Sheet*. London: Macdonald, 1991, 224 p.

BIARRITZ, FRANCE, AND LONDON, ENGLAND, APRIL 1909. It's springtime in Biarritz and playtime for Edwardian society. But that fast and fashionable world is suddenly shaken by the death of a high-class prostitute and by the extraordinary contents of her will. Topaz Brown, hostess to royalty, rakes, and roues, has left her considerable fortune to the suffragette movement. Nell Bray, committed suffragette but no stranger to society, is sent to Biarritz by Emmeline Pankhurst with instructions to claim the money, while keeping its embarrassing source obscure. But on arrival she becomes embroiled in a mystery surrounding Topaz's death. Did she commit suicide, or was she murdered? Nell finds herself cast in the role of detective, an ironic occupation for someone who has just come out of Holloway Prison after serving time for throwing a brick through the window of No. 10 Downing Street! Determined to discover the truth, Nell pursues her investigations through the tawdry slums and the elegant boulevards of Biarritz, encountering a circus, an indiscreet doctor and an exotic *soirée* at the villa of Topaz's rival. But all the while her task is hampered by antics of fellow suffragette Bobbie Fieldfare, who is bent on a mission of her own. With a gun in her traveling bag, Bobbie is stalking David Chester, Member of Parliament (MP), barrister and suffragette-hater, who was instrumental in Nell's recent incarceration. Associates: Roberta "Bobbie" Fieldfare, a fellow suffragette; Tansy Mills, Topaz Brown's maid; Jules Estevan, Topaz's friend; Rose. Historical Figure: Emmeline Pankhurst.

3. *Stage Fright.* London: Little, Brown, 1993, 188 p.

London, England, November, 1909. Although she has spent two terms in Holloway Prison for her suffragette activities, it is amateur sleuthing that is gaining Nell Bray a reputation. She has already solved two murders, and tales of her success are spreading throughout London, even reaching the ears of none other than George Bernard Shaw. The formidable playwright approaches Nell with a case: his leading lady is in danger, and Shaw wants to ensure that she makes it safely to curtain time. For his new play, *Cinderella Revisited*, Shaw has reworked a classic drama into a scathing attack on English marital law. The plot bears more than a passing resemblance to the life of its star, Bella Flanagan. Like her character, however, Bella is trapped in a loveless marriage to a man interested only in her money. It seems that her husband, Lord Penwardine, is no more willing to allow his wife to tread the stage than to give her any other freedom. Threats and sabotage have followed the actress throughout the rehearsals. With Nell's help, the play does finally open, but hardly without a hitch. Penwardine's cronies are out in full force, heckling, rioting, doing just about anything to get the production stopped. But would a hateful husband resort to murder? Someone does, and its up to Nell Bray to find the answer. Associate: Bella Flanagan, actress. Historical Figure: George Bernard Shaw.

4. *Widow's Peak.* London: Little, Brown, 1994, 210 p. As: ***An Easy Day for a Lady.*** New York: St. Martin's Press, 1995, 210 p.

London, England, and Chamonix, French Alps, July 1910. "An easy day for a lady" is a phrase well known to suffragette Nell Bray. The saying, notorious among mountain climbers, denotes something so effortless that it's hardly worth attempting. Where Nell is concerned, however, things are rarely that simple, and her unexpected visit to the French Alps proves to be no exception. An outraged Nell heads off to Chamonix after Britain's House of Commons smothers the bill that would at last have given women the vote. She's hoping that a climbing holiday will clear her head and calm the temper that once landed her in prison. Chamonix is a popular rendezvous for adventurous young Englishmen sampling the pleasure of a little light mountaineering in the shadows of Mont Blanc, while their womenfolk peruse the cafés and boutiques of the blossoming tourist town. For Nell it is an opportunity to rekindle old climbing skills, venturing above the snowline into the wilder regions of *bergschrund* and glacier and hitching up her skirts to cross treacherous crevasses on rickety wooden ladders. But such relaxing and restful pursuits are not to be hers: during one such excusion the feisty Nell chances upon a curious scene, a French rescue team chipping away at the glacier in order to remove a corpse, frozen solid in the mountain's chilly embrace. The inexorable, but painfully slow, descent of the glacier down the valley means that the body of Arthur Mordiford, missing and presumed dead since 1880, is only now being offered up by the mountain for burial; it is an apparently neat, if a little tardy, solution to a thirty-year-old mystery. However, Arthur's death may not have been as straightforward as the evidence seems to suggest, as the bilingual Nell begins to realize when she agrees to act as an interpreter for his family, recently arrived in Chamonix, and to help arrange for the body's return to England. Her suspicions mount as she witnesses the family's increasingly strange behavior. Why is Arthur's brother, Gregory, who was present the day he died, so keen to have the body taken home?—keen, that is, until he is mysteriously poisoned! And just what is the role of Madame Martin, the widow of a guide who perished with Arthur? The mountain maintains its impassive silence, so the resourceful Nell, flying as ever in the face of convention, decides to put more than her language skills into play. As the story unfolds, her powers of detection are tested to the limit. Associates: Pierre Martin, a French guide whose father was killed at the same time as Mordiford; "Easyday," a recluse rumored to be the black sheep of an English family—Nell becomes friendly with her and discovers she is actually Daisy Belford, Arthur's *fiancée*, who is reputed to have gone mad after his death; Bismarck, Daisy's faithful companion dog; Antoine Bregoli, an old guide who may remember something of the tragedy.

5. *Crown Witness.* London: Little, Brown, 1995, 218 p.

LONDON, ENGLAND, JUNE 1910. Detective Nell Bray once again finds herself in the midst of a mystery, as she and her fellow suffragettes organize a procession. The movement has decided to take advantage of the cheery atmosphere surrounding King George V's coronation to promote their cause with a peaceful five-mile-long march culminating in a rally at the Royal Albert Hall. Still, suffragette leaders have heard rumors about possible disruptions by protesters, so Nell is asked to keep watch for trouble. Since she is more than happy to avoid the pomp and circumstance of dressing for the procession, Nell accepts the job. All goes well until Nell spots an unusual float at the tail end of the procession. As she and her hapless friend Simon Frater move in to investigate, a fire breaks out on the float, confusion follows, and a shot is heard. When the crowd clears, Simon is left holding the gun and examining the body of the victim as the real suspects escape. The police arrive on the scene and ignore Nell's cries to follow the escaping criminals. Instead, they arrest Simon for murder and take Nell in, once again, for obstructing justice. Sentenced to thirty days in jail, Nell begins to piece together clues to prove Simon's innocence. But as Nell comes to learn the contents of the float and the identity of the murdered victim, her motive for discovering the truth takes on political as well as personal significance. Associates: Simon; "General" Flora Drummond, Mrs. Pankhurst's assistant; Inspecter Merit of Scotland Yard; Mr. Brust, Merit's assistant; Violet White, who is imprisoned at Holloway with Nell; Misery Minnie, warder at Holloway; Max Blume, journalist. Historical Figure: Emmeline Pankhurst.

6. *Dead Man's Music.* London: Little, Brown, 1996, 246 p. As: *Dead Man's Sweetheart.* New York: St. Martin's Press, 1996, 246 p.

PENNINE MOORS, AND LONDON, ENGLAND, 1913. Nell Bray is spending a few weeks with her brother's family in the Pennine Moors. A mystery surrounds the slaying of Osbert Newbiggin, squire of neighboring Crowberry Hall, a musical expert and pillar of the community. Davie Kendal, the dead man's protégé, has been tried, found guilty, and is currently languishing in jail awaiting the death sentence. Davie's barrister, Bill Musgrave, believes in his innocence, and Nell is quickly recruited to the cause. As she delves more deeply into the mystery, she discovers that the lives of both the dead man and his alleged killer were more complicated than they seem on the surface. Time is running out, and Davie soon will be executed, unless Nell can find incontrovertible proof of his innocence. Associates: Stuart; Pauline, his wife; Simon; Rose Mills, a *protégée* of Nell's; Tansy Mills, her sister, another protégé, of Nell's; Bill Musgrave, a criminal lawyer; Jimmy Kendal, Davie's brother. Historical Figures: Emmeline Pankhurst; Christabel Pankhurst, her daughter.

7. *Dance on Blood.* London: Virago, 1998, 250 p.

LONDON, ENGLAND, FEBRUARY–APRIL 1913. Nell Bray and her suffragettes would do almost anything to get the vote, but planting a bomb in a house belonging to David Lloyd George, Chancellor of the Exchequer, is where she draws the line. Her foolhardy friend, Bobbie, goes ahead with the mad scheme, their leader, Mrs. Pankhurst, takes the blame for it, and Nell inadvertently becomes a prime suspect in the ill-conceived plot. But Nell is even more horrified when a sinister Lloyd George gleefully offers her a deal she can't refuse: he will drop all charges against Nell if she agrees to recover some politically embarrassing letters from an infamous dancer! What's more, he just might take up the suffragette cause in Parliament. Nell is in no position to refuse the bizarre request. To make matters worse, it is now obvious that there is a mole within the movement, and Nell must uncover the spy's identity before he or she strikes again. An old unsolved murder, set up to resemble suicide, is the key to Nell's dilemma. Associates: Roberta "Bobbie" Fieldfair, a suffragette whose methods Nell opposes; June Price, Bobbie's naïve young *protégée*; Inspector Merit; Nell's old friend, journalist Max Blum. Historical Figures: David Lloyd George; Emmeline Pankhurst.

8. *The Perfect Daughter.* London: Virago, 2000, 308 p.

LONDON, ENGLAND, SUMMER 1914. In her family's eyes, naval officer's daughter Verona North was the perfect daughter—talented, brave, and attractive. But within a few months after leaving home to study art in London, she is found hanging in the family boathouse in Devon, an apparent suicide. Rumor has it that Verona had plunged rapidly from respectability into left-wing politics and a world of drugs and depravity. Her father, Ben, has no doubt who is to blame for all this: his cousin, the suffragette Nell Bray. Nell is certain she's not responsible, yet her sense of guilt at not paying closer attention to the young girl sets her on a trail to discover what really happened in the weeks leading up to Verona's death. Nell's search takes her from an enclave of Bohemian anarchists in Chelsea to an old run-down shop full of mysterious sea charts and maps. Piecing together clues, Nell soon discovers that Verona was leading a double life full of dangerous secrets in a world headed for war, and some of them involved people who couldn't let the girl's life—or Nell's either—stand in their way. Associates: Bill Musgrave; Commodore Benjamin "Ben" North and his wife, Alexandra, Verona's parents and Nell's cousins.

9. *Hanging on the Wire.* London: Little, Brown, 1992, 215 p.

LONDON, AND NANTGARREW MILITARY HOSPITAL, ENGLAND, JUNE 1917. Nell has unearthed the truth behind the mysterious death of one of France's most notorious courtesans. Now comes a plea from her old friend, Jenny Chesney. World War I is at its height, and Jenny is hard at work at Nantgarrew Military Hospital, surrounded by barbed wire, where Freudian analysis is a specialty. Her efforts are complicated by Mrs. Monica Minter, who is determined to express her disapproval of Freud's theories through petty acts of sabotage. But would Mrs. Minter resort to a potshot at one of the patients? It seems unlikely, but someone did. Nell holds no truck with either Dr. Freud or Mrs. Minter; neither does she approve of war, but attempted murder is another matter. So she heads for Nantgarrew, where she finds that mysterious behavior is a way of life. Mrs. Minter swoops down like lightning, bent on thwarting her schemes. Meanwhile, one poor soldier keeps a box of grenades and revolvers under his bed. Another is determined to reach Moscow by bicycle. And the doctors in charge are far less interested in these bizarre goings-on than in their patients' dreams. Nell's bafflement turns to horror when the would-be assassin finally aims true. Nantgarrew, devoted to healing, becomes the site of a murder, and Nell Bray, indomitable and irrepressible, is determined to solve it. Associates: Jenny Chesney, Nell's friend and a volunteer at Nantgarrew Military Hospital; Lieutenant David Ellrad, an old friend of Nell's who is also an inmate at Nantgarrew; Sergeant Jack Kelso, another inmate; Brigadier Moss, who is investigating irregularities at Nantgarrew. Historical Figure: Dr. Sigmund Freud (offstage).

10. *Blood on the Wood.* London: Virago, 2003, 311 p.

LONDON, ENGLAND, 1918. Nell Bray is dispatched to collect a valuable painting that had been left to the suffragette movement by Philomena Venn. The family of the dead woman reluctantly hand it over, but when Nell delivers it to Christie's for an evaluation, it turns out to be a fake. Shamefacedly, Philomena's husband admits to the deception but refuses to produce the genuine article. Against her better judgment, Nell agrees to attempt to liberate the painting, only to find herself caught red-handed with a corpse!

11. *Absent Friends.* London: Virago, 1999, 282 p.

LONDON, ENGLAND, NOVEMBER 1918. The Vote has been won at long last, the Great War is over, and suffragette Nell Bray is standing as a candidate in the first general election in which women will be allowed to vote. Everything seems to be falling into place for the dedicated activist. Yet, with just a month to go to the first general election, Nell is still without party backing, writing desperately to friends and contacts to drum up support for her cause. Further, the former Conservative candidate has been blown to bits at a fireworks party held to celebrate the Armistice, just before the campaign is set to open! His widow is now certain that her deceased husband is sending her messages through a haunted piano, and at least one person in the constituency has a murderous hatred of all politicians. To add to Nell's dismay, two men from her rather checkered past have just come home from the war. Nell finds herself in the midst of a baffling case, with the odds most definitely against her—both for election victory and survival. She must quickly find the killer while not losing her concentration on the rural constituency, which seems intent on throwing everything it can at her. Associates: Captain Musgrave, now home from the war; David Ellward, another old acquaintance and a rival with Bill for Nell's affections; Rose Mills Kendal, Nell's friend; her husband, Jimmy Kendal; Lucinda Sollers, who asks for

Nell's help. Historical Figures: Emmeline and Christabel Pankhurst; Prime Minister David Lloyd George.

MAUD STRETTON AND CECILIA BRIGHT SERIES

Scene of the Crime: London, England, in 1874.

Detective: Maud Stretton and Cecilia Bright.

Known Associates: Peter Pentland.

Premise: Two British women investigate a crime in nineteenth-century London.

Comment: Fashionable London is flocking to pay its last respects to the late Doctor Livingstone. Africa, with many of its riches and mysteries still unexplored, holds a potent magic, and feelings run high. Two women, strong-minded Maud Stretton and beautiful Cecilia Bright, meet and quarrel over Livingston's coffin as their husbands prepare to lead rival expeditions back to Africa. Reputations are at stake, in a world where reputation means more than life itself. But when death strikes, it takes an unexpected form, not in Africa but on a rainy night in a Westminster mission hall. The victim, a notorious coward and disgraced explorer, had claimed to know something that would convict one of the rival expedition leaders of behavior unbecoming an English gentleman. He dies on a public platform, seconds away from uttering his secret. The inquest jury's verdict is murder, and the poison that killed him came from Africa. Gossip, then worse than gossip, threatens Maud, Cecilia, and all around them. One man, Peter Pentland, has a particular reason for wanting to discover the truth: he promised both Stretton and Bright that he would look after their wives. That promise keeps him limping along more dangerous paths than anything to be encountered in Africa. Linscott vividly re-creates London and Africa at the height of Queen Victoria's empire.

Literary Crimes & Chimes: Linscott has a talent for creating convincing scenarios and equally convincing characters, particularly women. The constraints of Victorian society are evident everywhere, but the strong-minded ladies featured in this book let nothing stand in the their way in solving the murder. Great entertainment and great fun.

THE CASE

1. *Murder, I Presume.* London: Macmillan, 1990, 219 p.
   LONDON, ENGLAND, AND AFRICA, 1874. See commentary in this series.

LOVESEY, Peter (1936–). British.

<u>SERGEANT CRIBB SERIES</u>

Scene of the Crime: London, England, beginning in late 1879 and continuing into 1889.

Detective: Sergeant Wally Cribb, a member of the recently formed Detective Branch of the London Police Force. He is tall and thin, with bushy eyebrows, somewhere in his mid-forties when the series starts.

Known Associates: Constable Edward Thackeray, Cribb's assistant, a rotund man with a large, bushy beard, perhaps ten years junior to Cribb; Scotland Yard Detective-Inspector Jowett, Cribb's superior.

Premise: The London Police Force investigates crimes during the late Victoria era in Great Britain.

Comment: Lovesey's first novel, *Wobble to Death*, won a prize in a detective story contest, thereby inaugurating both the author's career and this eight-book sequence. The settings seem very authentic, with each entry in the series focusing on a pastime peculiar to the period. These books are framed as traditional British puzzlers. The murderers and their victims are presented without the psychodramatics typical of, say, the Anne Perry stories, which focus on the hypocrisy inherent in Victorian high society. The series is notable for having been among the first historical mysteries to be filmed for television, thereby vastly helping to popularize the subgenre.

Literary Crimes & Chimes: We never find out much about the workings of the London Police Force, or learn anything personal about either Cribb or Thackeray. Indeed, at one point Cribb remarks that he has never even met Thackeray outside of the job, and has no idea, really, of the kind of person he is or of what he does in his leisure time. Jowett makes no more than perfunctory appearances in most of the books. Hence, Lovesey's chief characters remain no more than ciphers in our minds, and the stories maintain interest only so long as each mystery remains unsolved. Perhaps this is why the series ended after only eight volumes: not even the author himself could sustain his attention.

THE CASES

1. *Wobble to Death.* London: Macmillan, 1970, 190 p.
LONDON, ENGLAND, NOVEMBER 1879. A six-day marathon race, a so-called wobble, turns deadly when one of the contestants drops dead of strychnine poisoning. Cribb and Thackeray must investigate the promoters

of the race, the dead man's widow and his trainer, and the other racers to determine who had the most to gain and the most to lose! Associate: Thackeray.

2. *The Detective Wore Silk Drawers.* London: Macmillan, 1971, 187 p.

LONDON, ENGLAND, JULY 1880. The illegal sport of bare-fist boxing is the focus of the second novel in the series, when the decapitated body of a well-known pugilist is found floating in the Thames. Constable Jago, the police boxing champion, is ordered by Cribb to infiltrate the underground sporting and gambling world. Associates: Thackeray; Jowett; Constable Jago.

3. *Abracadaver.* London: Macmillan, 1972, 220 p.

LONDON, ENGLAND, OCTOBER 1881. A series of bizarre jokes and puzzling public humiliations are afflicting the denizens of the London music halls. The police are drawn into the affray when a performer is murdered onstage during the midst of her disappearing act. Associates: Thackeray; Jowett.

4. *Mad Hatter's Holiday: A Novel of Murder in Victorian Brighton.* London: Macmillan, 1973, 192 p.

BRIGHTON, ENGLAND, SEPTEMBER 1882. A voyeur at Brighton Beach becomes involved with the beautiful wife of a doctor and then is drawn into a gruesome murder case when dissected body parts are discovered. The local authorities are so baffled by the events that they call in Scotland Yard detectives Cribb and Thackeray, who quickly solve the crime. Associate: Thackeray.

5. *Invitation to a Dynamite Party.* London: Macmillan, 1974, 188 p. As: *The Tick of Death.* New York: Dodd, Mead, 1974, 188 p.

LONDON, ENGLAND, MAY 1884. London is rocked by a series of anarchist bombings, and Cribb is ordered by Jowett to attend a class in bomb-making and dismantling. But when the detective is abducted by one of the Irish terrorists, he suddenly finds himself right in the midst of the Dynamite Party! Associates: Thackeray; Jowett.

6. *A Case of Spirits.* London: Macmillan, 1975, 160 p.

LONDON, ENGLAND, NOVEMBER 1885. Victorian spiritualists and spiritualism are the focus of this new book in the Sergeant Cribb series. When a medium is electrocuted during a séance, the detective must uncover the mystery from the Other Side and debunk the thought of otherworldly intervention. Associates: Thackeray; Jowett.

7. *Waxwork.* London: Macmillan, 1978, 239 p.

LONDON, ENGLAND, JUNE 1888. Madame Tussaud's "Chamber of Horrors" forms the centerpiece of the final mystery written in the series. The desire to include accurate representations of the world's most heinous murderers intersects with an actual murder case that Cribb is investigating.

Thackeray is completely absent from this book, while Jowett has now been promoted to Chief Inspector at Scotland Yard. Associate: Jowett.

8. *Swing, Swing Together.* London: Macmillan, 1976, 190 p.

LONDON AND THE THAMES RIVER, ENGLAND, SUMMER 1889. Several British schoolgirls discover a body while swimming nude in the River Thames. Meanwhile, Cribb and Thackeray must undertake a reenactment of Jerome K. Jerome's book *Three Men in a Boat*, after discovering that the chief suspects in the case have been following the very same route as that described in the bestseller. Associate: Thackeray.

BERTIE (PRINCE OF WALES) SERIES

Scene of the Crime: England, beginning in 1886 (however, the short story, "Bertie and the Boat Race," retrospectively tells the story of the Prince's days at Oxford).

Detective: Bertie, the nickname of Albert Edward, Prince of Wales, later King Edward VII of Great Britain.

Known Associates: Alexandra "Alix," Princess of Wales, later Queen of England.

Premise: The Prince of Wales reinvents himself as a sometime detective and solver of murder mysteries in Victorian England.

Comment: This is pretty lightweight stuff, even for Lovesey. We see overmuch of the rather aimless social existence of the British elite but very little in the way of actual character development. The stories are told in the first person by Bertie himself, and while the voice is certainly engaging enough, the prince is no more than a piece of fluff, not to mention dull and rather stupid. Alix has far more presence than her husband, which is not saying much, but the author makes relatively little of the possibilities. The puzzles are readily discernible.

Literary Crimes & Chimes: Can anyone actually believe that, even in Victorian times, the Prince of Wales could become involved in solving murders and not have that fact reported? Ahem. I mean, *really*, old chap!

THE CASES

1. "Bertie and the Boat Race," in *Crime through Time*, ed. by Miriam Grace Monfredo and Sharan Newman. New York: Berkley Prime Crime, 1997, p. 167–182.

OXFORD, ENGLAND, SUMMER 1860. Prince Bertie solves his first mystery while studying at Oxford University.

2. **"Bertie and the Fire Brigade,"** in *Royal Crimes*, ed. by Maxim Jakubowski and Martin H. Greenberg. New York: Signet Books, 1994.

LONDON, SUMMER 1870. Young Bertie becomes involved in investigating a serial arsonist.

3. ***Bertie and the Tinman: From the Detective Memoirs of King Edward VII.*** London: The Bodley Head, 1987, 208 p.

ENGLAND, NOVEMBER 1886. When well-known jockey Fred Archer, the so-called Tinman, is found dead, apparently by his own hand, the Prince of Wales takes it upon himself to investigate. A hint of scandal over potential horse race-fixing attends Archer's passing. Then Archer's business manager is murdered, and the Prince himself is left for dead in the same attack by ruffians. As Bertie delves ever more deeply into the financial stew that Archer's death has become, he becomes ever more puzzled over what he finds.

4. ***Bertie and the Seven Bodies.*** New York: Mysterious Press, 1990, 196 p.

DESBOROUGH, BUCKINGHAMSHIRE, ENGLAND, OCTOBER 1890. Bertie is invited to a shooting party at a country estate, where he anticipates a bit of fun with the ladies and a go at the birds, spoiled only by the fact that his dear Alix chooses to accompany him. But when the guests begin dropping dead in quite unpleasant ways, Bertie must put on his thinking cap to uncover a vicious serial killer. Associate: Alix.

5. ***Bertie and the Crime of Passion.*** London: Little, Brown, 1993, 245 p.

PARIS, FRANCE, MARCH 1891. While visiting France on holiday, Bertie investigates the murder of a male dancer shot down while performing at the Moulin Rouge. The dead man, Maurice, was a friend of actress Sarah Bernhardt, one of Bertie's current interests. But when Bertie identifies a suspect, Sarah is skeptical and pushes the prince to keep the investigation active. Finally, the real culprit is uncovered, and the innocent man released by the French police. Historical Figure: Sarah Bernhardt.

MISCELLANEOUS SERIES

Scene of the Crime: England, the Atlantic Ocean, Hollywood, and others, as noted below.

Detective: Various.

Known Associates: Various.

Premise: Various.

Comment: As with the other Peter Lovesey historical detective mysteries, these two novels and story collections are certainly entertaining fictions but a bit thin in other respects. *The False Inspector Dew* is as close to a comedy as the author has yet penned in this field and one of his most successful works.

Literary Crimes & Chimes: One does not expect deep psychological revelation from a Lovesey story.

THE CASES

1. *Keystone.* London: Macmillan, 1983, 255 p.

HOLLYWOOD, CALIFORNIA, 1915. A young British vaudevillian actor, Warwick Easton, goes to Hollywood to seek his fortune in the moving pictures. Mack Sennett promptly gives him a contract and starts calling him "Keystone," after the popular silent screen comedian cops. But Warwick soon witnesses a bizarre accident that may well have been a murder, and the actor must turn his movie persona into a real-life amateur detective in order to solve a fascinating potpourri of kidnapping, theft, blackmail—and murder!

2. *The False Inspector Dew.* London: Macmillan, 1982, 251 p.

LONDON, ENGLAND, AND AT SEA ON THE S.S. *MAURETANIA* IN THE ATLANTIC OCEAN, SEPTEMBER 1921. Performer-turned-dentist Walter Baranov is convinced by his new girlfriend, Alma Webster, to do away with his shrew of a wife, Lydia, who owns in her own name his house, his business, his entire life. Lydia has been pursuing an acting career, but roles are coming more slowly now that she's thirty-four. She wants to uproot their lives and move to America, where she's convinced she'll quickly become a movie star. Walter decides to dispose of his wife on their forthcoming cruise to the States, whereupon Alma, who has stowed away, will take Lydia's place. But someone spots the body being dumped out the porthole, the ship alters course, and the victim is retrieved. Walter, who has falsely registered himself as Walter Dew, is "recognized" by one of the passengers as the famous retired Scotland Yard Detective, Inspector Dew, and he's asked by the captain to investigate the woman's murder. When Walter inspects the body, he's shocked to discover that it's not his wife, and that the woman, whoever she is, has clearly been strangled. Meanwhile, Alma successfully poses as "Mrs. Baranov" but finds herself increasingly uncomfortable with what they have done together. In the end, "Inspector Dew" solves the crime and vanishes before his imposture can be discovered. This crime comedy is as good as anything Lovesey has ever penned, being filled with ironic twists and excellent plotting.

3. *Do Not Exceed the Stated Dose.* Norfolk, VA: Crippen & Landru Publishers, 1998, 212 p.

A collection of contemporary and historical short stories (as noted). CONTENTS: "Foreword"; "Because I Was There" (contemporary); "Bertie and the Boat Race" (Prince Bertie, Oxford, 1860); "Bertie and the Fire Brigade" (Prince Bertie, London, 1870); "The Case of the Easter Bonnet" (contemporary); "Disposing of Mrs Cronk" (contemporary); "The Mighty Hunter" (contemporary); "Murder in Store" (contemporary); "Never a Cross Word" (contemporary); "The Odstock Curse" (contemporary); "A Parrot Is Forever" (contemporary); "Passion Killers" (contemporary); "The Proof of the Pudding" (England, 1946); "The Pushover" (contemporary); "Quiet Please—We're Rolling" (contemporary); "Wayzgoose" (contemporary); "Mystery Novels and Stories by Peter Lovesey: A Checklist."

4. *The Sedgemoor Strangler and Other Stories of Crime.* Norfolk, VA: Crippen & Landru Publishers, 2001, 190 p.

A second collection of contemporary and historical short stories (as noted in the following). CONTENTS: "Foreword"; "The Sedgemoor Strangler" (contemporary); "The Perfectionist" (contemporary); "Interior, with Corpse" (contemporary); "Dr Death" (England, 1873); "The Four Wise Men" (Sherlock Holmes, London, 1895); "Away with the Fairies" (Wiltshire, England, 1938); "Showmen" (London, 1860); "The Word of a Lady" (contemporary); "Star Struck" (contemporary); "The Amorous Corpse" (contemporary); "The Kiss of Death" (contemporary); "The Stalker" (contemporary); "Ape" (contemporary); "The Usual Table" (contemporary); "The Problem of Stateroom 10" (Jacques Futrelle, at sea on the S.S. *Titanic*, April 1912); "Murdering Max" (contemporary); "A Peter Lovesey Checklist."

MARSTON, Edward (pseud. of Keith Miles) (1940–). Welsh.

RALPH DELCHARD AND GERVASE BRET OR DOMESDAY BOOK SERIES

Scene of the Crime: Norman England, beginning in 1086.

Detectives: Ralph Delchard, a Hampshire soldier, whose wife Elinor had died years earlier giving birth to a stillborn son; Gervase Bret (born 1061), a lawyer from Winchester, both in the service of a traveling Domesday tribunal of British King William I, called the Conqueror (1066–1087).

Known Associates: Canon Hubert of Winchester, a Benedictine monk, spiritual adviser to the Domesday tribunal; Brother Simon, his assistant; Gervase's wife, Alys; Ralph's wife, Golde; Aelgar, Golde's younger sister; Maurice Pagnal, a former soldier and now a commissioner from Dorset, replacing Hubert; Brother Columbanus, their scribe.

Premise: Two Normans become involved with solving crimes while conducting surveys of the local population for King William I in eleventh-century England.

Comment: Set in England twenty years after the Norman Conquest during the time of William the Conqueror, each novel draws upon an actual entry in the *Domesday Book*, a massive record compiled by tribunals sent by William into all areas of the kingdom in order to assess the taxes and survey the landholdings of all of the inhabitants of England. As Ralph and Gervase travel to each town or rural area, they become involved in solving crimes that occur along the way.

Literary Crimes & Chimes: Wherever the dynamic duo goeth, murder seemeth to follow! Excepting that one issue, however, the premise for this series is more interesting than most, and the author has certainly done his research. The inherent tensions between the Saxon natives and the Norman invaders create situations in which violence is a common outcome. Ralph and Gervase try always to calm the populations, settle political and land disputes (of which murder all too frequently is a part), while doing the bidding of their ultimate master, the King. Very entertaining and true to life.

THE CASES

1. *The Wolves of Savernake: A Novel.* New York: St. Martin's Press, 1993, 242 p.

    BEDWYN, ENGLAND, SUMMER 1086. The murder of a wealthy miller beckons two of King William the Conqueror's cleverest commissioners to the town of Bedwyn. There they find a community fraught with antagonism between Normans and Saxons and rife with intrigue among rival landowners from both factions. Then a mangled body is found in the woods that border the town, the corpse being torn and ravaged as if by teeth and claws. While attempting to settle disputes, collect taxes, and negotiate the town's tangled politics, Ralph and Gervase are drawn into the hunt for a killer who may or may not be human. Associates: Hubert; Simon; Alys.

2. *The Ravens of Blackwater: A Novel.* New York: St. Martin's Press, 1994, 245 p.

    MALDON, ESSEX, ENGLAND, SUMMER 1086. The small village of Maldon is controlled by the wealthy and rapacious Hamo, Lord Fitzcorbucion of Blackwater Castle. A volatile bully, Hamo has amassed wealth and land by questionable means, intimidating the villagers into silence. When his eldest son, Guy, is found murdered, an enraged Hamo demands justice and will stop at nothing to get it. Into this charged atmosphere arrives a tribunal led by soldier Ralph Delchard and lawyer Gervase Bret. While surveying Maldon's records, the tribunal detects irregularities in various deeds and plans to call Fitzcorbucion and his family to account. With tension high between Saxon and Norman factions, Ralph and Gervase unexpectedly find some relief in the gentler company of nuns. But Guy's murder and his father's quest for revenge force the two to deal with matters far more dangerous than their original duties. Associates: Hubert; Simon; Alys.

3. *The Dragons of Archenfield: A Novel.* New York: St. Martin's Press, 1995, 242 p.

    ARCHENFIELD, HEREFORDSHIRE, ENGLAND, 1086. The frontier zone of Archenfield is a no-man's-land that acts as a bulwark between Norman-controlled English soil and the Welsh border. Soldier Ralph Delchard and lawyer Gervase Bret arrive in Herefordshire for what looks like one of their more straightforward assignments from the Crown, to settle some conflicting claims to land in Archenfield. They are shocked to discover the murder of a principal witness, a wealthy landowner who has been burned alive in his own home. No clues remain except for an enigmatic depiction of a dragon, cut into the turf in front of the house. Documents essential to settling the land claims, including the landowner's will, appear to have been destroyed in the blaze. While attempting to settle the disputed land claims, Bret and Delchard are inevitably drawn into the search for a killer who has more than riches and wealth on his mind. Their mere presence in Archenfield stirs up additional hatred and sets into motion a deadly feud between two lords who will settle for nothing less than the death of the other. Gervase is now betrothed to Alys, and Ralph meets Golde in this novel. Associates: Alys; Hubert; Simon; Golde; Aelgar.

4. *The Lions of the North: A Novel.* New York: St. Martin's Press, 1996, 227 p.

YORKSHIRE, ENGLAND, 1086. Soldier Ralph Delchard and lawyer Gervase Bret lead a group of the King's finest commissioners into the war-torn lands of Yorkshire to settle land claims and compile *The Domesday Book*, a record of the realm's holdings. The battle-scarred country reminds Delchard of his own guilt in pillaging the shire years before while putting down a revolt against the Conqueror. However, one island of wealth and luxury remains in Yorkshire: the castle of merchant Aubrey Maminot, where the commissioners learn of two great terrors: the rogue Olaf Evil Child, a hero of the conquered Saxons, and the ravenous lions Maminot keeps on his estate as pets. The lions make a feast of an anonymous young man who dares to sneak into the castle, and Gervase begins to wonder why someone would commit such a suicidal act. As he and Ralph proceed with their investigations, however, both men find themselves agreeably distracted, Gervase by Inga, a young woman embroiled in a desperate struggle for her family's land, and Ralph by his companion, Golde, a Saxon woman who prods him to do more for the dispossessed. But Ralph and Gervase must first address a more urgent secret, which threatens their lives, their loves, and perhaps the Crown itself. Associates: Canon Hubert; Brother Simon; Inga; Golde; Tanchelm of Ghent, who comes to a very bad end.

5. *The Serpents of Harbledown.* New York: St. Martin's Press, 1998, 277 p.

CANTERBURY, ENGLAND, SUMMER 1086. When seventeen-year-old Bertha is found in a holly patch, dead from a snake bite, her premature death shocks and distresses the entire town of Canterbury. On the day that Bertha's body is discovered, Norman soldier Ralph Delchard and lawyer Gervase Bret arrive in Canterbury to settle a land dispute between the Archbishop and the head of the abbey. Newly married Ralph hopes to take ad-

vantage of their stay to tour the famous cathedral and surrounding countryside with his bride, Golde, a Saxon woman. But their honeymoon is cut
short, and Delchard's investigation into the property claims is upended,
when astonishing clues demonstrate that Bertha was in fact murdered. Ultimately, Delchard and Bret must look for a force far more vicious than a
mere snake. Associates: Golde; Aelgar; Hubert; Simon.

6. *The Stallions of Woodstock.* London: Headline, 1998, 275 p.

OXFORD, OXFORDSHIRE, ENGLAND, 1086. Just outside Oxford, three
powerful Norman lords and a downtrodden Saxon watch as their most valued horses race near the forest of Woodstock. A great deal of money and
even more prestige are at stake, and the owners are all desperate to win. The
race takes a deadly turn when one of the riders is stabbed and thrown from
his steed before he can cross the finish line. In the meantime, the King's
commissioners, Ralph Delchard and Gervase Bret, are on their way to Oxford, where they have been asked to settle a land dispute. When news of the
fatal race reaches them, the case of the rider's murder takes precedence over
their more mundane task. Plenty of people stand to gain from this death,
and Ralph and Gervase must ferret out the truth in a town determined to
keep its secrets. Canon Hubert, who is "indisposed," is here replaced by the
new commissioner, Maurice Pagnal. Associates: Golde; Maurice; Columbanus, replacing Simon.

7. *The Hawks of Delamere.* London: Headline, 1998, 246 p.

CHESTER, AND WINCHESTER, ENGLAND, 1086. Shortly after leading a
hunting party into the forest of Delamere, Hugh Lupus, Earl of Chester, is
outraged when his prized hawk is killed by an arrow. Two poachers are discovered close by, and the Earl demands that they be imprisoned, but unanswered questions linger. Meanwhile, Ralph Delchard and Gervase Bret are
guests of the Earl while settling a land dispute between church and state in
nearby Winchester. They discover a well-guarded prisoner in the castle dun-
geons: the Prince of Gwynedd remains under lock and key so that Hugh
can live free from the threat of a Welsh uprising. But was the hawk actually
the intended victim, or was the killer aiming for bigger game—the Earl himself! Associates: Hubert, now well again; Simon.

8. *The Wildcats of Exeter.* London: Headline, 1999, 275 p.

EXETER, DEVONSHIRE, ENGLAND, FALL 1086. In the gathering dusk of
the Devonshire countryside, Nicholas Picard is riding home when a snarling
wildcat attacks him. Neighbors find his lacerated body in the woods, but
when they also discover a slit in his throat, it soon becomes clear that human
hands are responsible for his demise. Picard's death complicates an already
difficult land dispute that Ralph Delchard and Gervase Bret have been sent
to settle in nearby Exeter. The murdered man had a stake in the outcome

of the claims, and now his widow, Catherine, believes that she should be the rightful owner of the land in question. However, Picard's mistress and the mother of a previous deed holder see things very differently. So determined is each woman to prove her claim that Ralph and Gervase begin to wonder whether one of them might just be capable of murder. Gervase marries Alys shortly after the action in this book. Associates: Simon; Hubert; Golde; Baron Hervey de Marigny; Alys.

9. *The Foxes of Warwick*. London: Headline, 1999, 320 p.

WARWICK, ENGLAND, DECEMBER 1086. Henry Beaumont keeps a renowned pack of foxhounds: quick, brave, and ruthless. During a winter hunt, the dogs uncover more than a fox in the woodlands. Brushing aside dead leaves, Beaumont finds the crushed body of Martin Reynard, a former member of his own household. Enraged, Henry swears to find the killer, although he is not trained in investigation. Before long, his hot head and rudimentary skills lead him to arrest a man of questionable guilt. Luckily, Ralph Delchard and Gervase Bret are in the area to settle a land dispute and are available to lend their expertise. Upon close consideration of the circumstances leading to the grisly murder, the two Domesday Commissioners begin a full-scale investigation designed to bring the true murderer to justice, whoever he may be. Associates: Alys; Golde; Archdeacon Theobald of Hereford, taking the place of Canon Hubert; Brother Benedict, taking the place of Brother Simon.

10. *The Owls of Gloucester*. London: Headline, 2000, 288 p.

GLOUCESTER, ENGLAND, WINTER 1087. The ordered calm of Gloucester Abbey is shattered by the disappearance of one of its monks. Two novices, Elaf and Kenelm, show little concern for the missing Brother Nicholas. Rebelling against monastic discipline, they indulge in secret midnight adventures. Fearing discovery, they hide in the bell tower, where they literally trip over the body of their missing colleague, his throat slit from ear to ear. The abbot is ill-equipped to deal with such a heinous crime and is reeling from his conversation with the local sheriff, who is convinced that one of the other monks is guilty of the crime. Ralph Delchard and Gervase Bret, the two Domesday Commissioners, present to resolve a land dispute, realize that the killing is just a symptom of a sinister presence that threatens the whole community. Associates: Hubert; Golde; Simon; Aelgar.

11. *The Elephants of Norwich*. London: Headline, 2000, 320 p.

NORWICH, ENGLAND, 1087. It is the juiciest piece of gossip the citizens of Norwich have heard for some time. The two elephants that robber baron Richard de Fontenel was using to lure the beautiful Adelaide into marriage have been stolen. Also missing is de Fontenel's steward, Hermer. Desperate to ignore this growing crisis are Domesday Commissioners Ralph Delchard and Gervase Bret, who are more interested in resolving a land dispute involving de Fontenel and Mauger, a man who is also trying to attract the fetching Adelaide. De Fontenel, however, refuses to cooperate until the thief is found. But is Hermer the steward really missing, or has something more sinister happened? In Ralph and Gervase's most baffling case yet, nothing is what it seems, and no one is above suspicion.

NICHOLAS BRACEWELL OR ELIZABETHAN THEATRE SERIES

Scene of the Crime: London and elsewhere in England, beginning in 1588.

Detectives: Nicholas Bracewell, a bookholder (a title far more prestigious than producer) for his acting company, Lord Westfield's Men.

Known Associates: Lord Westfield's Men, an acting troupe, including Lawrence Firethorn, the company's temperamental star, manager, and major stock owner; Margery Firethorn, his wife; Will Fowler, a leading actor murdered in *The Queen's Head*; Owen Elias, an actor and shareholder in the company; Roger Bartholomew, a playwright; Thomas Skillen, stagekeeper; Hugh Wegges, tireman; John Tallis, apprentice; Matthew Lipton, scrivener; Peter Digby, leader of the musicians; Richard Honeydew, actor; Alexander Marwood, landlord of the Queen's Head Inn, the company's base of operations; Sybil Marwood, his wife; Barnaby Gill, actor and shareholder; Edmund Hoode, playwright and shareholder; Lord Westfield, financial backer; Ralph Willoughby, playwright; George Dart, actor; Anne Hendrik, attractive widow of a Dutch emigrant, Jacob Hendrik and now Nicholas' landlady, friend, and occasional mistress; Preben van Lowe, Anne's neighbor and friend.

Premise: The manager of a traveling group of actors in Elizabethan England solves crimes associated with the theater.

Comment: Actor and playwright Edward Marston's Elizabethan Theatre Series anticipated such future successful tales as the award-winning film *Shakespeare in Love*. Historically grounded and theatrically sound, the Bracewell mysteries explore the face of Elizabethan England and reveal Marston's deep regard for its rich literary and dramatic heritage. Beginning with *The Vagabond Clown*, a very helpful Dramatis Personae is included. Maps are occasionally included in other volumes. The books are difficult to date internally, containing very few verifiable references to contemporaneous events; the death of Blanche Parry, the young Queen Elizabeth I's nurse and later her boon companion, in 1589 is one such event.

Literary Crimes & Chimes: Marston's knowledge of Elizabethan and contemporary stagecraft greatly enriches these books. One has the sense that the concerns expressed here by the characters are actually the concerns of most actors and theatricians in most eras. The absence of direct ties to an overabundance of historical figures actually lends credence to the novels. In fact, while many notables of the period undoubtedly attended performances at the London and provincial theaters, very few of them probably deigned to strike up conversations with the lowborn members of the performing communities. Here the crimes largely proceed from and to the theatrical world and make sense within their context. Marston also skillfully displays his knowledge of the Elizabethan era, a particularly dynamic period in English history. Overall, these books read very well indeed, both as entertainment and as an introduction to the early British theater.

THE CASES

1. *The Queen's Head.* London: Corgi Books, 1988, 236 p.

LONDON, ENGLAND, FEBRUARY 1587–MAY–JULY 1588. In 1587 Mary Queen of Scots dies by the executioner's ax. Will her death end the ceaseless plotting against Mary's red-haired cousin, Queen Elizabeth I? A year later, the year of the Spanish Armada, is a time of more terror and triumph, not just for Queen and court but for the whole of England. The turmoil is reflected in the theaters and under the galleries of inns like London's The Queen's Head, where Lord Westfield's Men perform. The scene there grows even more tumultuous when one of the actors is murdered by a mysterious stranger during a brawl. Nicholas Bracewell, the company's bookholder, faces two immediate repercussions. The company needs to secure a replacement actor acceptable to its temperamental star—and chief shareholder—Lawrence Firethorn, and second to keep his promise to the dying Will Fowler and catch the killer. Soon further robberies, accidents, and misfortunes assail Lord Westfield's Men as their onstage successes swell. Bracewell begins to suspect a conspiracy, not a single murderer's act, but where can he find proof? Then the players are rewarded with the ultimate accolade, an appearance at court, and the canny bookholder senses the end to the drama is at hand. The novel was nominated for the 1996 Edgar Award for Best Mystery Novel of the Year. Associates: Lawrence; Roger; Thomas; Hugh; John; Matthew; Peter; Richard; Alexander; Edmund; Barnaby; Lord Westfield. Historical Figure: British Queen Elizabeth I.

2. *The Merry Devils.* London: Corgi Books, 1989, 236 p.

LONDON, ENGLAND, 1588? Bookholder Nicholas Bracewell, fresh from his triumph in holding together his volatile players during a treasonous plot against Queen Elizabeth, is set to make the galleries at The Queen's Head ring with laughter with a new comedy, *The Merry Devils*, and his lugubrious lads will ensure that mischief will result. Nicholas sees only a harmless comedy that will summon up no devils but only two actors who are adept at tumbling. Why then, during the crucial scene, do three "devils" appear onstage, one of them looking disturbingly real? And what of the deviltry that follows, when one of the three is found dead beneath the stage? Associates: Hugh; Lawrence; Richard; Edmund; Barnaby; Ralph; Lord Westfield; George.

3. *The Trip to Jerusalem.* London: Corgi Books, 1990, 222 p.

LONDON AND ELSEWHERE IN ENGLAND, SUMMER 1589? Lord Westfield's Men face yet another troubling loss. A promising young actor, Gabriel Hawkes, comes to an untimely end. He may have been a victim of the cutthroat competition between London's theater companies, or perhaps a jealous rival has had his way. In the meantime, the city is experiencing a devastating outbreak of the plague. Many of the residents are shunning public places, so it makes sense for the troupe to go on tour in the provinces, where surely they will find friendly audiences, fresh air, and relief from their tribulations. Unfortunately, their most vicious rivals, Banbury's Men, have decided to do the same and are intent on stealing not only their venues but their plays as well. The two companies race toward York, accumulating a motley crew of camp followers along the way. Lead actor Lawrence Firethorn has an eye for the women, and Barnaby Gill, another actor in the company, prefers the boys. To complicate matters, the unsuspecting players may have unwittingly become involved in a Catholic plot to overthrow the queen! Associates: Lawrence; Barnaby; Edmund; Richard; Alexander; George; Anne.

4. *The Nine Giants.* London: Bantam Press, 1991, 235 p.

LONDON, ENGLAND, 1589? The fiery star, Lawrence Firethorn, is enamored of a lady, the wife of the Lord Mayor-Elect, and he arranges a tryst with her at London's Nine Giants Inn. Meanwhile, the lugubrious landlord of the actors' home base is laid even lower by a plot to take over ownership of the inn. A young apprentice actor is subjected to a horrible assault, and a waterman pulls a mangled corpse from the Thames. The drama comes to a climax at the annual Lord Mayor's show, as his barge moves grandly down the river. Associates: Lawrence; Anne; Barnaby; Edmund; George; Alexander.

5. *The Mad Courtesan.* London: Corgi Books, 1992, 252 p.

LONDON, ENGLAND, SUMMER 1589. Though the lusty star of Lord Westfield's Men, Lawrence Firethorn, is always ready to seduce the women bewitched by his art, the vicious rivalry that disrupts the acting troupe erupts between other players. Owen Elias is a surly, envious Welshman, while Sebastian Carrick is an open and attractive gentleman. Their onstage duels have become ever more realistic, but it is an ax that splits open Sebastian's head one night in a Clerkenwell Alley. Company bookholder Nicholas Bracewell, accustomed to handling damage control, begins to investigate the victim's death and learns that he was prone to make enemies, due to his weakness for women and his willingness to renege on his debts. A web of deception has been spun that stretches from lowborn to high-ranking courtesans, with a trail leading all the way to the Virgin Queen. And what of the horse Nimbus, destined to fly Pegasus-like from the very top of St. Paul's Cathedral? Associates: Lawrence; Peter; Barnaby; Edmund; George; Hugh; Richard; Anne. Historical Figure: Blanche Parry.

6. *The Silent Woman: A Novel*. New York: St. Martin's Press, 1994, 312 p.

LONDON, MARLBOROUGH, AND DEVONSHIRE, ENGLAND, 1589? When fire destroys their London theater during a performance, Lord Westfield's Men must seek out humbler venues in the countryside. Company manager Nicholas Bracewell is distracted by a shocking tragedy: a mysterious messenger from his native Devonshire is murdered by poison. Though the messenger is silenced, Nicholas understands that he must return to his birthplace and reconcile some unfinished business of the past, including dealing with a woman whom he had once hoped to marry. The rest of Westfield's Men are now penniless and dejected; they ride along with him on a nightmare tour. Their journey will perhaps become their own valedictory, dogged by plague, poverty, rogues, and thieves. Associates: Barnaby; Lawrence; Thomas; Edmund; Alexander; Anne.

7. *The Roaring Boy: A Novel*. New York: St. Martin's Press, 1995, 260 p.

ENGLAND, 1589? One member of Lord Westfield's Men has died. Their present production is a failure. Then an anonymous playwright hands company mainstay Nicholas Bracewell a chance for salvation: a new script that exposes a tragic miscarriage of justice in a murder case. News of the impending production of *The Roaring Boy* swiftly reaches high places. Long before rehearsals begin, the Company is menaced by enemies who destine both script and players for destruction. The new play establishes the innocence of the two people executed for the crime and points a bold finger at the real murderer. Not even Lord Westfield, the Company's powerful patron, can save the troupe from the mortal danger that now encompasses them.

8. *The Laughing Hangman: A Novel*. New York: St. Martin's Press, 1996, 248 p.

ENGLAND: 159– . Lord Westfield's Men are split down the middle: should they scorn the belligerent and sadistic playwright Jonas Applegarth, or should they perform his brilliant new drama, *The Misfortunes of Marriage*? When they decide to receive Applegarth, they unwittingly receive all of the man's enemies along with him. Actors, especially The Blackfriars, a rival troupe, are so scathingly portrayed in *The Misfortunes of Marriage* that revenge seems almost certain. When gruesome hangings plague both of the troupes, they speculate that it is just God taking out his wrath for the immorality portrayed in the theaters. But Nicholas Bracewell has heard the cackle of the "Laughing Hangman" and knows that the killer is closer to them than they think. Nick is also suffering his own "misfortunes of marriage": it has been a year since Anne refused his proposal and walked out of his life—but all's well that ends well. . . . Associates: Lawrence; Margery; Barnaby; Edmund; Owen; James Ingram; Richard Honeydew; Peter Digby; Alexander Marwood; Anne; Preben.

9. *The Fair Maid of Bohemia: A Novel.* New York: St. Martin's Press, 1997, 229 p.

LONDON, ENGLAND, AND PRAGUE, BOHEMIA, 159– . A plague is terrorizing Elizabethan England, and its theaters are empty as a result. Just as it seems that Lord Westfield's Men will be forced to disband, they receive an invitation to make a command performance at the Imperial Court in Prague, an event they believe will be their crowning achievement. The offer is from the fairest maid of Bohemia, a great-niece of Emperor Rudolph II, the alluring Sophia Magdalena. In confidence, their patron Lord Westfield has given Nicholas Bracewell a secret document to be delivered to an English doctor in Rudolph's court, Talbot Royden. While the troupe is en route to Prague, the brutal murder of an actor during their first performance turns their journey into a nightmare, especially when Bracewell realizes that he himself was the intended victim. After their arrival in Prague and after having been trailed through Europe by mysterious pursuers, the troupe discovers that the eccentric court of Rudolph II keeps its own perilous secrets and that instead of being the revered guest of the Court, Talbot Royden is languishing in a castle dungeon. In a harrowing subplot, Nicholas' beloved friend, Anne Hendrik, called to the deathbed of her father-in-law, Jan Hendrik in Amsterdam, is subsequently kidnapped, and Nicholas must come to her assistance as well. As the debut of their play, dedicated to Sophia Magdalena, nears, Bracewell needs all his wits to rescue the company from the whirlpool of deceit and danger into which they have plunged. Associates: Lawrence; Margery; Barnaby; Edmund; Richard; George; Owen; James; Thomas; Alexander; Anne Hendrik; Preben van Lowe, Anne's neighbor and friend; Lord Westfield. Historical Figures: Holy Roman Emperor Rudolph II; Conrad of Brunswick; Sophia Magdalena of Jankau.

10. *The Wanton Angel: A Novel.* New York: St. Martin's Press, 1999, 279 p.

LONDON, ENGLAND, 159– . All is not well, at least on the theatrical scene of Nicholas Bracewell's London. His players are being threatened with eviction from the Queen's Head Inn. Their landlord's unmarried daughter has become pregnant and will say only that her child's father is an actor. At the same time they are about to lose their theater venue when Queen Elizabeth's powerful Privy Council decides to shut down the groups, like Westfield's Men, that stage their works in the open yards of the inns. So they decide to build their own stage just outside the jurisdiction of the current edict. They cannot be surprised when their rivals begin to intervene with the construction process. Then, when Sylvester Pryde, a new member of the group, is found murdered at the site, Nicholas is forced to initiate an investigation into the crime. He himself is assaulted and other misfortunes begin to occur. In the meantime, a mysterious female benefactor, an acquaintance of Pryde's, has promised to underwrite the entire undertaking. Their prayers appear to have been answered, before things fall apart once again. It will take all of Bracewell's skills to discover the identity of Pryde's killer, as well as expose the secrets of the company's mysterious "angel." Associates: Lawrence; Edmund; Barnaby; Lucius; Alexander; Sybil, his wife; Rose, his wayward daughter; Owen; Richard; James; George; Ezekiel Stonnard, Marwood's lawyer; Lord Westfield; Anne. Historical Figure: British Queen Elizabeth I.

11. *The Devil's Apprentice: A Novel.* New York: St. Martin's Minotaur, 2001, 273 p.

ESSEX, ENGLAND, WINTER 159– . London is in the grip of an icy winter, and Lord Westfield's Men are out of work, when the troupe is suddenly invited to perform at Silvermere, Sir Michael Greenleaf's manor house in Essex. They accept willingly, even though the offer comes with two conditions: they must perform an entirely new play, and they must take on a young apprentice, Davy Stratton, son of Jerome Stratton, a rich merchant. At first the lad seems to be a talented and eager addition to the company. However, he soon disrupts the group's camaraderie when he quarrels with the other apprentices and runs away during a reconnaissance trip to Essex. Bracewell manages to hold the group together during rehearsals for the new play, *The Witch of Colchester*, by playwright Egidius Pye. But when the lead actor succumbs to a series of strange illnesses, identical to those that afflict his character in the play, some members of the troupe fear there may be a scoundrel among them. Then a prominent audience member dies during the opening night performance, and Nicholas must confront the deadliest foe of all. Associates: Alexander; Lawrence; Margery; Barnaby; Edmund; Owen; Anne.

12. *The Bawdy Basket.* New York: St. Martin's Minotaur, 2002, 262 p.

LONDON, ENGLAND, AUGUST 159? Lord Westfield's Men are enjoying good fortune in their native London. Their talented playwright, Edmund Hoode, is at work on his next opus, *The Duke of Verona*, set to open in a few short weeks, and Nick is looking forward to a calm and productive season. Unfortunately, his friendship with Francis "Frank" Quilter, a young actor who's just joined the troupe, is about to cause trouble. Frank's father has been arrested and accused of a murder he claims he didn't commit, and before anyone can figure out what to do, he is convicted and hanged for the crime. Devastated, young Frank swears to avenge his father, with disastrous results for the actors. Nicholas' loyalty is split between the company and his friend, and he agrees to help Frank on condition that he fulfills his acting obligations. An unlikely ally is the comely Moll Comfrey, a young peddler with more to sell than meets the eye. She has the key to the whole mystery hidden away in her "bawdy basket," and it's up to Nicholas to discover what secret she's hiding before the theater goes dark. Associates: Lawrence; Barnaby; Edmund; Owen; George; Lord Westfield; Alexander; Sybil; Anne; Preben van Loew.

13. *The Vagabond Clown.* New York: St. Martin's Minotaur, 2003, 292 p.

ON TOUR IN KENT, ENGLAND, 159? When unexpected disaster strikes Lord Westfield's Men during a packed performance, Nicholas Bracewell, the theater company's stage manager and all-around performer of miracles, must save the day once again. A melee caused by men in disguise is brought under control, but before the troupe can lament their destroyed set, Nicholas discovers a body in the stands with a knife sticking out of its back. They soon realize they are out one theater and one clown: Barnaby Gill, always hilarious on the stage and a hopeless curmudgeon off, has broken his leg. With long months of repairs facing them, Westfield's Men embark on a tour of the Kent countryside in order to salvage some of the downtime. They hire a stand-in for Gill, one Mussett, a gifted comedian and an even more gifted drunk. But it seems no clown is perfect, and while Gill has never been a barrel of laughs when not in front of an audience, Mussett simply doesn't seem to know when to quit being funny. Their major wound bandaged, albeit temporarily, Nicholas and the troupe are hoping to leave their troubles behind. But misfortune follows them at every turn, and the company finds that no matter what they do or where they go, someone very sinister is just moments behind. It's up to Bracewell to find out what's going on and exactly how it ties into their wayward comedian. Does the Vagabond Clown prophesy the end of Westfield's Men and perhaps the demise of Nicholas himself? Associates: Lawrence; Margery; Barnaby; Edmund; Owen; James; Rowland Carr; Francis Quilter (from *The Bawdy Basket*); George; Richard; Anne; Pieter Hendrik, her relative by marriage; Lord Westfield; Alexander.

14. *The Counterfeit Crank.* New York: St. Martin's Minotaur, 2004, 257 p.

LONDON, ENGLAND, 159– . Nicholas Bracewell, the bookholder and stage manager for the popular London theater troupe, Lord Westfield's Men, has a few problems on his hands. Edmund Hoode, the troupe's talented playwright, has fallen ill and is unable to complete his next opus. But is his illness from natural causes, or is something more sinister afoot? An absentee landlord seems to have coincided with a few unusual events at the inn the troupe calls home. A gambler has moved in upstairs and proceeds to take money off many of the actors, something the regular landlord would never have allowed to happen. Then the troupe's costumes are purloined from a locked storage cabinet, and they are forced to perform with makeshift clothing. When Nicholas meets a couple of down-on-their-luck young people who are making their way as con artists on the streets of London, helping them is almost too much for poor Bracewell. But he has a good heart and an inquisitive mind, and as usual he'll stop at nothing before he gets everything under control. After all, the show must go on! Associate: Edmund.

CHRISTOPHER REDMAYNE OR RESTORATION MYSTERY SERIES

Scene of the Crime: London, England, beginning in 1666.

Detective: Christopher Redmayne, an architect of the Restoration era; Jonathan Bale, a Puritan constable and Redmayne's close friend.

Known Associates: Sarah Bale, Jonathan's wife; Oliver and Richard Bale, Jonathan's sons; Jacob Vout, Christopher's servant; Henry Redmayne, Christopher's elder brother; Penelope Northcott, Christopher's paramour; Susan Cheever, Christopher's paramour; Sir Julius Cheever, Susan's father; Nicholas Cheever, Susan's brother; British King Charles II (1660–1685); Algernon Redmayne, Dean of Gloucester, Christopher's father; Tom Warburton, Jonathan's fellow constable.

Premise: A Restoration architect solves crimes in seventeenth-century England.

Comment: Christopher Redmayne is a true Restoration man: a well-connected scholar, soldier, philosopher, scientist, artist—and an eligible bachelor. Horrified at the scenes of destruction and tragedy wrought by the Great Fire of 1666 in London, he is also one of the architects working to restore the city to its vibrant and bustling state. Jonathan Bale is a Puritan constable who firmly believes that the fire would never have happened had Oliver Cromwell still been in power. Married with two children, Bale has an unshakeable sense of right and wrong, which has made him an excellent upholder of the law, a brave volunteer fireman, and a fierce critic of the newly restored Court's looser indulgences. At first sight, meeting by chance in the ashes of the ruined city, Redmayne and Bale would seem to the other to embody all that irritates them most in their fellow man; but they survive this encounter to become good friends and also to learn to respect each other's complementary skills at uncovering crimes.

Literary Crimes & Chimes: Again, Marston has done a superior job, both in creating an original premise and in developing a set of original characters. The crimes that are revealed in these tales fit within the context of the era and are solved in ways that are both relevant and believable. When measured, for example, with the historical novels of Paul Doherty, Marston's tales are so far superior in every respect that there is really no comparison possible between the two writers. Grand entertainment.

THE CASES

1. *The King's Evil.* London: Headline, 1999, 310 p.

LONDON, ENGLAND, SEPTEMBER 1666. The town house Christopher Redmayne has been commissioned to build by wealthy landowner Sir Ambrose Northcott is beset by thieving, and, between them, Christopher and Jonathan bring about an arrest. However, when Sir Ambrose is stabbed to death, leaving a distraught wife and daughter in Kent apparently ignorant of his new London base, it requires all Redmayne's flair and all of Bale's tenacity to unravel the complex and dangerous traces he has left behind, traces that lead to brothels and gaming dens, across the Channel, and to the private doors of the hedonistic Royal Court of King Charles. Christopher disguises himself as the King and attends a bawdy house, with Charles' connivance. Contains a helpful map of Restoration London, which is also repeated in the later books in the series. Associates: Sarah; Jacob; Henry; Penelope. Historical Figure: British King Charles II.

2. *The Amorous Nightingale.* London: Headline, 2000, 320 p.

LONDON, ENGLAND, 1667. Acclaimed beauty and singer Harriet Gow has earned a position envied by every available performer of the Restoration period: she has become the King's favorite mistress. After seeing her perform, architect Christopher Redmayne is also captivated. The impression Harriet made is still lingering pleasantly in his mind when he is summoned urgently by Charles II. Harriet has been kidnapped, and Redmayne, with the help of his friend Jonathan Bale, is engaged to look into this delicate affair. The facade of elegance and gentility soon begins to crumble in the face of their investigation. Harriet is, indeed, an amorous nightingale, the fabric of her life entangled with jealousy, avarice, and lust. Just as Redmayne and Bale start to question whether she is really a victim or the guilty party, a brutal murder provides the answer. Associates: Henry; Oliver; Richard; Algernon; Jacob. Historical Figure: British King Charles II.

3. *The Repentant Rake.* London: Headline, 2002, 306 p.

LONDON, ENGLAND, SUMMER 1668. Christopher Redmayne and Jonathan Bale find themselves embroiled in the hunt for the murderer of

Nicholas, the "repentant rake" of the story, son of Sir Julius Cheever. Could his death be connected with the fact that a blackmailer is terrorizing London high society? Divided by politics but united in their quest for justice, Jonathan and Christopher take on the challenge, but how can they exploit the scandals of others, when the victims themselves will do anything to maintain their anonymity. And what of Nicholas? Many feel that the lad must have been the victim of his own debauched appetites, while others talk of his newfound repentance. With only lies, rumors, and gossip to work with and facing several attempts on their lives, the two detectives must navigate their way through a maze of corruption and political intrigue. Associates: Sir Julius; Henry; Susan; Nicholas; Tom.

4. *The Frost Fair.* London: Allison & Busby, 2004, 284 p.

LONDON, ENGLAND, DECEMBER 1669. During one of the coldest winters in years, the Thames is frozen over from bank to bank; London celebrates with a traditional frost fair held on the broad thick ice of the river itself. Revelers come from far and wide to enjoy the spectacle; an ox is roasted, booths are set up, and entertainers gather to amuse the crowds. Young architect Christopher Redmayne escorts Susan Cheever, the daughter of one of his clients, with whom he has formed a romantic attachment. There they meet Redmayne's friend, Constable Jonathan Bale, attending the fest with his family. Bale's son Richard gets into trouble when he slides onto thin ice and is in danger of falling into the freezing water. Christopher and Jonathan rescue the boy but in the process make a grim discovery—the frozen corpse of a man embedded in the ice. The dead man is Jeronimo Maldini, an Italian fencing master, who has been missing for some time. Christopher is inclined to dismiss the case and leave the investigation to Bale; but all that changes when his brother, Henry Redmayne, is charged with the murder and thrown into prison. Henry had been drunk the night of the disappearance and had been overheard arguing with the Italian. Christopher must now risk all he holds dear, both personally and professionally, in order to uncover the truth about his (possibly) worthless brother. Associates: Henry; Susan; Richard; Sir Julius; Sarah.

INSPECTOR ROBERT COLBECK SERIES

Scene of the Crime: London and elsewhere in England, beginning in 1851.

Detective: Police Inspector Robert Colbeck, who has a love for locomotives and a knowledge of railroading far beyond the average.

Known Associates: Police Commissioner Richard Mayne, Head of the Detective Department of Scotland Yard; Superintendent Edward Tallis, Colbeck's dyspeptic superior, who disapproves of the Inspector's methods and is less concerned about justice and more involved with his own image; Sergeant Victor Leeming, Colbeck's assistant, who intensely dislikes railway travel; Brendan Mulryne, a shady former policeman from the Devil's Acres, who is enlisted by Colbeck to help with his investigations; Madeleine "Maddy" Andrews, daughter of the injured railroad engineer, Caleb Andrews; she becomes very close to the Inspector while helping him to solve this case.

Premise: A British policeman solves railway crimes in nineteenth-century London.

Comment: The London-to-Birmingham mail train is robbed and derailed, injuring the driver and several other people aboard. Inspector Robert Colbeck knows that this is a case that won't be easily solved, when he is faced with the question of how the robbers got into a safe with two keys that were secured on opposite sides of the country. To get to the bottom of the mystery, he enlists the aid of veteran former policeman Brendan Mulryne behind his Superintendent's back to search out the culprits in the notorious Devil's Acre, a cluster of gambling dens in the shadow of Westminster Abbey. However, Mulryne may create more trouble than he can solve. Things get even more complicated when the beautiful daughter of the injured train driver, Miss Madeleine Andrews, comes forward to provide additional information, unwittingly drawing the unwanted attention of the crooks. With the attempting bombing of a railroad tunnel and a dynamite plot mounted against the locomotive exhibit at the Great Exposition, the Inspector realizes that he is dealing with the most driven and powerful criminals that he has ever faced in his career. With Madeleine kidnapped and held hostage against his investigation, Colbeck must race against time to save the woman and catch the perpetrators before they leave England.

Literary Crimes & Chimes: Once again, Marston manages to create an interesting twist on the standard historical mystery, providing a unique setting and unique detective to complement his other series. It's interesting to compare this book with Crichton's *The Great Train Robbery*, which was based on an actual crime and has a somewhat more cynical take on mid-Victorian England. Crichton focuses on the larger-than-life criminal Edward Pierce, whose charm and *savoir-faire* make him almost a sympathetic character. Marston's villains are upper-crust ex-Army officers who carry a grudge against the incursion of the British railway lines into the beautiful English countryside. Inspector Colbeck also belongs to the aristocracy, but he originally joined the police force (somewhat beneath his station) to bring criminals to justice, after his *fiancée* was murdered. His loneliness seems destined to be assuaged in future offerings in this series. By the end of *The Railway Detective*, which is what the press is now calling him, it appears that he will likely be delegated to deal with any new crimes that affect the railroad companies. Judging by his obvious love for, and knowledge of, the great locomotives that ride the rails in Great Britain, this seems to be good match for both him and his readers.

THE CASE

1. *The Railway Detective.* London: Allison & Busby, 2004, 261 p. LONDON, ENGLAND, 1851. See commentary in this series.

MEDAWAR, Mardi Oakley. American.

TAY-BODAL SERIES

Scene of the Crime: Western United States, beginning in 1866.

Detective: Tay-bodal, a Kiowa Indian healer, age about thirty-two in 1866.

Known Associates: Crying Wind, Tay-bodal's second wife and White Bear's widowed cousin (from *Death at Rainy Mountain*), whom he loves deeply, even when her assertiveness exasperates and confounds the former bachelor; Skywalker, an Owl Doctor, who becomes Tay's best friend and devoted disciple when Tay successfully treats his painful migraines (also from *Death at Rainy Mountain*); the great Chief White Bear (whom the whites call Satanta), the wise and wily leader of the Rattle Band, to which Tay becomes attached through his marriage.

Premise: A Kiowa Indian healer solves crimes affecting his tribe in mid-nineteenth-century America.

Comment: Tay-bodal, a Kiowa healer, does not follow the usual healer's code, nor does he, by choice, belong to either the Owl Doctors or the Buffalo Doctors, principally because he does not strictly adhere to their methods of healing. Because Tay has become so notorious (and even respected) within the tribes for his propensity for "thinking outside the box," he is often called upon by the wily Chief White Bear to investigate certain events that threaten the stability of the tribe and to seek out the true facts in each case. Skywalker, also a healer and White Bear's influential cousin, befriends

Tay and works with him to right wrongs and solve crimes. Tay-bodal is a modern-thinking Kiowa healer, whose study of anatomy and physiology has set him apart from other tribal doctors of his time. He is unique for the period in which he operates, in that he approaches his investigations by using deductive and inductive reasoning, rather than finding traditional and mystical solutions. Medawar, of Cherokee background herself, presents her Native Americans as totally believable characters and draws effectively from her own background and personal knowledge to present a comprehensive look at historical Kiowan life and values.

Literary Crimes & Chimes: This series is utterly delightful! What a great pity it now seems defunct. Medawar succeeds brilliantly in her accurate portrayal of the culture of a nineteenth-century tribe in their sometimes desperate struggle to survive and redefine themselves in the post–Civil War era. The introspective Kiowa healer, Tay-bodal, speaking in his own unique voice, tells us more of the ways and mores of his people than any dry history book could ever convey. Skillfully weaving irony, pathos, and black humor throughout her straightforward plots, Medawar creates an irresistible tapestry, rich with the insidious foibles of desire, revenge, and jealousy that can destroy a community—and the nobler values of courage, integrity, and wisdom that are needed to set things right again. Although a sprinkling of glaring typographical errors detracts somewhat from the otherwise graceful storytelling skills of the author (Tay—while halting his pony—notes that "I *reigned* up" in *The Ft. Larned Incident*), this series is a "must" read for all fans of the historical mystery novel.

THE CASES

1. ***Death at Rainy Mountain.*** New York: St. Martin's Press, 1996, 262 p.
    RAINY MOUNTAIN, NORTH TEXAS, SUMMER 1866. The separate bands of the Kiowa Nation gather at sacred Rainy Mountain to elect a successor to Little Bluff, the recently deceased principal chief. Three men are put forward as candidates, each the chief of a major Kiowa band. When the Cheyenne Robber, the handsome nephew of one candidate, White Bear, is accused of killing Coyote Walking, the nephew of another candidate, in rivalry for the hand of his beloved White Otter, the nation finds itself divided; no matter how the council rules in the matter, one band is sure to declare war on the other. Although he had challenged his rival in front of witnesses, the young man swears he didn't kill the victim. Modern-thinking Kiowa healer Tay-bodal, whose study of anatomy and physiology sets him apart from other tribal doctors, is asked by Chief White Bear of the Rattle Band, whom the whites call Satanta, to help find the true murderer. Break-

ing tribal tradition, Tay-bodal examines the body of the dead man and discovers that he was strangled and his neck subsequently broken. This is a particularly cowardly killing method, and Tay-bodal wonders why any decent Kiowan would have used it. The healer must find compelling evidence proving the guilt of the actual murderer to avert a war, which could destroy the Kiowa Nation. In doing so, he rights old wrongs and earns the tribe's respect and gratitude for his services, in addition to acquiring a new wife and son! Associates: Owl Man, leader of the Owl Doctors, religious and spiritual healers of the tribe; Skywalker; Crying Wind; Lieutenant "Hawwy" Haw-we-sun (actually Harrison), a Blue Jacket doctor who goes against tradition by seeking out and marrying White Bear's niece, Cherish—Tay wishes to learn "doctoring" from him. Historical Figure: Chief White Bear (Satanta).

2. *Witch of the Palo Duro: A Tay-bodal Mystery.* New York: St. Martin's Press, 1997, 224 p.

PALO DURA CANYON, TEXAS (THE KIOWAN WINTER RETREAT), WINTER 1866. For the first time in two years, the Kiowas return to their traditional winter retreat at the Palo Dura Canyon in northern Texas. But when Tay-bodal's friend, the renowned healer and seer Skywalker, mysteriously disappears and two horses are found killed, the camp becomes convinced it is the work of a shape-shifter. When Tay-bodal's spouse, Crying Wind, accidentally overmedicates an ailing infant, she is rumored to be an evil witch. Tay begins an investigation to find his missing friend and discover what is behind the mishaps, in order not only to save the life of his spouse but to save the tribe from descending further into chaos. Associates: Crying Wind; Skywalker. Historical Figure: Chief White Bear (Satanta).

3. *Murder at Medicine Lodge: A Tay-bodal Mystery.* New York: St. Martin's Press, 1999, 262 p.

MEDICINE LODGE, KANSAS (OSAGE COUNTY), OCTOBER 1867. Lone Wolf, newly elected Chief of the Kiowa tribes, leads his people to Medicine Lodge, Kansas, along with the Comanche, Arapaho, Apache, and Cheyenne tribes, in order to meet with representatives of the U.S. government and to sign peace treaties. But not all of the Kiowa agree that the peace treaty is a good thing, and tensions between them and the Army Blue Jackets run high. When the army bugler ("Buug-lah") disappears and White Bear, chief of the Rattle Band and Tay-bodal's mentor, finds the bugle out on the plains, the army commandant assumes he has killed the soldier in order to steal the instrument. To make matters worse, the bugler's body is later found murdered on the plains. The army is set to try White Bear for murder, and the Kiowa are determined to go on the warpath if he is not found innocent. Tay is charged by Lone Wolf to investigate the murder and clear

White Bear's name. With very little time before the army tribunal is held, Tay must find out the truth about the victim, a man he doesn't know, and what might have actually happened out there on the plains. Associates: Crying Wind; Skywalker; Hawwy, the Blue Jacket doctor; Billy (Returned to Us), a half-breed who has lived as a white but now returns willingly to the tribe; Henry M. Stanley, a Welsh-born journalist who is seeking to learn more about the Indians. Historical Figures: Chief White Bear (Satanta); Commissioner of Indian Affairs Nathaniel Taylor; Senator John B. Henderson; the Washington delegation to the treaty negotiations, including William S. Harney, Alfred H. Terry, S. F. Tappan, J. B. Sanborn, and C. C. Augur.

4. *The Ft. Larned Incident.* New York: St. Martin's Minotaur, 2000, 270 p.

MEDICINE LODGE CREEK, KANSAS, AND FT. LARNED, OKLAHOMA, SUMMER 1868. Following the signing of the Medicine Lodge Treaty, things are not going well for the Kiowa. Their promised lands actually went to another tribe, their promised goods have not yet arrived, and the bored and tense warriors are becoming more and more unruly, especially when whiskey is made available to them. Colonel Jesse Henry Leavenworth, the Indian agent assigned to Tay-bodal's band, once again fails to live up to his promises, and is run off by a furious White Bear. Leavenworth's exasperated assistant declares they must go to Ft. Larned if they are to receive their annual annuities. Meanwhile, Tay, a healer and a member of the Rattle Band, is undergoing a personal crisis. A disagreement with his wife has escalated to the point where he has moved out. She has been seen with another man, and divorce seems inevitable. Tay is therefore not in the best frame of mind when he is called upon to investigate the murder of Three Elks, the son of another chief, and one he had called friend. Complicating matters further, the man accused of killing him is not only a member of the Rattle Band but also the man who was trying to steal Tay's wife! If Tay-bodal cannot put aside his personal concerns and prove that the accused man is innocent, there may be war between the bands, which could tear apart what remains of the Kiowa nation. Interestingly, the *dénouement* that completes the tale takes place fifty years after the episode in question and provides a poignant, yet entirely appropriate, summing up of the life and times of Tay-bodal and his friends and loved ones. Associates: Crying Wind; Skywalker; Returned to Us (Billy), the band's half-breed interpreter; Hawwy, the white army officer who marries a Kiowa and becomes Tay's friend. Historical Figure: Chief White Bear (Satanta).

MEYERS, Annette (1934–). American.

Olivia Brown Series

Scene of the Crime: New York, New York, beginning in the 1920s.

Detective: Olivia (nicknamed Oliver) Brown, was orphaned long ago; her guardian, Jonas Avery, an elderly bachelor, was somewhat baffled by the ways of a young girl, so she was brought up by Mattie Timmons, Mr. Avery's housekeeper. Olivia lost her fiancé, Franklin Prince, in the war. The 1918 influenza pandemic that followed the war took the lives of her guardian and her beloved teacher, Miss Sarah Parkman. Olivia then sank into a depression, and when she came out of it, she had her long red hair bobbed and moved (along with Mattie) to Greenwich Village. Olivia sells poetry, acts in a small theater, and sometimes helps a detective with his private inquiries.

Known Associates: Mattie Timmons, a good friend who also acts as her housekeeper; Harry Melville, her tenant and mentor; Mr. Brophy, a policeman; Whitney Sawyer, a cast-off lover; Edward Hall, the magazine publisher who first published her poems; Stephen Lowell, a poet Olivia admires; Jig Cook, director/manager of the Provincetown Playhouse; the Hudson Dusters, a street gang.

Premise: A poet solves crimes in early-twentieth-century New York City.

Comment: Olivia's Great Aunt Evangeline kicked over the traces of polite society long ago; she married another young woman (Alice) in a "Boston marriage" and became a private detective in Greenwich Village. Harry Melville had worked for her, in fact was trained by her, and became her tenant for life. He now runs his detective agency out of the ground floor flat in the building that Olivia inherited. (As she puts it, she inherited Harry as well, in a codicil to Great Aunt Evangeline's will.) Olivia's family never spoke of "Vangie" (as Harry calls her), and Olivia never even knew that she existed. Olivia is passionate about life in Greenwich Village; she feels that the creative work and the creative lives of the people there are the best that the world has to offer. She sleeps until the afternoon, rises when she wishes, writes, goes to the theater to act in avant-garde plays, visits speakeasies with her friends, and often takes home a young man for the night. Harry has been training her in the ways of detection, and when she is in danger, she works to discover the villains who are murdering her friends. Olivia lives on her nerves, wine, gin, and very little food and sleep. Her only strong relationships are with her friend and housekeeper, Mattie, and her mentor,

Harry Melville. She falls in love at least twice in a book but is ultimately dedicated primarily to her poetry.

Literary Crimes & Chimes: This series provides a pleasant diversion for the reader of historical mysteries, providing much period detail on the Roaring Twenties. The narrative is punctuated by samples of Olivia's poetry, in which it is evident that her muse is Edna St. Vincent Millay. Olivia's sleuthing is logical and interesting; she follows up clues in a surprisingly thorough and straightforward manner; although the final revelations always seem to come when she is most in jeopardy. The books feature everything from speakeasies to the Black Hand (the precursor of the Mafia).

THE CASES

1. *Free Love.* New York: Mysterious Press, 1999, 240 p.

GREENWICH VILLAGE, NEW YORK, 1920. Drunk and sloshing through puddles outside of Chumley's speakeasy, Olivia falls over a corpse. The police are called, and the speakeasy warned (so that the booze can be hidden and the teacups brought out). The murder victim turns out to be an acquaintance of Olivia, made up to look just like her. This raises the obvious question: just who did the murderer intend to kill? Associate: Andrew (Antonio).

2. *Murder Me Now.* New York: Mysterious Press, 2001, 290 p.

NEW YORK, NEW YORK, 1920s. A weekend house party of bright young people includes games that devolve into vicious attacks, lovers' meetings that end in attempted murder, and the discovery of a corpse in a tree. Olivia finds the verdict of suicide difficult to believe, and she and Harry begin a dangerous investigation. Associates: Paulo; Fordy Vaude; Celia Gillam; Kate; Daisy; Susan Glaspell. Historical Figures: Edmund "Bunny" Wilson; Monk Eastman.

3. **"Timor Mortis,"** in ***The Mammoth Book of Roaring Twenties Whodunnits,*** ed. by Mike Ashley. London: Robinson Publishing; New York: Carroll & Graf, 2004, p. 3–32.

GREENWICH VILLAGE, NEW YORK, MARCH 1921. Harry's crazy cousin, Fania, has shaved her head, painted her scalp blue, and departed for parts unknown, accompanied only by her imaginary friend. Olivia thinks it would be interesting to meet her, and Harry would like to locate the woman to reassure her family (and himself) that she's safe. They take time out from their sleuthing to attend a "Feather Ball" (a costume ball in which each outfit incorporates feathers) and are stunned to see Fania riding in on a white horse, acting as Lady Godiva, completely naked save for a frosting of white feathers. The arrow that suddenly strikes her down is also feathered, but it kills her quite dead just the same. Associates: Harry Melville; Maggie; Detective Gerry Brophy; Ding Dong; Red Farell; Kid Yorke; Edward Hall; Kendall. Historical Figure: Jack Dempsey.

MEYERS, Maan (pseud. of Annette Meyers [1934–] and Martin Meyers). American.

TONNEMAN FAMILY SERIES

Scene of the Crime: The series covers both intrigues and criminal cases investigated by several generations of the Tonneman family. The series follows the evolution of New York as much as the descendants of Pieter Tonneman, beginning during the period in which New York, New York, was called New Amsterdam in 1664 with *The Dutchman*, and continuing through 1895 with *The House on Mulberry Street*.

Detective(s): Different novels in the series focus on different protagonists. In *The Dutchman* and *The Dutchman's Dilemma* the detective is Pieter Tonneman, the "*schout*" (a position similar to that of Sheriff) of New Amsterdam. Pieter was born in 1621 in Holland, and he and his wife, Maria, immigrated to New Amsterdam. Maria died just before the events recounted in *The Dutchman*, and Pieter has developed a habit of deadening his grief with liquor. Throughout much of the action in that first book, his skills are hampered by his drunkeness, and he is distracted by the pain he still feels over his wife's death. The events in *The Dutchman's Dilemma* occur about a decade later; Pieter has given up law, gone into business, and remarried. He is forced back into acting as a detective by an obligation to a man he hates, someone he suspected of complicity in the crime he uncovered in *The Dutchman*.

In *The Kingsbridge Plot*, Pieter Tonneman's great-great-grandson, John Peter Tonneman (born 1746), returns to New York on his father's death. He has been living in England, having thought that his sympathies lay with the "Loyalists," but as the country erupts into war, he finds that his heart is with the American "Rebels." He is a doctor, as was his father. His father's old position of coroner falls to him, and so he finds himself investigating suspicious deaths, first for the Crown, and then for himself.

In *The High Constable*, John Peter Tonneman's son, Peter Tonneman (born 1789), brings the family to the brink of disgrace, partly through the family curse of weakness for alcohol. He redeems himself partly through the family penchant for heroic rescues and in 1808 is made a constable, a job for which he has an inherited talent. He advances to the position of Captain of the Night and Day Police before he retires in 1848.

In *The Lucifer Contract* Pete Tonneman (born 1837), Peter Tonneman's grandson, is an investigative reporter for the *Evening Post*. The Civil War gives rise to both intrigue and scandal, and all are grist for the newspapers.

In *The House on Mulberry Street* John "Dutch" Tonneman (born 1867), Pete's son, is a young police detective starting out in a city that's rife with corruption. He's Irish through his mother's side of the family (the Clancys), and is accepted (but kept at arm's length) by the Irish cops in the Police Department.

Known Associates: Pieter Tonneman's best friend (and later business partner) is Conraet Ten Eyck. Conraet's wife, Antje, treats Tonneman as a brother, and Conraet and Antje's son Pieter is Tonneman's godson. Pieter Tonneman's first wife was Maria; they had one child, Anna, who lived to adulthood. She married Johan Bikker before the events of the first book. By the time of *The Dutchman's Dilemma*, Pieter Tonneman has remarried. His second wife is Racquel Mendoza, and they have four children: Moses, Maria, Benjamin, and Daniel.

John Peter Tonneman (in *The Kingsbridge Plot*) stayed many years in England to escape all contact with his ex-fiancée, Abigail, who jilted him and married Richard Willard. John Peter feels he must return to New York when he receives word that his father, Peter Tonneman, has died. When John Peter comes back to New York, he brings along his best friend, Maurice "Jamie" Jamison. John Peter is given the position of coroner and investigates suspicious deaths with the assistance of Constable Goldsmith; by the end of the book, Quintin Brock is assisting with the investigation and also acting as John Peter's cook and head housekeeper. John Peter also hires Molly, a reformed prostitute; she helps him keep house as well. John Peter marries Mariana Mendoza, and by the time of the events of *The High Constable*, they have had five children: William, David, Peter, Gretel, and Leah.

The High Constable is a continuation of the story told in *The Kingsbridge Plot*. The main protagonist is Peter Tonneman, John Peter's son, but some scenes are told from the point of view of his father and mother, the protagonists of *The Kingsbridge Plot*. Most of the characters in *The Kingsbridge Plot* reappear, seen now from Peter's perspective. The next generation comes to the fore; for instance, Abigail's son, George Willard, plays a major role. Peter begins work for High Constable Jake Hays and works with Constable Bill Duffy; Peter becomes romantically involved with Hays' widowed kinswoman, Charity Boenning.

The Lucifer Contract features Pete Tonneman, "Old Peter" Tonneman's grandson. Pete lives with his grandparents, Peter and Charity Tonneman; his newspaper editor is Everett Miller. In this book he meets the woman he eventually marries, Meg Clancy.

In *The House on Mulberry Street* John "Dutch" Tonneman, son of Pete Tonneman, is on the force with many of his cousins (most of them Irish, from his mother's side of the family). In the course of the story he also works with the photographer Esther Breslau.

Premises: In *The Dutchman* Pieter Tonneman is a peace officer and, in that capacity, investigates New Amsterdam's crimes. In *The Dutchman's Dilemma* he is asked to investigate the murder of a horse, a request he finds politically impossible to refuse. In *The Kingsbridge Plot* John Peter Tonneman begins an investigation in his capacity as New York's Coroner; the case takes an unfortunate personal turn when someone near him is targeted by the killer. In *The High Constable* Peter Tonneman assists in the investigation of a murder when he is appointed as a town constable. In *The Lucifer Contract* Pete Tonneman learns of a plot to burn New York. He's less interested in stopping the plot than in filing a story. In *The House on Mulberry Street* Dutch Tonneman works as a policeman, trying to fight crime in New York despite corruption at the highest levels of government.

Comment: It is very difficult to divide this series' characters into "associates" and real-life historical figures. The authors use names that are the names of actual persons who lived at the time. There was indeed a Peter Tonneman, and he actually served as *Schout* of New Amsterdam in 1664. However, the character is fleshed out with a weight of detail that could not possibly have come from extant historical records; for purposes of classification within this work, he is treated as a fictional character. Similar decisions have been made for Asser Levy, whose name is recorded as that of a butcher in New Amsterdam, and Nicasius De Sille. They are included herein as fictional characters, not as historical figures, because every personal observation made of them, aside from their names and Tonneman and Levy's professions, was invented by the authors. It was determined that Clubber Williams would be recorded as a Historical Figure, even though the specific crimes attributed to him in *The House on Mulberry Street* are fictional, simply because they are entirely within the keeping of all that is known of him, and these paltry additions could not further blacken his character.

Literary Crimes & Chimes: These books not only are rich in period detail but include elements that make it seem as if the author had actually witnessed the events in question. Most historical novels offer information that appeals to the senses: information on sights, textures, smells, and sounds. These mysteries certainly do that, but they also mention the everyday dramas and absurdities that convey a strong sense of the people and their community. For instance, when relating how the townspeople fought a fire, not only are the buildings and the geography underlying the city depicted, but also the treatment of the Jews of New Amsterdam; and then the narrative goes into great detail: the buckets that are supposed to be set out at all times to battle fires are missing, because some rascal stole them (a recurring theme in the series); the faces of the people fighting the fire look grotesque in the fire's light; the excitement of the children as they get underfoot, one child yelling to his mother that he wants to carry a bucket of water, is described; and so forth. Highly recommended for all lovers of historical mystery fiction.

THE CASES

1. *The Dutchman.* New York: Doubleday, 1992, 306 p.

NEW AMSTERDAM, NEW YORK (later called NEW YORK, NEW YORK), 1664. Pieter Tonneman, New Amsterdam's *Schout*, has crawled into a bottle after the death of his wife; when he finds the body of his best friend, Pieter is so sunk in misery that it doesn't occur to him to question the apparent suicide. Pieter has to almost literally fall over the next murder victim before he realizes that crimes are being committed in his town. The murdered man's corpse is moved to implicate the Jewish community in his death, and Pieter finds his job complicated by his co-religionists' prejudices, as well as by his fascination with a young Jewish woman. Associates: Pos; Foxman; Nicasius and Geertruyd De Sille; Jan Keyser; David Mendoza; Asser Levy. Historical Figure: Pieter Stuyvesant.

2. *The Dutchman's Dilemma.* New York: Bantam Books, 1995, 254 p.

NEW-YORK [*sic*], New York, 1675. When a magnificent horse is killed and a piece of it left on the church altar in the *Book of Common Prayer*, Pieter Tonneman is hired to solve the crime. The madman who is killing the animals moves on to maiming and killing people, and the rumor mill attributes the crimes to witchcraft. Pieter's wife's work as a healer leaves her vulnerable to those who would claim that she is a witch, and Pieter realizes that he must solve the crimes quickly. Associates: Foxman; Nicasius and Geertruyd De Sille; Jan Keyser; Asser Levy.

3. *The Kingsbridge Plot: An Historical Mystery.* New York: Doubleday, 1993, 321 p.

NEW-YORK [*SIC*], NEW YORK, 1775. John Tonneman, recently returned from England, is made Coroner and given the job of investigating a grisly crime, the death and beheading of a young woman. He discovers not only a serial killer but also a plot to assassinate General George Washington. This story is based on the actual historical events that formed the basis of the Hickey Plot. Associates: Arthur "Jamie" Jamison; Gretel; Abigail; Constable Goldsmith; Molly; Quintin Brock. Historical Figures: General George Washington; Thomas Hickey; Samuel Fraunces; David Matthews; James Rivington; David Bushnell.

4. *The High Constable: An Historical Mystery.* New York: Doubleday, 1994, 307 p.

NEW-YORK [*SIC*], NEW YORK, 1808. The draining of Collect Pond reveals a number of corpses, victims of crimes recent and old. High Constable Jake Hays sees promise in Peter Tonneman, a young man who had seemed dedicated to becoming a wastrel. Peter seizes the chance to become a Constable and is so determined to succeed that he puts himself in grave peril. Associates: Leah Tonneman; Arthur "Jamie" Jamison; Constable Goldsmith; Molly; Quintin Brock; Bill Duffy; Charity Boenning. Historical Figures: Jake Hays; Aaron Burr.

5. **"The High Constable and the Visiting Author,"** in *Crime through Time*, ed. by Miriam Grace Monfredo and Sharan Newman. New York: Berkley Prime Crime, 1997, p. 184–199.

NEW-YORK [*SIC*], NEW YORK, FEBRUARY 1842. Charles Dickens visits New-York, and High Constable Jake Hays and Captain Peter Tonneman take him on a walk through the city (where he sees an attempted mugging) and to visit the Tombs prison (where he sees a successful jailbreak). Historical Figure: Charles Dickens.

6. **"The High Constable and the Rochester Rappers,"** in *Crime through Time II*, ed. by Miriam Grace Monfredo and Sharan Newman. New York: Berkley Prime Crime, 1998, p. 192–215.

NEW-YORK [*SIC*], NEW YORK, JUNE 1850. Jake Hays and Peter Tonneman (both retired) attend a séance with the intention of exposing the mediums as charlatans. Associate: Charity. Historical Figure: Horace Greeley.

7. *The Lucifer Contract: A Civil War Thriller.* New York: Bantam Books, 1998, 268 p.

MANHATTAN, NEW YORK, 1864. Pete Tonneman, a journalist who has recently returned from covering the Civil War, learns of a plot to torch New York on Election Day. Unfortunately, word of the plot has already been leaked to the newspapers, and the amused populace is treating it as a bizarre conspiracy theory. This novel was based on an actual historical incident, commonly called "The Incendiary Plot." Associates: Margaret "Meg" Clancy; Claudia Albert; Patrick Duff; Leah Tonneman; Philip Tonneman. Historical Figures: Police Superintendent John A. Kennedy; Mayor C. Godfrey Gunther; Horace Greeley; Edwin, Junius; John Wilkes Booth.

8. *The House on Mulberry Street.* New York: Bantam Books, 1996, 305 p.

MANHATTAN, NEW YORK, 1895. New York seems overrun by crime; it intrudes even at the wake honoring "Old Peter" Tonneman. Corruption reaching into the highest level of government protects the guilty rather than the innocent. When an afternoon's worth of exposed photographic plates is targeted by criminals, Dutch Tonneman realizes that their next target may be the photographer: she must be protected from people on all sides of the law. Associates: Margaret "Meg" Tonneman; Ned Clancy; Robert Roman; Father Duff; Esther Breslau. Historical Figures: Police Commissioner "Moose" Teddy Roosevelt; Police Commissioner "Peacock" Andrew D.

Parker; Chief of Detectives Thomas Byrnes; Clubber Williams; "Marm" Frederika Mandelson; Jack West.

MONFREDO, Miriam Grace (1940–). American.

Scene of the Crime: New York, New York, beginning in 1848, at a time when women were finally gaining civil rights in America (the Married Women's Property Act was passed in New York in 1848), and moving into the Civil War era.

Detective: Glynis Tryon always meant to be a spinster. She and all her friends in the Young Ladies Sewing Society made a pact when they were twelve or thirteen years old that they would never marry but would send each other friendship quilts (each of the group contributing a patch) for their respective thirtieth birthdays. Two of the group kept their pledge and chose to get an education instead of getting married. (At this time it was necessary for women to choose one or the other path.) The series starts the month that Gladys, the librarian in Seneca Falls, first receives her quilt. Glynis is the main protagonist through the first four books of the series. Bronwen Llyr, Glynis Tryon's niece, is the protagonist for the second part of the series. In *The Stalking Horse* Bronwen is a Pinkerton Detective; Glynis goes south to assist her in a dangerous investigation. The Pinkertons fire Bronwen, telling her that she is "undisciplined and not suitable material for a detective." However, her work has been admired by Rhys Bevan, who is hiring investigators for a Special Detective Unit, and she becomes an undercover agent for the U.S. government. She and Glynis work together again in *Must the Maiden Die?*. By *Sisters of Cain* Bronwen is the principal protagonist.

Known Associates: Glynis boards at Harriet Peartree's boardinghouse; she has a terrier named Duncan. Harriet Peartree's other boarder is Dictras Fyfe. Glynis holds her position as librarian for Seneca Falls through a yearly contract approved through the Library Board. Her assistant is Jonathan Quant. The town constable (and Glynis' best friend) is Cullen Stuart. Other townspeople who appear in most of the Glynis' Tryon part of the series include Jeremiah Merrycoyf, an attorney; hardware store owner Abraham Levy; Abraham's wife, Neva Cardoza-Levy; and the sisters, Aurora and Vanessa Usher. Historical Figures who appear prominently in the early books in the series include Elizabeth Cady Stanton and Susan Brownell Anthony; later books include depictions of Abraham Lincoln and General George McClellan. Bronwen's closest associates are the members of her family, starting with her sister Kathryn, who volunteers as a nurse in the War between the States; her brother, Seth, a soldier in the Union Army; her cousin, Emma, married and more or less settled by the beginning of the war; and her Aunt, Glynis. Bronwen's boss is Rhys Bevan; he organizes agents to conduct espionage for the Union. Bronwen works for him, as does Kerry O'Hara; they also work with Tristan "Marsh" Marshall. Bronwen's sister Kathryn works for Dr. Gregg Travis. Kathryn befriends Natty, a child of the streets, and eventually he is introduced to Bronwen as well. In the course of her investigations Bronwen is occasionally helped by Alain Farrar. Historical figures that show up repeatedly in the "Cain Trilogy" (the last three books of the series) include President Abraham Lincoln; Union spy Elizabeth Van Lew; Major William Norris, the head of the Confederate Secret Service Bureau; and his agent, Colonel Dorian de Warde, who seems unstoppable.

Premise: A woman and her niece investigate crimes and act as agents for the U.S. government in antebellum and Civil War America.

Comment: At the opening of the series, Seneca Falls is a growing city of 4,000 people. This is a time of social upheaval. While slavery is practiced in the United States, many citizens regard it as an evil. Some abolitionists have begun likening the position of women to a type of slavery, since a woman is essentially her husband's property. Advances in technology are changing the way that everything is done, from killing (new and better guns), to farming (machinery takes some of the jobs previously performed by men). Glynis Tryon is caught up in the social changes. Her friend, Elizabeth Cady Stanton, is working to organize the first Woman's Rights Convention (which takes place in the first book), and Glynis assists her. Glynis is painfully aware that many people regard a woman who chooses a profession over a marriage as unnatural. She's also aware of the precariousness of her position. If the Library Board finds her political stance offensive, she will lose her job, and it is unlikely that she will find another. She finds herself a part of society, but also strangely outside of it, fitting nowhere. She feels a special affinity for the downtrodden and the dispossessed; when she is asked to help them, she cannot say "no." This series shows very clearly the fine line that women had to walk as they attempted to fight for their rights without alienating those in power (i.e., men). As Glynis circulates a petition relating to the Woman's Rights Conference, townswomen give her a multitude of reasons for not being willing to sign. One states that she doesn't need any more rights and doesn't know what she would do with them if she had them, since her husband gives her everything she needs. Another tells Glynis that she would sign, but that to do so seems disloyal to her husband. One of the most compelling "characters" in the series is Elizabeth Cady Stanton, whose rash outspokenness often gives voice to sentiments that could be championed by modern-day women.

Literary Crimes & Chimes: Chapters are prefaced with quotes from documents of the time, often providing an interesting insight on how issues were viewed then. This series is very well researched (the author used to be a librarian); background notes at the end of each book give readers some of the pertinent historical facts. The narrative moves back and forth between the detective's point of view and that of others (usually just one or two others per book). Some of the novels have so many plot threads running that they are difficult for the uninitiated to follow. Characterizing women in such a way that they remain true to their time while not frustrating modern readers is difficult. There are times when Glynis' inherent shyness is extremely aggravating, as is the fact that a good many of the men she meets seem captivated primarily by her beauty (but have times really changed that much?). Bronwen, on the other hand, is sometimes unreasonable and even shrewish; there are moments when a reader can only agree that she is hopelessly unprofessional. Still, the view of this society provided through both of these female narrators is interesting and unusual and ultimately well worth the extra investment of energy on the part of the reader.

THE CASES

1. *Seneca Falls Inheritance.* New York: St. Martin's Press, 1992, 259 p.

NEW YORK, NEW YORK, 1848. Friedrich Steicher has died in an apparent accident, without leaving a will but leaving his affairs in utter disorder. Within a few weeks a new heir makes herself known to the family, and soon afterward she too is found dead in the canal near the library. Her murder is just the first in a series of seemingly unrelated crimes. Associate: Jacques Sundown. Historical Figure: Elizabeth Cady Stanton.

2. *North Star Conspiracy.* New York: St. Martin's Press, 1993, 332 p.

NEW YORK, NEW YORK, 1854. Glynis Tryon is extremely busy, preoccupied with the question of marriage, embroiled in efforts to acquire and open a local theater, and working on a state assembly election campaign for a candidate who favors women's rights. All of these concerns pale beside a friend's request to help a slave escape to freedom. Murders, both past and present, must be solved before the murderer strikes again to keep his secrets. Associates: Owen; Gwen; Katy; Bronwen; Seth; Emma; Niles; Kiri; Zeph; Jacques Sundown. Historical Figures: Frederick Douglass; Sojourner Truth; Matthew Brady.

3. *Blackwater Spirits.* New York: St. Martin's Press, 1995, 328 p.

NEW YORK, NEW YORK, 1857. In a time of social reform Glynis Tryon takes a stand against the racism directed at the Seneca Iroquois Indian tribe.

When a local farmer is murdered, suspicion falls naturally on Jacques Sundown, who has been a good friend to Glynis. Local prejudice complicates the investigation, and Glynis, sure that her friend is being framed for a crime that he did not commit, determines to investigate. Associates: Zeph; Jacques Sundown.

4. *Through a Gold Eagle: A Glynis Tryon Mystery.* New York: Berkley Prime Crime, 1996, 386 p.

NEW YORK, NEW YORK, 1859. On a train bound for Seneca Falls a fatally wounded man, fleeing from his assailant, whispers a cryptic message to Glynis and then drops a pouch into her lap. The contents of the container lead to an investigation of counterfeiting, slave revolts, and murder. Associates: Emma; Zeph; Fleur Coddington; Rhys Bevan. Historical Figures: Frederick Douglass; John Brown; Anne Brown.

5. *The Stalking Horse.* New York: Berkley Prime Crime, 1998, 340 p.

ALABAMA, 1861. Bronwen, Glynis' niece, has left school to become a detective in training for the Pinkerton Agency. She overhears several conspirators plotting and guesses that there will be an attempt to assassinate President-elect Abraham Lincoln. Frantic and believing that someone has guessed that she may be an agent, Bronwen sends a message to Glynis asking for her help. Associates: Thaddeus Dowling; Guy Seagram; Tristan Marshall; Rhys Bevan; Jacques Sundown; Glynis. Historical Figures: Abraham Lincoln; Mary Todd Lincoln; Elizabeth Van Lew; Allan Pinkerton.

6. *Must the Maiden Die?* New York: Berkley Prime Crime, 1999, 366 p.

NEW YORK, NEW YORK, 1861. Glynis' niece Emma is preparing for her wedding but is also struggling with the question of how she can marry without losing control of her shop. Glynis' involvement in the planning is interrupted when a prominent businessman is murdered, and suspicion falls on a woman who has had difficulty defending herself from accusations. Associates: Emma; Adam MacAlistair; Bronwen; Professor Lowe; Kathryn; Robin; Jacques Sundown; Rhys Bevan; Glynis.

7. *Sisters of Cain.* New York: Berkley Prime Crime, 2000, 368 p.

WASHINGTON, DC, 1862. The conduct of the Civil War is changing, with iron boats about to be launched. General McClellan is proposing an invasion of Viginia and the capture of Richmond. Rhys Bevan has been asked to train his operatives in espionage techniques, and Bronwen is sent to learn the battle plans of the Confederate Army. Associate: Jacques Sundown. Historical Figures: Joseph Maddox; Hattie Lawton; General George McClellan.

8. *Brothers of Cain.* New York: Berkley Prime Crime, 2001, 323 p.

VIRGINIA, 1862. When Bronwen's brother Seth is captured by the Rebels, she knows that she must go undercover to Richmond to see if she can save him. Bronwen has already seen a Pinkerton agent hanged by the

Rebels; if the wrong people realize that Seth is Bronwen's brother, he is sure to share that fate. Associate: Seth.

9. *Children of Cain*. New York: Berkley Prime Crime, 2002, 335 p.

UNITED STATES, 1862. Allan Pinkerton, inordinately proud of his investigators and styling them as the Union's Secret Service, refuses to believe that Bronwen, an agent he has dismissed, has learned information vital to the war effort. She fights to get word to McClellan as the war rages on. Historical Figures: General Robert E. Lee; General Stonewall Jackson; Allan Pinkerton; General George McClellan.

NEWMAN, Sharan (Elizabeth) (1949–). American.

CATHERINE LEVENDEUR SERIES

Scene of the Crime: Europe (mostly France), beginning in 1139 and continuing into the 1140s.

Detective: Catherine LeVendeur (born 1122). When the series opens, she is a novice at the Paraclete Convent.

Known Associates: In *Death Comes as Epiphany*, Catherine is sent by Héloïse into the world to investigate in secret, with a cover story for her family and friends. She soon gains an ally in Edgar of Wedderlie, a student of Abelard, who becomes her husband in *The Devil's Door*; they work together with Solomon ben Jacob, her cousin. One of her father's men, Jehan of Blois, loathes her and eventually threatens her family; he appears in the books throughout the series. Other continuing characters are members of Catherine's, Edgar's, and Solomon's families. Most prominent is Catherine's father, Hubert LeVendeur, who leaves to join the community at Arles at the end of *The Difficult Saint*; nonetheless, he appears in some of the later volumes, *To Wear the White Cloak* and *The Outcast Dove*; Catherine's sister, Agnes, is a pivotal character and plays a major role in *The Difficult Saint*. The carefully quiet lives of Solomon's uncle and aunt, Eliazar and Johannah, provide insight into the dangers faced by the Jewish community in medieval France; those dangers drive plots and subplots within the series. Edgar's sister joins their household in *Cursed in the Blood*, and Catherine gives birth to James in 1143 and to Edana in 1145. Catherine's mother, Madeleine, is prominent in *Death Comes as Epiphany* but retires to a convent in *The Devil's Door*. Her brother and his wife, Guillaume and Marie, are also prominent in *Death Comes as Epiphany* and appear intermittently in the series. Historical figures prominent in the books include Peter Abelard (until he dies in 1142), Héloïse, and their son, Astrolabe. Other historical personages, from clerks to prelates, are interwoven into the background of the stories.

Premise: A young woman solves crimes in twelfth-century France.

Comment: The novice nun Catherine LeVendeur has delayed taking her final vows, partly because she fears that she may love books more than she loves the Lord! The voice that speaks to her is not the voice of God, nor of the saints; instead, it is her own troubled conscience coupled with her relentless logic. Catherine notices discrepancies in what are essentially crime scenes, and her inner voices will not leave her alone until she resolves the conflicts thus created. In this hierarchical world where a woman's silence is valued almost as much as her obedience, Catherine has a difficult time. Her assets as an investigator and as a chronicler of her time and place are many. Through her father's dealings with Abbot Sugar and her own affiliation with the Paraclete Convent, Catherine has ties to the religious community. Through her father's trade partners, she has access to another group, the Jews of Paris. Through her own studies and Abbess Héloïse's relationship with Peter Abelard, she has ties to the community of scholars and students. The different books in the series provide insights into the daily lives in each of these communities. How could any reader not love a character who is afraid that she enjoys reading overmuch? Catherine is a warm, if somewhat impetuous, woman whose ruthless logic balances her susceptibility to romantic notions. Newman was a graduate student of medieval history when she wrote the first book in the series. The meticulous research underlying these books ensures an accurate picture of medieval life, and the vibrant writing allows the reader to step back into that time. The series turns darker with the fifth book, *Cursed in the Blood*, when some of the merriment leaves Edgar. He and Catherine become more adult in the following books, although still giving, thoughtful, and determined; they become more conscious of their responsibilities. The series is best read in order. The stories mostly center on the activities of Catherine and her family, the exceptions being the short story "Solomon's Decision" and the novel *The Outcast Dove*; Solomon ben Jacob is the protagonist in both.

Literary Crimes & Chimes: Newman's strengths include her careful attention to historical accuracy and to the details of medieval life. Through these books the reader can see the sights, hear the sounds, and smell the odors of twelfth-century Europe. Her characters are remarkable; these are not modern people in fancy dress but individuals with their own doubts, ideas, fears, and beliefs, all perfectly in tune with their time. The crimes result from acts of desperation brought about by the beliefs of the criminals and of their victims; everything is of a piece and works together to allow the reader to experience the medieval world. Solomon, Edgar, and Catherine play different roles in the investigations. Solomon's faith has put him at risk all of his life; as he states in *The Wandering Arm*, he was born a Jew and is therefore a foreigner everywhere (p. 33). He has become used to looking for hidden motives and is always careful. Edgar is an outsider to French society; he questions the societal conventions that he sees (giving the author a chance to explain) and, as a young man and a scholar, has access to areas that are off-limits to Catherine. On the other hand, Catherine can enter areas forbidden to men, and she has those troublingly logical voices! The conclusions of the books often hinge on an open confession by the guilty party, made after Catherine has uncovered the reason for the crimes and the likely perpetrators. Newman's first medieval mystery, *Death Comes as Epiphany*, won the Macavity for Best First Mystery of 1993, and *Cursed in the Blood* won the Herodotus Award for Best Historical Mystery of 1998.

THE CASES

1. **"Conventional Spirit,"** in *Malice Domestic 5*, ed. by Phyllis A. Whitney. New York: Pocket Books, 1996, p. 1–17.

PARACLETE CONVENT, FRANCE, 1137. As penance for her unorthodox claim (based on a letter of St. Ambrose) that St. Jerome had nagged St. Paula to death, Catherine is set to scrub the mud off the oratory floor. When she finds muddy footprints reappearing the next morning, she realizes that someone is entering the locked convent at night. Associates: Bertrada; Emelie; Felicitia.

2. **Death Comes as Epiphany.** New York: Tor, 1993, 319 p.

PARIS, FRANCE, 1139–1140. Rumors reach Abbess Héloïse that a psalter created at the Paraclete Convent as a gift for Abbot Sugar was examined at the library of Paris' Abbey of St. Denis and found to contain heretical writings; if true, this could cause the Nunnery to be disbanded. Héloïse sends one of the novices who worked on the psalter, Catherine LeVendeur (who has family in Paris), to check the book. Catherine discovers evil beyond the false witness of the psalter, evil that includes blackmail, theft, and murder. Associates: Bertrada; Edgar; Solomon.

3. **The Devil's Door.** New York: Forge, 1994, 384 p.

FRANCE, 1140. Knowing that she is grievously wounded, the Countess Alys of Tonnerre seeks the safety of the Paraclete Convent. Alys uses her last breath to commend her soul to God and to take her vows as a nun. Catherine rejoices in the woman's saving of her immortal soul but can't let go of the question of who assaulted the Countess, not just once, but repeatedly over many years. Associates: Bertrada; Edgar; Solomon.

4. _The Wandering Arm._ New York: Forge, 1995, 351 p.

FRANCE, 1141. When the Jews of Paris fall under suspicion because one of their community has been dealing in stolen Christian religious artifacts, melting them down and resetting the jewels, Edgar is asked to pose as a masterless metalsmith to draw out the thieves. The amount of money at stake and the punishment for the heresy of stealing from the Church ensure that the thieves will go to any lengths to conceal their crimes; but if the guilty parties are not found, and suspicion falls on the Jewish community in Paris, there could be a massacre. Associates: Edgar; Solomon.

5. "Solomon's Decision," in _Crime through Time_, ed. by Miriam Grace Monfredo and Sharan Newman. New York: Berkley Prime Crime, 1997, p. 54–69.

SPAIN, 1146. On a trading mission Solomon visits at the house of Yishmael. There he meets a brilliant young scholar with a passion for the truth. Solomon tries to help the scholar with a little matchmaking, but murder puts a stop to all such plans. Detective: Solomon. Associate: Mayah.

6. _Strong as Death._ New York: Forge, 1996, 384 p.

SPAIN, 1142. Catherine's prophetic dream sends her and her family on a pilgrimage to Spain to petition Saint James to add his voice to their prayers for a son. They travel with a group of other pilgrims, who have a surprising variety of motives for making the journey. One of them has a particularly impious goal—revenge and murder! Associates: James; Aaron; Edgar; Solomon.

7. _Cursed in the Blood._ New York: Forge, 1998, 348 p.

SCOTLAND, 1143. Edgar is called home after two of his brothers are ambushed and murdered. Someone is exacting revenge against the entire Wedderlie family. Catherine must uncover the reasons for this vendetta, if she is to find a way to stop the massacre before Edgar is claimed. Associates: Adalisa; Edgar.

8. "Death before Compline," in _Death Dines at 8:30_, ed. by Claudia Bishop and Nick DiChario. New York: Berkley Prime Crime, 2001, p. 239–258.

PARACLETE CONVENT, FRANCE, 1146. The corpse of a young man is discovered at the Paraclete Convent; he was ex-communicant and had not returned to the fold. The nuns grieve not only for the loss of his life but also for the loss of his soul. Catherine's son James finds a vital clue to the murder. A recipe for Feast Day Fish Stew is included! Associates: James; Edgar.

9. *The Difficult Saint.* New York: Forge, 1999, 352 p.

GERMANY, 1146. Agnes was delighted with the idea of a marriage to a German man, as happy at the prospect of never setting eyes on her family again as in the hope of a good marriage. When her new husband is murdered, she is seized and held pending her execution. Agnes sends to her grandfather for an advocate; as soon as Catherine's family hears of the accusations against her, they rush to Agnes' side. Associates: Bertrada; Agnes; Edgar; Solomon.

10. *To Wear the White Cloak.* New York: Forge, 2000, 367 p.

FRANCE, 1147. Catherine and her family return to Paris after their year-long sojourn to rescue Agnes in Germany. They find Paris in tumult, filled with men anxious to join the Crusades and kill the non-Christians. Catherine's family and the Jews of Paris are particularly anxious not to call attention to themselves; when Catherine and Edgar find the corpse of a Crusader in their home, they must solve the murder quickly. Associates: Edgar; Agnes; Solomon.

11. *Heresy: A Catherine LeVendeur Mystery.* New York: Forge, 2002, 352 p.

FRANCE, 1147. A group of peasants and runaway serfs live in the forest, followers of a charismatic madman who believes that he is the son of God. When a band of knights attacks the group, murdering a woman whom they were sheltering, they try to frame Astrolabe for the crime. Catherine and Edgar must work against powerful men to clear him of suspicion. Associates: Astrolabe; Edgar; Solomon.

12. *The Outcast Dove.* New York: Forge, 2003, 432 p.

FRANCE AND SPAIN, 1148. Edgar, uneasy about his wife, has turned back from a trading expedition, but Solomon continues on. In Toulouse Solomon finds his old enemy, Jehan, his Uncle Hubert, who stumbles across a murdered man, and his father, who may accuse Hubert of apostasy and ruin Hubert's family. Crowning all of this is the news that a woman he admires, Mayah, has been taken as a slave. Solomon soon joins a party traveling to rescue her. Detective: Solomon. Associates: James; Caudiza; Anna; Aaron; Mayah; Edgar.

13. *The Witch in the Well.* New York: Forge, 2004, 352 p.

BOISVERT CASTLE, FRANCE, 1148? Catherine's grandfather sends for his family to tell them their well is going dry. This is alarming news, because the family's wealth depends on its status; if the well goes dry, the castle will fall. Grandfather expresses a deeper fear, however, in a mysterious woman who is either old or young, dead or alive, depending on whom one asks. Catherine does not share her family's belief in such superstititions or the legend that they are descended from a liaison between one of Charlemagne's knights and a faerie. When dead bodies start turning up, Catherine knows she's right and must uncover the secrets of the witch in the well in order to save her family's birthright. Associates: Grandfather; Edgar; Solomon.

CRIME THROUGH TIME ANTHOLOGY SERIES

Scene of the Crime: Various.

Detective: Various.

Known Associates: Various.

Premise: The editors have compiled three anthologies featuring historical mystery stories from various eras.

Comment: Both of these authors are well-known fiction writers in their own right, with major story and novel credits in the subgenre. These three books feature mostly American writers of historical detectives, with a sprinkling of top-name British practitioners. The majority of the tales are original to the volumes in question.

Literary Crimes & Chimes: As might be expected, Monfredo and Newman have produced a set of high-quality volumes. All of the major writers in the field, particularly on the American side of the Atlantic, are included. These are books that any fan of the historical mystery story will want to own.

THE CASES

1. *Crime through Time,* ed. by Miriam Grace Monfredo and Sharan Newman. New York: Berkley Prime Crime, 1997, 373 p.
   An anthology of general historical detective stories. CONTENTS: "Introduction," by Miriam Grace Monfredo and Sharan Newman; "Death of a Place-Seeker," by Lynda S. Robinson; "Archimedes' Tomb," by Steven Saylor; "Solomon's Decision," by Sharan Newman; "Murder at Anchor," by Edward Marston; "The Hangman's Apprentice," by Leonard Tourney; "Suffer a Witch," by Miriam Grace Monfredo; "The Lullaby Cheat," by Kate Ross; "Anything in the Dark," by Edward D. Hoch; "Bertie and the Boat Race," by Peter Lovesey; "The High Constable and the Visiting Author," by Maan Meyers; "Look to the Lady," by Alanna Knight; "Mrs Hudson's Case," by Laurie King; "Exit Centre Stage," by M. J. Trow; "Decision of the Umpire," by Troy Soos; "Uncle Charlie's Letters," by Anne Perry; "Killing the Critic," by Gillian Linscott; "Portrait of the Artist as a Young Corpse," by Barbara Paul; "The Mamur Zapt and the Kodaker's Eye," by Michael Pearce; "Storm in a Tea Shoppe," by Carola Dunn; "The Enemy," by Ken Kuhnken; "The Soldier and His Dead Companion," by Nicholas A. DiChario.

2. *Crime through Time II,* ed. by Miriam Grace Monfredo and Sharan Newman. New York: Berkley Prime Crime, 1998, 352 p.

A second anthology of general historical detective stories. CONTENTS: "Introduction," by Antonia Fraser; "Preface," by Sharan Newman and Miriam Grace Monfredo; "Murder One," by Walter Satterthwait; "The Etruscan House," by John Maddox Roberts; "Domesday Deferred," by Edward Marston; "The Movable City," by Edward D. Hoch; "The Case of the Santo Niño," by Anne Perry; "Anna and the Mirror," by Dianne Day; "Mizu-Age," by Laura Joh Rowland; "A Scientific Education," by Nancy Kress; "A Mule Named Sal," by Miriam Grace Monfredo; "Sense and Sensuality," by Robert Barnard; "The High Constable and the Rochester Rappers," by Maan Meyers; "The Ballad of Gentleman Jem," by Gillian Linscott; "The Hungry Ghost of Panamint," by William F. Wu; "The Promised Land," by Sharan Newman; "Mesmerizing Bertie," by Carole Nelson Douglas; "A Man of My Stature," by Jan Burke; "Fearful," by Sarah Smith; "Unsinkable," by Elizabeth Foxwell; "Dorothy Past and Present," by Michael Coney.

3. *Crime through Time III,* ed. by Sharan Newman. New York: Berkley Prime Crime, 2000, 332 p.

A third anthology of general historical detective stories. CONTENTS: "Introduction," by Anne Perry; "Preface," by Sharan Newman; "The Consul's Wife," by Steven Saylor; "Merchants of Discord," by Laura Frankos; "Farmers' Law," by Harry Turtledove; "The Case of the Murdered Pope," by Andrew Greeley; "Lark in the Morning," by Sharyn McCrumb; "The Weeping Time," by Maureen Jennings; "The Irish Widower," by Leonard Tourney; "Smoke," by William Sanders; "The Episode of the Water Closet," by Bruce Alexander; "Suspicion," by Michael Coney; "Murder in Utopia," by Peter Robinson; "Dr. Death," by Peter Lovesey; "Dinner with H.P.B." by Eileen Kernaghan; "The Haunting of Carrick Hollow," by Jan Burke and Paul Sledzik; "Howard," by H.R.F. Keating; "Come Flit by Me," by Elizabeth Foxwell; "Murder on the Denver Express," by Margaret Coel; "A Single Spy," by Miriam Grace Monfredo.

NOLAN, William F(rancis) (1928–). American.

THE BLACK MASK BOYS SERIES

Scene of the Crime: California, beginning in 1935.

Detective: Real-life mystery writers Dashiell Hammett, Erle Stanley Gardner, and Raymond Chandler.

Known Associates: Although the writers encounter the usual denizens of Southern California urban life in the depression era, including some real-life historical figures, there are no "Associates" as such.

Premise: Three famous detective authors solve crimes together, with a different writer narrating each of the three stories.

Comment: Nolan, a well-known writer of mystery, science fiction, and horror stories and novels, produces an original take on Hollywood of the 1930s, combining the talents of three detective writers of the period to solve the crimes of which they become aware or in which they are personally involved. The author deliberately did not try to copy the literary styles of the writer-characters telling the stories but does include some very clever and very well composed one-liners of his own. Nolan's research is meticulous, and we have a sense of being thrust into a period that is now almost as alien to us as the 1850s. Well-crafted and well-written, these novels are way above the ordinary for historical mysteries of the period. Three further tales in the series were planned but were never actually published: *Once a Pinkerton* (narrated by Hammett), *Killer's Moon* (narrated by Chandler), and *Material Witness* (narrated by Gardner).

Literary Crimes & Chimes: As with all of the historical mysteries of this type, which are based on real-life figures as the central narrators of the story, one wonders how any of the writer-detectives could have actually been involved in such goings-on without the public becoming aware of the crimes. All of these individuals spent way too much time in the public eye to have escaped the scrutiny of the press. Having said this, though, Nolan does an excellent of convincing us that these stories *could* have taken place. The mysteries themselves are well-wrought puzzles worthy of the analytical minds who ultimately unravel them.

THE CASES

1. *The Black Mask Murders: A Novel Featuring the Black Mask Boys: Dashiell Hammett, Raymond Chandler, and Erle Stanley Gardner.* New York: A Thomas Dunne Book, St. Martin's Press, 1994, 214 p.
   HOLLYWOOD, CALIFORNIA, DECEMBER? 1935. A jeweled skull, the so-called cat's eye, has been stolen, and several individuals involved with the artifact murdered, drawing the three writers together for the first time to solve this intricate puzzle. Narrated by Dashiell Hammett.

2. *The Marble Orchard, Starring: Raymond Chandler.* New York: A Thomas Dunne Book, St. Martin's Press, 1996, 230 p.
   CALIFORNIA, 1936. The "Black Mask Boys" solve several murders involving the "Vampire Queen," a well-known horror star of the screen who

sends Raymond Chandler searching for her missing sister. The action moves swiftly from the coastal splendors of Hearst Castle, to the abandoned canals of Venice by the Sea, to an ornate hotel on Coronado Island off San Diego to the rococo Victorian mansions of Bunker Hill in Los Angeles. Narrated by Raymond Chandler.

3. *Sharks Never Sleep: A Novel Featuring the Black Mask Boys: Dashiell Hammett, Raymond Chandler, and Erle Stanley Gardner.* New York: A Thomas Dunne Book, St. Martin's Press, 1998, 242 p.

HOLLYWOOD, CALIFORNIA, 1937. The "Black Mask Boys" are back in action once again. This time Gardner is arrested for murder and must defend himself in court, *à la* his own literary creation, Perry Mason. Hammett and Chandler provide vital assistance in proving him innocent of the crime. Narrated by Erle Stanley Gardner.

PAIGE, Robin (pseud. of Susan Wittig Albert [1940–] and William J. Albert). American.

KATE ARDLEIGH SERIES

Scene of the Crime: Essex, England, beginning in 1894 and continuing into the early 1900s.

Detective: Kathryn "Kate" Ardleigh, Irish American author of "penny-dreadfuls" written under the pseudonym of "Beryl Bardwell." She relocates to Essex in order to claim her ancestral home, the Georgian estate known as "Bishop's Keep."

Known Associates: Sir Charles Sheridan, later Baron of Somersworth, a renowned photographer, amateur scientist, and skilled detective and Kate's husband from *Death at Devil's Bridge*; Sabrina Ardleigh and Bernice Jaggers, Kate's aunts, who bring her to England—their mysterious deaths in the first volume (*Death at Bishop's Keep*) are not only mysteries to be solved by Kate but leave her, as their only living heir, the new owner of Bishop's Keep estate; Eleanor and Bradford Marsden, brother and sister, Kate's neighbors at Bishop's Keep; Sarah Pratt, the cook at Bishop's Keep; Lawrence and Amelia, the Sheridans' servants (from *Death at Gallows Green*; Amelia is Sarah Pratt's niece); Police Constable Edward "Ned" Laken, Sir Charles' boyhood friend (from *Death at Gallows Green*); Albert Edward "Bertie," Prince of Wales, later King Edward VII of Great Britain, who from time to time calls on Kate and Sir Charles to assist in solving some urgent problem of state.

Premise: A young American writer inherits an estate in rural England and begins solving real-life crimes in turn-of-the-century Britain.

Comment: Kate Ardleigh, a twenty-five-year-old Irish American writer of crime fiction, is everything an English gentlewoman is not—outspoken and freethinking. After relocating to Essex, England, at the behest of her aunt, Sabrina Ardleigh, she begins looking for situations in the English countryside that will provide fodder for the lurid mysteries she writes as "Beryl Bardwell." Inevitably, she captures the interest of her aunt's neighbor, Sir Charles Sheridan, as they begin their first case together. Each case centers around a different physical scene or *milieu,* and each involves a crime or murder with close historical and/or literary ties. For instance, the first book, *Death at Bishop's Keep,* features a body recovered at an archeological dig associated with the secret occult society, the Order of the Golden Dawn. In the second book, *Death at Gallows Green,* Kate is assisted by a shy young woman who introduces herself as Beatrix Potter. Other sequences include "characters" such as Rudyard Kipling, Arthur Conan Doyle, and Jack London, among many others relying heavily on precedents set by the modern Gothic *genre,* the authors have created a spunky and attractive young American-born neophyte, Kate, who is gently and successfully guided through daunting adventures by her strong male counterpart, Sir Charles. Manor houses and ghoulish moors abound. Susan Wittig Albert is also the author of the popular "China Bayles" mystery series, and Bill Albert is the coauthor, with his wife, of more than sixty novels for young adults.

Literary Crimes & Chimes: The authors have done their research, delving through various and sundry historical events in order to provide fodder for their imaginative extrapolations (much as Kate herself researches the crimes and murders *she* encounters as inspiration for her own potboiling efforts). Beginning with the second book, *Death at Gallows Green,* "Historical Notes," "Authors' Notes" and/or "References" are appended that provide background information on the real-life characters and circumstances in the story at hand. Beginning with the fourth book, *Death at Devil's Bridge,* a helpful "Major Characters" or "Cast of Characters" list is also included. The books are an entertaining romp, especially for those who will enjoy the literary and historical tie-ins and allusions. There is a progression in the series, as Kate and Charles meet, fall in love, and marry, so the books should be read in order. There's nothing very deep here, and the plots often seem contrived, but the stories are fast-paced and the characters attractive, even if they are reminiscent of the "usual suspects," English country, "drawing-room," or "cozy" mystery genre.

THE CASES

1. *Death at Bishop's Keep.* New York: Avon Books, 1994, 266 p.

NEW YORK, NEW YORK, AND BISHOP'S KEEP, ESSEX, ENGLAND, 1894. American mystery writer Katherine "Kate" Ardleigh arrives in England at the invitation of her deceased father's elder sister, Sabrina Ardleigh; but the household at Bishop's Keep, especially her straitlaced younger aunt, Bernice Jaggers, is shocked by the young woman's self-assured progressive approach to her new surroundings. When a fresh corpse is discovered at a nearby archeological dig, Kate eagerly takes part in the investigation, convinced that the find will provide a perfect premise for her latest crime novel. But she is unprepared for the surprises in store for her, especially when the trail leads her to a secret occult society known as the Order of the Golden Dawn. Then the affair turns even deadlier with the mysterious poisoning of both her aunts. Kate, as their only living heir, inherits the manor and estate of Bishop's Keep—and thus stands to gain immensely from the untimely deaths. Another old family retainer, the cook Sarah Pratt, comes under suspicion, and Kate is forced to solve the double murders in order to clear both their names. During her investigations she meets and captures the attention of amateur sleuth Sir Charles Sheridan, and they join forces to seek answers to the mysteries confronting them. Associates: Sabrina Ardleigh, Kate's aunt, who brings her to Bishop's Keep; Bernice Jaggers, her less supportive aunt; Charles; Kate's friend and neighbor; Eleanor; Bradford; Sarah; Mudd, the butler; Vicar Barfield Talbot. Historical Figures: Arthur Conan Doyle; Oscar Wilde; William Butler "Willie" Yeats, all members of the Order of the Golden Dawn.

2. *Death at Gallows Green.* New York: Avon Books, 1995, 267 p.

MELFORD HALL, SUDBURY, SUFFOLK; GALLOWS GREEN, ESSEX, ENGLAND, 1895. Kate is settling into her new role as mistress of Bishop's Keep, a rambling Georgian estate that includes a holding of some 700 acres. At her friend Eleanor's suggestion, Lady Hyde-Parker of Melford Hall has invited Kate to spend several weeks at her estate near Sudbury in Suffolk. She agrees, hoping to find fodder for the newest book by "Beryl Bardwell," Kate's *nom de plume.* She is initially bored with the outing, but things pick up when she makes the acquaintance of "Bea" and her charming pets. The brutal demise of a local constable, Sergeant Arthur Oliver, in Mr. McGregor's garden on the Marsden estate, is discovered by Kate's servant Amelia. The grisly murder, coupled with the disappearance of a child, bring the sleuthing couple together again. With the assistance of the shy young woman who calls herself Beatrix Potter, Kate and Sir Charles follow a trail of deadly greed and mischief to a successful conclusion. Associates: Charles; Eleanor

Fairley *née* Marsden; Bradford; Sarah; Constable Laken; Amelia; Amelia's beau, Lawrence. Historical Figure: Beatrix Potter.

3. *Death at Daisy's Folly.* New York: Berkeley Prime Crime, 1997, 274 p.

EASTON LODGE, GREAT DUNMOW, ENGLAND, 1896. The Countess of Warwick, known affectionately as "Daisy," is the subject of endless rumors about her "unladylike" ways and temperament. But what happens during a weekend party at her Easton estate is uglier than any rumor. First, Harry Gordon, young groom to the Prince of Wales, is killed. Then a nobleman, Reggie Wallace, is murdered outside Daisy's well-known trysting spot. Seeking to avoid the inevitable scandal, Daisy's "friend" and protector, "Bertie," the Prince of Wales, orders Sir Charles to solve the case. He and Kate soon discover, however, that even the highest levels of society cannot be protected from the deadliest of deeds. Associates: Charles; Eleanor; Bradford; Lawrence; Amelia; Andrew Kirk-Smythe, an Officer of the Guards and secretly bodyguard to the Prince of Wales. Historical Figures: Albert Edward "Bertie," Prince of Wales; Lady Frances "Daisy" Brooke, Countess of Warwick; Daisy's husband, Lord Francis Brooke, Earl of Warwick.

4. *Death at Devil's Bridge.* New York: Berkeley Prime Crime, 1998, 274 p.

BISHOP'S KEEP, ESSEX, ENGLAND, 1897. The attraction between Charles and Kate has turned to affection and then to love, as they solved the murders at the Countess of Warwick's weekend house. Now they are newlyweds and have settled into Kate's estate at Bishop's Keep, where she plans to devote herself to her writing while Charles tends to the responsibilities of the landed gentry. He agrees to host an automobile exhibition and balloon race, which will be attended by Europe's foremost investors and inventors, among them the young Charles Rolls and Henry Royce. Speed, competition, and money prove to be more explosive than gasoline and even more deadly, as the couple are drawn once more into mystery and intrigue. Associates: Charles; Bradford; Patsy Marsden, Bradford's sister; Sarah; Mudd, the butler; Vicar Barfield Talbot, who married the Sheridans; Constable Laken; Coroner Harry Hodson; Lawrence Quibbley; Amelia, now married to Lawrence. Historical Figures: Charles Stewart "Charlie" Rolls and Henry Royce, automobile pioneers.

5. *Death at Rottingdean.* New York: Berkeley Prime Crime, 1999, 290 p.

SEABROOKE HOUSE, ROTTINGDEAN, NEAR BRIGHTON, ENGLAND, LATE SUMMER 1898. Kate's husband, Sir Charles Sheridan, following the untimely death of his elder brother Robert the preceding Christmas, has become Baron of Somersworth and has moved with Kate to the family mansion in London to take up his duties and his seat in the House of Lords. Kate is exhausted by her social obligations and life in the big city. She is devastated when her early pregnancy fails, especially when it is revealed she will never again be able to conceive. The Sheridans decide to take a much-needed seaside holiday to forget their tragedy, taking with them only their trusted servants, Lawrence and Amelia. They arrive at Seabrooke House in Rottingdean, a quaint hamlet known locally as "Smuggler's Village," which straddles a labyrinth of 100-year-old tunnels through which contraband goods were once moved in and out of England. When the body of a coastal guard is discovered on the beach, the couple suspect that the town is still plying its illicit trades of the past. With the assistance of an imaginative young writer named Rudyard Kipling, they are about to discover that something is indeed "rotten" in the town of Rottingdean. The authors note that their "German invasion of Britain" plot was inspired by Sir George Chesney's 1871 novella, *Battle of Dorking*, a bestseller of its time. Associates: Charles; Lawrence and Amelia; Patrick "Paddy," an eleven-year-old waif who witnesses the murder— the Sheridans informally adopt him at the end of the book; Constable Jack "Fat Jack" Woodhouse of Rottingdean; Chief Constable Sir Robert Pinkney of Brighton, British Coast Guard Captain Reynold Smith; Count Ludwig Hauptmann, Cultural Representative of the Kaiser; Arthur and Reuben Sassoon, wealthy residents of Brighton. Historical Figures: Edward and Georgiana "Georgie" Burne-Jones, the Pre-Raphaelite painter and his wife; their nephew, the writer Rudyard "Rud" Kipling and his wife Caroline; Stanley and Lucy Baldwin; Bertie, Prince of Wales.

6. *Death at Whitechapel.* New York: Berkeley Prime Crime, 2000, 276 p.

BISHOP'S KEEP, ESSEX, LONDON, ENGLAND, OCTOBER 1898. Kate is becoming accustomed to her new role in society as Baroness of Somersworth. She meets kindred spirit Jennie Jerome Churchill, whose carefree lifestyle has made her the target of the tabloids. Kate soon discovers that Jennie is being blackmailed by someone who has made a heinous accusation. Someone claims to have proof that Jennie's husband, Lord Randolph Churchill, father of her son Winston, was none other than the notorious Jack the Ripper! Kate and Charles must put a stop to the scandal, which threatens Winston's future political career. Their investigations lead them to the highest levels of society for the incredible answer to murders long unsolved. Associates: Charles; Bradford; Constable Laken; George Cornwallis-West, Jennie's lover; Walter Sickert, artist and friend to Prince "Eddy"; Sister Ursula, registrar at Saint Saviour's Chapel; Sarah. Historical Figures: Jennie Jerome Churchill, widow of Randolph Churchill; Lieutenant Winston Churchill, Jennie's son.

7. *Death at Epsom Downs.* New York: Berkeley Prime Crime, 2001, 292 p.

EPSOM DOWNS; BISHOP'S KEEP, ENGLAND, MAY–SEPTEMBER 1899. Lord Charles is planning to photograph the Derby Day races at Epsom Downs with his new camera, while his wife, Kate, watches from the stands. It's a thrilling day for the Sheridans, made more so when the race ends abruptly with a jockey's death. When her husband is called to investigate the incident, Kate travels to the countryside, where she is scheduled to interview world-renowned actress Lillie Langtry for a magazine article. As Kate puzzles over the long-ago theft of the actress' jewels, she is not surprised when Charles' own investigation begins to turn in Lillie's direction. Sorting through rumors of bitter rivalries and torrid love affairs, Kate and Charles embark on a race for justice that may turn out to be a photo finish. Associates: Charles; Patrick, now an apprentice jockey; Lawrence and Amelia; Bradford; Edith Hill; Bradford's *fiancée*; Lord Reginald Hunt, owner of the racehorse Gladiator. Historical Figures: Jennie Churchill; "Bertie," Prince of Wales; Lillie Langtry; Jeanne-Marie Langtry, Lillie's daughter; Hugo de Bathe, Lillie's future husband.

8. *Death at Dartmoor.* New York: Berkeley Prime Crime, 2002, 324 p.

DARTMOOR PRISON, ENGLAND, MARCH 1901. Although the Sheridans have heard truly awful things about Britain's most notorious prison at Dartmoor, Kate hopes to find inspiration for her latest novel within its mist-shrouded environs. Charles will accompany her in order to implement a new fingerprinting program at the prison and arrange a meeting with one of its most infamous inmates, Samuel Spencer. Charles is convinced that Spencer, a Scotsman who admitted to killing his wife, is, in fact, innocent. What's more, he believes he has the evidence to prove it. Spencer not only continues to maintain his guilt, he confirms it by staging a daring prison escape! Charles and his acquaintance, Arthur Conan Doyle, are most perplexed by this turn of events. And when a body turns up on the moor, it's up to the two men, assisted by the clever Kate, to discover if the missing convict is connected to the new murder. Associates: Charles; Patsy Marsden, their friend; Samuel "Sam" Spencer, the accused; William Crossing, who is compiling a guidebook on Dartmoor; Fletcher Robinson, Doyle's *protégé*; Constable Chapman; Major Cranford, Sheridan's assistant on the fingerprinting project. Historical Figure: Arthur Conan Doyle.

9. *Death at Glamis Castle.* New York: Berkeley Prime Crime, 2003, 338 p.

HOUSESTEADS, NORTHUMBERLAND; GLAMIS CASTLE, ENGLAND, AUGUST 1901. Kate and Sir Charles are on another archeological dig, this time excavating the ruins at Hadrian's Wall, when they are summoned to Glamis Castle by King Edward VII. Nestled in the rugged Grampian Mountains, Glamis is the most historic castle in all of Scotland, a place teeming with dark secrets and haunting shadows. While Kate wends her way through the ancient manor, seeking inspiration for her next Gothic novel, Charles is made aware of the reason behind their journey. Prince "Eddy," rightful heir to the throne until his purported death in 1892, has actually been alive all these years. Deemed unfit to rule, he has been living secretly at Glamis under an assumed name. But now he has disappeared, on the very morning the body of one of his servants was found, her throat slashed in a manner reminiscent of the Ripper's! The sleuthing couple must find Eddy and clear his name, while keeping his true identity a secret. Associates: Charles; British Intelligence officer Andrew Kirk-Smythe, the King's bodyguard; Flora MacDonald, housemaid at Glamis and friend to "Lord Osborne"; Angus Duff, estate factor at Glamis Castle; Constable Oliver Graham; German Intelligence officer Count Ludwig von Hauptmann. Historical Figures: British King Edward VII; Princess Victoria "Toria"; First Counselor Friedrich von Holstein, the German Kaiser's "Grey Eminence"; Prince Albert Victor Christian Edward "Eddy," Duke of Clarence; Lady Glamis (Cecilia Bowes-Lyon), wife of Lord Glamis; Lady Elizabeth Bowes-Lyon (later wife of King George VI and mother of Queen Elizabeth II).

10. _Death in Hyde Park._ New York: Berkley Prime Crime, 2004, 296 p.

ENGLAND, 1901. A bomb meant for England's new King Edward and Queen Alexandra reveals a terrorist plot and raises an urgent question: in a world full of spies and counterspies, who might be responsible for this latest threat? Jack London, an American author and well-known Socialist, is drawn into the multilayered plot, and Kate and Sir Charles are drawn in as well, to untangle it. Associate: Charles. Historical Figures: British King Edward VII; Queen Alexandra; Jack London.

PARRY, Owen (pseud. of Ralph Peters) (1952–). American.

CAPTAIN ABEL JONES SERIES

Scene of the Crime: The "scene of the crime" shifts from book to book. The focus of the series is always the American Civil War and the battlefronts thereof, as well as the places adjoining or supplying those battlefronts, beginning in 1861.

Detective: Abel Jones looks unimpressive, but he's very tough. He was born in Wales, Merthyr Tydfil, in 1828. He served in Queen Victoria's army in India; his short stature coupled with his great fierceness surprised his compatriots, and he rose to the rank of Sergeant. He reevaluated the situation when he was ordered to lead bayonet practice on bound prisoners. He refused to kill any more captives. His commander, Colonel Tice-Rolley, had regarded him as heroic and did not want to see him hanged, so he convinced the surgeon to write Jones up as "mad of a fever" and unfit for duty and sent him home. The woman who had waited for him, Mary Myfanwy, determined that they would immigrate to America to escape local gossip. They love America and were happily settled (Abel was working as a clerk), when the Civil War broke out. He determined to stay out of the conflict, but when he saw the neighbor boys drilling with boundless incompetence, he could not stand back and let them go forth to be slaughtered. Jones stepped in and trained the troops and then led them at the First Battle of Bull Run, where he was badly injured. He was too stubborn to let the surgeon take his leg and too tough to die; he refused to return home. No longer fit for fighting, he's now working as a clerk dedicating himself to ensuring that the troops receive needed supplies.

Known Associates: Dearest to Abel Jones is his wife, Mary Myfanwy, a woman with the ability to think through a problem and spot inconsistencies. He thinks of her and the son he hardly knows, John, every day, and he visits home as often as he can. When they have a chance to talk, Mary's recommendations are extremely useful; she uses her common sense to set herself up as a seamstress, after Jones purchases for her a Singer machine, asking Jones' permission in *Call Each River Jordan*; her business is thriving in *Bold Sons of Erin*. Jones' ward, Frances Raeburn, joins the household in *Honor's Kingdom*. In the field and at the front Jones is assisted by his friends: Evans, a good Glamorgan man who works in the War Department's Telegraph office; Dr. Michael Tyrone, a man driven to save as many people as he can; and Jimmy Molloy, whom Jones discovered to be a thief when they served together in India but who is trying to make something of himself in America. Other recurring characters include Mrs. Schutzengel, Jones' landlady; and Annie Fitzgerald, who began work for Mrs. Schutzengel in *Faded Coat of Blue*, and married Molloy in 1862.

Premise: A Welsh-American soldier solves crimes during the American Civil War.

Comment: Jones is working as a clerk when General McClellan sends for him and asks him to investigate a politically sensitive murder. Jones protests that he does not have the skill, but he does learn from his mistakes as the series progresses. In the course of that first investigation he finds that the basis of the recommendation was the belief that Jones could be easily led. McClellan soon discovers that he was misinformed. Jones' honesty and tenacity bring him to the attention of President Lincoln, who promotes him to Major (*Faded Coat of Blue*), and Lincoln's office takes over assigning his investigations. When Abel faces death in *Faded Coat of Blue*, he writes a letter to his wife and then speaks to his landlady about hiring a girl that he met in his investigations, a girl who has lost her job and who will be turned out of her lodgings onto the street if she does not find another. He tells his landlady, "You said yourself that justice would only come in America. But it will never come if we don't make it come, see." This is Abel Jones in a nutshell: the determination, the compassion, the methodical care of everyone, even of a woman whom he just met as he faces his own death. He sees himself as plodding and does not view his integrity and compassion as at all heroic; but he remains a memorable and admirable character. Jones' stated views on people of other ethnicities, other races, and on women are certainly not admirable, but they were the views of most of the men of the 1860s and do reflect the popular wisdom of that time. Jones does indeed repeat many vile stereotypes, but in his actions he is always compassionate and thoughtful. He thinks in the vernacular of his era, but he also sometimes rises above it.

Literary Crimes & Chimes: The language of the narrative harks back to the painfully beautiful language found in Civil War letters, a time when words were used to convey more than simple facts, a time when the ways in which words were put together was somehow more thoughtful, with ideas and philosophy bound up in them. Even when Abel Jones is being cynical, his language is tempered with moral conviction and with humor, as in, "Our government bled money to buy the things that soldiers needed, but the relationship between payment and delivery seemed to have broken down. There was not an excess of honesty among the manufacturers, if I may be pardoned the frankness, and not a few seemed to regard the war first and foremost as a splendid opportunity to bolster their fortunes. Nor was our government composed entirely of innocents" (*Faded Coat of Blue*, p. 9). The colorful language spices up both the dialogue and the narrator's voice, as in Jones' observation when Major Campbell, the adjutant, is shown the corpse of a murdered man: " 'Well, I'll be damned and resurrected,' he said, and I am certain that he was half correct" (*Faded Coat of Blue*, p. 4). The characters also shine with humanity, most having some good in them as well as weakness; and the men (mostly men) themselves determine whether that weakness will rule them or whether they will be virtuous (or mostly virtuous) in spite of it. The first novel in the series, *Faded Coat of Blue*, won the 1999 Herodotus Award for Best First U.S. Historical Mystery. The series is best read in straight order, since the relationships between the continuing characters evolve over time.

THE CASES

1. *Faded Coat of Blue.* New York: Avon Books, 1999, 338 p.

WASHINGTON, DC, AND PHILADELPHIA, PENNSYLVANIA, NOVEMBER 1861. Anthony Fowler was a hero in abolitionist circles, a golden boy who spoke passionately about the cause. He was also an ordnance officer who may have stumbled upon proof of corruption so vile that it verges on treason. When he is found shot beside a Union encampment, Abel Jones is asked to conduct an inquiry. Was Fowler killed by raw recruits nervously firing into the storm in the night, by "Southron" agents desperate to silence a powerful advocate for abolition, or by businessmen bent on burying a scandal so that they could continue to profit through the war? The First Battle of Bull Run is recounted. Associates: Mr. Cawber; Mr. Gowen. Historical Figures: General George McClellan; President Abraham Lincoln.

2. *Shadows of Glory.* New York: William Morrow, 2000, 311 p.

NEW YORK, NEW YORK, 1862. Abel Jones sets forth to investigate rumors of an Irish insurrection; he must step very carefully, for the body of the last investigator, another federal agent, has been found tortured and foully murdered. The Battles of Fort Henry and Fort Donelson are recounted through Mick Tyrone's letters. Associate: Nellie Kildare. Historical Figures: Mr. Seward; Frederick Douglass; Elizabeth Cady Stanton; Susan B. Anthony.

3. *Call Each River Jordan.* New York: William Morrow, 2001, 321 p.

TENNESSEE, 1862. Forty runaway slaves are found massacred by the Union Army as it advances. Abel Jones rides into Tennessee under a flag of truce to find justice for those who died. The Battle of Shiloh is fought. Associates: Francis Raines; Mr. Barnaby; Mrs. Barclay. Historical Figures: General Ulysses S. Grant; General William Sherman.

4. *Honor's Kingdom.* New York: William Morrow, 2002, 328 p.

LONDON, ENGLAND, AND GLASGOW, SCOTLAND, 1862. The Union is losing agents who are trying to stop the completion and delivery of a battleship commissioned from England by the Confederate administration. Jones is sent to investigate their murders and the conspiracy behind them. In England Jones finds himself haunted by ghosts from his past, ghosts that he thought he had laid to rest; but they're not as dangerous as the old enemies still living on British soil. Associates: Colonel Tice-Rolley; Earl of Thretford. Historical Figures: Charles Francis Adams; Henry Adams; Benjamin Disraeli; William Gladstone; Lord Palmerston.

5. *The Bold Sons of Erin.* New York: William Morrow, 2003, 335 p.

PENNSYLVANIA, FALL 1862. Jones is sent to investigate the murder of a general, a murder strangely and too quickly solved. The man who has admitted to the deed was proclaimed dead of cholera within hours of his confession and buried quickly for fear of contagion. Jones believes that the killer has actually fled and determines to get to the bottom of the matter through a little midnight grave robbing. He expects to find an empty casket; instead, he uncovers the body of a young woman, several months dead, and no one will admit that anyone is missing. The Battle of Fredericksburg is observed. Associates: Mrs. Dolly Walker; Matt Cawber. Historical Figures: Jack Kehoe; Mr. Gowen; Mr. Seward; General Meagher; Daniel Patrick Boland.

PAUL, Raymond (1940–). American.

LON QUINNCANNON SERIES

Scene of the Crime: New York and New England, beginning in January 1832.

Detective: Lon Quinncannon, Irish American criminal attorney, tall, with a close-cropped black moustache and a roguish nature to fit. He appears to be about thirty-five or forty years of age in his earliest appearance in the series.

Known Associates: Quinncannon employs different young associates as his assistants in each of the stories: David "Davy" Cordor, a reporter for the *New York Sun*, in *The Thomas Street Horror*; Christopher "Christy" Randolph, a newly annointed attorney, in *The Tragedy at Tiverton*; and Tobias "Toby" Brendon, another new attorney, in *The Bond Street Burlesque*.

Premise: A criminal attorney solves a series of horrendous murder cases through his spirited legal defense of several falsely accused individuals and through his detailed knowledge of the New York criminal underworld and humanity in general.

Comment: The author became interested in accounts of old murder cases both from contemporaneous printed sources (early newspapers and the like) and from actual trial transcripts; and eventually decided to employ the records of real sensational murder cases in New York City and New England as the bases for three extraordinary mystery novels. Not only do the real-life settings of these books give them an immediacy and authenticity sometimes lacking in the historical mysteries of other writers, but they also enable the author to comment on the curiosities of life in early metropolitan America. The mix works extraordinarily well, and the reader is left wishing that the series had lasted a tad longer than it did.

Literary Crimes & Chimes: Lon Quinncannon is a larger-than-life figure, an immigrant to America who has succeeded in adapting to urban life almost better than the natives. Handsome, wealthy, blessed with a tremendous insightfulness and superior legal skills, Quinncannon will take on any client, even those obviously guilty of their crimes, for the proper fee. In each of the three novels, his understudy is a young man still trying to find his way in the world, a professional who is both repelled and attracted by what Quinncannon has to offer. And what the Irishman brings to the table is an education in real-life law and in the realities of American society of the time. By the end of each novel, the "juniors" have all learned valuable lessons, both about life and about themselves. If Quinncannon sometimes seems a little too accomplished to be true, one must remember that such figures dominated New York politics and social life during the nineteenth century. Quinncannon does have a sense of justice and draws the line at doing certain activities—just not very many! First-rate fiction by any standard.

THE CASES

1. *The Tragedy at Tiverton: An Historical Novel of Murder.* New York: Viking Press, 1984, 352 p.

    NEW YORK, NEW YORK, PROVIDENCE, RHODE ISLAND, AND BOSTON, MASSACHUSETTS, 1832–1833. A poor, pregnant millworker is found strangled to death, and a respected and respectable Methodist minister is accused of the crime. Quinncannon and his young friend, Christy Randolph, agree to defend the man, despite his pomposity and general uncooperativeness, but begin to doubt their own judgment as more and more revelations regarding the reverend's exceedingly bad conduct begin coming to light. Their client fails to help matters any with his stubbornness and unwillingness to provide vital information. Despite this, Quinncannon is able to use his legal skills to uncover the real murderer, in a classic courtroom *dénouement*. Associate: Christy.

2. *The Thomas Street Horror: An Historical Novel of Murder.* New York: Viking Press, 1982, 322 p.

    NEW YORK, NEW YORK, 1835–1836. Helen Jewett, the undisputed "Queen of the Pave" in New York City, is found brutally murdered with an ax, her beautiful body left burning. The police immediately arrest a likely suspect and charge him with the crime. Davy Cordor, an acquaintance of the victim and a cub reporter for the *Sun*, covers the crime for his newspaper. He soon joins forces with rogue attorney Quinncannon, the man who has agreed to represent in court the not-so-innocent rapscallion accused of the crime. One revelation after another follows during the sensational trial, where once again Quinncannon uncovers the real murderer using his skills as an investigator and interrogator. Includes excerpts of actual newspaper accounts published during the mid-1830s of the murder and the murder victim. Associate: Davy.

3. *The Bond Street Burlesque: An Historical Novel of Murder.* New York: W. W. Norton, 1987, 363 p.

    NEW YORK, NEW YORK, 1856–1857. The miserly owner of a New York building is found murdered, and his jilted mistress and tenant is accused of the crime, together with a supposed male accomplice. Toby believes the woman guilty, but Quinncannon keeps everyone guessing, until he finally solves the crime at the last moment and brings the real culprits to justice. Once again Raymond Paul uses an actual murder case as the basis for a thrilling legal battle. Nicely illustrated with contemporaneous woodcuts of the principals. Associate: Toby.

PENMAN, Sharon Kay (1945–). American.

JUSTIN DE QUINCY OR THE QUEEN'S MAN SERIES

Scene of the Crime: England, beginning in 1192.

Detective: Justin, the bastard child of a wanton who died at his birth, had been taken in many years earlier by the Bishop of Chester, Aubrey de Quincy. At least, that's the story that Justin was always told. While working for Lord Fitz Alan, Justin looks for information about his mother and discovers that she was no wanton, but instead a young woman lead astray by the Bishop of Chester himself. Justin confronts the Bishop and then leaves in a fury, repudiating the cleric's help. Justin rides off with little money, fewer prospects, and no surname. On the road he comes across a scene of ambush and murder; he cannot save the dying merchant but determines to fulfill the man's last wish and carry out his mission of delivering a letter to Queen Eleanor.

Known Associates: Justin is helped in his investigations by Fitz-Alan's Serjeant Jonas and by Luke de Marston, Undersheriff of Winchester. There is some friction between Justin and de Marston over Justin's admiration for Luke's betrothed, Aldith Talbot. Justin also feels bitter over his father, Aubrey de Quincy, who has spent a lifetime concealing their relationship and who fears that any scandal will ruin his career in the church. Justin becomes entangled with Claudine de Loudun, a lady-in-waiting to Queen Eleanor of Aquitaine, in *The Queen's Man*; she is pregnant with a child (maybe Justin's) in *Cruel as the Grave*. Justin lives on Gracechurch Street; his neighbors include Nell, Gunter, and Agnes. Justin's enemies include Prince John and Durand de Curzon, a knight in the pay of Prince John and others.

Premise: A young natural son of a cleric solves crimes and works as an agent in twelfth-century England.

Comment: Justin de Quincy comes to the attention of Eleanor of Aquitaine when he manages to deliver a letter that discloses that King Richard I the Lion-Hearted has been captured and is being held prisoner. The entire country is awash with rumors that Richard has died while voyaging home from the Crusades; in fact, some people seem to be sowing these stories to further their own political ends. Queen Eleanor learns the tale of Justin's birth within an hour of meeting him. She begins calling him Justin de Quincy and soon wins his complete loyalty. Queen Eleanor is in desperate need of trustworthy allies; her son John is scheming to take the Crown from Richard, and she must find some way to stop her youngest son. She makes Justin "the Queen's Man," her personal agent, to investigate the murder of her secret courier. Justin is, frankly, not really cut out to be a great detective, nor is he naturally expert at intrigues and spying. He has a good heart, a strong arm, and a susceptible nature and quickly loses his *naiveté*, but it is his dogged persistence that sees him through his investigations. He travels a great deal between London and Winchester (which gives the reader a chance to explore the countryside and the customs, particularly the legal customs, of medieval England). He is ably assisted by Luke de Marston, Hampshire's Undersheriff, a man well able to conduct an investigation. At times Justin's detection technique is difficult to differentiate from flailing around. The research is worked in well enough so that it does not disrupt the stories.

Literary Crimes & Chimes: This series is at its best in the verbal fencing matches between Prince John and Justin; they are extraordinary, bone-chilling exchanges. Penman is a well-established author of historical novels; this series benefits from her experience at writing and research. She has stated that she always wanted the opportunity to explore Queen Eleanor's dysfunctional family, and she makes the most of it in these books. Each book ends with an Author's Note in which Penman explains whatever liberties she took with the known history and occasionally some of the unresolved mysteries that she uncovered in her research. The first book was nominated for an Edgar Award for Best First Mystery from the Mystery Writers of America.

THE CASES

1. *The Queen's Man: A Medieval Mystery.* New York: Henry Holt, 1996, 291 p.
   WINCHESTER AND LONDON, ENGLAND, 1192–1193. Riding out of Winchester on Epiphany morning, Justin interrupts a murder. The dying victim presses a letter for Queen Eleanor into Justin's hands and bids him deliver it. Justin does so, and the Queen hires him to get to the bottom of the crime, knowing that her youngest son, Prince John, may well be behind the murder. Historical Figures: Will Longsword; British Queen Eleanor; Prince John.

2. *Cruel as the Grave: A Medieval Mystery.* New York: Henry Holt, 1998, 242 p.

LONDON, ENGLAND, APRIL–JUNE 1193. Justin is asked to clear the nephew of Agnes, one of his neighbors, of the charge of murder; that investigation is interrupted when Queen Eleanor sends him on a mission to thwart Prince John's incipient treason. Justin penetrates into Prince John's besieged stronghold, with a "secret" offer for the Prince. The Queen knows that Prince John will reject an offer of clemency but will be irresistibly drawn into intrigue! While Prince John can be deadly, his men, even those who are secretly in the pay of the Queen, can be just as dangerous. Historical Figures: Will Longsword; William Marshal; British Queen Eleanor; Prince John.

3. *Dragon's Lair: A Medieval Mystery.* New York: G. P. Putnam's Sons, 2003, 322 p.

WALES, JULY–OCTOBER 1193. King Richard I is imprisoned in Germany, and word has leaked that the Holy Roman Emperor is willing to ransom him. Queen Eleanor works frantically to raise the funds, while Prince John works just as hard (though not as openly) to build his own treasury, reasoning that if a great deal of money can buy Richard's freedom, even more money can ensure his permanent captivity—or worse. When a group carrying funds to Chester is ambushed and robbed, Eleanor sends Justin to find the culprit (and the money); and so he begins a dangerous race with Prince John. Associates: Bennett; Molly; Rhun. Historical Figures: Welsh Prince Davydd ab Owain; Emma of Anjou; Llewelyn ab Iorwerth; British Queen Eleanor; Prince John.

PÉREZ-REVERTE, Arturo (1951–). Spanish.

MISCELLANEOUS SERIES

Scene of the Crime: Spain, in 1471, 1868, and 1990.

Detective: Various.

Known Associates: Various.

Premise: Various.

Comment: Pérez-Reverte's research is impeccable, and his psychological portrayals of both contemporary and historical characters are first-rate. The crimes he depicts are rooted in the *milieux* of each period, as well as in the perceptions of the "investigators." That crimes have taken place is without refute, but the true nature of the transgressions often remains hidden until revealed through a careful peeling away of multiple layers of deception and of the masks of the complex individuals involved. *The Flanders Panel* in particular is a masterpiece that interweaves both past and present into one seamless mystery, the uncovering of which reveals the links between medieval and modern, between the characters of the murdered knight and the murdered art dealers. This is as good as it gets with the historical mystery genre.

Literary Crimes & Chimes: As well written as these books are, some few flaws remain. It strains belief that this particular painting (in *The Flanders Panel*), depicting three historical figures, two of them playing chess, should surface just at this time and this place, so as to have a maximum influence on the psyches of the modern-day players. The police in both books are depicted as particularly idiotic, almost caricatures of officialdom. Both novels might also be considered as extended literary games, having deliberately been fashioned by the author as puzzles within puzzles. Still, both as entertainment and as mystery, these fictions work very well indeed. *¡Ola!*

THE CASES

1. *The Flanders Panel,* trans. by Margaret Jull Costa from *La tabla de Flandes*. New York: Harcourt, Brace & Co., 1994, 294 p.

SPAIN, 1471, 1990. Julia, a modern-day art specialist, is given a 1471 painting to restore. *The Game of Chess*, also known as *The Flanders Panel*, proves unusual in several respects. X-rays reveal a hidden inscription on the bottom of the work, apparently painted over by the artist shortly after his completion of the work. The tableau depicts a ruling duke and a knight playing chess, with the duchess hovering in the background. "Who killed the knight?" asks the artist, and it appears that the question is a deadly serious one. An expert whom the restorer consults is found murdered in his apartment. But as Julia investigates the historical background of the characters shown on *The Game of Chess*, and as she explores the game being played itself, she is pulled deeper and deeper into the mystery. Who murdered whom, both in 1471 and in 1990? The answer to one puzzle may provide the answer to the other. Absolutely first-rate, one of the best historical mysteries ever written.

2. *The Fencing Master,* trans. by Margaret Jull Costa from *El maestro de esgrima*. New York: Harcourt, Brace & Co., 1999, 245 p.

MADRID, SPAIN, SUMMER 1868 (the Prologue is set in December 1866). During a time of revolution and civil unrest, with Queen Isabel II tottering on her throne, fencing master Jaime Astarloa receives an unusual request. He is approached by a woman, Adela de Otero, who asks him to teach her a killing thrust with the foil, a move that he invented some years earlier and has since kept a close secret. Instructing any woman is unthinkable in his profession, but she demonstrates a unique ability with the sword, with a greater knowledge and proficiency than his usual run of pupils. Reluctantly he agrees, and she learns the special tactic most readily. Not long thereafter, another of his pupils, the Marqués de los Alumbres, is found dead in his house, killed by the thrust of a foil through the neck. Jaime immediately suspects the lady, but then a body resembling her is found floating in the river. As he investigates the crime, he suspects that Adela is still alive and that she lies at the heart of a conspiracy to shake the very foundations of the Spanish royal government.

PERRY, Anne (originally Juliet Marion Hulme) (1938–). British.

CHARLOTTE AND THOMAS PITT SERIES

Scene of the Crime: London, England, beginning on April 20, 1881, and continuing into the 1890s.

Detective: Thomas Pitt (born about 1846), London police inspector, later Superintendent of the Bow Street Police Station (beginning with *The Hyde Park Headsman*), still later a member of Special Branch (beginning with *The Whitechapel Conspiracy*); he is tall, dark, hook-nosed, and somewhat untidy in his dress and hair; Charlotte Ellison Pitt (born about 1858), Thomas' wife (beginning with *Callander Square*), forthright and honest, assists her husband privately in his investigations.

Known Associates: Thomas and Charlotte's children, Jemima (born 1883) and Daniel (born 1886); Gracie, the Pitts' maid (from *Rutland Place*); Emily Ellison Ashworth (born about 1862), Charlotte's younger sister, married to George March, Viscount Ashworth (from *Callander Square* to *Cardington Crescent*), and second to Jack Radley, M.P. (mentioned from *Cardington Crescent*, married in *Bethlehem Road*), mother of Edward March, Viscount Ashworth, and Evangeline Radley (born about 1889); Caroline Ellison (born about 1830), Charlotte and Emily's mother, married to Edward Ellison (dead about 1888), and later to actor Joshua Fielding; Grandmama, Edward's elderly mother; Lady Vespasia Cumming-Gould (born about 1808), great-aunt of George and compatriot to Emily and Charlotte (from *Paragon Walk*); Superintendent Micah Drummond, Pitt's superior from *Bethlehem Road* to *Farriers' Lane*; Assistant Commissioner Giles Farnsworth, Pitt's superior from *The Hyde Park Headsman* to *Traitors Gate*; Captain Superintendent (later Assistant Commissioner) John Cornwallis, Pitt's superior from *Pentecost Alley* to *The Whitechapel Conspiracy*; Victor Narraway, Head

of Special Branch (an early version of the secret service), Pitt's superior from
The Whitechapel Conspiracy, Inspector Samuel Tellman, Pitt's friend and
member of the Bow Street Station force, enamoured of Gracie; the Inner
Circle, a secret group of high-level officials determined to gain control of
the British government and impose a republic (from *Belgrave Square*), in
opposition to the Masons.

Premise: In late Victorian England, London Police Inspector Thomas
Pitt, son of a country estate game manager, becomes a police constable and
gradually rises through the ranks of the London Police Force, being helped
in his investigations by his wife, Charlotte, the latter's sister, Emily, and occasionally by others. However, his career is later sidetracked by the Inner
Circle, and he is forced into service with the Special Branch in 1892.

Comment: Anne Perry's inaugural series was a milestone in the history
of the historical mystery novel, being one of the first major success stories
of the genre. Her books focus on the dichotomy between the outward ve-
neer of Victorian society, the staid, complacent life of virtue trumpeted by
church and state, and the corruption that underlay both the higher and
lower classes, leading on occasion to carousing, high jinks, or even crime.
Other tensions are created by juxtaposing the relative freedom of men in society compared with the straitlaced strictures governing the conduct of
women, and the inherent unfairness of the situation. These combined tensions often cross in Perry's tales to create unbearable fractures in the social
strata that ultimately lead to murder. The reluctance of the upper classes to
reveal their true selves and motivations to Pitt and his assistants presents the
police with their greatest challenges, particularly since the resulting deaths
are sometimes horrendous in their violence and viciousness.

Literary Crimes & Chimes: Even in the 1890s, it is sometimes difficult
for the reader to believe that Charlotte Pitt, her sister, and other compatriots would be able to find the relative freedom of operation within and without society that Perry demonstrates in her fictions. These foragings for truth
are what enable Pitt to reach some just conclusion in each novel, although
as the series progresses, the reckonings become ever dearer and the conclusions less sure. There is a clear advancement of the characters and their sensibilities throughout the decade encompassed by the novels; the reader is
therefore urged to read the books in the order that they have been written.

THE CASES

1. *The Cater Street Hangman*. New York: St. Martin's Press, 1979, 247 p.
   LONDON, ENGLAND, APRIL–NOVEMBER 1881. On fashionable Cater
Street, the Ellison family is drawn into a series of brutal stranglings of local
young women, culminating in the death of Sarah Ellison (Mrs. Dominic

Corde), the oldest daughter of the family. Suspicion swirls around the male relatives as Inspector Pitt attempts to unravel the puzzle. Finally, Charlotte provides the answer in an astonishing *dénouement*. By the end of the novel, George asks for Emily's hand, and Thomas proposes to Charlotte. Associates: Caroline; Emily; George; Dominic; Edward; Grandmama.

2. *Callander Square.* New York: St. Martin's Press, 1980, 221 p.

LONDON, ENGLAND, OCTOBER 1883. The bodies of two young children are found buried in a garden in fashionable Callander Square, with the implication that they are illegitimate offspring of the local gentry. Charlotte furthers the investigation by having herself hired as an assistant to one of the local residents, retired General Balantyne, who wishes to pen his military memoirs. Associates: Emily; Balantyne.

3. *Paragon Walk.* New York: St. Martin's Press, 1981, 204 p.

LONDON, ENGLAND, SUMMER 1884. When a young lady of fashion is found raped and murdered in Paragon Walk, Pitt must dig deeply into the family connections of the dead woman to uncover a grisly secret. Great-Aunt Vespasia makes her first appearance in the series. Associates: Emily; Vespasia; George.

4. *Resurrection Row.* New York: St. Martin's Press, 1981, 204 p.

LONDON, ENGLAND, JANUARY 1885. A corpse is discovered sitting upright in a hansom cab; even worse, the dead man has apparently been exhumed from his grave and placed on public display for some unknown reason. And then it happens again, with exactly the same body! Dominic, widower of Charlotte's sister, Sarah, makes his second appearance in the series as the prime suspect for the desecrations. Associates: Dominic; Vespasia.

5. *Rutland Place.* New York: St. Martin's Press, 1983, 235 p.

LONDON, ENGLAND, MARCH 1886. A series of what appear to be petty thefts turns ominous as Charlotte realizes that each of the items stolen could seriously compromise the victims. When blackmail and murder become part of the equation, Pitt is called in to unravel the puzzle. Gracie makes her first appearance in the series. Associates: Caroline; Grandmama; Edward; Gracie; Emily.

6. *Bluegate Fields.* New York: St. Martin's Press, 1984, 308 p.

LONDON, ENGLAND, SEPTEMBER 1886. A boy has been viciously raped and murdered, the body being dumped in a sewer. Pitt must uncover the hidden world of homosexual prostitution and the systematic abuse of adolescents of both sexes to solve this vicious crime. Associates: Vespasia; Caroline; Dominic; Grandmama.

7. *Death in the Devil's Acre.* New York: St. Martin's Press, 1985, 248 p.

LONDON, ENGLAND, JANUARY 1887. When the sexually mutilated body of a socially prominent doctor is found in the Devil's Acre, Pitt must interrogate the physician's neighbors and acquaintances, including a retired military officer, General Balantyne, making his second appearance in the series. Soon the bodies begin piling up, and it's clear that a serial killer is at work. Associates: Emily; George; Balantyne.

8. *Cardington Crescent.* New York: St. Martin's Press, 1987, 314 p.

LONDON, ENGLAND, JUNE 1887. Emily discovers her womanizing husband dead in bed. When murder is suspected, Pitt must investigate all of George's friends and connections, with houseguest Jack Radley becoming the major suspect in the crime. Jack's first appearance in the series. Associates: George; Emily; Vespasia; Jack.

9. *Silence in Hanover Close.* New York: St. Martin's Press, 1988, 341 p.

LONDON, ENGLAND, DECEMBER 1887. Pitt is ordered by Ballarat to investigate a three-year-old burglary and killing with political overtones. But his questioning of the surviving witnesses leads to one of them being murdered, making him suspect that Very Important Personages will do anything to prevent the truth from appearing. Associates: Jack; Vespasia; Emily; Gracie; Superintendent Ballarat.

10. *Bethlehem Road.* New York: St. Martin's Press, 1990, 309 p.

LONDON, ENGLAND, APRIL 1888. When a Member of Parliament is found hanging from Westminster Bridge, his throat slit, Pitt considers the murder an isolated incident. Then a second official is found, and it's clear that motives both vicious and personal are driving the killer. Also, Emily marries Jack, thereby losing her courtesy title, and they exit on their honeymoon to Europe. Associates: Emily; Jack; Gracie; Vespasia; Micah.

11. *Highgate Rise.* New York: Fawcett Columbine, 1991, 330 p.

LONDON, ENGLAND, SEPTEMBER 1888. An arson fire kills the wife of a prominent London physician. Pitt has two problems: he must first determine the intended target of the blaze, and second unravel the web of gossip surrounding the private lives of Dr. Shaw and his family. Associates: Emily; Caroline; Vespasia; Grandmama; Gracie.

12. *Belgrave Square.* New York: Fawcett Columbine, 1992, 361 p.

LONDON, ENGLAND, SUMMER 1889. Pitt investigates the murder of a small-time crook, William Weems, who has been blackmailing Lord Sholto Byam, a friend of Micah. Pitt uncovers a web of high finance, homosexuality, and hidden influence interwoven with the workings of the Inner Circle, which intervenes to protect its own. Micah and Jack face a crisis of faith and love. Associates: Emily; Micah; Jack; Vespasia.

13. *Farriers' Lane.* New York: Fawcett Columbine, 1993, 374 p.

LONDON, ENGLAND, FALL 1889. Caroline Ellison's young paramour, the actor Joshua Fielding, may be involved in the murders of several prominent jurists and their friends. Pitt must unravel one of his most baffling cases, while uncovering old secrets that have been covered up for decades. Vespasia renews her friendship with Theloneus Quade. Associates: Caroline; Joshua; Vespasia; Gracie; Micah; Theloneus.

14. *The Hyde Park Headsman.* New York: Fawcett Columbine, 1994, 392 p.

LONDON, ENGLAND, SPRING 1890. Not long after Pitt is promoted to Superintendent of the Bow Street Station, he investigates a beheading in Hyde Park that enmeshes him in the seamy tentacles of a long-buried family scandal. Jack decides to run for Parliament and is later elected. Associates: Emily; Jack; Vespasia; Micah; Farnsworth; Tellman.

15. *Traitors Gate.* New York: Fawcett Columbine, 1995, 411 p.

LONDON, ENGLAND, MAY 1890. The death of Sir Arthur Desmond, owner of the estate on which Pitt was raised, involves the Superintendent in a web of conspiracy concerning the leaking of secret information from the Foreign Office and ultimately focuses Pitt's attention once again around the activities of the Inner Circle. Associates: Vespasia; Farnsworth; Tellman.

16. *Pentecost Alley.* New York: Fawcett Columbine, 1996, 405 p.

LONDON, ENGLAND, AUGUST 1890. The murder-mutilation of a prostitute implicates the scion of a wealthy family, and Pitt is called in. But when he nabs a suspect and the man is convicted and executed, suddenly another murder victim appears, killed in exactly the same fashion. Has the wrong man been hanged? Associates: Jack; Emily; Vespasia; Gracie; Tellman; Cornwallis.

17. *Ashworth Hall.* New York: Fawcett Columbine, 1997, 373 p.

LONDON, ENGLAND, OCTOBER 1890. A policeman's assassination is tied to the "Irish Problem," and Pitt is ordered to protect the lives of the Protestant and Irish attendees at a political conference called to find a solution. But the bodies begin piling up, and unless Pitt can unravel the puzzle, the British government may fall and Ireland may disintegrate into Civil War. Associates: Jack; Emily; Vespasia; Gracie; Tellman; Cornwallis.

18. *Brunswick Gardens.* New York: Fawcett Columbine, 1998, 389 p.

LONDON, ENGLAND, MARCH 1891. Charles Darwin's theory of evolution underlies the murder of the attractive and assertive feminist assistant to Reverend Parmenter, who opposes everything that Darwin stands for. Pitt must discern whether the girl's death is political, religious, or personal. Dominic's fourth appearance in the series. Associates: Dominic; Vespasia; Tellman; Cornwallis.

19. *Bedford Square.* New York: Ballantine Books, 1999, 330 p.

LONDON, ENGLAND, JUNE 1891. The discovery of a murder victim outside General Balantyne's door leads Pitt into the investigation of a possible corruption scandal. Someone has been making a killing through the leaking of privileged financial data, and the blackmail of former high-ranking military and political figures is definitely involved. Balantyne's third appearance in the series. Associates: Gracie; Vespasia; Theloneus; Balantyne; Tellman; Cornwallis.

20. *Half Moon Street.* New York: Ballantine Books, 2000, 312 p.

LONDON, ENGLAND, SEPTEMBER 1891. The manacled body of a French diplomat is found floating in the Thames. The ensuing investigation leads Pitt into the seamy world of Victorian pornography and the underside of the professional theater. Associates: Caroline; Joshua; Vespasia; Tellman.

21. *The Whitechapel Conspiracy.* New York: Ballantine Books, 2001, 341 p.

LONDON, ENGLAND, APRIL 1892. After testifying successfully against a member of the Inner Circle, who is convicted and sentenced to death, Pitt is discredited in the press and removed from his position at the Bow Street Station. He is temporarily delegated to Special Branch to investigate an anarchist threat in Whitechapel. Suddenly the two cases begin to converge, as an Inner Circle plot to overthrow the monarchy is revealed. Associates: Vespasia; Gracie; Tellman; Cornwallis; Narraway.

22. *Southampton Row.* New York: Ballantine Books, 2002, 326 p.

LONDON, ENGLAND, JUNE 1892. Despite Pitt's successful conclusion of the Whitechapel affair, he is prevented from returning to Bow Street by the Inner Circle, being permanently assigned to Special Branch, the equivalent of the Secret Service. Now he must fight a new conspiracy aimed at bringing the leader of the Inner Circle back into power. Associates: Jack; Emily; Vespasia; Cornwallis; Narraway.

23. *Seven Dials.* New York: Ballantine Books, 2003, 345 p.

LONDON, ENGLAND, AND EGYPT, SEPTEMBER 1892. For the first time in his career, Pitt must travel abroad to investigate the death of a minor diplomat by an Egyptian woman. Soon he finds himself examining the massacre of a native group by English soldiers, the scandal of which may ignite a general uprising among the Egyptians against the British occupiers of their land. Associates: Emily; Vespasia; Gracie; Grandmama; Tellman; Narraway.

WILLIAM MONK AND HESTER LATTERLY SERIES

Scene of the Crime: London, England, beginning on July 30, 1856, and continuing into the 1860s.

Detective: William Monk (born about 1816), who is dark-complected and very intense, an inspector with Peel's Metropolitan Police Force, later (from *Dangerous Mourning*) a private investigator, whose amnesia and blunt manner frequently cause him problems; Hester Latterly (born about 1827), Monk's wife (from *The Twisted Root*), very tall for a woman, frank and outspoken in nature, a nurse who had formerly served with Florence Nightingale during the Crimean War (1855–1856); she later worked as a nurse in London, both in hospitals and privately, and opened her own free health clinic in Coldbath Square catering to poor women prostitutes (from *Death of a Stranger*).

Known Associates: Lady Callandra Grey Daviot (born about 1800), the widowed sister of the late Lord Shelburne and aunt of the present holder of that title and a friend of Hester from about 1849; Inspector (later Superintendent) Runcorn (born about 1816), Monk's immediate superior in the Police Force, and later a potential rival; Sergeant John Evan, Monk's police assistant and later his friend; Sir Oliver Rathbone, attorney, friend, and sometime paramour to Hester; Henry Rathbone, Oliver's father, a retired pedant; Kristian Beck, physician and friend to Callandra; Charles Latterly, Hester's brother; Margaret Ballinger, Hester's friend and fellow nurse at Colbath Square.

Premise: An amnesiac ex-policeman and a strong-minded nurse solve crimes in early Victorian England.

Comment: Inspector William Monk of the London Metropolitan Police Force suffers an accident in which his memories are erased. He gradually recovers bits and pieces of faces and incidents over the years, enough to regret the man he once was, but never gains the knowledge fully to understand his personal past. After leaving the police force, he establishes himself as a private investigator. One of his sometime caregivers, Hester Latterly, a former nurse in the Crimean War, finds living and working in London in the 1850s a difficult adjustment, particularly since nurses are held in such low esteem in early Victorian England. She gradually forms an attachment with William, eventually becoming an essential adjunct to his criminous investigations. From its very inception, the Monk/Latterly series was significantly darker in tone than Perry's books featuring Thomas and Charlotte Pitt. The plots focus directly and personally on violations of individuals and the society to which they belong. Monk's lack of identity, his inability to recover everything that made him who and what he was, the terror of the London Police, is both a blessing at times (he finds himself revolted by some of his earlier actions) and a curse. Hester's difficulty in adjusting to the difference between her position in the Crimea, where she was a necessary adjunct to the medical services being provided to the British soldiers there, and her uncertain life in London as an itinerant nurse and unmarried spinster, creates similar tensions within her own personality. The ongoing relationship between two very strong-minded individuals is a continuous source of interest and occasional conflict. These books contain some of Anne Perry's best writing, most devious plots, and most gut-wrenching suspense. The books reflect accurately the nuances of the period in which they're set. It doesn't get much better than this for fans of historical mysteries.

Literary Crimes & Chimes: Ironically, while this series includes some of Perry's best works of fiction, it also features her worst novel (see the books' descriptions), with several others that are below par. Perry has a tendency to stray from the scenarios and environments that she knows best into other parts of the world with which she is clearly less familiar. This might matter less to another writer's criminous creations, but the author's focus on the psychological environment in which her criminals and detectives live and work, as the essential backdrop to machinations of her plots, quickly uncovers any defects in perception. As with the Pitt series, even though Hester experiences many more difficulties in living and working than the more privileged Charlotte Pitt ever did, she nonetheless possesses a freedom of action in these novels that is a trifle unrealistic for a female citizen of London at the time. To be sure, women in Victorian England did think feminist thoughts; very few, however, were able to express such ideas openly without repercussions that would have severely limited their access into elite society, and such access is often a key to solving the mysteries presented herein. Still, these are first-rate psychological stories, filled with complex characters and complex plot situations. They can be read over and over again with great pleasure.

THE CASES

1. *The Face of a Stranger.* New York: Fawcett Columbine, 1990, 328 p.

LONDON, ENGLAND, JULY 1856. Policeman William Monk suffers an accident that robs him of his memories but decides to hide his disability from his superiors. He begins investigating the death of a Crimean War hero, Joscelin Grey. But Grey's death is more than it seems, and as he probes further, Monk uncovers a scandal involving the misuse of funds and the ruining of the fortunes of the Latterly family. Associates: Callandra; Runcorn; Evan; Charles; Callandra.

2. *Dangerous Mourning.* New York: Fawcett Columbine, 1991, 330 p.

LONDON, ENGLAND, NOVEMBER 1856. Monk investigates the stabbing death of the daughter of Sir Basil Moidore. The evidence points toward a particular suspect whom Monk believes is innocent. When ordered to arrest the man, Monk refuses and is thereby immediately dismissed from the Police Force. Lady Callandra hires him to solve the mystery, and when he does so successfully, offers to provide the funding for Monk to establish himself as a private inquiry agent. Associates: Callandra; Runcorn; Evan; Oliver.

3. *Defend and Betray.* New York: Fawcett Columbine, 1992, 385 p.

LONDON, ENGLAND, APRIL 1857. General Thaddeus Carlyon impales himself on a decorative suit of armor in an apparent accident, but the police establish that Carlyon could not have fallen without assistance. When his wife, Alexandra, confesses to the crime, Hester begs Oliver to represent a woman whom she believes is innocent. But Alexandra refuses to cooperate, and Oliver hires Monk to unravel the mystery. Associates: Oliver; Evan.

4. *A Sudden, Fearful Death.* New York: Fawcett Columbine, 1993, 383 p.

LONDON, ENGLAND, SUMMER 1857. A talented nurse who had served with Hester under Florence Nightingale during the Crimean War is found strangled to death, and Kristian Beck, a foreign physician working at the facility, is suspected in the crime. Oliver agrees to represent the doctor, with Monk doing the supplemental investigation. Suddenly the case turns widdershins when letters from the nurse to a hospital administrator surface, suggesting a personal connection between the doctor and the nurse and implicating both of them as part of the underground abortion mill. It's left to Monk and Hester to unravel the true motives of both murderer and victim. Associates: Callandra; Kristian; Oliver; Evan; Runcorn. Historical Figure: Florence Nightingale.

5. *The Sins of the Wolf.* New York: Fawcett Columbine, 1994, 374 p.

LONDON, ENGLAND, AND EDINBURGH, SCOTLAND, OCTOBER 1857. Hester takes a position as personal nurse to an elderly Scottish lady, but on the train trip back to London, the old woman is found murdered in her coach bed. Hester is immediately charged with poisoning the lady and is returned to Scotland for trial. Oliver cannot represent her there, because the Scottish legal system has its own set of rules and qualifications. As the evidence mounts against her, and as Monk strives mightily to find any shred of evidence to exonerate her, Hester's future looks ever more bleak as the days pass. The ending of this novel is unprecedented in Perry's fiction for its simultaneous combination of tension, fear, and poignancy. The author's best novel to date. Associates: Callandra; Oliver. Historical Figure: Florence Nightingale.

6. *Cain His Brother.* New York: Fawcett Columbine, 1995, 390 p.

LONDON, ENGLAND, JANUARY 1859. Genevieve Stonefield pleads with Monk to locate her missing husband, Angus. By all accounts Angus is an extraordinary individual, loving and caring to both family and employees alike. His identical twin brother, Caleb, however, a man known for his perversity, wickedness, and general criminous behavior, is the obvious suspect for Angus' disappearance and possible murder. However, something very unseemly links the two men, and Monk is determined to find the connection, wherever it takes him. A bit obvious, what? Associates: Callandra; Oliver.

7. *Weighed in the Balance.* New York: Fawcett Columbine, 1996, 355 p.

LONDON, ENGLAND, AND VENICE, ITALY, SUMMER 1859. Rathbone, who has recently been knighted by Queen Victoria, is engaged by Countess Zorah Rostova to defend her against a suit for slander being brought by Princess Gisela of the German state of Felzburg, widow of the late Crown Prince Friedrich. Zorah has accused Gisela in public of murdering her husband, who had renounced his rights to the throne in order to marry beneath his station. At the heart of the dispute is the potential status of the kingdom in a German federation dominated by Prussia. Friedrich had opposed the idea of union; his younger brother Waldo, now the heir apparent, favors it. Rathbone hires Monk to investigate, and the detective must soon travel to Venice to interview one of the principals. But the deeper he probes, the more obscure the case seems to become! By far the least of the Monk books (and perhaps the author's worst fiction), this novel simply fails to capture the ambience or the political or social situations of the twenty-five semi-independent German states that later (after 1871) constituted the German Empire. Associate: Oliver.

8. *The Silent Cry.* New York: Fawcett Columbine, 1997, 361 p.

LONDON, ENGLAND, JANUARY 1860. A well-known solicitor, Leighton Duff, is found beaten and murdered in a London slum, the battered, but living, body of his son, Rhys, lying next to him. As the bodies mount up, the police are baffled by the series of brutal assaults. Then Monk uncovers a connection between the Duffs and a series of rapes affecting local prostitutes. The evidence points to Rhys having killed his own father. Can Monk save the day? Associates: Oliver; Evan; Runcorn.

9. *A Breach of Promise.* New York: Ballantine Books, 1998, 374 p. As:
   Whited Sepulchres. London: Headline, 1997, 282 p.

LONDON, ENGLAND, SPRING 1860. Two socialites file suit against the young architect, Killian Melville, alleging that he had broken a promise to marry their daughter, Zillah Lambert. Despite intense pressure from the courts, from his attorney, Sir Oliver Rathbone, and from the girl's parents, Killian declares that he cannot marry her but will absolutely not say why. Rathbone hires Monk to investigate the architect. As the trial opens, Melville seems determined to lose both his good name and his fortune—and then his murdered body is discovered! At story's end, Monk finally proposes to Hester, and she accepts. Associate: Oliver.

10. *The Twisted Root.* New York: Ballantine Books, 1999, 346 p.

LONDON, SUMMER 1860. Monk is hired to trace a groom's *fiancée*, the widow Miriam Gardiner, whose coach has been found abandoned and the driver murdered. But as Monk and Hester investigate, they uncover a deeply buried family secret and an even older series of deaths—and an ancient injustice that they must now try to put right. Associates: Callandra; Kristian; Oliver.

11. *Slaves of Obsession.* New York: Ballantine Books, 2000, 344 p.

LONDON, ENGLAND, WASHINGTON, DC, AND MANASSAS, VIRGINIA, JUNE 1861. The onset of the American Civil War creates opportunities for the likes of London arms dealer Daniel Alberton, who is becoming a very wealthy man indeed. He boasts of his accomplishments at a dinner party that Monk and his new bride attend. But when one of the guests is murdered, and two others suddenly disappear, along with Alberton's entire inventory of weapons, Monk is hired to track down the assassin and thief and uncover the mystery behind the crime. Their journey takes them overseas to war-torn America and the First Battle of Bull Run and then back again to Britain, where the hidden motives of the characters are finally revealed. Associate: Oliver.

12. *Funeral in Blue.* New York: Ballantine Books, 2001, 344 p.

LONDON, ENGLAND, AND VIENNA, AUSTRIA, SEPTEMBER 1861. When Kristian's wife and an artist's model are found murdered together, the foreign-born doctor immediately becomes the prime suspect. But when Monk begins investigating the not-so-happy couple, he discovers that their domestic life had been a lie and that both had been previously and heavily involved in the revolutionary movement of 1848 on the European continent. To make matters worse, Hester's brother Charles appears to be connected in some way to the crime; his wife has been gambling away the family fortune in a den near the scene of the killing. Monk finally decides that the answers lie elsewhere and travels to Austria to investigate the Becks' past and unravel the puzzle. Associates: Charles; Kristina; Callandra; Runcorn.

13. *Death of a Stranger.* New York: Ballantine Books, 2002, 337 p.

LONDON, AND DERBYSHIRE, ENGLAND, SPRING 1863. The mysterious death of British magnate Nolan Baltimore in a sleazy neighborhood brothel, not far from Hester's newly established clinic catering to the health needs of London's prostitutes, leads Monk to be engaged by the *fiancée* of an executive in the Baltimore and Sons railway company. What she wants to know is this: was the firm (and her husband-to-be) engaged in fraudulent business practices? Monk's investigation leads him directly into his own past, because the detective's first patron, Arrol Dundas, had been unfairly convicted of a very similar crime many years before and had eventually died in prison, despite Monk's best efforts to exonerate him. This had decided Monk on becoming a policeman. As William rushes to complete his investigate before the new railroad line is inaugurated, he comes to realize that he will either solve the case and simultaneously vindicate Dundas or die trying. Absolutely first-rate, one of the best books in the series, with a stunning climax. Associates: Oliver; Margaret.

14. *The Shifting Tide.* New York: Ballantine Books, 2004, 328 p.

LONDON, ENGLAND, OCTOBER 1863. Although Monk knows London's underworld exceedingly well, the River Thames and its docks might as well be a foreign country to him. Shipping magnate Clement Louvain hires the detective to investigate the theft of a cargo of African ivory from one of his docked ships. The crime suggests an "inside job," but Monk is stymied at every turn by his ignorance of criminal practice along the river. Simultaneously, Hester and her nurses become trapped in their own clinic when one of their patients, a relative of Louvain, develops the plague. Anyone visiting the facility must be confined there until the disease finally runs its course. Monk cannot help his wife and seems to be making very little progress in solving the heist, until the link between the two seemingly isolated events suddenly becomes clear. Another extraordinary work of high drama and enormous tension. At the end of the novel, Oliver proposes marriage to Margaret, but she fails to give him her answer. Associates: Oliver; Margaret.

JOSEPH AND MATTHEW REAVLEY SERIES

Scene of the Crime: Great Britain, beginning in June 1914, and continuing through 1918.

Detectives: Joseph Reavley, a Professor at Cambridge University; his brother, Matthew Reavley, an officer in the British Intelligence Service.

Known Associates: The Reavleys' two sisters, Judith and Hannah.

Premise: Two brothers seek to prevent the onset of World War I and to discover a traitor in the British government.

Comment: Perry uses the real-life character of her grandfather, Captain Joseph Reavley, as the basis for this limited series of five novels centered around World War I, each apparently set in a different year. The first book deals with the circumstances surrounding the onset of World War I. The Austrian Archduke Ferdinand is assassinated in Sarajevo, not long after the murders of the parents of Joseph and Matthew Reavley. John Reavley had been carrying a secret document that would have allied Germany and Britain, breaking a long-standing political arrangement that linked the British Isles with France and Russia. The Reavleys are successful in locating the now abrogated agreement, but the result in any case is the outbreak of World War I, and the knowledge that the traitor lurking within the bowels of British government is still and secure—and able to wreak further mischief.

Literary Crimes & Chimes: With the publication of only two books in this series out of the five planned, it's impossible to judge its final overall impact. Perhaps the sum of the whole will indeed prove greater than the parts. Thus far, however, this sequence runs a poor third to Perry's other two series, both in setup and in execution. It lacks the tension of those books and lacks also the verisimilitude of place and time. What makes Perry's books work best is the underlying dynamic between the way society appears and the way it actually functions. The lies, the hypocrisy, the cover-ups are the fuel that power her fictions. These are mostly lacking here, and the result is a series that seems, at best, a shadowy imitation of the author's best writing.

THE CASES

1. *No Graves As Yet: A Novel of World War I.* New York: Ballantine Books, 2003, 339 p.

ENGLAND, JUNE–AUGUST 1914. John and Alys Reavley are killed in a terrible car accident, leaving their four adult children bereaved. Then Joseph, a British Intelligence agent, reveals that their father had been on his way to London to deliver a secret document that could disgrace England forever and change the course of history. The two brothers investigate the circumstances of their parents' passing and discover that the Reavleys were murdered. At the same time, Joseph is faced with the seemingly unconnected murder of his most gifted student, Sebastian Allard. Are the three deaths connected? Can the Reavleys locate the missing document? Associates: Judith; Hannah.

2. *Shoulder the Sky: A Novel.* New York: Ballantine Books, 2004, 338 p.

LONDON, ENGLAND, AND NORTHERN FRANCE, APRIL 1915. Joseph Reavley is now a chaplain serving in the British trenches in war-torn France. In the no-man's-land between the opposing lines, Joseph finds the body of a war correspondent, Eldon Prentice, a nephew of a British general. Prentice was despised for his attempts to turn the reading public against the war. He appears to have been murdered by friendly troops. Who hated the man enough to kill him? Meanwhile, Matthew Reavley, an intelligence officer in London, continues searching for the sinister enemy known as the Peacemaker, who is also trying to undermine the war effort. The Peacemaker kills with impunity, and the Reavley family must bend all their efforts to thwart his schemes. Associate: Judith, now an army driver.

PETERS, Elizabeth (pseud. of Barbara Louise Mertz) (1927–). American.

AMELIA PEABODY SERIES

Scene of the Crime: Egypt and England, beginning in 1884, and continuing through the 1910s.

Detective: Amelia Peabody, feminist, archeologist, wife, and mother, intended to die a spinster until she met Radcliffe Emerson (*Crocodile on the Sand-*

bank). She is a handsome woman: dark-haired, with eyes of steely gray, a voluptuous figure, and a decided manner. In the initial book she reveals that she is thirty-two at the time these chronicles begin. About the time that she begins coloring her hair, she also begins altering her personal calendar; she is not a woman who will surrender to anything, not even time, without a battle!

Known Associates: Amelia's husband, Radcliffe Emerson, whom she meets in *Crocodile on the Sandbank*; their children, Ramses (from *The Curse of the Pharaohs*) and Nefret (from *The Last Camel Died at Noon*); their ward, Sennia (from *The Falcon at the Portal*); Amelia's in-laws, Walter and Evelyn; their "Egyptian family," Abdullah (through *The Ape Who Guards the Balance*); his youngest son, Selim (from *The Mummy Case*); his nephew, Daoud (from *The Curse of the Pharaohs*); his widowed daughter-in-law, Fatima (from *The Ape Who Guards the Balance*); his grandson, David (from *The Hippopotamus Pool*); the cat Bastet (from *The Curse of the Pharaohs* through *The Hippopotamus Pool*).

Premise: An archeologist solves crimes in late-nineteenth- and early-twentieth-century Egypt.

Comment: When Amelia Peabody inherits a fortune from her scholarly father, she determines to visit the places that he had studied. The ancient ruins in Egypt capture her imagination, and she decides to become an archeologist. Archeological fervor has inspired many to treat the excavations as a search for buried treasure rather than a search for knowledge; many Egyptians see no reason that they should refrain from plundering their past while the rest of the world runs amok searching for tombs. In early books in this series elaborate plots designed to frighten off tourists, locals, and officials are all foiled by Amelia, who is less likely to faint at the sight of an apparition than she is to arm herself with a parasol and chase after it. In the later novels Amelia, her family, and even her parasol have gained a reputation that often attracts trouble. The series was partly inspired by (rather than based on) the activities of real women in the Victorian era. Amelia Edwards did sail up the Nile in a *dahabiyeh* and wrote a travel book, *A Thousand Miles up the Nile*, based on her experiences. Her companion became known as "Hakim Sitt" for the medical assistance she rendered during their travels. Lady Hilda Petrie (William Petrie's wife) accompanied her husband on archeological digs. The author holds a doctorate in Egyptology from the University of Chicago; her novels are filled with details on the methods and attitudes of archeologists, and her historical research is impeccable. The adventures chronicled in the early books in the sequence are reminiscent of the novels of H. Rider Haggard, being full of humor and fantastical crimes.

The novels that cover the war years include more realistic crimes and more frightening villains.

Literary Crimes & Chimes: The great joy in these books is the voice of the narrator. Amelia Peabody's humor is never overt; it comes through the contrast between her statements and her actions. She is both strong and pragmatic; her actions reveal a romantic imagination and a warm heart. The result is both touching and funny. From *Seeing a Large Cat* forward the narration is divided between Amelia's voice and "Manuscript H," text written from Ramses and Nefret's point of view. Amelia mellows slightly in the later books, but Ramses changes a great deal throughout the series. The novels are best read in order. The series alters in voice and mood with *The Deeds of the Disturber* and *The Last Camel Died at Noon*, but the later entries return to the mood and locations of the early volumes in the series. In a November 2003 speech at the Library of Congress, the author stated that she plans to continue the series at least to the point of Howard Carter's discovery of King Tut's tomb but that some of the future books will be "prequels" that fill in gaps in the chronology.

THE CASES

1. *Crocodile on the Sandbank.* New York: Dodd, Mead, 1975, 273 p.

EGYPT, 1884. Amelia sallies forth to explore the worlds her late father had studied. On the way to Egypt she rescues Evelyn and hires her as a companion. Sinister events fail to daunt these women; they join the Emerson's archeological exploration of the site of Khuenaten's royal palace, and when they see a mummy walking by moonlight, Amelia characteristically leaps forward to chase it down! Associates: Evelyn; Radcliffe.

2. *The Curse of the Pharaohs.* New York: Dodd, Mead, 1981, 357 p.

EGYPT, 1892. Bad luck haunts the excavators that opened a previously undiscovered tomb in the Valley of the Kings, culminating in the death of their leader, Sir Henry Baskerville. Lady Baskerville (who used to be *very* well acquainted with Emerson) pleads for Emerson to brave the Pharaoh's curse and take over the excavation of the tomb. When the Emersons' dig is beset by suspicious accidents, Amelia begins to sleuth. Associates: Kevin O'Connell; Cyrus Vandergelt; Karl von Bork; Mary Berengeria; Radcliffe; Ramses.

3. *The Mummy Case.* New York: Congdon & Weed, 1985, 313 p.

EGYPT, 1894. Ramses accompanies his parents to excavate the "pyramids" of Mazghunah (long since reduced to piles of rubble) and proves to be a natural archeologist. The season is complicated by zealous missionaries, a gang of thieves, and vanishing and reappearing mummy cases! Associates: Sethos; M. de Morgan; Radcliffe; Ramses.

4. *Lion in the Valley: An Amelia Peabody Mystery.* New York: Atheneum, 1986, 291 p.

EGYPT, 1895. An attempted abduction of Ramses (now eight years old) and the murder of a criminal from their past occur before the Emersons arrive at Dahshoor to excavate the Black Pyramid. This site is one that Amelia has long dreamed of, but she approaches it with a dark foreboding, one that proves prescient when she is captured. Emerson must duel the Master Criminal to try to free her. Associates: Sethos; Donald Fraser; Enid Debenham; Major Ramsay; Emerson; Radcliffe; Ramses.

5. *The Deeds of the Disturber: An Amelia Peabody Mystery.* New York: Atheneum, 1988, 289 p.

ENGLAND, 1896. A night watchman at the British museum is found dead, his face set in a mask of terror, and sightings of archaically clad Egyptian priests who seem to appear and disappear at will are reported. Amelia and Emerson's sleuthing takes them through a London opium den, where Amelia meets a woman who causes her to question her husband's loyalty. Even an attempt at a day of vacation from crime, escorting her son, her niece, and her nephew to Madame Tussaud's waxworks, ends in crime, fear, and fury. Associates: Kevin O'Connell; James Peabody; Percy; Violet; Miss Minton; Inspector Cuff; Ayesha; Emerson; Radcliffe; Ramses.

6. *The Last Camel Died at Noon.* New York: Warner Books, 1991, 352 p.

EGYPT, 1897. The Emersons set out to excavate in the ruins of the ancient Cushite capital of Napata; before long, however, they are seduced by the fascination of searching for a lost culture and of rescuing the explorer Willoughby Forth and his wife. Associates: Kemit; Tarek; Prince Natasen; Amenit; Murtek; Emerson; Radcliffe; Ramses; Nefret.

7. *The Snake, the Crocodile, and the Dog.* New York: Warner Books, 1992, 340 p.

EGYPT, 1898. Amelia and Emerson set off for Luxor without the children, just like old times. Before their excavations begin, Emerson is kidnapped and seriously injured; Amelia struggles to help him, guard him, and avenge him. The activities of the Master Criminal complicate everything. Associates: Sethos; Mr. Vincey; his cat Anubis; Cyrus Vandergelt; Bertha; Karl von Bork; Emerson; Radcliffe; Ramses; Nefret.

8. *The Hippopotamus Pool.* New York: Warner Books, 1996, 384 p.

EGYPT, 1900. A mysterious stranger seeks out the Emersons and offers information on the tomb of Queen Tetisheri in Drah Abu'l Naga. His explanation that he knows the location of the site through his attachment to the Queen (in his first incarnation) is received by the irascible Emerson just as one might expect. Associates: Abd el Hamed; Layla; Sir Edward Washington; Kevin O'Connell; Cyrus Vandergelt; Howard Carter; Bertha; Matilda; Emerson; Radcliffe; Ramses; Nefret.

9. *Seeing a Large Cat.* New York: Warner Books, 1997, 386 p.

EGYPT, 1903. Was the terse message to stay away from tomb Twenty-A a warning or a lure? Twenty-A's mummy is found, somewhat embalmed, but wrapped in nineteenth-century petticoats. As Abdullah might say, such a "fresh" corpse (he has no prejudice against mummies of a proper vintage) can only mean that a murderer is at hand. Associates: Miss Dolly Bellingham; Mr. and Mrs. Donald Fraser; Cyrus Vandergelt; Howard Carter; Mrs. Katherine Whitney-Jones; Radcliffe; Ramses; Nefret.

10. *The Ape Who Guards the Balance: An Amelia Peabody Mystery.* New York: Avon Twilight, 1998, 376 p.

ENGLAND AND EGYPT, 1906. Daring daylight robberies and attempted abductions inform the Emersons that the scope of the criminal activities that plagued them in Egypt has expanded to England. To Egypt they go, where Ramses alters his protective coloring (in England he played a man-about-town; in Egypt he disguises himself as Ali the Rat) to investigate the illegal antiquities trade. They expect to uncover a thief, but unfortunately they uncover a murderer. Associates: Sethos; Miss Christabel Pankhurst; Kevin O'Connell; Lia; Howard Carter (Amelia cheers him up by predicting that he will one day make an interesting find); Edward Ayrton; Sir Edward Washington; Layla; Bertha; Matilda; Ramses; Emerson; Radcliffe; Ramses; Nefret.

11. *Guardian of the Horizon.* New York: William Morrow, 2004, 399 p.

EGYPT, 1907–1908. The Emersons set out once more for the Holy Mountain in response to an urgent message that Tarek is ill. Even before they arrive, they suspect that the messenger, Merasin, has not been entirely truthful. This book offers an interesting explanation for Nefret's resistance to Ramses. Associates: Merasin; Tarek; Daria; Ramses; Emerson; Nefret; Radcliffe.

12. *The Falcon at the Portal: An Amelia Peabody Mystery.* New York: Avon Twilight, 1999, 366 p.

EGYPT, 1911. David has often risked himself to protect Ramses. Now a different kind of danger haunts David: he is accused of returning to the illegal antiquities trade to gather funds for Egypt's nationalists. The Emerson's hands are full with combating those suspicions, excavating the pyramids at Zawaiet el 'Aryan, and solving a new murder. Associates: Percy Peabody; Kevin O'Connell; Jack Reynolds; Maude Reynolds; Karl von Bork; Wardani; Geoff Godwin; Mr. Russell; Emerson; David; Radcliffe; Ramses; Nefret; Sennia.

13. *He Shall Thunder in the Sky: An Amelia Peabody Mystery.* New York: William Morrow, 2000, 400 p.

EGYPT, 1914. Feelings run high as the Great War (World War I) begins in Europe. The Emersons continue to excavate, attempting to recover and protect information from past civilizations as the current civilization seems to disintegrate. A gigantic statue is uncovered in an unlikely location. Does Sethos' idea of "delicate attentions" include moving mountains to offer artifacts to Amelia? Ramses takes part in the war effort by trying to wage peace and spying to prevent a massacre. Associates: Percy; Mrs. Fortescue; Mr. Russell; Major Ewan Hamilton; Miss Melinda Hamilton; Miss Nordstrom; El-Gharbi; Sethos; Emerson; Ramses; Radcliffe; Nefret; Sennia.

14. *Lord of the Silent.* New York: William Morrow, 2001, 404 p.

EGYPT, 1915. The Emersons conspire to remove Ramses from the vicinity of people interested in his clandestine activities of the previous season. While Amelia and Radcliffe continue the excavation of the *mastabas* at Giza, Ramses and Nefret are sent to warn off tomb robbers in Luxor. Murder, espionage, and romantic rescues (both past and present) abound in this entry in the series. Associates: Howard Carter; Miss Minton; Jamil; Jumana; Cyrus and Katherine Vandergelt; Bertie; Alain Kuentz; George Barton; the Honorable Algernon Bracegirdle-Boisdragon; Sethos; Emerson; Ramses; Nefret.

15. *The Golden One.* New York: William Morrow, 2002, 429 p.

EGYPT, 1917. The rains of the last year proved particularly effective in uncovering traces of a previously unscathed tomb; our heroes know this because artifacts from the tomb are being offered for sale by the dealers in illegal antiquities. The find sets off an absolute fever of tomb hunting, even in such seasoned archeologists as Emerson and Vandergelt, who are working Medinet Habu and Deir el Medina. Ramses has determined to devote himself to archeology, but the Secret Service makes him an offer he cannot refuse. Associates: Jamil; Jumana Cyrus and Katherine Vandergelt; Bertie; the Honorable Algernon Bracegirdle-Boisdragon; Sethos; El-Gharbi; Sahin Pasha; Esin; Major Cartright; Lieutenant Chetwode; Sir Edward Washington; Emerson; Ramses; Radcliffe; Nefret; Sennia.

16. *Children of the Storm.* New York: William Morrow, 2003, 400 p.

EGYPT, 1919. The goddess Hathor seems an unlikely criminal; it is unclear if her activities are motivated by revenge, affection, or a desire to halt the excavations of the village at Dier el Medina. The Emersons attempt to focus on their work but must assist Cyrus Vandergelt when priceless artifacts that were held in his keeping are stolen. The accumulation of odd and mysterious circumstances resolves in abduction and attempted piracy. Walter's criminal instincts help the Emersons carry the day. Associates: Cyrus;

Katherine; Bertie; Walter; Evelyn; Lia; Evvie; Charla; Davy; Dolly; the Honorable Algernon Bracegirdle-Boisdragon; Matilda; Maryam; Sethos; Radcliffe; Ramses; Nefret; Sennia.

ASSOCIATIONAL VOLUME

Amelia Peabody's Egypt: A Compendium, ed. by Elizabeth Peters and Kristen Whitbread, with contributions by numerous authors. New York: William Morrow, 2003, 334 p.

This companion volume of "facts" about Amelia Peabody and her excavations serves a reference work for the series. It provides character lists (including information on times and places of real-life excavations), essays on Egyptology, photographs, and excerpts from the unpublished journal of Professor Radcliffe Emerson.

PETERS, Ellis (pseud. of Edith Mary Pargeter) (1913–1995). British.

BROTHER CADFAEL SERIES

Scene of the Crime: The Brother Cadfael mysteries are set in Britain in the twelfth century (1120–1145), amid the chaos of a nineteen-year period of weak contenders vying for the British Crown. The settings are focused on Shrewsbury, England, and environs for most of the stories but occasionally venture to Wales, the Thames Valley, Chester, Worcester, and Oxfordshire.

Detective: After an adventurous life as a sailor and as a crusader with Godfrey de Bouillon, Brother Cadfael, the Welshman Cadfael ap Meilyr ap Dafydd, joins the Benedictine monks at Shrewsbury. Born in 1080, Cadfael is ready to turn his back on war and seek to mend the ills of mankind rather than continue as a warrior. He is unaware that he may have progeny afoot in the world. Upon his arrival at Woodstock, Cadfael enters the parish church, forgetting to leave his sword outside. When a treble voice remonstrates, " 'Sir, should not all weapons of war be laid aside here?' " Cadfael responds, " 'Sir, You may very well be right.' " *A Rare Benedictine.* Cadfael is tolerant, understanding, even-tempered, humble, and caring. He is fortunate in the abbots who rule at St. Peter's, both of whom are intelligent, open-minded, generous, and kind. Cadfael, age fifty-seven when we first meet him, demonstrates a keen mind and observant senses. Through his series of chronicles he gains reader's respect and admiration.

Known Associates: Cadfael is assisted in many of his investigations by Deputy (later Sheriff) Hugh Beringar, who is married to Aline; their child, Giles, is Cadfael's godson. Monks with whom Cadfael lives include Brother Oswain, Brother Mark, Brother Jerome, and Brother Rhun (after the events chronicled in *An Excellent Mystery*). Sister Magdalen, a Benedictine nun at Godric's Ford, is a friend. Other associates include Sheriff Gilbert Prestcote (until after the events chronicled in *Dead Man's Ransom*) and, after the events chronicled in *The Virgin in the Ice*, Olivier de Bretagne. The books also include many historical figures that appear on- or offstage throughout the series: King Stephen, grandson of William I and husband of Queen Matilda of Boulogne; Empress Maud, daughter of King Henry I and Matilda, half sister to Robert, Earl of Gloucester, widow of Henry V of Austria and wife to Geoffrey, Count of Anjou, mother of King Henry II of England; Robert, Earl of Gloucester, illegitimate son of Henry I of England; William and Philip are his sons (Robert and William are in Maud's camp, but Philip will defect to Stephen); Archbishop Theobald of Canterbury; Geoffrey de Mandeville, outlaw; Bishop Roger de Clinton; Owain ap Gwynedd; Cadwaladr; Gilbert, Bishop of St. Asaph in Wales; Bishop Meurig of Bangor; William FitzAlan; the Earl of Chester, Ranulf, poisoned by Peverel family; Hugh Bigod, first Earl of Norfolk; Robert Bossu de Beaumont, Earl of Leicester; Humphrey de Bohun, who served the Empress; Roger, Earl of Hereford, appointed in 1143, but who lost his honor when Henry II became king; Henry of Blois, Bishop of Winchester, King Stephen's younger brother; Abbot Radulfus, at Shrewsbury in 1137; Prior Robert Pennant; Abbot Heribert; St. Winifred.

Premise: A monastic herbalist heals the sick and solves crimes in twelfth-century England.

Comment: Cadfael learned something of potions and medicines during his travels in the Middle East and is thus assigned as the abbey's herbalist and physician upon his arrival there. Between this work and his years of battle, Cadfael has extensive experience in the physical manifestations that different types of death leave on a corpse. His occupations also provide him with some freedom of movement and an opportunity to investigate deaths. He works with Sheriff Hugh Beringar, who becomes Cadfael's fast friend and confidant, to help solve murders and determine causes of death, quickly demonstrating his expertise to help the law bring the malefactors to justice. The countryside harbors many desperate people whose homes and livelihood have been destroyed by the civil war. Even monasteries and priories have been razed by roaming bodies of armed men. Like a shifting terror, ubiquitous and unpredictable, the civil war in England casts a shadow on all villages, institutions, and civil life. The devastation and fear are palpable as armies attack at random and highwaymen prowl the countryside. Religious faith is a given, and the church is just awakening to the "danger" of alternative ideas about God, Jesus, and so on. Not all clerics depicted in these books think alike: witness, for example, the polar natures of Abbot Radulfus and Prior Robert. Aline Beringar and Sister Magdalen both voice issues faced by the women of the twelfth century.

Literary Crimes & Chimes: These tales not only are well written but also immerse us in the background details of twelfth-century England and the war that consumes it. There are no rigid formulas here. The murders sometimes come late in the story, and means and motives vary. Because of his calling, Cadfael is usually the one individual best able to render a crime scene and discover the ultimate truth about any particular death. The characters are so well defined over a series of stories that one can almost predict how they will react and think. The author's writing at times approaches the poetic: "trees, darkening now over her head and dropping, silently and moistly, the occasional withered leaf, the tears of the aging year."—*The Hermit of Eyton Forest*. A wealthy landowner's gift to the abbey is a "prudent precaution to acquire merit for his soul." "A shadow no bigger than Liliwin's, there behind them black against the slanting sun of mid-afternoon, and yet he cast such a darkness over them as they could hardly bear."—*The Sanctuary Sparrow*. Such passages and others like them lift these tales above the average for the historical mystery story and make them enjoyable reading over and over again. Ellis Peters was one of the chief factors in popularizing the genre in the 1980s and 1990s, both through the publication of her books and through the television versions that were made of about half of these novels. Highly recommended.

THE CASES

1. **"The Light on the Road to Woodstock,"** in *A Rare Benedictine*. London: Headline, 1988, p. 7–39.

   ENGLAND CHANNEL AND SHREWSBURY, ENGLAND, 1120. We meet Cadfael ap Meilyr ap Dafydd, a Welsh former Crusader and soldier for King Henry I of England, as he is returning to England after Henry has won th⸍ Duchy of Normandy. Chance intervenes when Cadfael aids Prior Herib in gaining title to lands that Cadfael's commanding officer had hor add to his booty. Cadfael then realizes he must embrace "a new and monstrous" change to give his life back its meaning. Associates: Prior Heribert; Roger Mauduit; Eadwina; Alard; Goscelin.

2. **"The Price of Light,"** in *A Rare Benedictine*. London: Headline, 1988, p. 45–76.

SHREWSBURY, ENGLAND, CHRISTMAS 1135. Beginning as if it were a fairy tale, this story is one of the most humorous and enjoyable of all of Peters' fictions. A wealthy landowner bestows a gift to the Abbey of St. Peter in his spirit of "prudent precaution to acquire merit for his soul," after a lifetime of overindulgence, selfishness, and brutality. When the gift disappears, Cadfael becomes involved and finds the charity of others very fulfilling. Associates: Abbot Heribert; Alard; Hamo FitzHamon of Lidgate; Lady FitzHamon, "smiling on the world in scarlet and brown, like a robin, and just as confidently."

3. **"Eye Witness,"** in *A Rare Benedictine*. London: Headline, 1988, p. 99–118.

SHREWSBURY, ENGLAND, 1136. An attempted murder is foiled, and an ingenious trap is set to catch the guilty thief. The background of twelfth-century Shropshire is highlighted through its daily life and customs. Associates: Mad Dog of the Dead Boat; Brother Ambrose; William Rede; Jacob of Bouldon; William Harefoot; Rhodri Fychan, a beggar.

4. *A Morbid Taste for Bones: A Mediaeval Whodunnit.* London: Macmillan, 1977, 192 p.

SHREWSBURY, ENGLAND, AND WALES, 1137. Robert, Prior of the Benedictine Abbey of St. Peter and St. Paul, seizes upon an opportunity to gain favor with the Benedictine hierarchy by arranging the transfer of Welsh St. Winifred's relics to St. Peter's. A Welsh leader who is opposed to the move is murdered, and a young "outlander" or "*alltud*" (foreigner) is suspected of the crime. Brother Cadfael, because he is Welsh and can translate back and forth between the languages, accompanies the mission to Wales and helps in solving the crime. He surreptitiously resolves the dispute in a way that he believes is in accordance with the wishes of a Higher Authority. Associates: Brother John; Brother Columbanus; Brother Richard; Urien, a chaplain; Bened, a smithy; Sioned; Risiart; Annest; Padrig; Marared; Cai; Engelard; Cadwallon; Peredur; Dame Branwen; Father Huw.

5. *One Corpse Too Many: A Mediaeval Whodunnit.* London: Macmillan, 1979, 191 p.

SHREWSBURY, ENGLAND, SUMMER 1138. When King Stephen's forces are victorious in the Battle at Shrewsbury, the monks of St. Peter and St. Paul Abbey offer to bury the dead who fought for Empress Maud; and Brother Cadfael notices there is an extra corpse, not a casualty of war, but a murdered youth. Who is the young man, and who murdered him, and for what reason? We meet Aline Siward and Hugh Beringer for the first time. Associates: Abbot Heribert; Godith Adeney; Nicholas Faintree; Petronilla; Flesher; Torold Blund; Ulf; Sheriff Prestcote. Historical Figure: British King Stephen.

6. *Monk's Hood: The Third Chronicle of Brother Cadfael.* London: Macmillan, 1980, 223 p.

SHREWSBURY, ENGLAND, DECEMBER 1138. Abbot Heribert is summoned by the papal legate (probably due to the war's frequent floundering from one side to the other), and Prior Robert's ambitions suddenly shine forth. Cadfael meets a dear friend dating from his pre-Crusade adventures. Monk's-hood from Cadfael's herbarium provides the means for murder. Associates: Abbot Heribert; Abbot Radulfus, whom we meet for the first time; Brother Mark; Sheriff Gilbert Prestcote; Brother Jerome.

7. *Saint Peter's Fair: The Fourth Chronicle of Brother Cadfael.* London: Macmillan, 1981, 220 p.

SHREWSBURY, ENGLAND, JULY–AUGUST 1139. St. Peter's annual fair in the abbey town attracts merchants, customers, revelers, politicians, and even murderers, many of whom travel there via the Severn River. Beautiful young Emma, niece of a wealthy merchant, becomes involved in the web of murder and intrigue. Simultaneously, the Empress Maud and her half brother, Robert of Gloucester, attempt to wrest the throne from King Stephen's tenuous grasp. The countryside is fraught with danger and lawlessness, and recent skirmishes and battles have left poverty and starvation in their wake. A few months after this tale concludes, Maud lands at Arundel. Associates: Provost Geoffrey Corviser; his son, Philip Corviser; Sheriff Gilbert Prestcote; Watt (Walter Renold), tavern owner; Cadfael's helper, Brother Mark; Rhodri ap Haw, a Welsh merchant who speaks no English and communicates via Brother Cadfael; Thomas of Bristol, a wine importer in favor with Robert of Gloucester; Emma Vernold, his niece; Ivo Corbiere, from manor Stanton Cobbold in Cheshire; Turstan Fowler, Corbiere's archer and falconer; Ewald, Corbiere's groom; Fulke Adeney. Historical Figure: Abbot Radulfus, who has been abbot at St. Peter for six months.

8. *The Leper of Saint Giles: The Fifth Chronicle of Brother Cadfael.* London: Macmillan, 1981, 223 p.

SHREWSBURY, ENGLAND, OCTOBER 1139. A wealthy squire has arranged to wed the lovely Iveta, forty years his junior and a ward of her uncle and aunt. Another suitor challenges the wedding and then is accused of thievery and murder. With the help of a leper from nearby St. Giles hospital, Brother Cadfael unravels the mystery. Associates: Sheriff Gilbert Prestcote; Brother Mark; Brother Oswain; Lazaarus (Guimar de Massard); Iveta; Huon de Domville; Jocelin Lucy; Godfrid Picard; Agnes Picard; Avice of Thornbury.

9. *The Virgin in the Ice: The Sixth Chronicle of Brother Cadfael.* London: Macmillan, 1982, 220 p.

LUDLOW, ENGLAND, NOVEMBER–DECEMBER 1139. The devastation and lawlessness resulting from the ongoing war for the Crown is a sobering backdrop to the events thrust upon the religious and secular communities. Three evacuees from the Worcester area disappear, and a monk who was their companion for a short time is found beaten almost to death. Cadfael is dispatched to treat the injured cleric and meets a young man, the son of Mariam of Antioch. Associates: Sheriff Gilbert Prestcote; Brother Mark; Brother Oswain; Yves Hugonin; Ermina Hugonin; Mariam; Sister Hilaria; Prior Leonard; Brother Edmund; Elyas; John Druel; Evrad Boterel; Alain la Gaucher; Olivier de Bretagne.

10. *The Sanctuary Sparrow: The Seventh Chronicle of Brother Cadfael.* London: Macmillan, 1983, 221 p.

SHREWSBURY, ENGLAND, SPRING 1140. Like baying hounds, the townsmen chase Liliwin, a young servant to the goldsmith, into the chapel at St. Peter's, where he is given sanctuary according to law and custom. They accuse him of robbery and murder, but Cadfael investigates and uncovers a fabric of mistrust, hate, greed, and also love. Life in a class-stratified society gives readers food for thought. Associates: Liliwin; Walter Aurifaber, goldsmith; Daniel, his son; Juliana, his grandmother; Margery Bele, Daniel's bride; Griffin, a locksmith's son; Susanna Aurifaber; Rennilt, a maid; Cecily Corde, Daniel's mistress; Iestyn, a journeyman to Aurifaber; Sheriff Prestcote (offstage); Geoffrey Corviser, town provost; Mad Dog of the Dead Boat.

11. *The Devil's Novice: The Eighth Chronicle of Brother Cadfael.* London: Macmillan, 1983, 191 p.

SHREWSBURY, ENGLAND, SEPTEMBER 1140. A well-to-do landowner, suspecting that his son has committed murder, sends the recalcitrant youth to St. Peter's Abbey. The on-again, off-again war between Stephen and Maud continues, and the countryside has once more become unsafe. Bishop Henry's envoy has disappeared, and Meriet seems implicated. Associates: Brother Oswin; Brother Paul; Roswitha Linde, *fiancée* of Nigel Aspley; her brother, Janyn Linde; Father Leoric Aspley; Meriet; Canon Eluard of Winchester; Peter Clemence.

12. *Dead Man's Ransom: The Ninth Chronicle of Brother Cadfael.* London: Macmillan, 1984, 189 p.

SHREWSBURY, ENGLAND, AND WALES, FEBRUARY 1141. Turmoil and terror reign in the countryside as the soldiers of Stephen and Maud vie for hegemony. When Sheriff Prestcote and a Welsh fighter are captured, an attempt at a prisoner exchange is made, but the plan is complicated by murder and by love. Associates: Sister Magdalen Avice of Thornbury; Sheriff Gilbert Prestcote; Melicent, his daughter; Elis ap Cynan.

13. *The Pilgrim of Hate: The Tenth Chronicle of Brother Cadfael.* London: Macmillan, 1984, 190 p.

SHREWSBURY, ENGLAND, MAY 1141. King Stephen is being held prisoner after the Battle of Lincoln. The Empress Maud is living in London, and their factions are fighting throughout the shires, threatening the safety of the civilians. The occasion for pilgrims to throng to Shrewsbury is the anniversary of St. Winifred's translation. Among the varied mix are devout pilgrims, cripples, thieves, robbers, and even a murderer who is not what he seems. Associates: Brothers Anselm; Edmund; Jerome; Oswain; Provost Corviser; Wat the Taverner; Daniel Aurifaber; William Hales; Walter Bagot; John Shure.

14. *An Excellent Mystery: The Eleventh Chronicle of Brother Cadfael.* London: Macmillan, 1985, 190 p.

SHREWSBURY, ENGLAND, AUGUST 1141. Amid the turmoil of Empress Maud's and King Stephen's battle for the throne of England, a beautiful maiden goes missing. Is she lost, kidnapped, murdered, or just in hiding? Does Brother Cadfael himself harbor a personal secret? Associates: Brother Oswain; Brother Rhun; Brother Urien; Nicholas Harnage; Reginald Cruce; Mad Dog of the Dead Boat; Adam Heriet; Sister Magdalen.

15. *The Raven in the Foregate: The Twelfth Chronicle of Brother Cadfael.* London: Macmillan, 1986, 201 p.

SHREWSBURY, ENGLAND, DECEMBER 1141–JANUARY 1142. When Bishop Henry of Winchester sends Father Ailnoth as vicar to Holy Cross parish to replace the beloved Father Adam, the Holy Cross flock is enraged by Ailnoth's rigorous interpretation of Papal law. Then Ailnoth is found dead in the mill-race. In the turmoil of people's shifting allegiances for either Empress Maud or King Stephen, a young retainer of Maud is suspected of murdering the prelate. Associates: Brother Jerome; Deputy Alan Herbard; Torold Blund; Godith Adeney.

16. *The Rose Rent: The Thirteenth Chronicle of Brother Cadfael.* London: Macmillan, 1986, 190 p.

SHREWSBURY, ENGLAND, SPRING 1142. How does a white rose bush become the focus of two murders and tie two shy townspeople together in romance? What options are open for a widow in medieval society other than the cloister or living with her adult children? Associates: Brother Rhun; Sister Magdalen; Provost Geoffrey Corvisier; Philip Corvisier, shoemaker; Mad Dog of the Dead Boat; Brother Anselm.

17. *The Hermit of Eyton Forest: The Fourteenth Chronicle of Brother Cadfael.* London: Headline, 1987, 224 p.

SHREWSBURY, ENGLAND, OCTOBER 1142. The shifting fortunes of England's battle of cousins tests the allegiances of those who have much to gain or lose in the struggle. We witness defection and loyalty among the mighty and the lowly. A widow plots to control the future of her son; a hermit is not what he seems; and Cadfael is challenged by three murders. Associates: Brother Paul; Brother Jerome; Dane Dionisia; John of Longwood; Hilltrude; Fulke Astley; Cuthred; Rinaud Bouchier; Eilmund; Hyacinth; Drogo Bosiet; Rafe of Coventry, falconer; Richard Ludel.

18. *The Confession of Brother Haluin: The Fifteenth Chronicle of Brother Cadfael.* London: Headline, 1988, 205 p.

SHREWSBURY, ENGLAND, WINTER 1142–1143. In this shocking winter tale, we meet someone who is truly evil. Brother Haluin's confession sends Cadfael on an adventure that leads to murder, betrayal, and, yes, also constancy, pity, and love. Associates: Brother Haluin, book illuminator; Brother Rhun; Philip Corvisier; Adelais de Clary, Audemar, her son; Lothair, groom; Luc, his son; Cenred Vivers, manor lord; Hellisende Vivers, daughter, who is betrothed to Jean de Perronet; Roselin, squire to Audemar.

19. *The Heretic's Apprentice: The Sixteenth Chronicle of Brother Cadfael.* London: Headline, 1989, 279 p.

SHREWSBURY, ENGLAND, JUNE 1143. This tale begins dramatically with the arrival of a corpse just before the annual anniversary of the transformation of St. Winifred. Elave, the companion of William of Lythwood, who lies dead in the cart, brings an ornately carved box to Fortunata, adopted daughter of William. Elave is accused of heresy, thus introducing the reader to a capsule discussion of church controversy: faith, good works, original sin, and predestination. And yes, there are murders. Associates: Brother Jerome; Brother Rhun; Elave; Girard of Lythwood; Fortunata; Aldwin; Conan; Gerbert of Canterbury.

20. *The Potter's Field: The Seventeenth Chronicle of Brother Cadfael.* London: Headline, 1990, 309 p.

SHREWSBURY, ENGLAND, JULY–NOVEMBER 1143. A woman's body is found when the Brothers of St. Peter plow a newly acquired field. Who is she? How did she come to be buried in unhallowed ground, yet shrouded and clasping a cross to her chest, as if in Christian burial? Amid the turmoil and desecration of civil war, questions are cleverly raised in the narrative regarding women's positions or lack thereof in medieval society. Associates: Deputy Alan Herbard; William Warden, officer; Walter Renold (Wat), tavern owner; Brother Oswain at St. Giles; Brother Matthew, accountant.

21. *The Summer of the Danes: The Eighteenth Chronicle of Brother Cadfael.* London: Headline, 1991, 311 p.

SHREWSBURY AND CHESTER, ENGLAND, AND CLWYD VALLEY, WALES, SUMMER 1144. While King Stephen and Empress Maud's forces are entrenched respectively in the southeast and southwest of England, the archbishop, in order to secure his domain, has created a new bishopric in Wales.

Brother Cadfael accompanies the courier Brother Mark with the appropriate gifts and message of welcome. Their journey unravels when Owain ab Gwynedd is attacked by Danish mercenaries under Otil, who has been encouraged by Cadwaladr, Owain's brother. Murder, romance, courage, daring, and courtly love complete the tale. Associates: Hywel Owain's son, Canon Meirion; Heledd, his daughter; Cuhelyn ab Einion; Gwion; Bishop Meurig; Gledri ap Rhys; Turcaill; Ieuan, the bridegroom chosen for Heledd; Brother Mark.

22. *The Holy Thief: The Nineteenth Chronicle of Brother Cadfael.* London: Headline, 1992, 282 p.

SHREWSBURY, ENGLAND, FALL 1144. Subprior Herlium of neighboring Ramsey Abbey flees to St. Peter's after Geoffrey de Mandeville's outlaws sack and burn Ramsey. The River Severn floods, and donations collected for Ramsey are intercepted on the way by outlaws. A slave maiden owned by a troubadour plays a role in naming the murderer of an innocent servant. Cadfael's secret regarding the St. Winifred's reliquary is in jeopardy. Associates: Abbot Walter of Ramsey; Sulien Bount; Donata Blount; Brother Rhun. Historical Figure: Robert Bossu Beaumont, Earl of Leicester.

23. *Brother Cadfael's Penance: The Twentieth Chronicle of Brother Cadfael.* London: Headline, 1994, 276 p.

SHREWSBURY, COVENTY, AND THE THAMES VALLEY, ENGLAND, WINTER 1145. Cadfael gains temporary leave from the abbey to attend a futile meeting between Stephen and Maud called by Bishop Roger de Clinton and to find his son, who has been hidden as a pawn after the surrender of Faringdon. Ives is accused of murder, and Cadfael is drawn into the civil war and is present at Maud's siege of La Musarderie. What becomes of Olivier de Bretagne, Brien de Soules, and Philip of Gloucester? Will Cadfael be admitted back into the contemplative life of a monk after having an active role in secular affairs? Associates: Brother Edmund; Yves Hugonin; Brien de Soulis; Olivier de Bretagne. Historical Figures: Bishop Roger de Clinton of Coventry and Lichfield (1129); Reginald FitzRoy, half brother to Empress Maud; King Stephen; Empress Maud; Hugh Bigod, Earl of Norfolk; Robert Bossu Beaumont, Earl of Leicester; Earl Ranulf of Chester; Humphrey de Bohun, servant to the Empress; Roger, Earl of Hereford (appointed in 1143); Henry of Blois, Bishop of Winchester and King Stephen's younger brother; Robert, Earl of Gloucester, Empress Maud's half brother; William, his son; and Philip, the younger son, who fought on King Stephen's side.

24. *A Rare Benedictine.* London: Headline, 1988, 125 p.

A collection of short stories featuring Brother Cadfael. CONTENTS: "The Light on the Road to Woodstock"; "The Price of Light"; "Eye Witness." The individual stories are covered separately above.

ASSOCIATIONAL BOOKS

1. *Cadfael Country: Shropshire & the Welsh Borders,* by Rob Talbot and Robin Whiteman. London: Macdonald, 1990, 192 p.

This book is a celebration of the world of Ellis Peters and the medieval sleuth she has created. It takes the form of a historical pilgrimage through the wild border country of Shropshire.

2. *The Cadfael Companion: The World of Brother Cadfael.* London: Macdonald, 1991, 392 p.

A background encyclopedic guide to the people, places, and things associated with Ellis Peters' popular medieval detective, Brother Cadfael.

3. *Brother Cadfael's Herb Garden: An Illustrated Companion to Medieval Plants and Their Uses,* by Robin Whiteman and Rob Talbot. London: Little, Brown, 1996, 200 p.

This covers the history of herbal remedies and monastic herb gardens such as Cadfael's and features a complete A-to-Z guide to the medical uses of every herb and plant mentioned in the Ellis Peters books.

PRONZINI, Bill (i.e., William John) (1943–). American.

CARPENTER AND QUINCANNON SERIES

Scene of the Crime: The American West, beginning in 1893.

Detective: John Frederick Quincannon, an operative with the U.S. Secret Service and later a partner in his own private investigation service in San Francisco, Carpenter and Quincannon. He appears to be in his mid-forties. He has a problem holding his liquor.

Known Associates: Sabina Carpenter, a Pinkerton Detective Agency operative and later Quincannon's partner in detection. She appears to be about ten years younger than Quincannon.

Premise: Two private detectives operate out of their San Francisco office in the 1890s, after resigning from their respective agencies in the introductory book to the series.

Comment: Pronzini is one of the best in the business at generating a believable atmosphere in a historical setting. The characters are both depicted as strong, intelligent, handsome, and true to their era. Quincannon finds himself attracted to Carpenter initially for her skills as a detective but then comes to have romantic designs on her as well, designs that Sabina carefully deflects. Their on-again, off-again relationship never really advances beyond the surface. The mysteries they have to solve are also well constructed, often focusing around issues peculiar to the period. Pronzini enjoys and employs many locked-room mystery scenarios.

Literary Crimes & Chimes: Sabina perhaps exercises a little more latitude than a woman of her time might actually have been capable of doing, although this is, after all, San Francisco in the Gay Nineties. The crimes often draw Quincannon (in particular) away from the big city into the less populated areas of California and the West, while Sabina usually remains close to their home office. Both Carpenter and Quincannon are complex but attractive individuals, making one wish that Pronzini had spent less time with his better-known Nameless Detective and more with surfing the 1890s.

THE CASES

1. *Quincannon.* New York: Walker & Co., 1985, 175 p.

SAN FRANCISCO, CALIFORNIA, AND SILVER CITY, IDAHO, 1893. The initial volume in the series introduces Quincannon as an operative with the U.S. Secret Service and Sabina as an agent with the Pinkerton Detective Agency. They encounter each other while working separate cases at the mining community of Silver City, Idaho, near the junction of the state lines of Utah, Idaho, and Oregon. Quincannon is investigating a counterfeiting ring operating through the West when one of his informants is murdered in San Francisco. He follows a lead to Silver City, where his chronic alcoholism eventually endangers both his own life and that of Carpenter. Sabina is simultaneously investigating a pyramid scheme operated by one of the mine owners at Silver City. The violent *dénouement* shocks Quincannon out of his boozey depression and ultimately changes his life. After sobering up and returning home to San Francisco, he wires Carpenter in Denver to suggest that they both resign their positions and form a joint detective agency based in Northern California. Sabina agrees to a business relationship only.

2. *Beyond the Grave,* with Marcia Muller. New York: Walker & Co., 1986, 236 p.

SOUTHERN CALIFORNIA, 1846, 1894, 1986. This curious hybrid contains alternating chapters written by Pronzini and his wife, the mystery writer Marcia Muller. The Pronzini sections feature John Quincannon investigating a case in 1894, while the Muller pieces focus on the parallel investigation of Santa Barbara museum director Elena Oliverez in 1986. In 1846 the Mexican ranchos in California were overrun by American rebel soldiers invading from the north. The Velasquez family hid their treasures somewhere near their farmhouse in the mountains outside Santa Barbara, before the place was burned and looted in the fighting, leaving the descendants of the clan almost impoverished. Both investigators, each working 100 years apart from the other, seek to discover the location of the missing gold. This curious hybrid nonetheless manages to engage the reader and solve the mystery, with Quincannon's delvings eventually providing the essential clues for Elena to complete the 150-year-old puzzle. Sabina is mostly offstage in this story.

3. *Carpenter and Quincannon, Professional Detective Services.* Norfolk, VA: Crippen & Landru Publishers, 1998, 202 p.

CALIFORNIA AND NEVADA, DECEMBER 1894–1899. A collection of short stories featuring the two detectives, working together and/or separately. CONTENTS: "No Room at the Inn" (Quincannon only, an inn in the Sierra Nevada Mountains, December 1894); "Burgade's Crossing" (Quincannon only, Sacramento River Delta, date unknown); "The Cloud Cracker" (Quincannon only, Delford, California, 1895); "Lady One-Eye" (Quincannon and Carpenter, Grass Valley, California, 1899); "Coney Game" (Quincannon and Carpenter, San Francisco, California, date unknown); "The Desert Limited" (Quincannon and Carpenter, on the train between Needles and Barstow, California, date unknown); "The Horseshoe Nail" (Quincannon only, a lumber camp in the Sierra Nevada Mountains, near Verdi, Nevada, date unknown); "Medium Rare" (Quincannon and Carpenter, San Francisco, California, date unknown); "The Highbinders" (Quincannon and Carpenter, San Francisco, California, date unknown).

4. *Burgade's Crossing: Western Stories.* Waterville, ME: Five Star, 2003, 226 p.

CALIFORNIA AND NEVADA, DECEMBER 1894–1899. A second collection of short stories featuring the two detectives, working together or separately, mostly reprinted from *Carpenter and Quincannon.* CONTENTS: "Burgade's Crossing" (Quincannon only, Sacramento River Delta, date unknown); "Lady One-Eye" (Quincannon and Carpenter, Grass Valley, California, 1899); "Coney Game" (Quincannon and Carpenter, San Francisco, California, date unknown); "The Desert Limited" (Quincannon and Carpenter, on the train between Needles and Barstow, California, date unknown); "The Highgraders" (Quincannon only, a mine in the Sierra Nevada Mountains, date unknown); "No Room at the Inn" (Quincannon only, an inn in the Sierra Nevada Mountains, December 1894); "The Horseshoe Nail" (Quincannon only, a lumber camp in the Sierra Nevada Mountains, near Verdi, Nevada, date unknown); "The Highbinders" (Quincannon and Carpenter, San Francisco, California, date unknown). Only one of these stories, "The Highgraders," is original to this volume.

Zachary McQuestion Series

Scene of the Crime: Yukon Territory, Canada, and San Francisco, California, in 1897.

Detective: Zachary McQuestion, a Corporal in the Canadian North West Mounted Police, born 1869 in Manitoba.

Known Associates: None.

Premise: Corporal McQuestion uses his skills as a tracker and hunter to trace the brutal killers of the manager of a trade post.

Comment: McQuestion finds the body of roadhouse keeper Molly Malone and her two helpmates foully murdered by persons unknown. Tracking the killer south, he heads through Yukon Territory into Alaska, and eventually down the Pacific Coast to San Francisco, where he finally corners the perpetrator near Petaluma. Well written and authentic in every detail, *Starvation Camp* was intended, according to the author's introduction in the 1994 reprint edition, to be the first volume of a trilogy, most of the later part of the series to be set in the United States. For various reasons, the other two books were never written, leaving this historical mystery novel an orphan. Still, *Starvation Camp* does very well on its own. The characters are compelling, the action nonstop, and the settings true to life.

Literary Crimes & Chimes: Pronzini has a knack of putting the reader into the minds of his main characters. Although the narrative is told in the third person, we feel like we're actually there in the Yukon in midwinter, the cold and ice closing in upon us, while we chase the equally brutal denizens of this unforgiving climate. At the end of the book, McQuestion resigns from the Mounted Police and presumably will become what John Quincannon became just a year later in Pronzini's *oeuvre*: a private operative based in San Francisco. Indeed, one can see an almost direct link between the development of the two characters. Both, for example, have fathers who were members of the law enforcement clan, and both belong to official government organizations before resigning their positions for personal reasons (neither fits into an organizational structure). This is quality work of the first level.

THE CASE

1. *Starvation Camp.* Garden City, NY: Doubleday & Co., 1984, 180 p. Reprinted with a new introduction by Pronzini, "The Challenge of the Yukon." Cedar Rapids, IA: Mystery Scene, 1994, 180 p.
   Yukon Territory, Canada, and San Francisco, California, March 1897. See commentary in this series.

REED, Mary, and Eric Mayer. American.

Scene of the Crime: Constantinople, from 525 through the reign of the Emperor Justinian (which ended in 565).

Detective: John the Eunuch is tall, lean, and handsome. As a young man he studied philosophy but left the contemplative life to became a soldier. He then served as a mercenary in Bretania. He follows the religion of many soldiers of his time, worshipping Mithra. His military career has left him relatively unscathed, save for an abiding fear of deep water (he once witnessed the drowning of a comrade). He has lived in Alexandria, Egypt, traveling with his lover Cornelia, who was an acrobat who performed as a bull jumper. He expected to eventually retire there as a farmer with Cornelia. His plans were destroyed when he was captured by the Persians, castrated, and sold into slavery. He is sensitive to, and embarrassed by, the physical difficulties of other men who have been castrated; he abhors the softness of many of them, and he works to remain strong. He passed through the household of at least one owner before he was sold to the Palace in Constantinople. Through his investigative skills he rose to the position of Lord Chamberlain to the Emperor Justinian I.

Known Associates: Most of John's confidants are other believers in the outlawed religion of Mithra. Anatolius is the Emperor's Secretary; Felix is the Captain of the Excubitors (Palace Guard); Gaius, the Emperor's doctor. Theodora, the woman who rose from "actress" (read courtesan) to Empress loathes John, and one of her pages, Hektor, delights in plotting against him.

Isis is the madam of the best brothel in the city; it's not a place that John has much use for, but Isis comes from Alexandria and regards John as a fellow countryman in a strange land. Members of John's household include Peter, who is hired as John's servant at some point between "Beauty More Stealthy" and *One for Sorrow*. By the end of *Two for Joy*, Hypatia, also a servant, has joined the household.

Premise: A eunuch solves crimes and serves as an agent for the Emperor in sixth-century Byzantium.

Comment: The Byzantine Emperor Justinian I regards John as brilliant, trustworthy, and expendable, an attractive combination, since Justinian can order John to find answers and yet sacrifice him as a scapegoat if any of these answers cause the government political problems. Many of John's investigations are undertaken at the direct command of the Emperor. The Empress Theodora also orders John to investigate on several occasions. It is less certain whether she wants John to succeed or to fail. She hates John and is usually as acidulous in her descriptions of what will happen to him if he fails to solve a case as she is in her instructions on what she wants discovered. John also initiates some of his own investigations, motivated by his own need for seeing justice done. The fact that he is Lord Chamberlain to Justinian gives him enough power to compel suspects and witnesses to speak to him. This is a fascinating time and an interesting and unusual place for a detective to operate. The Christian Church is rising, but there are adherents to different forms of the doctrine who passionately regard all other Christian sects as the enemy. There are also many followers of the old religions, which technically have been outlawed. Unrest is present at every level of the society, made manifest in the constant palace intrigues, riots in the streets, and even in scurrilous writings that mock the Empress and Emperor. We also see the scientific marvels of the age, such as automatons and water clocks. The society depicted is both rich and strange, a great setting for these mysteries.

Literary Crimes & Chimes: This series combines intricate puzzles, strong characters, and fascinating historical details. The authors' research is impeccable; some situations in the books derive directly from the histories of the time. John is a character of great discipline and reserve. We experience this as we see John's thoughts and fears. John does not dwell overmuch on his "condition," but he has a bone-deep abhorrence of some of the habits of the typical eunuchs he encounters. He maintains himself with a military discipline, avoiding becoming soft. The reader can see his horror of what has happened to him; but John maintains emotional discipline to control his own thoughts and feelings. Reminders of his affliction creep up unexpectedly, as when John feels grateful that Anatolius does not uncomfortably look away when he and John talk in the baths. Less skillful writers would have had John afraid of the stares of friends and strangers. Mary Reed and Eric Mayer instead give us a man of great dignity who has managed to come to terms with being maimed, one who demands respect and refuses pity.

THE CASES

1. *Four for a Boy.* Scottsdale, AZ: Poisoned Pen Press, 2003, 328 p.

CONSTANTINOPLE, 525. While Byzantine Emperor Justin I lies on his deathbed, the heir presumptive, his nephew Justinian, is wracked by a suspicious illness and plagued by rumors that he arranged the death of a prominent citizen. Justinian suspects that someone is plotting against him, using magic, poison, or both to prevent him from succeeding his uncle as Emperor; and so chooses the most unlikely of champions, a eunuch, to conduct an investigation and clear his name. John the Eunuch knows that he will gain the next Emperor's favor if he succeeds, but if he fails his best hope will be for a quick death, and the barbaric palace guard ordered to assist him is not likely to be much help. Associates: Felix; Lady Anna; Avis. Historical Figures: Byzantine Emperor Justin I; Byzantine Emperor Justinian I.

2. "A Mithraic Mystery," in *The Mammoth Book of Historical Detectives,* ed. by Mike Ashley. New York: Carroll & Graf Publishers, 1995, p. 103–119.

CONSTANTINOPLE, 525–532. A young disciple of Mithra is found dead, in what is obviously a Mithraeum. The Empress commands John to investigate. Does she know that he is an initiate? It's difficult to say who is more dangerous: the murderer or the Empress Theodora. Historical Figure: Empress Theodora.

3. "Beauty More Stealthy," in *Classical Whodunnits: Murder and Mystery from Ancient Greece and Rome,* ed. by Mike Ashley. New York: Carroll & Graf Publishers, 1997, p. 317–345.

CONSTANTINOPLE, 525–532. John's friend Anna is found dead, and he suspects murder. The most likely suspect is her new slave, Hypatia, a gardener, an herbalist, an Egyptian—and a likely poisoner; but John cannot believe that the Hypatia would first try the poison out on a cat. Eventually, John finds unsatisfying answers, but very satisfying justice. Associates: Peter; Hypatia; Anna.

4. "A Byzantine Mystery," in *The Mammoth Book of Historical Whodunnits,* ed. by Mike Ashley. New York: Carroll & Graf Publishers, 1993, p. 99–105.

CONSTANTINOPLE, 532. Constantinople is ablaze with riots, and John is given a task of such delicacy and cloaked in such secrecy that he must conduct his investigation without revealing its object to those he questions! Historical Figure: Ecumenical Patriarch Epiphanios.

5. "A Lock of Hair for Proserpine," in *Chronicles of Crime: The Second Ellis Peters Memorial Anthology of Historical Crime*, ed. by Maxim Jakubowski. London: Headline Book Publishing, 1999, p. 117–131.

Kateros was rumored to have dabbled in the black arts, but the brothel-keeper Isis believed him to be of reasonably good character, and so she sold him Nefret to be his wife. When he is struck dead, Nefret fears some magical agency is at work and tries to protect his soul. John suspects a more human villain and seeks to preserve Nefret's life.

6. "Leap of Faith," in *Ellery Queen's Mystery Magazine* (November 1998): 24–38.

In some ways this story is the opposite of a locked-room mystery. A stylite (a holy man who lives out his life on the top of a marble column) is murdered while he stands in splendid isolation on top of a smooth-sided, forty-five-cubit-high column, in full view of a large crowd of people. The Empress gives John until nightfall to find the murderer and informs him that if he fails to do so, he will permanently replace the dead stylite at the top of the column. Historical Figure: Empress Theodora.

7. *One for Sorrow.* Scottsdale, AZ: Poisoned Pen Press, 1999, 292 p.

CONSTANTINOPLE, 535. John's investigation into a friend's murder uncovers a struggle between men who are religious, men who are greedy, and men who are both, all attempting to gain possession of a holy relic—in fact, the Holy Grail itself. John is not sure if the Knight whose quest touched off the race for the Grail is a true believer or a con man. By this point, it no longer matters. When something of such value is at stake, many in Constantinople regard blood (at least the blood of others) as a trivial price to pay. Associates: Thomas; Europa; Cornelia; Berta; Ahasuerus.

8. *Two for Joy.* Scottsdale, AZ: Poisoned Pen Press, 2000, 345 p.

CONSTANTINOPLE, NOVEMBER 537. A holy man prophesies that four men will be struck down by God unless Justinian makes him co-ruler of the empire. That night three stylites are burned to death in the middle of a rainstorm. John must solve the murders before he is exiled or killed. Associates: Aurelius; Philo; Lucretia; Balbinus.

9. "The Finger of Aphrodite," in *The Mammoth Book of Roman Whodunnits*, ed. by Mike Ashley. New York: Carroll & Graf Publishers, 2003, p. 473–500.

ROME, 537. John arrives in Rome, carrying Justinian's congratulations to General Belisarius, who has just conquered that city, but while the Goths are laying siege to his forces. There are more dead men in the city than can be counted; but one was an acquaintance of John's, and they were staying at the same inn. John is well on the trail of the murderer before he stops to ask: just who was the intended victim here? Historical Figure: Count Belisarius.

10. *Three for a Letter.* Scottsdale, AZ: Poisoned Pen Press, 2001, 368 p.

CONSTANTINOPLE, 539. Anatolius' Uncle Zeno hosts a spectacular feast for Theodora; the entertainments include a reenactment of the story of Jonah and the whale, for which a fantastical mechanical whale has been constructed. The script calls for Barnabus the dwarf, playing Jonah, to appear in the mouth of a mechanical whale; instead, the mouth opens to reveal the mangled body of one of the royal twins being held hostage. The dwarf has disappeared, and the other twin is in deadly peril. Associates: Gadaric; Sunilda; Zeno; Barnabus; Hero.

11. **"And All That He Calls Family,"** in *The Mammoth Book of More Historical Whodunnits,* ed. by Mike Ashley. New York: Carroll & Graf Publishers, 2001, p. 97–114.

CONSTANTINOPLE, BETWEEN 539 and 542. Damian has died recently, and his household is afraid that his infant son will soon follow him. It's not just that the baby is sickly but that a curse tablet has been found, and a ghost has been seen walking the garden. John must investigate hatreds both new and old in order to lay the curse and the ghost to rest.

12. *Five for Silver.* Scottsdale, AZ: Poisoned Pen Press, 2004, 259 p.

CONSTANTINOPLE, 542. Plague decimates the city, filling Samsun's Hospice with the dying and the streets with the dead. Those not yet stricken find opportunities to help or to profit during the reign of the deadly disease. Hypatia seeks to help, nursing a badly burned youth; Peter seeks vengeance, asking John to help by discovering who murdered Peter's old comrade-in-arms. Associates: Hektor; Thomas; Europa; Cornelia; Lucretia; Balbinus; Ahaseurus; Xanthe; Crinagoras; Scipio; Hypatia; Peter.

ROBB, Candace (M.) (1950–). American.

OWEN ARCHER SERIES

Scene of the Crime: York, England, beginning in 1363.

Detective: Owen Archer was Captain of the bowmen in the service of Henry of Grosmont. When he lost the sight in his left eye, he no longer trusted his ability in the field, so he spoke to the Duke and was given a new position. The Duke had Owen educated so that he could write and read messages, and Owen was assigned to act as a spy. When the Duke died, Owen thought that he would be dismissed from service. Then John

Thoresby, Lord Chancellor of England and Archbishop of York, notified Owen that he was going to honor the old Duke's request to give Owen a new position. He allows Owen a choice: either to serve him or to serve the new Duke, John of Gaunt. Owen chooses Thoresby. In 1364 John of Gaunt realized that the 1361 plague had killed too many of his archers, and so he recalled Owen to service. This infuriated Owen, who had never been in the service of Gaunt. Owen asked Thoresby for his help, and Thoresby saved him. Owen thus regards himself as beholden to Thoresby, and when he is summoned, he feels that he must act on his behalf. Owen marries Lucie Wilton in 1364; they have a daughter, Gwenllian (b. 1366), and son, Hugh (b. 1368).

Known Associates: Lucie Wilton, who is widowed in the first book of the series and who later becomes Owen's wife; Bess Merchet, Lucie's best friend; Tildy, Lucie's serving girl; Lucie's father, Sir Robert D'Arby (through, one way or another, *A Spy for the Redeemer*); Lucie's Aunt Phillippa; Jehannes, Owen's friend, who is also in service to the Archbishop (*The King's Bishop*). Other frequently appearing characters include the Infirmarian, Brother Wulfstan (through *Riddle of St. Leonards*); Archbishop Thoresby's secretary, Brother Michaelo; Magda the Riverwoman (a midwife); Jasper, an orphan, who joins Owen and Lucie's household in 1366. John Thoresby, Archbishop of York from 1352 to 1373, is a prominent character throughout the series.

Premise: A former archer serves as agent to the Lord Chancellor of England, simultaneously solving crimes in fourteenth-century England.

Comment: At the beginning of the series Owen tries to believe that he will be content as an assistant to an apothecary, but he loves challenges and would feel confined if he knew that he had to live out the rest of his life in one place. His friends try to help him, encouraging their lord to offer him work as a soldier; but, much as Owen misses that life, without the use of both of his eyes he does not trust his own skills. The place of a spy suits him admirably, no matter how much he resents being summarily summoned and sent forth to do the Archbishop's bidding. In his work he often solves puzzles (which include murders) and engages in both clandestine and open activities. He has acted as messenger, spy, and bodyguard as well as detective; but his skills in detection are necessary to each of his adventures. This is one of the few series covering medieval life that thoroughly incorporate the importance of the Guilds. Their influence not only is economic but extends to every aspect of society. They are shown in these books to have had power in law; for instance, Lucie's guild demands that she not change her name when she remarries. The guilds are shown to provide a safety net for their members, the merchant guilds caring for their own sick and elderly. Guilds even color the thinking of their members: Owen is dismayed at the standards for loyalty that seem to be the norms for wool merchants.

Literary Crimes & Chimes: The author's notes at the back of each book offer some of the historical facts that underlie the narratives. These books are rich in period detail and full of colorful, engaging characters. The unusual setting and premise make for a compelling series of historical mystery novels.

THE CASES

1. *The Apothecary Rose: A Medieval Mystery.* New York: St. Martin's Press, 1993, 256 p.
   YORK, ENGLAND, 1363. Brother Wulfstan, worried about the illness of a nameless pilgrim, asks Nicholas Wilton, the Master Apothecary, for a remedy. This is given to the pilgrim, but he dies anyway. When the same medicine is given to a man in less dire straits, he also dies, and suspicions are raised. Owen Archer is asked to investigate. Associate: Nicholas Wilton.

2. *The Lady Chapel: An Owen Archer Mystery.* New York: St. Martin's Press, 1994, 287 p.
   YORK, LONDON, AND WINDSOR, ENGLAND, 1365. A merchant is killed within the shadow of York Minster, an orphaned boy being the only witness. The boy disappears, and the severed hand of the murdered man is found on the floor of a room at the inn. The most recent occupant of that room had donated a goodly sum to the Lady Chapel, and Owen is furious when Thoresby sends the spy to gently question him, while ignoring the danger to the boy. Historical Figures: British King Edward III; Alice Perrers; Thoresby.

3. *The Nun's Tale: An Owen Archer Mystery.* London: Heinemann, 1995, 354 p.
   YORK, ENGLAND, 1366. A year earlier a young nun had died of fever; the fear of contagion caused her body to be buried in haste. Now she has returned, seemingly risen from the grave, but some around her are meeting their own untimely deaths. Owen is sent to investigate. Associate: Lief; Gaspare. Historical Figures: Geoffrey Chaucer; John of Gaunt.

4. *The King's Bishop: An Owen Archer Mystery.* London: Heinemann, 1996, 350 p.
   YORK, ENGLAND, 1367. When a man who seemed to be paying court to Ned Townley's betrothed is found dead, Ned falls under suspicion. Some believe that his jealousy drove the victim to drink, precipitating an accident, while others simply think that Ned committed murder. Owen must pierce through the mystery to save his friend. Associate: Ned Town-

ley. Historical Figures: Alice Perrers; Queen Phillippa; Sir William of Wyndesore.

5. *The Riddle of St. Leonard's: An Owen Archer Mystery.* London: Heinemann, 1997, 303 p.

YORK, ENGLAND, 1369. A child dies on a Sunday's eve; then by the next Sunday, five of the city's inhabitants were also dead, the contagion having taken hold. A different kind of plague seems to have struck St. Leonard's. Two corrodians have perished in three weeks. (Corrodians are people who deed some of their property to a religious house in return for housing and medical care in their declining years.) The Master of St. Leonard's hospital asks the Archbishop for assistance, and Owen is sent to investigate. Associate: Alisoun Ffulford. Historical Figure: Thoresby.

6. *A Gift of Sanctuary: An Owen Archer Mystery.* London: Heinemann, 1998, 303 p.

WALES, 1370. The war with France is not going well, and news has come to John of Gaunt that the French have found a Welsh mercenary willing to help raise Wales against its English lords. Owen is sent to Wales to determine where the people's allegiances lie. When he finds his contact murdered, he knows that his mission is even more dangerous than he thought. Associate: Sir Robert D'Arby. Historical Figures: Geoffrey Chaucer; Owen Lawgoch; Dafydd ap Gwilym.

7. *A Spy for the Redeemer: An Owen Archer Mystery.* London: Heinemann, 1999, 318 p.

WALES AND YORK, ENGLAND, 1370. The Archdeacon of St. David's demands that Owen identify the murderer of a stonemason before Owen returns to his home in England. In England rumors start that Owen has forsaken his family to remain in his native Wales. Lucie, trying to take care of the responsibilities she once shared with Owen in England, hires several assistants, one of whom fatally betrays her. Historical Figure: Owain Lawgoch.

8. *The Cross-Legged Knight.* London: Heinemann, 2002, 327 p.

YORK, ENGLAND, 1371. Bishop Wykeham is almost killed by a falling tile. Is this an accident or an attempted murder? Since Owen was supposed to be protecting the man at the time, he has an interest in resolving the matter but finds it difficult to bring the attacker Wykeham to justice. Owen must set a trap to ensure that the killer, no matter if he be Knight, Bishop, or King, will be caught. Associate: Alisoun Ffulford.

MARGARET KERR SERIES

Scene of the Crime: Perth and Edinburgh, Scotland, beginning in 1297.

Detective: Dame Margaret Kerr is not yet twenty years of age when the series begins. She has red-gold hair, hazel eyes, and freckles that make her look even younger. She's strong-willed, good-hearted, sharp-witted, and too stubborn for her own good. She's been married two years to a merchant who spends most of the time away from home. She's disappointed that he pledged fealty to the murdering English King Edward (Edward Long-shanks); she favors John Balliol as King of Scotland. When husband Roger goes missing, she asks for help; when it becomes clear that any such help has failed to appear, she ventures forth herself.

Known Associates: Margaret's brother, Father Andrew, is a monk at Holyrood (near Edinburgh). Margaret left her younger brother, seventeen-year-old Fergus, in Perth to see to the business and take care of the house; she does not have the funds to hire someone with more experience. Margaret's father is Malcolm; her mother, Christiana, is either a visionary or mad. Margaret's maid (and friend) is Celia.

Premise: A woman seeks her husband and solves crimes in thirteenth-century Scotland.

Comment: Scotland is at war, Edinburgh being occupied by the English. Soldiers patrol the streets. The country is unsafe for everyone, but most of all for travelers. Margaret's husband, Roger, had no choice but to venture forth, since he's a merchant. He disappeared in November 1296, and his cousin, Jack Sinclair, went to Edinburgh to find him. Jack has returned in a shroud, stabbed to death. Margaret resolves to go to Edinburgh herself to search for her husband. Everyone counsels her to go north, as far from the English soldiers as she can. It's good advice, but Margaret is too stubborn to take it. This is a time and place of such tribulation that divided loyalties within a family are not surprising. The heroine is appealing, the dialogue interesting, and the period details make the setting vivid.

Literary Crimes & Chimes: This series has a heroine with her own opinions and decided loyalties, scoundrels, war, and mystery. The author uses enough Scotch words to spice the narrative without making it unreadable and provides a handy glossary in each book. Each of the books end with a Historical Note, giving some of the background to the period in which the volumes are set. Good entertaining reading.

THE CASES

1. *A Trust Betrayed: First Chapter of Margaret Kerr of Perth.* London: Heinemann, 2000, 240 p.
   SCOTLAND, SPRING 1297. Margaret's husband has been missing since last November; his cousin Jack, sent to Edinburgh to find him, is found murdered. Margaret then makes the journey to Edinburgh herself. There she

discovers more about Jack's death and about Roger's life and must decide upon her own course of action. Associates: James Comyn; Jack; Roger. Historical Figures: Robert Bruce, Earl of Carrick; Adam, Abbot of Holyrood.

2. *The Fire in the Flint.* London: Heinemann, 2003, 315 p.

EDINBURGH AND ENGLAND, SUMMER 1297. A raid and murder on the Kerr property brings Margaret and her Uncle Murdoch to the malefic attention of the English. The sudden reappearance of Roger gives Margaret the chance to escape from Edinburgh. Together they make for Perth, but soon she begins to suspect that Roger's newfound enthusiasm for their marriage is nothing more than a foil for a mission for Robert the Bruce. Margaret is troubled and confused, and then her father returns from Bruges, bringing more trouble and discord in his wake. What was it the raiders sought from Margaret's property? And what of her mother, Christiana's visions, which all sides are keen to interpret? Can Margaret trust either her husband or her father? Associates: Roger; Murdoch; Christiana; Malcolm. Historical Figure: Robert the Bruce.

ROBERTS, David. British.

LORD EDWARD CORINTH AND VERITY BROWNE SERIES

Scene of the Crime: England, Spain and the *Queen Mary*, beginning in 1935, with flashbacks to 1917.

Detective(s): Lord Edward Corinth, younger brother of the Duke of Mersham. Born at the turn of the century, six feet tall, good-looking, with a title, £12,000 a year, and no responsibilities. Verity Browne, card-carrying member of the Communist Party, reporter for the *Daily Worker* (the official organ of the Communist Party), and, by the end of the first book, also a correspondent for Lord Weaver's *New Gazette*. She stands five-foot-three (five-foot-four when angry), and is an idealistic twenty-five-year-old in 1936.

Known Associates: Gerald, Duke of Mersham, Edward's older brother; Connie, Gerald's wife; Frank, Connie and Gerald's son, Edward's nephew; Fenton, Edward's manservant; David Griffiths-Jones, Verity's commander in the Communist Party; Joe, Lord Weaver, owner of the newspaper the *New Gazette*; Chief Inspector Pride of Scotland Yard, always eager to spot the easy answer; Major Stille, an agent of Hitler's, a charming and ruthless man; Adrian and Charlotte Hassel, friends of Verity's; Major Ferguson, a policeman for the Special Branch; Lord Benyon, a well-known economist, and Inna Benyon, his wife.

Premise: A British lord and a young female reporter who is a member of the Communist Party form an uneasy alliance and work together to solve crimes.

Comment: The passions (communist and nationalist) that preceded the Second World War are at the forefront of this series. The admiration that many in the British aristocracy had for the Nazis will surprise some readers. The wounds from World War I are still healing, and it seems as if most of the world is willing to turn a blind eye to Germany's aggression. England is slow to respond to the threat and America is determined to never again involve herself in European wars. This series cover the years that the Communists and others fought *Gereralisimo* Francisco Franco in Spain. Even though there is evidence that Germany is involved in the war, supporting Franco, most people prefer to believe that Spain's war is an internal conflict, and thus avoid any moral imperative to become involved. Both Verity and Edward value truth and both acknowledge that Germany is using Spain to hone its battle strategies. They agree that England is in peril. However, they have very different responses. Verity goes to Spain to try to gain enough information for her news stories to rouse the world to defeat Franco. Edward believes that defeating Franco would simply clear the way for the Communists, and he believes that they would install a totalitarian regime that would be different, but no less oppressive, than rule under the Fascists.

Literary Crimes & Chimes: The puzzles in these mysteries are good, but sometimes the detection seems haphazard. The preferred method of getting enough evidence to convict seems to be to catch murderers in the act, in one case long after the identity of the most-likely villain has been uncovered. The social history of pre-World War II England is shown well. Roberts brings to life the mounting societal tension along both class lines and political beliefs, the mounting political tension as England's leaders try to believe that Germany will never attack the British Isles, and the idealism, even fanaticism, of those who journey to Spain to fight Franco.

THE CASES

1. *Sweet Poison.* New York: Carroll & Graf, 2001, 277 p.

ENGLAND, 1935. Edward's brother Gerald (the Duke of Mersham) is desperately trying to stave off the next war by bringing the parties together over a dining table and trying to help them reach a common understanding. His "peace dinner" goes horribly wrong when one of his guests dies, by poison. Verity, at the table under false pretences, has a wonderful scoop for the *Daily Worker*; Edward determines to find out the truth about the death. Associates: Gerald, Duke of Mersham; Connie; David Griffiths-Jones;

Joe, Lord Weaver; Blanche, Lady Weaver; Hermione Weaver; Peter Larmore; Baron Von Friedberg; Amy Pageant; Chief Inspector Pride; Major Stille; Max, Verity's dog; Cecil Haycraft, Bishop of Worthing; Adrian Hassel; Reverend Tommie Fox; General Craig; Colonel Philips; Captain Gordon; Charlie Lomax.

2. *Bones of the Buried.* New York: Carroll & Graf, 2001, 342 p.

ENGLAND AND SPAIN, 1936 (prologue is at Eton in 1917). Edward is asked to travel to Spain to help clear a man he loathes of murder charges; he does so by finding evidence that the "victim" is still alive, or rather, was alive until the day Edward located him. An emergency at home calls him back to England where he becomes embroiled in another murder investigation; gradually realizing that it is not an isolated crime, but that he is on the trail of a man who has murdered before and will murder again, unless Edward finds him quickly. Associates: Gerald, Duke of Mersham; Connie; Frank; David Griffiths-Jones; Joe, Lord Weaver; Amy Pageant; Chief Inspector Pride; Stephen Thayer; Charles Thayer; Harry Bragg; Ben Belasco.

3. *The Hollow Crown.* New York: Carroll & Graf, 2002, 309 p.

ENGLAND, 1936. Letters stolen from the jewel case of Mrs. Wallis Simpson could, if published, seriously embarrass King Edward VIII. Molly Harkness, a woman Edward met and, in a way, rescued in Africa, is attempting to blackmail Mrs. Simpson into returning to America. Edward is asked to convince Molly to return the letters. Edward only has a chance to talk to her briefly before she is murdered and the letters stolen. Everyone except Edward seems more concerned with finding the letters than with bringing Molly's murderer to justice. Associates: Joe, Lord Weaver; Blanche, Lady Weaver; Chief Inspector Pride; Major Stille; Leo Scannon, Catherine "Dannie" Danhorn; Adrian Hassel; Charlotte Hassel; Sir Richard Carstairs; Sir Geoffrey Hepple-Keen; Lady Hepple-Keen; Larry Harbin; Ruth Conway; Lord Benyon; Inna Benyon; Major Ferguson. Historical Figure: Mrs. Wallis Simpson.

4. *Dangerous Sea.* New York: Carroll & Graf, 2003, 248 p.

VOYAGE ON THE *QUEEN MARY*, 1937. An attempt on Lord Benyon's life makes it clear that there are people who would go to any lengths to keep him from a clandestine meeting in which he will ask President Franklin D. Roosevelt to aid England. Lord Edward is asked to help guard Lord Benyon on a dangerous voyage. By chance Verity is crossing on the same ship; going to meet with labor leaders in the United States. They are faced with a baffling series of crimes, from murder to attempted murder, while being distracted by the complexities of more than one shipboard romance. Associates: Lord Benyon; Frank; Marcus Fern; Tom Barrett; Henry Fawcett; Sam Forrest; Warren Fairley; Jane Barclay; Senator George Earl Day; Bernard Hunt; Mrs. Roosevelt, a distant cousin of the U.S. President; Perry Roosevelt, her son; Philly Roosevelt, her daughter; Professor Dolmen; Major Cranton; Captain Peel.

5. *The More Deceived*. London: Constable and Robinson, 2004, 246 p.

ENGLAND, BILBAO, AND GUERNICA, 1937. This is a story of facing reality and altering course. Leaders in England are not ready to do that, they are hoping to avoid a confrontation with Germany, and are taking too long to ready for a possible war. The Foreign Office is furious that a rabble-rouser named Winston Churchill is incorporating state secrets into his speeches as he tries to rouse England's populace. Edward is asked to find out who is passing Churchill sensitive information; he takes on the job, but quickly comes to the conclusion that Churchill is right. Edward alters course and focuses his investigation on the disappearance of one worker from the Foreign Office's Industrial Intelligence unit. Midway through his investigation he is overcome by the conviction that Verity is in terrible danger. He races to Spain and accompanies her to Guernica, where they witness a new kind of fighting, something called a *blitzkrieg*. The unarmed village is first bombed, and then aircraft guns are used to massacre the fleeing civilians. Verity is wounded, but not killed. Edward takes her back to England, and during her convalescence she helps him solve a case of murder and treason. By the end of the book Verity has realized that she was intentionally sent to Guernica to be killed because her superiors in the Communist Party did not like her investigation of Communist Party actions. Associates: Fred Cavens; Sir Robert Vansittart; Chief Inspector Pride; André "Bandi" Kavan; Gerda Meyer; Guy Baron; David Griffiths-Jones; Adrian Hassel; Charlotte Hassel; Reverend Tommie Fox; Marcus Fern; Bernard Hunt; Charlie Westmacott; Matilda Westmacott; Alice Westmacott; Georgina Hay; Desmond Lyall; James Lyall; Mildred Hawkins; Jane Williams; Harry Younger; Angus McCloud; Sir Vida Chandra; Jack "Spotty" Spot. Historical Figure: Winston Churchill.

ROBERTS, John Maddox (1947–). American.

SPQR (OR DECIUS CAECILIUS METELLUS) SERIES

Scene of the Crime: Late Roman Republic, beginning in 70 BC and continuing to about 27 BC.

Detective: Decius Caecilius Metellus the Younger, born circa 100 BC, a rising politician from a prominent Roman family.

Known Associates: Rome is full of Caecilii Metelli; they make up a large enough voting block so that one of their own can ususally get voted into office. Decius' father, Decius Caecilius Metellus the Elder (also known as old Cut-Nose), wants his son to succeed and suspects that Decius' inquisitiveness is going to ruin his political prospects. In most books in the series Decius the Elder appears to work toward his son's advancement, often by offering him extensive criticism. In *The Sacrilege* Decius' Uncle Lucius gives Decius a slave named Hermes, who is Decius' companion through the rest of the series. Asklepiodes, a Greek physician with a knowledge of wounds, helps Decius in most of the investigations.

Premise: A Roman official solves crimes in late Republican Rome.

Comment: Metellus relates the stories of his youthful investigations in ancient Rome from the perspective of his old age, circa 27 BC. By his own admission, he had during his earlier years a "propensity for snooping into things others would prefer to remain hidden." In the intrigue-ridden Roman Republic, this is both a useful and occasionally dangerous trait. His investigations tend to derive from the intrigues surrounding the statesmen and chief political figures of the day, some of them well-known historical names. He generally succeeds in bringing the murderers to justice, but the men who actually plot the crimes behind the scenes are often left untouched. By the end of each novel, Metellus relates who committed the infractions, how they occurred, and why the crimes were committed. However, the detective is often left without the necessary evidence or political clout to convict the real criminals, the creatures manipulating events at the very heart of the dying republican government. The device of having an old man relate his memoirs allows the author to place the events into a broader context. Roberts limits the "had I but known" moments to a few striking instances; however, this kind of narration sometimes creates problems of its own, particularly in the first novel in the series. For example, at one point of supposedly high suspense, Metellus breaks his narration to offer a detailed discourse on the three types of streets common to Rome. One can imagine the detective teetering almost on the edge of senility while expounding on his treatise, but the effect breaks down the action and tension of the scene, interrupting the flow of the story. The author usually avoids this mistake in the sequels. Indeed, one can see a great improvement in the writing and plotting as the series advances.

Literary Crimes & Chimes: The narratives are sometimes interrupted by the insertion of historical facts (more of a problem in the initial novel than in the rest). In some volumes the actual "mystery" seems slight and the perpetrator easy to guess, particularly if one knows anything about the history of the period. On the other hand, Roberts demonstrates an excellent adherence to known history, providing a thoughtful interpretation of the characters and their motivations. The narrator's attitudes and fears seem appropriate for someone of that time and place. Each volume includes a useful map and a short glossary of Latin terms.

THE CASES

1. *SPQR*. New York: Avon, 1990, 229 p. As: ***SPQR I: The King's Gambit***. New York: Thomas Dunne Books, St. Martin's Minotaur, 2001, 274 p.

ROME, 70 BC. When Commissioner Metellus is told that documents relating to the investigation of the activities of a foreign importer have been sealed by the Senate and placed for safekeeping in the Temple of Vesta, he realizes that the murder that he has been asked to investigate is potentially dangerous—both to his political career and to his health! One crime leads to another: first a gladiator is killed, then the importer, then a wealthy freedman. Finally, Metellus uncovers a conspiracy against General Lucius Lucinius Lucullus, after being seduced, drugged, murderously attacked, and arrested. His reward for revealing the truth is a Triumph, of sorts. Associate: Asklepiodes. Historical Figures: Titus Annius Milo; Pompey; Crassus; Clodius; Clodia; Cicero; Julius Caesar.

2. ***SPQR II: The Catiline Conspiracy***. New York: Avon, 1991, 216 p.

ROME, 63–62 BC. Metellus, now promoted to Quaestor of the Treasury, is struck by a number of unusual conversations he overhears at the parties he's forced to attend and also notices a number of rather odd political alliances forming. When he discovers a cache of arms within the city walls, he realizes that a revolution may be in the works and that the only way to determine the truth is to join the conspiracy himself! Associate: Asklepiodes. Historical Figures: Catalina; Cicero; Clodius; Clodia; Crassus.

3. ***SPQR III: The Sacrilege***. New York: Avon, 1992, 216 p.

ROME, 62 BC. Metellus is appointed to the Senate and given a new slave, Hermes. He attends a party where the gatekeeper and host are murdered, and an attempt is made upon his own life. Then Clodius is caught in female garb attending the *Bona Dea* ceremony, which by law can be celebrated only by women, an event that causes both public outrage and hilarity. Metellus is the only person to suspect a sinister reason for Clodius' presence at the *fête*. Soon he knows exactly who was in the house of the Pontifex Maximus during the ceremony and why it was worth murder to keep their presence a secret. Associates: Asklepiodes; Julia Minor; Ambassador Lisas. Historical Figures: Caius Julius Caesar; Clodia, Appius Claudius Nero; Quintus Lutatius Catulus; Capito; Catullus; Metellus Celer, Lucius Licinius Lucullus; Cato; Titus Annius Milo; Fausta; Cicero; Crassus; Fulvia, betrothed to Clodius; Pompey.

4. *SPQR IV: The Temple of the Muses.* New York: Avon, 1992, 215 p.

ALEXANDRIA, EGYPT, 60 BC. Senator Metellus joins a diplomatic mission to the Kingdom of Egypt. He suspects that a philosopher is being less than truthful in response to idle questions about the man's work. Before he has a chance to investigate further, however, the pedant is murdered. Metellus contrives to have King Ptolemy XII name him as investigator and in the course of his probing uncovers an Alexandrian plot to throw off the protectorship of Rome. Associates: Rufus; Julia Minor; Asklepiodes. Historical Figures: Fausta; Berenice; Cleopatra; Egyptian King Ptolemy XII.

5. "**The Statuette of Rhodes,**" in *Classical Whodunnits: Murder and Mystery from Ancient Greece and Rome,* ed. by Mike Ashley. London: Robinson Publishing, 1996; New York: Carroll & Graf, 1997, p.96–112.

ISLAND OF RHODES, 60 BC. Senator Metellus enlivens his exile on the island of Rhodes with a little sightseeing. While roaming about the ruins of the great Colossus, he witnesses the discovery of the remains of Telemachus, high priest of Helios (the sun god). His investigation of the murder weapon uncovers a Roman general's plot to control the island, as well as the identity of the killer.

6. *SPQR V: Saturnalia.* New York: Thomas Dunne Books, St. Martin's Minotaur, October 1999, 275 p.

ROME, 59 BC. Senator Metellus returns to Rome in response to his father's urgent summons: their relative, Quintus Caecilius, has been foully murdered, the chief suspect being the victim's wife, the notorious Clodia. The investigation encompasses the Saturnalia festival, during which the masters serve their slaves. Clodius requests that Metellus find the killer to clear Clodia of suspicion. A major subplot here is the practice of the "old religion" of Roman witchcraft. Associates: Asklepiodes; Julia Minor; Ambassador Lisas. Historical Figures: Clodia; Clodius; Caesar; Marcus Antonius; Crassus; Vatinius; Fulvia; Fausta; Titus Annius Milo; Cicero; Creticus; Scipio.

7. *SPQR VI: Nobody Loves a Centurion.* New York: Thomas Dunne Books, St. Martin's Minotaur, 2001, 276 p.

GAUL, 57 BC. With Clodius now serving Rome as Tribune, Senator Metellus escapes the city to the comparative safety of the Gallic Wars, serving under General Julius Caesar. Metellus displays his customary respect for authority by interfering with the discipline prescribed by the First Spear of the Tenth, Titus Vinus. When the despicable Vinus is abruptly killed, the Senator must undertake an investigation in order to clear his own men of the charge of murder. Associates: Gnaeus Quintilius Carbo; Lucius Burrus. Historical Figure: Caesar.

8. *SPQR VII: The Tribune's Curse.* New York: Thomas Dunne Books, St. Martin's Minotaur, 2003, 248 p.

ROME, 55 BC. Crassus, anxious to prove himself militarily, manages to maneuver the Senate into giving him a command. There is no legal way now to prevent him from becoming a general; Tribune Caius Ateius Capito, finding that the law can't stop Crassus from assuming his military post, invokes the gods, uttering a terrible curse that includes the secret name of Rome. Rome's Virgo Maxima and the Senate work to avert the curse and charge Decius with finding the villain who had helped Ateius with his sorcery. Associates: Julia Minor; Ambassador Lisas; Asklepiodes. Historical Figures: Crassus; Titus Annius Milo; Fausta; Clodius; Cato; Pompey.

9. *SPQR VIII: The River God's Vengeance.* New York: Thomas Dunne Books, St. Martin's Minotaur, 2004, 290 p.

ROME, 53 BC. When a five-story insula collapses, killing most of its tenants, Aedile Decius Caecilius Metellus the Younger is struck by the fact that the building was new, not old enough to have succumbed to decay and termites. Decius plunges into an investigation of the corrupt building trade and realizes the power of those involved only when his evidence disappears and his witnesses begin dying. Associates: Asklepiodes; Julia Minor. Historical Figures: Marcus Antonius; Titus Annius Milo; Cato.

10. "Mightier Than the Sword," in *The Mammoth Book of Historical Whodunnits*, ed. by Mike Ashley. London: Robinson Publishing; New York: Carroll & Graf, 1993, p. 28–43.

ROME, 53 BC. Plebian Aedile Metellus stumbles across a body while conducting routine building inspections. His investigation leads him to uncover one of the crimes considered most heinous by the Roman people.

11. "The Etruscan House," in *Crime through Time II*, ed. by Miriam Grace Monfredo and Sharan Newman. New York: Berkley Prime Crime, 1998, p. 20–45.

ROME, 52 BC. His aedileship completed, the middle-aged Senator Metellus investigates the death of a fellow senator in Rome amid a series of political controversies.

12. "The King of Sacrifices," in *The Mammoth Book of Historical Detectives*, ed. by Mike Ashley. London: Robinson Publishing, 1993; New York: Carroll & Graf, 1995, p. 52–69.

ROME, CIRCA 27 BC. At age seventy-three, Senator Metellus is asked to investigate the body of a murdered man who had recently been chosen to be elevated to patrician status, with the First Citizen's daughter being directly implicated.

ROBINSON, Lynda S(uzanne) (1951–). American.

LORD MEREN SERIES

Scene of the Crime: Ancient Egypt, beginning circa 1350 BC.

Detective: Lord Meren, Chief Investigator for Pharaoh Tutankhamun and heir to one of the oldest noble families in Egypt, is considered the eyes and ears of a living god. Years before, Pharaoh Akhenaten had demanded that the worship of the old gods end; Meren's father had refused and was then executed for his beliefs. At the age of eighteen Meren was marked for death. Vizier Ay convinced the Pharaoh to give Meren a chance to serve Aten as his god, in the person of Akhenaten. Meren complied to save himself and learned to conceal his thoughts and feelings and eventually his suspicions about Akhenaten's death. He became a survivor at court.

Known Associates: Meren's associates are the highest-ranking people of Egypt. The man who saved his life is Vizier Ay (later Pharaoh). Horemheb, who has been a friend of Meren since they were in training to be warriors, is General of the King's army. Maya, head of the treasury, is a man whose chief ambition is efficiency rather than advancement. Meren's family includes his adopted son, Kysen, and Kysen's son, Remi. He is joined by his unmarried daughters, Bener and Isis, beginning with *Murder at the Feast of Rejoicing*. In *Drinker of Blood* Isis goes to live with her married older sister, Tefnut.

Premise: An investigator for the Pharaoh solves crimes in Ancient Egypt.

Comment: King Tutankhamun's father, Akhenaten, had upset the existing social order when he denounced the old gods and demanded that his subjects worship the one true god, Aten. Then Akhenaten died under suspicious circumstances. Tutankhamun, aged fourteen at the beginning the series, was Akhenaten's second successor as Pharaoh. His position is precarious. Many of his nobles and priests hated his father and would be happy to see Tutankhamun interred in his tomb. Armies from neighboring countries have begun to harry Egypt, believing that the king is young and weak. Meren knows that his duty is to protect Tutankhamun; he not only follows orders but also tries to mentor the boy-king.

Literary Crimes & Chimes: This series demonstrates the intrigue and politics of court life at a time when Egypt's kingdom and throne were particularly vulnerable. At the beginning of *Drinker of Blood* the author includes a historical note, explaining the deficiencies of the historical records from that time and setting forth the bare facts of the accounts that she used as a basis for these books. Robinson creates interesting characters interacting through believable relationships. Individual fears and hopes, petty insecurities and great loves, are all shown to great effect, making the people we encounter seem quite real. The author frequently employs changes in points of view to show the ways in which the victims and criminals are thinking. We also catch personal glimpses of Meren's and Kysen's lives.

THE CASES

1. **"Death of a Place-Seeker,"** in *Crime through Time*, ed. by Miriam Grace Monfredo and Sharan Newman. New York: Berkley Prime Crime, p. 1–24.

EGYPT, YEAR FOUR OF TUTANKHAMUN'S REIGN (1330 BC). When the greedy Lord Userhet is found dead, his stepson, Surero, a "child of the nursery" (someone who has been the Pharaoh's friend since birth), is the most likely suspect. Meren finds it unlikely that Surero is the killer. The young man is intelligent enough to have arranged a more plausible accident. Associate: Surero. Historical Figure: Egyptian Pharaoh Tutankhamun.

2. *Murder in the Place of Anubis.* New York: Walker & Co., 1994, 190 p.

EGYPT, YEAR FIVE OF TUTANKHAMUN'S REIGN (1329 BC). The repellent scribe, Hormin, is found murdered, stabbed in the neck with an embalming knife. His body has desecrated the sacred place of embalming. Since insurrection is a greater threat to the throne than another murder, this crime must be solved quickly, before the priests can use it as leverage against the boy-king Tutankhamun. Associates: Ahmose; Pawero; Ankhesenamun; Parenfer, High Priest of Amun. Historical Figure: Egyptian Pharaoh Tutankhamun.

3. *Murder at the God's Gate: A Lord Meren Mystery.* New York: Walker & Co., 1995, 236 p.

EGYPT, YEAR FIVE OF TUTANKHAMUN'S REIGN (1329 BC). It's bad enough that a priest has fallen to his death, but it's even worse when he has toppled from the top of a King's statue. Worst of all, he's not even a simple priest, but one of Meren's aide's informers. What was the man doing climbing monuments? How can Meren keep those who support a Hittite invasion from using this death to their own benefit? Associates: Prince Tanefer; Ebana; Parenefer.

4. *Murder at the Feast of Rejoicing: A Lord Meren Mystery.* New York: Walker & Co., 1996, 229 p.

EGYPT, YEAR FIVE OF TUTANKHAMUN'S REIGN (1329 BC). Lord Meren, on a secret mission, returns home with the excuse that he wishes to be with his family. His sister plans a surprise party for his homecoming, with a great feast of rejoicing. She invites all of his relatives, including a few people that he had hoped never to see again. Then the Pharaoh sends word that he is joining them, and Meren knows that his danger is escalating. Associates: Sennefer; Ra. Historical Figure: Egyptian Pharaoh Tutankhamun.

5. *Eater of Souls: A Lord Meren Mystery.* New York: Walker & Co., 1997, 229 p.

EGYPT, YEAR FIVE OF TUTANKHAMUN'S REIGN (1329 BC). Meren had discovered that the Pharaoh's sister-in-law, the great and beautiful Nefertiti, widow of the late Pharaoh Akhenaten, did not die of the plague, as was popularly supposed, but was poisoned. He suspects that the person who ordered the murder still lives and would just as easily kill the young Pharaoh Tutankhamun. Meren's investigations are complicated when a serial killer, the Eater of Souls, begins stalking the city. The mystery in this novel is continued in *Drinker of Blood.* Associate: Prince Djoser. Historical Figures: Egyptian Pharaoh Tutankhamun; Queen Nefertiti.

6. *Drinker of Blood.* New York: Mysterious Press, 1998, 290 p.

EGYPT, YEAR FIVE OF TUTANKHAMUN'S REIGN (1329 BC). The narrative moves back and forth in time, from the reign of Amenhotep to that of Tutankhamun. During the joint reign of Amenhotep and his son, Akhenaten, Nefertiti is first struck down with a suspicious illness and then dies after Akhenaten succeeds to the throne. Under the reign of Tutankhamun, Meren secretly continues his investigation into her death. Her murderer guesses his aim, and the counterattacks begin. Associates: Prince Djoser; Irzanen; Tefnut; Ebana. Historical Figures: Egyptian Pharaoh Tutankhamun; Nefertiti; Akhenaten; Amenhotep.

7. "Disease-Demon," in *Chronicles of Crime: The Second Ellis Peters Memorial Anthology of Historical Crime,* ed. by Maxim Jakubowski. London: Headline Press, 1999, p. 305–326.

EGYPT, YEAR FIVE OF TUTANKHAMUN'S REIGN (1329 BC). A physician finds the death of one of his clients suspicious and asks Lord Meren to investigate. The man's heirs are less sure, however, that an investigation will be profitable. Associates: Sa; Roan; Pentu.

8. *Slayer of Gods.* New York: Mysterious Press, 2001, 244 p.

EGYPT, YEAR FIVE OF TUTANKHAMUN'S REIGN (1329 BC). The knowledge that Nefertiti was murdered has opened up old wounds at court. The Pharaoh knows that he will have no peace until her murderer is discovered, and he gives Meren the charge. As Meren gets closer to the truth, the murderer grows more bold. Associates: Anath; Irzanen. Historical Figures: Egyptian Pharaoh Tutankhamun; Nefertiti.

9. "Heretic's Dagger," in *The Mammoth Book of Egyptian Whodunnits*, ed. by Mike Ashley. New York: Carroll & Graf Publishers, 2002, p. 199–227. EGYPT, YEAR FIVE OF TUTANKHAMUN'S REIGN (1329 BC). The corpse of a peasant is found during a military training exercise. The Pharaoh insists on leading the hunt to find the killer and finds a murder weapon engraved as if it belonged to his dead brother and father, Akhenaten. Associate: Sa. Historical Figure: Egyptian Pharaoh Tutankhamun.

ROOSEVELT, Elliott (1910–1990). American.

ELEANOR ROOSEVELT MYSTERIES

Scene of the Crime: Washington, DC, beginning in 1933.

Detective: Eleanor Roosevelt, wife of the President of the United States, affectionately called "Babs" by him.

Known Associates: Franklin Delano Roosevelt, President of the United States; Inspector Sir Alan Burton of Scotland Yard (*The White House Pantry Murder, Murder at the Palace*); Washington, DC police lieutenant Edward "Ed" Kennelly; Secret Service agent Stanislaw "Stan" Szczygiel; Gerald "Jerry" Baines, Head of the White House Secret Service Detail; Lawrence Pickering, a legal investigator (*The Hyde Park Murder, Murder at Midnight*).

Premise: Following the events recorded in the "Blackjack" Endicott series (see next series under Elliot Roosevelt), Eleanor Roosevelt, the President's wife, is called upon to solve various crimes and misdemeanors in order to keep scandal and controversy out of the public eye, thereby protecting both her husband and his presidency and, at the same time, aiding various of her less powerful friends and acquaintances who have come under suspicion. From time to time she enlists the assistance of her husband and his influential cronies and colleagues to point her in the right direction. She is not above using her position and celebrity to pave the way for her investigations.

Comment: Elliott Roosevelt, youngest son of President Franklin Delano Roosevelt and his wife, Eleanor Roosevelt, was a prolific writer and gentleman rancher. He made excellent use of his behind-the-scenes knowledge of the people, places, and events prominent in the headlines during the years of his father's tenure in the White House, from 1932 to 1945. At the time of Elliott Roosevelt's death in 1990, a stash of completed and partially completed manuscripts was supposedly discovered, enabling his publishers to continue the series posthumously. One does wonder, however, how often certain unnamed collaborators may have lent a hand in completing these books, even before Roosevelt's demise—outside of the final book in the sequence, which is clearly credited to William Harrington for the benefit of "the Elliott Roosevelt estate." Yet the books sold well enough to generate twenty volumes plus two prequels, making it one of the longest sequences of historical mysteries yet published. They are not, however, anywhere near the best.

Literary Crimes & Chimes: Roosevelt's literary agility is limited. He often repeats descriptive adjectives or their variants in the same paragraph and has a tedious tendency to describe the clothing and accessories worn by his characters *ad nauseam*, as if to convince his audience that, yes, he actually was there and, yes, saw (and, more importantly, registered) every slight detail and nuance of the varied and stylish wardrobes of his beautiful people. If the reader can get beyond some of the silliness and buy into the premise that Eleanor Roosevelt was not only a magnificent First Lady but also an astute detective who stumbled time and again, Jessica Fletcher-like, into murder and mayhem in and around the White House, the series can be an enjoyable romp (*Murder at Hobcaw Barony* contains quite delicious send-ups of Bogart, Crawford, and Tallulah Bankhead, for example, the latter of whom comes across as completely insane). As is the case with many of these historically based series, however, the writer's necessity to skew the known facts in order to shoehorn in the necessary suspense elements can result in some inevitably risible *dénouements*. Roosevelt's regretable tendency to rely heavily on known events and celebrated figures to flesh out his plots and make the action seem more plausible than it is succeeds only sometimes—and sometimes it just doesn't. This is the case in *Murder in the Château*, which employs a patently absurd premise, that FDR actually sent his wife into war-torn Europe in the midst of World War II to conduct secret negotiations on his (and the United States) behalf with known Nazis! While it must be assumed that the younger Mr. Roosevelt knew the truth of much of which he speaks, we must also be aware that many of these fictionalized exploits are presented from the point of view of a loving son who believed his mother was not only brilliant but indestructible as well. *Caveat emptor.*

THE CASES

1. *Murder at Midnight: An Eleanor Roosevelt Mystery.* New York: St. Martin's Press, 1997, 216 p.

WASHINGTON, DC, MAY 1933. Judge Horace Blackwell, a friend and adviser to the President, is found stabbed to death in his White House suite. The obvious suspect is a black maid, Sara Carter—yet the young woman swears she is innocent. As police officials cart Sara off to jail, Eleanor promises the girl a fair hearing. She gains the confidence of lead investigator Lawrence Pickering and begins to take an active role in the search. A second murder in the White House calls into question the safety of FDR himself. Can Eleanor ferret out the real killer before he strikes again? Eleanor crosses paths with everyone from writers to military generals as she seeks out the truth. Associate: Lawrence Pickering. Historical Figures: President Franklin D. Roosevelt; William Faulkner; Gertrude Stein; General Douglas MacArthur; Major Dwight D. Eisenhower, later President of the United States; retired Supreme Court Justice Oliver Wendell Holmes; James Farley; Missy LeHand.

2. *For the Estate of Elliott Roosevelt, Murder at the President's Door: An Eleanor Roosevelt Mystery.* New York: Thomas Dunne Books, St. Martin's Minotaur, 2001, 232 p.

WASHINGTON, DC, MAY 1933. The President and the First Lady have just settled into the White House to face a nation in the depths of the depression and a world on the brink of war. But chaos erupts in their own home when the body of a White House police officer is discovered lying at the President's bedroom door. Eleanor Roosevelt is convinced that the crime must be solved internally without attracting the attention of the press or the FBI. Firmly committed to her husband's safety, she enlists the confidential assistance of a few faithful associates to aid in her investigation. With their connivance, Eleanor is able to keep up appearances at her many social engagements while managing the secret investigation and examining clues behind the scenes. Faced with a trail of evidence leading to stolen nights of passion in the White House, underground tunnels, insider trading, mob connections, and speakeasies, Eleanor uncovers suspicious characters and motives galore. It takes discreet ingenuity and social propriety to continue rubbing elbows with famous contemporaries and fulfilling her duties as First Lady while keeping a top secret assassination investigation in full swing. Can Eleanor stop the killer before he makes another attempt on FDR's life? You betcha! The chronology of this tale appears to conflict with that of the preceding book in the series. Associates: Police Lieutenant Edward "Ed" Kennelly; Secret Service Agent Stanislaw "Stan" Szczygiel. Historical Figures: President Franklin D. Roosevelt; J. Edgar Hoover; Louis Howe; Harry Hopkins; Marguerite "Missy" Lehand [*sic*].

3. *Murder in the Oval Office.* New York: St. Martin's Press, 1989, 247 p.

WASHINGTON, DC, JULY 1934. Who shot Alabama Congressman Winstead Colmer to death in the Oval Office of the White House? With all the windows and doors bolted from within, it appeared to be a suicide. But too many people around Capitol Hill were breathing relieved sighs over the Banking Subcommittee Chairman's timely demise for his passing to be so neatly dismissed. With FBI Director J. Edgar Hoover mucking up the investigation, feisty First Lady Eleanor Roosevelt decides to try her hand, taking time from her busy schedule to solve a rather nasty puzzle that could scandalize the country and cause irreparable harm to her husband's New Deal administration. Associates: Lorena "Hick" Hickock, Eleanor's friend; Gerald "Jerry" Baines, Head of the White House Secret Service detail; Tommy Thompson. Historical Figures: President Franklin D. Roosevelt; James Farley; Harry Hopkins; Louis Howe; Missy LeHand; J. Edgar Hoover; General Douglas MacArthur; Bing Crosby; Jean Harlow; Bob Hope.

4. *The Hyde Park Murder.* New York: St. Martin's Press, 1985, 231 p.

HYDE PARK, NEW YORK, AND WASHINGTON, DC, MAY 1935. Eleanor Roosevelt puts on her investigative cap when a Hyde Park neighbor, Alfred Hannah, is indicted in a multimillion-dollar stock swindle. But just as his son's *fiancée*, Adriana van der Meer, turns to "Aunt Eleanor" for help, the case darkens, and financial fraud becomes murder most foul. Mrs. Roosevelt hasn't a clue as to the killer's identity, but from Wall Street to Washington she has all the right connections—all with hot tips for the First Lady. Soon she's well on her way to solving a killing in the market and tracing the deadly destination of a trail of hard cold cash. A mediocre plot is further burdened with a wholly contrived conclusion. Associates: Adriana van der Meer, Eleanor's young neighbor; her *fiancée*, Robert "Bob" Hannah, son of the accused; Harry Bledsoe, an ex-cop hired as a bodyguard for Hannah; Lawrence Pickering, a legal investigator. Historical Figures: President Franklin D. Roosevelt; Sara Delano Roosevelt, FDR's mother; James "Jim" Farley; Louis McHenry Howe; Marguerite "Missy" LeHand; Gus Gennerich, the President's bodyguard; Arthur Prettyman, the President's valet; Joseph P. Kennedy; New York Mayor Fiorello La Guardia; Supreme Court Justice Louis Brandeis.

5. *Murder in Georgetown: An Eleanor Roosevelt Mystery.* New York: St. Martin's Press, 1999, 230 p.

WASHINGTON, DC, FEBRUARY 1935. When the newest member of the Federal Treasury Board is found naked in his Georgetown townhouse with a hole in his head and an earring belonging to his latest mistress on the floor next to him, the police are convinced they're looking at an easy conviction. This probably would have been the case if Eleanor Roosevelt hadn't gotten involved. Jessica Dee, the dead man's mistress, claims she had nothing to do with the murder. Mrs. Roosevelt believes her, which gives her no choice but to open her own investigation. She gradually uncovers a trail of clues that lead from the bloody back alleys of Washington to the genteel duplicity of the Boston banking world, a web of deceit and passion that centers on a mysterious woman with flaming red hair and a fondness for murder. Associate: Police Lieutenant Edward "Ed" Kennelly. Historical Figures: President Franklin D. Roosevelt; Joseph P. Kennedy; the Marx Brothers; Sara Delano Roosevelt, FDR's mother; Missy LeHand.

6. *Murder in the West Wing: An Eleanor Roosevelt Mystery.* New York: St. Martin's Press, 1992, 247 p.

WASHINGTON, DC, MARCH 1936. As storm clouds gather over Europe, Eleanor is thrust into danger much closer to home. One of the President's staff has been found dead, poisoned by cyanide mixed in his evening bourbon. Even worse, the accused killer is another White House aide, diminutive beauty Thérèse Rolland. Although the police are determined to pin the crime on Thérèse, Eleanor is immediately convinced she is innocent. Calmly but firmly, the First Lady uncovers a web of lies and secrets swirling around the Louisiana political machine, until another shocking murder is discovered. Suddenly, the investigation is taking Eleanor places no proper First Lady should ever go—to the darkest underside of society and toward a shattering truth that lies within the White House itself! Associates: Police Lieutenant Edward "Ed" Kennelly; Secret Service Agent Stanislaw "Stan" Szczygiel. Historical Figures: John Lowell "Blackjack" Endicott; President Franklin D. Roosevelt; Albert Einstein; Joseph P. Kennedy; Eliot Ness; James Farley.

7. *Murder in the Rose Garden.* New York: St. Martin's Press, 1989, 232 p.

WASHINGTON, DC, JULY 1936. Someone has planted a corpse among the White House's world-famous roses—the body of prominent hostess Vivian Taliafero is discovered strangled just beneath the Cabinet Room window. Before her demise, the popular socialite had been a very busy blackmailer, seducing, then photographing powerful politicos in extremely compromising positions. The list of murder suspects reads like a who's who, with the military and every branch of the federal government well represented. But FDR is out boating and J. Edgar Hoover is crime-busting in gangland, so it falls to First Lady Eleanor Roosevelt to expose the killer before the seamy revelations of this seedy case brings Washington's rosy *façade* tumbling to the ground. Associates: Secret Service Agent Stanislaw "Stan" Szczygiel; Police Lieutenant Edward "Ed" Kennelly. Historical Figures: President Franklin D. Roosevelt; Harry Hopkins; Missy LeHand; Mary McLeod Bethune, Negro leader and President of Bethune-Cookman College.

8. *Murder in the Red Room.* New York: St. Martin's Press, 1992, 249 p.

WASHINGTON, DC, JANUARY 1937. The President and Mrs. Roosevelt are hosting a glittering, white tie affair for the members of the Supreme Court. With a string orchestra playing and the State Room decked with flowers and sparkling with jewelry, thoughts of murder and mayhem are the farthest thing from anyone's mind, until, of course, a dead body is found on the floor of the Red Room. The victim is a notorious Cleveland mobster who was certainly not an invited guest. Eleanor Roosevelt leads the investigation through the darkest mazes of the government elite to discover what scandalous connection exists between the underworld and the Roosevelt White House. Associates: Secret Service Agent Stanislaw "Stan" Szczygiel; Police Lieutenant Edward "Ed" Kennelly. Historical Figures: President Franklin D. Roosevelt; Chief Justice Charles Evans Hughes; Missy LeHand.

9. *Murder at Hobcaw Barony.* New York: St. Martin's Press, 1986, 233 p.

HOBCAW BARONY, NEAR GEORGETOWN, SOUTH CAROLINA, FALL 1937. Mrs. Roosevelt has accepted an invitation for a holiday of fun and socializing with some of Hollywood's greats at Bernard "Bernie" Baruch's famed South Carolina estate, Hobcaw Barony. But on the very first night, Mrs. Roosevelt and the other guests are horrified when the mansion is rocked with a violent explosion that leaves a prominent, though despised, film producer dead, and Eleanor facing yet another mysterious murder. A dazzling cast of supporting players joins forces with the First Lady to solve the mystery in a decidedly illegal, yet eminently satisfactory, manner. Associates: Robert Wilkes, Eleanor's Secret Service Guard; George, Baruch's houseman. Historical Figures: President Franklin D. Roosevelt; Bernard Baruch; Humphrey Bogart; Joan Crawford; Darryl F. Zanuck; a startlingly nude Tallulah Bankhead.

10. *A First Class Murder.* New York: St. Martin's Press, 1991, 261 p.

AT SEA ON THE S.S. *NORMANDIE*, A FRENCH LINER ON THE ATLANTIC OCEAN, SEPTEMBER 1938. Following Eleanor's visit to France to receive an award, the French government compensates her and her secretary with a magnificent first-class suite for her return trip home. The world is on the brink of war, and Eleanor has been urged by the President and his advisers to quietly, and behind the scenes, observe what is said by her various shipboard companions. During the Atlantic crossing, the Russian ambassador, Boris Troyanoskii, dies from poisoning after drinking a glass of tainted wine. It is up to Eleanor Roosevelt to investigate the shipboard crime, with the assistance of a young John F. Kennedy. Associates: Malvina "Tommy" Thompson, Eleanor's secretary; Moira Lasky, an acquaintance from home; Monsieur Edouard Ouzoulias, the *Normandie*'s "house" detective. Historical Figures: John F. Kennedy, son of U.S. Ambassador to the Court of St. James, Joseph P. Kennedy; Franklin D. Roosevelt, President of the United States; Anna Roosevelt, FDR's daughter; Secretary of State Cordell Hull; William O. Douglas, Chairman of the Securities and Exchange Commission; shipboard passengers including Charles A. Lindbergh; Henry Luce; Jack Benny and his wife, Mary Livingstone; Josephine Baker.

11. ***Murder in the Executive Mansion.*** New York: A Thomas Dunne Book,
St. Martin's Press, 1995, 197 p.

WASHINGTON, DC, JUNE 1939. As the story opens, Washington is
buzzing with activity when the King and Queen of England arrive for a visit.
In all the confusion, Lucinda Robinson, an assistant to the First Lady, can't
be found. Two days later, she turns up strangled in a linen closet on the
third floor of the White House. Horrified, Eleanor is fast on the trail. The
desperate letters from an embittered lover of Lucinda's point to a young
Washington lawyer who has also recently disappeared. Suspecting that the
girl has been killed elsewhere—and that she was far from innocent—Eleanor
disguises herself as "Martha Broderick," a Washington Homicide Detective,
and enters an underworld of speakeasies, mobsters, and tangled sexual liaisons. She's shocked to discover a German spy ring working from within
the White House! America's national security is at risk. With the dark specter
of war in Europe looming and various celebrities wending their ways to the
White House to visit FDR, Eleanor is running out of time to stop a killer
who can do more harm than murder. Associates: Henrietta Nesbitt, White
House housekeeper; Malvina "Tommy" Thompson, the First Lady's secretary; Edith Helm, the First Lady's social secretary; Gerald "Jerry" Baines,
Secret Service agent; Washington Police Captain Edward "Ed" Kennelly;
Police detective Fred Mariott. Historical Figures: President Franklin D. Roo-
sevelt; Harry Hopkins; Missy LeHand; Arthur Prettyman, the President's
valet; British King George VI and Queen Elizabeth; Ernest Hemingway;
William Faulkner; Lou Gehrig; Babe Ruth.

12. ***Murder and the First Lady.*** New York: St. Martin's Press, 1984, 227 p.

WASHINGTON, DC, AUGUST 1939. An employee of the ushers staff at the
White House has become a crime victim, and the matter is complicated by
the fact that he was the rather unsavory son of a high-powered congressman. Pamela Rush-Hodgeborne, one of the First Lady's secretaries, is suspected and immediately arrested. The girl's former employer, a member of
the nobility, asks Mrs. Roosevelt to take a hand in the matter on Pamela's
behalf, since the crime appears to be related to an earlier unsolved mystery,
the theft of jewels belonging to the Earl of Crittenden. When a tainted bottle of bitters is found in Pamela's apartment, she is implicated even further.
Eleanor must go undercover to discover who besides Pamela had access to
the bottle. Associate: Edward Kennelly. Historical Figures: President
Franklin D. Roosevelt; Harry Hopkins; Missy LeHand; J. Edgar Hoover;
Sir Alan Burton.

13. ***Murder in the East Room.*** New York: St. Martin's Press, 1993, 201 p.

WASHINGTON, DC, JUNE 1940. The world is at war. The British have
been defeated at Dunkirk, and France is collapsing. While FDR agonizes

over a possible third term, fine food and drink are not a major topic of concern at the White House. But bad bubbly isn't the reason Senator Vance Gibson staggers away from a state dinner. Moments after his departure, the man is found dead in the East Room, his throat slit from ear to ear. With the White House invaded by movers, shakers, and plotters, the First Lady can't help but investigate the murder of Senator Gibson, a man who was irresistible to women. Examining the suspects, from jealous husbands to corrupt politicians, Eleanor finds herself in a steamy world of sex and secrets. But for the President's wife, the most shocking truth is yet to come! Associates: Chief of the Homicide Division Police Captain Edward Kennelly; Gerald Baines. Historical Figures: President Franklin D. Roosevelt; Greta Garbo; Missy LeHand; Harry Hopkins; James Farley; Arthur Prettyman; Henry Stimson; Alfred Landon; Alice Roosevelt Longworth.

14. *A Royal Murder.* New York: St. Martin's Press, 1994, 234 p.

BAHAMAS ISLANDS, SEPTEMBER 1940. At FDR's request, Eleanor travels to the Bahamas, where the United States is hoping to establish air and naval bases to thwart Hitler's plans for expansion. The Duke of Windsor, who has been appointed Governor of the islands, receives Eleanor cordially and entertains her royally among the other celebrities in residence on the islands. Eleanor must use her diplomatic skills to convince the Duke and Duchess not to visit to the United States, since rumors have surfaced about their pro-Nazi sympathies. Meanwhile, the First Lady becomes embroiled in various complicated and subversive schemes hatched by wartime profiteers. And she is startled to learn that plans are afoot to make the Bahamas—as well as all of Latin America—into a Nazi stronghold! The resourceful First Lady faces one of her most challenging mysteries as she encounters smuggling, defection, disloyalty, murder—and even attempts on her own life. Associates: Kenneth Krouse; Secret Service Agent Alexander Zaferakes; Tommy Thompson. Historical Figures: President Franklin D. Roosevelt; Edward, Duke of Windsor; Wallis, Duchess of Windsor; Missy LeHand; Assistant Secretary of State Adolf Berle; Judy Garland.

15. *Murder in the Château: An Eleanor Roosevelt Mystery.* New York: St.
     Martin's Press, 1996, 200 p.

FRANCE, AND WASHINGTON, DC, APRIL 1941. FDR chooses Eleanor to negotiate on his behalf at a top-secret meeting of anti-Nazi leaders, including Field Marshal Erwin Rommel; the gathering is to be held in a lovely, pre-Revolution French château. Other denizens on the estate include a female Jewish terrorist (disguised as a maid) and an Irish mercenary bodyguard. When an S.S. officer, Artur Brandt, is found with a slug in his head, the First Lady finds herself prowling through the château's elegant rooms in search of his elusive killer. Associates: Colonel William J. "Wild Bill"

Donovan; Victoria Klein. Historical Figures: President Franklin D. Roosevelt; German Field Marshal Erwin Rommel; Missy LeHand.

16. *The White House Pantry Murder: An Eleanor Roosevelt Mystery.* New York: St. Martin's Press, 1987, 231 p.

WASHINGTON, DC, CHRISTMAS 1941. Christmas promises to be a bleak affair in the nation's capital. The country is in the grip of a terrible war, and the holiday season is rife with rumors of sinister international intrigue. On a personal note, the president's mother, Sara Delano Roosevelt, has died the previous September. White House security, in anticipation of a visit from British Prime Minister Winston Churchill, is tighter than ever, but not tight enough, it seems! For when a mysterious stranger turns up brutally murdered in the White House refrigerator—followed days later by another suspicious death—it becomes clear to First Lady Eleanor Roosevelt that unless she unravels the deadly plot quickly, FDR and Sir Winston will receive gifts they'll be in no condition to return! Associates: Henrietta Nesbitt, White House cook; Gerald "Jerry" Baines, Secret Service Agent; Don Deconcini, Baines' assistant; Inspector Sir Alan Burton of Scotland Yard; Lieutenant-Commander George Leach, Churchill's personal aide. Historical Figures: President Franklin D. Roosevelt; Harry Hopkins; Missy LeHand, now ill and impaired from a stroke; British Prime Minister Winston Churchill; Lord Beaverbrook.

17. *Murder in the Blue Room.* New York: St. Martin's Press, 1990, 213 p.

WASHINGTON, DC, MAY 1942. Who bludgeoned a pretty young Press Office secretary to death, right in the Blue Room of the White House? That's what a shocked Eleanor Roosevelt aims to find out. A friend, a lover, and even a Rockefeller are being questioned, along with the White House staff. But with a house full of visiting Russian diplomats headed by Soviet Foreign Minister Molotov, the First Lady's sleuthing may take a dangerous turn. Molotov may know something his hosts don't know, but questioning the Russians about murder may shatter some delicate negotiations and tip the balance of world power! Associates: Chief of the Homicide Division Police Captain Edward Kennelly; Dom Deconcini. Historical Figures: President Franklin D. Roosevelt; Soviet Foreign Minister Vyacheslav Mikhailovich Molotov.

18. *Murder at the Palace.* New York: St. Martin's Press, 1987, 232 p.

BUCKINGHAM PALACE, LONDON, ENGLAND, OCTOBER 1942. In blitz-ravaged London, while Winston Churchill is preparing a surprise offensive that could bring an end to World War II, the most hated man in England is bludgeoned to death at a Buckingham Palace cocktail party. The murder has all the marks of an inside job. But the task of finding the killer falls to the only outsider on the scene, the famous American First Lady, Eleanor Roosevelt, who is in London at Churchill's request. Associates: Colonel Oveta

Hobby, Head of the Women's Army Corps; Inspector Sir Alan Burton of Scotland Yard, Mrs. Roosevelt's bodyguard in Britain; Tommy Thompson. Historical Figures: Lieutenant Colonel Elliott Roosevelt, now stationed in London; President Franklin D. Roosevelt; Harry Hopkins; British King George VI and Queen Elizabeth; British Prime Minister Winston Churchill.

19. *Murder in the Map Room: An Eleanor Roosevelt Mystery.* New York: St. Martin's Press, 1998, 251 p.

WASHINGTON, DC, FEBRUARY 1943. While World War II rages on, the White House is aflutter with preparations for the visit of Madame Chiang Kai-shek, beautiful wife of China's leader and a well-loved celebrity both at home and in the States. Eleanor Roosevelt accompanies the smooth-tongued General's wife from social functions to congressional sessions. The First Lady must find a delicate balance between Madame Chiang's nationalistic demands with the best interests of the United States. But diplomacy is put in jeopardy with the discovery of the dead body of George Shen, an American Chinese shoe salesman in the President's top-secret Map Room! With enormous amounts of opium in his bloodstream and a photograph of a beautiful Asian woman in his pocket, the corpse presents questions that are not easily answered. Now the First Lady must smoke out a sinister killer with a twisted political agenda. Associates: District of Columbia Police Captain Edward "Ed" Kennelly; Secret Service Agent Robert Kirkwal; Captain David Bloom, Naval Intelligence; Malvina "Tommy" Thompson, Eleanor's secretary. Historical Figures: President Franklin D. Roosevelt; Harry Hopkins; Madame Chiang Kai-shek, wife of China's wartime leader.

20. *Murder in the Lincoln Bedroom: An Eleanor Roosevelt Mystery.* New York: Thomas Dunne Books, St. Martin's Press, 2000, 228 p.

WASHINGTON, DC, MAY 1943. On the eve of the Trident Conference, a highly classified council attended by FDR, Winston Churchill, and Dwight Eisenhower with the purpose of planning an Allied invasion into Western Europe, the White House is aflutter with preparations and swarming with extra Secret Service agents and soldiers. So when a body is discovered in the Lincoln Bedroom while the conferees are in session, Eleanor Roosevelt knows that in order to keep the murder (as well as the conference) a secret from the prying eyes of the press, not to mention foreign agents, she must solve it herself. The victim, Paul Weyrich, was a White House employee—one of the President's top advisers—who had been having an affair with his secretary. So at first glance, it looks to be a simple crime of passion instigated by Weyrich's refusal to marry the girl. However, the deeper Eleanor digs into the case, the more clouded and uncertain the outcome becomes. Gradually, Eleanor discovers that the victim was part of a plot to assassinate the President, and she embarks on a daring plan of her own to trap the assassin, using FDR as bait. Now, Eleanor's skills will be put to the ultimate test as she races to solve the mystery before the assassin can strike again. Associates: Stanislaw Szczygiel; Captain Edward Kennelly. Historical Figures: President Franklin D. Roosevelt; British Prime Minister Winston Churchill; Sarah Churchill; General Dwight D. Eisenhower.

"BLACKJACK" ENDICOTT MYSTERIES

Scene of the Crime: Washington, DC, and elsewhere in 1932.

Detective: John Lowell "Blackjack" Endicott, companion to, and protector of, politician Franklin Delano Roosevelt.

Known Associates: Franklin Delano Roosevelt, Governor of New York, later President of the United States.

Premise: "Blackjack" Endicott, FDR's old boarding-school chum, is handpicked by him to combat various threats to his life and presidential campaign in 1932.

Comment: These two books may be considered a prequel to Roosevelt's more popular series of books dealing with his mother, Eleanor Roosevelt, and share many of the same plusses and minuses (indeed, Endicott appears as a character in one of the Eleanor Roosevelt series). However, the basic setup here is at least more plausible than in the other sequence, in that Endicott's specific task is to protect presidential candidate Roosevelt from would-be assassins and political opportunists who would rather see someone else nominated as Herbert Hoover's opponent in 1932.

Literary Crimes & Chimes: As with the previous series featuring Eleanor Roosevelt, the "Blackjack" Endicott books are filled with "guest" appearances by a large number of the famous and infamous personalities of the period. While these lend some small measure of verisimilitude to the proceedings and are certainly possible (if rather a tad improbable) under the circumstances (with several murders being investigated), too much of this sort of thing becomes mere name-dropping in a very obvious sort of way and doesn't really lend much to the development of either story line. While the quality here is better overall than with the Eleanor Roosevelt books, that really isn't saying very much. As thin as an Oreo cookie, but without the frosting inside.

THE CASES

1. *The President's Man: A "Blackjack" Endicott Novel.* New York: St. Martin's Press, 1991, 247 p.
   CHICAGO, ILLINOIS, NEW YORK, NEW YORK, AND WASHINGTON, DC, JULY 1932. At New York's Stork Club, a well-dressed gentleman meets a

known gangster, while celebrities sip their drinks two tables away. Prohibition is doomed. New York Governor Franklin D. Roosevelt is destined to become the next president. And only a few insiders are aware of an incredible secret: someone in the East Coast underworld has vowed Roosevelt won't reach the Chicago Democratic Convention alive. After a series of death threats, a calm FDR handpicks his boarding-school chum "Blackjack" Endicott as his emissary into a world of high society and big-time crime, confident that the dashing, handsome man of the world has the guts to take on the hit men of Tammany Hall—and the skill to solve a mystery of murder and the mob. Associate: Oscar Carter. Historical Figures: Franklin D. Roosevelt, Governor of New York; Lucky Luciano; Al Capone; Dutch Schultz; F. Scott Fitzgerald; Rudy Vallee; Will Rogers; Missy LeHand.

2. *New Deal for Death: A "Blackjack" Endicott Novel.* New York: St. Martin's Press, 1993, 251 p.

CHICAGO, ILLINOIS, CALIFORNIA, AND WASHINGTON, DC, JULY 1932. After having already saved FDR from bootlegging gangsters who plotted against him, "Blackjack" Endicott again is called upon to investigate angry—and possibly deadly—labor racketeers who fear Roosevelt will establish a labor bill and crush their profits. Using all of his masterful wit and guile, "Blackjack" intrepidly battles against major crime figures as varied as Meyer Lansky, who say "no deal" to Roosevelt's New Deal. Historical Figures: Franklin D. Roosevelt, Governor of New York and future President of the United States; Meyer Lansky; Al Smith; Dutch Schultz; Lucky Luciano; Lucy Mercer Rutherfurd, FDR's mistress; William Randolph Hearst; Marion Davies.

ROSS, Kate (i.e., Katherine J. Ross) (1956–1998). American.

JULIAN KESTREL SERIES

Scene of the Crime: England, beginning in 1824.

Detective: Julian Kestrel, a young man in his mid-twenties, is a headliner in upper-class English society because of his style, taste, and wit, but a man of mystery whose origins and family are wholly unknown. He lives as a gentleman, breaking his fast each morning (well, afternoon) halfway through the arduous process of dressing. He attends parties, clubs, or "gaming hells" on most nights. He lives quietly, renting rooms in London.

Known Associates: Julian was orphaned as a child. His closest connection now is his manservant, Thomas Stokes, called Dipper, a (somewhat) reformed pickpocket. Dr. MacGregor (met in *Cut to the Quick*) initially considers Julian a useless young man but comes to see that he is much more than a dandy; they become fast friends. Another friend is a very young lady,

Philippa Fontclair, also met in the course of his first case, whom he treats as a younger sister.

Premise: A seeming fop solves crimes in nineteenth-century England.

Comment: Julian Kestrel has known both poverty and wealth. His father was the son of a Yorkshire country squire but was cut off without a penny when he married an actress. She died in childbirth, and Julian was raised as a gentleman by his father. His father died when he was a teenager, and Julian stayed briefly with a relative of his mother's, before leaving England to explore the world. He worked abroad until a friend settled enough money on him so that he could live as a gentleman. Julian has never succumbed to the rich man's fiction that all misery is earned. He has great sympathy for the unfortunate; his innate kindness, sensitivity, and intelligence drive him to help whenever he can. He applies these qualities when he sees young Hugh Fontclair, a novice in a gaming hall, looking desperate and very drunk. Julian extricates Hugh before he loses much of his fortune. Hugh asks his benefactor to visit the Fontclair estate while the Fontclairs entertain the family of Hugh's betrothed. (Hugh's family is being blackmailed into the match by the father of his bride-to-be, so Hugh expects an uncomfortable visit.) Circumstances conspire to embroil Julian in the investigation of a murder; he uncovers every secret connected with the crime. This gives him the confidence eventually to aid a woman who is being victimized. His success in both of these ventures leads to the usual gossip in high society, as more and more people ask him for investigative help. This is a time and a place in which the individual's reputation was paramount, in which scandals must be avoided at all cost, in which every household and every person within that family strives to present a perfect image of respectability. Julian's investigations pierce through the *façades*, exposing the dark underpinnings and shameful secrets lying beneath the surface. His kindness and empathy give him insights, but they also exact a price. He is driven to work for justice, a true justice far beyond the narrow-minded rectitude generally offered to the unfortunate of his time; but his nature does not limit his sympathy to the victims of the crimes. At times he also feels intense empathy for the perpetrators, and, while this does not keep him from exposing their actions, it does make him suffer for it. "Dipper" adds a touch of humor and irreverence to the stories, providing another perspective on high (and low) society.

Literary Crimes & Chimes: Julian is a sensitive man, and the secret scandals and crimes he uncovers are horrific. The books never fall into the trap of moralizing or becoming cloyingly sweet. Part of this is due to the protagonist's humor and wit; part is due to his companions, the gruff Dr. Mac-

Gregor and the artless Dipper. Julian's expertise and confidence as an investigator increase during the course of these books, and the secrets of Julian's past are tantalizingly revealed in stages. It is best to read the books in order. The series was cut off by the death of its creator, Kate Ross, a young trial lawyer with an amazing talent, who died in 1998.

THE CASES

1. *Cut to the Quick.* New York: Viking, 1993, 337 p.

ENGLAND, APRIL 1824. Julian wonders why the proud Fontclairs agree to a marriage between their eldest son and the daughter of a stable hand who was dismissed from the family's employment. Julian's resolve to stay out of their business must be discarded when a murdered girl is found in his bed, and his manservant Dipper is suspected of having a hand in her death. Associate: Dipper.

2. *A Broken Vessel.* New York: Viking, 1994, 289 p.

LONDON, ENGLAND, OCTOBER 1824. Dipper's long-lost sister, a London prostitute, makes a habit of stealing small souvenirs from her gentlemen. At the end of a long evening she has gathered three handkerchiefs, and with them a note from a desperate woman who is being held against her will. Dr. MacGregor warns Julian that she'll be trouble, and in a way he is right; before they are done, she will put herself into danger trying to help the unfortunate woman. Associates: Sally Stokes; Dipper; MacGregor.

3. *Whom the Gods Love.* New York: Viking, 1995, 382 p.

LONDON, ENGLAND, MAY 1825. Alexander Falkland is murdered at his own New Year's Eve party, with his guests reveling in one room while he was being bludgeoned to death in another. Months later, when it's apparent that the Bow Street Runners are stymied, Sir Malcolm, Alexander's father, asks Julian to investigate. Associates: Peter Vance; Verity Clare.

4. **"The Lullaby Cheat,"** in *Crime through Time*, ed. by Miriam Grace
   Monfredo and Sharan Newman. New York: Berkley Prime Crime, 1997,
   p. 125–149.

LONDON, ENGLAND, JULY 1825? A governess is accused of an unspeakable crime, attempting to murder the infant who's been placed under her care. Julian investigates and uncovers a complex plot involving fraud, threatened kidnapping and accusations of murderous intent. Associate: Peter Vance.

5. *The Devil in Music.* New York: Viking, 1997, 447 p.

MILANO, ITALY, SEPTEMBER 1825 (the Prologue is dated March 1821). Marquis Lodovico Malvezzi apparently died of heart failure, but the reality is somewhat different, and the authorities have decided to cover up the crime. Four and a half years later, Julian is visiting Italy when the scandal comes out in the newspapers; Julian is fascinated by the situation and driven to investigate. He finds the investigation dangerous in a great many ways.

ROWLAND, Laura Joh (1954?–). American.

SANO ICHIRŌ SERIES

Scene of the Crime: Edo Japan, during the Genroku Period; the first book takes place in Genroku Year one, Month nineteen (Tokyo, Japan, in January 1689).

Detective: Sano Ichirō, son of Sano Shutarō. The family has fallen on hard times; Sano Shutarō once ran a school for martial arts training, and Ichirō taught there and also did some tutoring to bring extra money into the family. Shutaro calls in a generations-old debt to the family and asks that Katsuragawa exert his influence to gain a well-paying position for Ichirō. Thus, the son becomes a police commander; although he feels painfully unprepared for the work, to have refused the position would have brought shame upon his family. At the onset of the series, Ichirō feels inept and overwhelmed. Other police commanders who should be his colleagues treat him harshly, angry that this upstart should be given a position equal to theirs. (Customarily, these administrative posts are inherited.) The new commissioner is both shunned and belittled, and no attempt is made to train him. However, by observing his colleagues' actions, he comes to the conclusion that they delegate almost all the work anyway and that they have little real concern about whether justice is actually achieved. He refuses to emulate them. His only assets are his driving curiosity and his unwillingness to condemn the innocent. These are enough to bring him to the attention of the Shogun in the first book, *Shinjū*, and he is made the Shogun's *sōsakan-sama*, Most Honorable Investigator of Events, Situations, and People.

Known Associates: Dr. Ito Genboku, once physician to the Imperial family, now disgraced and forced to live out his life in the Edo Morgue, is someone whom Sano Ichirō admires and respects. Dr. Ito uses the forbidden foreign knowledge that caused his downfall to determine how each crime victim actually died. In *Shinjū*, Ichirō is assisted by Tsunehiko; in subsequent books, by Hirata. In *Bundori* Ichirō agrees to a marriage contract offered by Magistrate Ueda, father to Reiko, thereby gaining a respected ally; the couple are married in *The Concubine's Tattoo*. Almost from the first moment they meet, and at least by the time of the events depicted in

Bundori, Chamberlain Yanagisawa becomes Ichirō's implacable enemy, being jealous of the Shogun's attention to the commissioner; while the former's wife, encountered for the first time in *The Pillow Book of Lady Wisteria*, is sometimes seized with the demented belief that she could have had Reiko's happiness if only she can destroy Reiko's life.

Premise: A police commissioner solves crimes in seventeenth-century Japan.

Comment: Sano Ichirō is a good man who works at following the correct spiritual path to bring honor to his family. He knows little about detection but has an uncanny sense for danger, has been trained with weapons, and persists in his determination to find the truth. His investigations proceed logically, and he cannot be pressured into giving up the hunt. His questioning mind and honorable nature will not allow him to settle for only those answers that will please his superiors. His inability to compromise the most essential part of himself puts him at constant risk. The societal pressures of seventeenth-century Japan provide much of the tension of the stories. After hundreds of years of war, peace in Japan is ruthlessly enforced. Everyone has a specific role in the stable hierarchy. Anything other than immediate obedience to one's superior is unacceptable. Criticism or even questioning of superiors is seen as a form of treason. Through the course of these books the reader sees Sano's gradual disillusionment as he serves the dissolute ruler of a corrupt regime.

Literary Crimes & Chimes: This series takes place in a setting both unfamiliar and fascinating to Western readers. The neighborhoods of Edo (the old name for Tokyo) are well described. The author switches point of view to give her readers insights into the crimes, opening many of the books with a Prologue covering the initial murder. This technique makes the convoluted investigations relatively easy to follow, since readers know something about the mind and motivations of the criminal. Sano Ichirō is a likable protagonist, unsure of himself, but always striving to do what is right. However, his acceptance of his wife as an investigative partner (*The Concubine's Tattoo*) is a bit difficult to believe.

THE CASES

1. **Shinjū.** New York: Random House, 1994, 367 p.
   EDO, JAPAN, 1689. Yoriko Sano Ichirō was given his post partly because his superiors were certain that a man so inexperienced and aware of the social consequences of the displeasure of the powerful would be easy to control. Sano's unwillingness to certify a verdict of Shinjū, a ritual double suicide performed by star-crossed lovers, infuriates both his superior and his patron. He continues his investigations even after he is forbidden to do so and un-

covers a sinister plot aimed at the highest levels of government. Associates: Lady Wisteria; Tsunehiko; Magistrate Ogyu; Midori.

2. *Bundori: A Novel of Japan*. New York: Villard, 1996, 339 p.

EDO, JAPAN, 1689. A grisly trophy of war, a head staked to a board, is found in the city, where there has been no war for over a century. Sōsakan-sama Sano is charged with finding the killer, and as the murderer strikes again and again, political enemies focus on destroying Sano, rather than supporting his investigations. Eventually, Sano understands their motives, but not before two separate assassins have been instructed to kill him. Associates: Sano Shutarō (deceased); Aoi; archivist Noguchi Motoori; Hirata; Ueda; Reiko; Yanagisawa.

3. "Mizu-Age," in *Crime through Time II*, ed. by Miriam Grace Monfredo and Sharan Newman. New York: Berkley Prime Crime, 1998, p. 114–130.

YOSHIWARA, JAPAN, 1689. Sano attends a celebration of a young courtesan's coming-of-age. The honor of being her first client has been auctioned off to the highest bidder. When the child is found murdered, her client, feeling cheated, asks Sano to investigate. Associate: Yoriki Hayashi.

4. "The Iron Fan," in *Chronicles of Crime: The Second Ellis Peters Memorial Anthology of Historical Crime*, ed. by Maxim Jakubowski. London: Headline Book Publishing, 1999, p. 195–213.

EDO, JAPAN, 1689. Sano is charged with protecting the life of an honest magistrate. The man has convicted the members of a criminal gang and is afraid that, while he takes his ill wife on a pilgrimage to seek a cure, he will himself be murdered.

5. *The Way of the Traitor: A Samurai Mystery*. New York: Villard, 1997, 307 p.

NAGASAKI, JAPAN, 1690. With the Shogun ill, the treacherous Chamberlain Yanagisawa Yoshiyasu orders Sano to conduct an inspection tour of Nagasaki, a task that will probably keep him away from the Shogun's side for many months. Nagasaki is the one place where Japanese and foreigners may meet, and the town is watched assiduously for signs of sedition by missionaries and arms merchants. When the Director of Trade for the Dutch East India Company disappears, Sano must investigate; any security breach in Nagasaki mandates an automatic death sentence on all involved. Associates: Dr. Nicolaes Huygens; Iishino; Old Carp; Yanagisawa.

6. *The Concubine's Tattoo*. New York: St. Martin's Press, 1998, 326 p.

EDO, JAPAN, 1690. A concubine dies in the palace. The Shogun, more afraid of contagion than villainy, sends Sano to "prevent the evil spirit of disease" from reaching him. Even though the case separates him from his new bride, Sano must obey. Soon he realizes that the woman did not die of natural causes. Associates: Dr. Kitano; Eri; Lady Keisho-in; Midori; Danzaemon; archivist Noguchi Motoori; Reiko.

7. **"Onnagata,"** in *More Murder, They Wrote*, ed. by Elizabeth Foxwell and Martin H. Greenberg. New York: Berkley Boulevard Books, 1999, p. 231–262.

EDO, JAPAN, 1691. A young Kabuki actor is murdered in the middle of a performance. The Shogun's mother, who at first thought that the death was staged, demands that Reiko, who had accompanied her to the theater, solve the murder. Associates: Lady Keisho-in; Reiko.

8. *The Samurai's Wife.* New York: St. Martin's Minotaur, 2000, 203 p.

MIYAKO, JAPAN, 1691. When one of the Shogun's spies is killed, Sano is sent out to hunt the murderer and neutralize any potential threats. Rumor has it that the man was murdered using the "spirit cry," a scream that can strike an opponent dead. Sano, Reiko, and an unexpected ally work together trying to solve the murder and protect each other from harm. Associates: Marume; Fukida; Jokyōden; Hoshina; Reiko.

9. *Black Lotus.* New York: St. Martin's Minotaur, 2001, 341 p.

EDO, JAPAN, 1693. One of the greatest dangers in a city of wooden buildings is fire; when an arsonist torches the Black Lotus Temple, Sano is sent to investigate. There he and Reiko find crimes of all sorts, including murder. Associates: Haru; Midori; Lady Keisho-in; Hiroko; Reiko.

10. *The Pillow Book of Lady Wisteria.* New York: St. Martin's Minotaur, 2002, 292 p.

EDO, JAPAN, 1693. When the Shogun's cousin, the heir to the throne, is found dead after a night of debauchery, Sano is sent to investigate. The Shogun's rage is horrible, and Sano must locate the killer quickly. Associates: Hoshina; Lady Wisteria; Lady Keisho-in; Midori; Lord Niu; Lady Yanagisawa; Kikuko.

11. *The Dragon King's Palace.* New York: St. Martin's Minotaur, 2003, 340 p.

EDO, JAPAN, 1694. Lady Keisho-in determined to take a trip to Mount Fuji and demands that Reiko, Midori, and Lady Yanagisawa attend her. Reluctantly they join her, only to be kidnapped from their palanquins on the orders of a madman. Sano must work with his greatest enemies to save his wife. Associates: Hoshina; Lady Keisho-in; Midori; Lord Niu; Lady Yanagisawa; Kikuko; Dr. Kitano; Marume; Fukida; Reiko.

12. *The Perfumed Sleeve.* New York: St. Martin's Minotaur, 2004, 326 p.

EDO, JAPAN, 1694. Sano's help is requested to solve a murder; the man making the request is the victim, and Sano feels that he cannot refuse. His investigation is complicated by the political maneuvering of two different factions, each striving to gain the advantage in control of the military government. Each side watches the investigation, eager to see Sano condemn the other. Associates: Hoshina; Lady Yanagisawa; Kikuko; Midori; Dr. Kitano; Marume; Fukida.

SAYLOR, Steven (1956–). American.

GORDIANUS THE FINDER (OR ROMA SUB ROSA) SERIES

Scene of the Crime: Italy (primarily Rome), from the year 674 from the founding of Rome (80 BC), when Sulla is dictator, through 48 BC, the time of Julius Caesar.

Detective: Gordianus, born 644 from the founding of Rome (110 BC), called "Deductus" (the Finder), due to his commitment to the truth, the perspicacity of his observations, and the fact that people find it difficult to resist confiding in him. He is helped in many of his cases by one of his adoptive sons, Eco.

Known Associates: Bethesda, born in Alexandria of an Egyptian mother and a Jewish father in 106 BC, sold as a slave to Gordianus in 90 BC, manumitted and married to Gordianus in 70 BC. At the end of *Roman Blood* Gordianus takes in a mute boy, Eco (born 90 BC); he begins to speak again in *Arms of Nemesis*. In 63 BC Eco marries Menenis; their twins, Titus and Titania, are born in 60 BC. Meto (born 79 BC) is purchased and given to Gordianus at the end of *Arms of Nemesis* and is manumitted and adopted; he becomes a soldier in *Catilina's Riddle* and is featured in the books sporadically after that. Gordianus' youngest child, Diana, is born to him and Bethesda in 70 BC. Belbo is Gordianus' slave at the end of the events in "Little Caesar and the Pirates," until he dies during the action of *Murder on the Appian Way* In that book Gordianus acquires two more slaves, Mopsus and Androcles, as well as a son-in-law, Davus. In *Rubicon* Diana and Davus have had a son; his name is Aulus. At the end of *Last Seen in Massilia*, Gordianus has added the most fortunate scapegoat in the world, Hieronymus, to his household; and in *Mist of Prophecies* he adds Rupa, the mute brother of Cassandra.

Premise: A detective solves crimes in late Republican Rome.

Comment: In the slippery world of Roman politics, cleverness counts more than wisdom, rhetoric more than truth. This sickens Gordianus, whose passion for truth drives him to solve the mysteries that are presented to him. This pleases the advocates who hire him, at least when the truth upholds the positions they wish to take. Cicero points out to him in *Murder on the Appian Way:* "The important thing about tomorrow's hearing is not to determine who did what to whom on the Appian Way. The important thing, the absolutely vital thing, is that at the end of the day, Milo must go free. If the truth hinders that objective, then it must be dispensed with. It serves no purpose" (p. 345). No matter what he is hired to do, Gordianus cannot rest until he is satisfied that he has learned the truth. Until Eco marries and sets up his own household, he acts as Gordianus' companion in detection. The activities of his son Meto involve Gordianus in political intrigue. Meto finds trickery exhilarating, while Gordianus finds deception abhorrent. The author, who received a degree in history from the University of Texas, has stated about this period of Roman history: "There's political intrigue, courtroom drama, sexual scandal, extremes of splendor and squalor, and no shortage of real-life murder mysteries" (preface to "Archimedes' Tomb" in *Crime through Time*). Although some of his plot points seem a bit far-fetched, Saylor's background research is excellent, and his books may include everything from verbatim passages from actual speeches given by Roman politicians to scurrilous verse created at the time to embarrass the rich and powerful. In some cases Gordianus' dealings with historical figures seem quite natural. What could be more reasonable, for example, than Cicero hiring an investigator to gather material for a legal defense? In others the historical figures are treated with compassion and insight. Throughout the series Saylor's treatment of Clodia is particularly interesting. In a few cases Gordianus' presence as witness to events does seem forced, however, almost a Forest Gump-like insertion into history; his presence at Catilina's last battle and his witness to Pompey's execution fall into this category. Gordianus is viewed with suspicion by all; Pompey says to him in *Rubicon:* " 'the most honest man in Rome,' Cicero called you once. No wonder no one trusts you!"

Literary Crimes & Chimes: The harshness of the society depicted in *Roman Blood* is utterly repellent, and this image does not improve with subsequent entries in the series. What does change is the sphere of Gordianus' influence. Gordianus is a gentle, thoughtful man with great empathy and deep compassion. Where he has influence, the world is not only more just but more merciful. Without the safe haven that is created by his actions, the books would be intolerable; with it they are a joy to read. Any reader dismayed by *Roman Blood* should continue the series at least through *Catilina's Riddle*. The relationships between Gordianus, his family, the members of his household, and his friends are complex. To understand the underlying tensions and love that develop, it is perhaps best to read the novels in order. Most of the short stories cover the years between *Roman Blood* and *Arms of Nemesis*; these develop some of Gordianus' relationships with Eco and Lucius Claudius. Several of the stories are referred to in the novels, the events of 90 BC related in "The Alexandrian Cat" are alluded to in *The Venus Throw*, and those in "The House of the Vestals" are mentioned in *Catalina's Riddle*.

THE CASES

1. *Roman Blood.* New York: St. Martin's Press, 1991, 357 p.

ROME, 80 BC. Gordianus is hired by Cicero, who is defending a man against the accusation of parricide. In the course of the investigation, Gordianus uncovers unimaginable depravity and cruelty; the purest plea he receives is from a young mute boy named Eco, who wants Gordianus and Tiro to avenge an attack on his mother. They do. Associates: Rufus; Tiro; Eco. Historical Figure: Cicero.

2. "Death Wears a Mask," in *The House of the Vestals: The Investigations of Gordianus the Finder*. New York: St. Martin's Press, 1997, p. 1–34.

ROME, 80 BC. Eco is enjoying his first attendance at a Roman festival, and Gordianus is enjoying showing it to him. An actor is murdered backstage during a performance, and Eco solves the case before Gordianus! Associate: Eco.

3. "Tale of the Treasure House," in *The House of the Vestals: The Investigations of Gordianus the Finder*. New York: St. Martin's Press, 1997, p. 35–48.

ROME, 80 BC. Bethesda tells Gordianus a story of the cleverness of women. The woman in the story traps a thief who stole silver from King Rhampsinitus' treasure house. Associate: Bethesda.

4. "If Cyclops Could Vanish in the Blink of an Eye," in *Ellery Queen's Mystery Magazine* (August 2003): 72–78.

ROME, CIRCA 80 BC. Under cover of darkness, while the household is sleeping, someone enters Eco's room and steals the small clay figurines that he's earned working for a potter. Bethesda suggests that they have become animate and have left on their own, but Gordianus is not satisfied with that explanation. Associates: Bethesda; Eco.

5. **"A Will Is a Way,"** in *The House of the Vestals: The Investigations of Gordianus the Finder*. New York: St. Martin's Press, 1997, p. 49–74.

ROME, 78 BC. A bored patrician (Lucius Claudius) hires Gordianus to explain the puzzle of how a man who died two days ago could be spotted shopping in the marketplace. He is satisfied with the explanation that the detective finally provides, but not with Gordianus' conclusion that nothing can be done to correct the situation. He proves that Gordianus is wrong, and the two men begin a lifelong friendship. Associate: Lucius Claudius.

6. **"The Lemures,"** in *The House of the Vestals: The Investigations of Gordianus the Finder*. New York: St. Martin's Press, 1997, p. 75–110.

ROME, 78 BC. In the aftermath of Sulla's death, Rome seems to be haunted by *lemures*, the unquiet dead. One of the men proscribed and beheaded by Sulla seems to be walking once more, terrorizing the people who purchased his mansion for a paltry 1,000 *sesterces*. At the same time, *lemures* of men killed by one of Sulla's soldiers return to torment him. Associate: Lucius Claudius.

7. **"Little Caesar and the Pirates,"** in *The House of the Vestals: The Investigations of Gordianus the Finder*. New York: St. Martin's Press, 1997, p. 111–150.

ITALY, 77 BC. Area pirates are becoming bolder, and the story of Julius Caesar's retribution against them is the talk of Rome. When a ransom note is delivered to the parents of Spurius, Gordianus is asked to carry the money to the kidnappers; it is understood that he will then do his best to get it back.

8. **"The Disappearance of the Saturnalia Silver,"** in *The House of the Vestals: The Investigations of Gordianus the Finder*. New York: St. Martin's Press, 1997, p. 151–174.

ROME, 77 BC. Traditionally, on Saturnalia, Romans give each other gifts, and the masters serve their slaves. Gordianus reports to Bethesda on what he has done that day, but he also witnesses Lucius Claudius' dismay at the theft of his Saturnalia gifts. Bethesda acts as Gordianus would, solving the mystery. Associates: Lucius Claudius; Bethesda.

9. **"The Consul's Wife,"** in *Crime through Time III*, ed. by Sharan Newman. New York: Berkley Prime Crime, 2000, p. 2–27.

ROME, 76 BC. Consul Decius Brutus hires Gordianus to uncover a plot to assassinate him, a plot that he believes is being concocted by his wife and her lover. Gordianus finds nothing and so cannot collect the second half of his fee, at least not from the consul.

10. **"King Bee and Honey,"** in *The House of the Vestals: The Investigations of Gordianus the Finder.* New York: St. Martin's Press, 1997, p. 175–201.

LUCIUS' ETRUSCAN FARM, ITALY, 76 BC. Lucius, Gordianus, and Eco's vacation is interrupted by a visit from a passionate couple, Titus Didius and his wife, Antonia. With the Pleiades rising, it is time to harvest the honey, a task that is fascinating to Gordianus and Eco but fatal to someone else. Associates: Lucius Claudius; Bethesda; Eco.

11. **"The White Fawn,"** in *Classical Whodunnits: Murder and Mystery from Ancient Greece and Rome,* ed. by Mike Ashley. New York: Carroll & Graf, 1997, p. 72–95.

EASTERN SPAIN, 76 BC. Gordianus travels to eastern Spain to convince the grandson of a Senator to leave the camp of the rebel Sertorius and return to Rome. In Sertorius' camp there is a white fawn through which the goddess Diana is believed to speak. When the virgin who tended the fawn is found murdered and the fawn gone, Sertorius asks Gordianus for his help.

12. **"Archimedes' Tomb,"** in *Crime through Time,* ed. by Miriam Grace Monfredo and Sharan Newman. New York: Berkley Prime Crime, 1997, p. 25–52.

SYRACUSE, SICILY, 75 BC. Cicero spends an evening lecturing his Syracusan guests about their own history, specifically about Archimedes. His lecture bears unexpected fruit, not only Cicero's own determination to restore Archimedes' tomb, but also a murder! Historical Figure: Cicero.

13. **"Death by Eros,"** in *Past Poisons: An Ellis Peters Memorial Anthology of Historical Crime,* ed. by Maxim Jakubowski. London: Headline, 1998, p. 65–86.

NEAPOLIS, ITALY, 75 BC. Gordianus is asked by a heartbroken father to investigate the death of his son. The boy was extraordinarily beautiful, gifted, and heartless. His companions believe that the victim was struck down by the god Eros and that it was justice.

14. **"The Alexandrian Cat,"** in *The House of the Vestals: The Investigations of Gordianus the Finder.* New York: St. Martin's Press, 1997, p. 202–224.

ROME, 74 BC. Gordianus tells Lucius Claudius about a case he solved in Alexandria in 90 BC, in which Gordianus solved a mystery, and the Alexandrian mob killed a man for murdering a cat. Associates: Lepidus; Lucius Claudius.

15. **"The House of the Vestals,"** in *The House of the Vestals: The Investigations of Gordianus the Finder.* New York: St. Martin's Press, 1997, p. 225–250.

ROME, 73 BC. Gordianus is called upon to solve a murder in the House of the Vestals. The death of a man is a tragedy anywhere, but the murder

of a male citizen in a sanctuary where even the presence of a man is sacrilege is much worse. If Gordianus does not find the evidence that will clear
two other men of wrongdoing, one of the Vestals will be buried alive. Associates: Fabia; Licinia; Rufus. Historical Figures: Cicero; Crassus; Catilina.

16. **"A Gladiator Dies Only Once,"** in *The Mammoth Book of Roman
    Whodunnits*, ed. by Mike Ashley. New York, Carroll & Graf, 2003,
    p. 27–74.

ETRURIA, 73 BC. Gordianus has often been asked to help discover a murderer. This case, however, is highly unusual: a beautiful young Nubian
woman wants him to investigate a resurrection! Historical Figure: Cicero.

17. *Arms of Nemesis.* New York: St. Martin's Press, 1992, 305 p.

BAIAE, ITALY, 72 BC. Roman law allows all the slaves in a man's house
to be put to death if that man is murdered and the culprit cannot be identified. Spartacus' slave rebellion is the talk of Italy, and Crassus believes he
will gain politically by ostentatiously following that law while he seeks the
approval of the Senate to raise an army to destroy the rebellion. Gordianus
has five days, until the funeral games of Lucius Licinius, to solve Licinius'
murder, or ninety-nine men, women, and children will die. Associates: Crassus; Marcus Mummius; Apollonius.

18. **"Poppy and the Poisoned Cake,"** in *The Mammoth Book of More His-
    torical Whodunnits*, ed. by Mike Ashley. New York: Carroll & Graf,
    2001, p. 3–26.

ROME, 70 BC. Gordianus is hired by the public censor to determine how
a slave of his was poisoned. Gordianus uncovers a plot against the censor
himself but sees the information he gathered put to an unusual use.

19. *Catilina's Riddle.* New York: St. Martin's Press, 1993, 430 p.

ETRUSCAN FARM, ITALY, 63 BC. Gordianus is looking forward to spending some time on the estate left to him by Lucius Claudius; his peace is interrupted by the demands of his friends, the enmity of some of his neighbors,
and a series of headless corpses. Cicero sends Marcus Caelius to ask Gordianus to open his home to Cicero's rival Catilina and to spy upon him.
Gordianus finds more to admire in Catilina than he has recently found in
Cicero. Unfortunately, so does Meto, and he leaves to become a soldier. Associates: Rufus; Marcus Mummius; Apollonius; Caelius; Meto. Historical
Figures: Cicero; Catilina.

20. *The Venus Throw.* New York: St. Martin's Press, 1995, 308 p.

ROME, 56 BC. Gordianus' old teacher, Dio of Alexandria, appears out of
a stormy night disguised as a woman to ask for Gordianus' help; later that
night Dio is murdered. Dio was the last of a delegation of 100 men from
Alexandria come to ask that the Senate remove Ptolemy the Flute Player
from the throne of Egypt in favor of Queen Berenice. Clodia takes an interest in the philosopher's death, asking Gordianus to prove that the lover

who abandoned her, Marcus Caelius, is guilty. Associates: Clodia; Caelius. Historical Figures: Dio; Cicero; Egyptian King Ptolemy XII.

21. *A Murder on the Appian Way.* New York: St. Martin's Press, 1996, 304 p.

ROME, 52 BC. When Clodius is murdered on the Appian Way, his wife, Fulvia, and Pompey, patron of the chief suspect, both ask Gordianus to investigate the crime. Gordianus and Eco leave their homes and families in the care of bodyguards, with the Roman mob so close to rioting that it is necessary to safeguard their families. They expect to be gone for a few days, but a (relatively) innocent man is so frightened of the truth that he plans their abduction and murder. Associates: Fulvia; Sempronia; Clodia; Clodius; Caelius; Milo; Eco. Historical Figures: Pompey; Lepidus; Cicero.

22. *Rubicon.* New York: St. Martin's Press, 1999, 276 p.

ITALY, 49 BC. Caesar's forces have crossed the Rubicon and are marching toward Rome; the Senate passes the Ultimate Decree, effectively putting Rome under martial law. As Pompey's partisans flee the city, one of Pompey's agents is murdered in Gordianus' garden. Pompey demands that Gordianus uncover the murderer and conscripts Davus to force Gordianus to do so. Associates: Tiro; Davus. Historical Associates: Pompey; Caesar.

23. *Last Seen in Massilia.* New York: St. Martin's Minotaur, 2000, 277 p.

MASSILIA, ITALY, 49 BC. When Gordianus receives word of Meto's death, he can't bring himself to believe the news. Davus accompanies him to Massilia only to find it under siege by Caesar's troops. At the risk of their lives, they don armor and join a sneak attack on the city so that they can search for news of Meto. Associates: Meto; Trebonius; Vitruvius; Gaius Verres; Milo; Davus. Historical Figure: Caesar.

24. *A Mist of Prophecies.* New York: St. Martin's Minotaur, 2002, 270 p.

ROME, 48 BC. Gordianus first saw Cassandra when she collapsed in front of the House of the Vestals. Soon the prophetess is known throughout Rome, and the women left behind while their husbands, brothers, and lovers are at war look to her for information on the present and on the future. Then she dies in the marketplace, poisoned, and Gordianus is determined to find her killer. Associates: Terentia; Antonia; Cytheris; Fulvia; Fausta; Calpurnia; Clodia; Caelius; Milo.

25. *The Judgment of Caesar: A Novel of Ancient Rome.* New York: St. Martin's Minotaur, 2004, 290 p.

ALEXANDRIA, EGYPT, 48 BC. Bethesda believes that her illness will be cured if she bathes in the Nile, so Gordianus takes her to Alexandria, accompanied by Rupa, Mopsus, and Androcles. There they encounter the survivors of the Battle of Pharsalus. Pompey has been driven almost to madness by his defeat. Someone tries to poison Caesar, and a member of Gordianus' family becomes the chief suspect. Associates: Bethesda; Rupa; Mopsus; Androcles. Historical Figures: Pompey; Cornelia; Egyptian King Ptolemy XII; Caesar; Egyptian Queen Cleopatra VII.

SEDLEY, Kate (pseud. of Brenda Margaret Lillian Clarke) (1926–). British.

ROGER THE CHAPMAN SERIES

Scene of the Crime: England, beginning in 1471 during the Wars of the Roses.

Detective: Roger the Chapman, an itinerant peddler.

Known Associates: Richard, Duke of Gloucester, with whom Roger shares a birthday (October 2, 1452) and who becomes his mentor; Timothy Plummer, the Duke's man, whom Roger saves from a pieman and is forever grateful; Margaret Walker, mother of Roger's deceased first wife, Lillis; Elizabeth, his daughter; Adela, his long-suffering second wife; Nicholas, her son; Alderman Alfred Weaver and his daughter, Alison, who return again and again to assist Roger and to ask for his help; William Burnett, Alison's betrothed; Master Gilbert Parsons, a London Sheriff's officer; Philip Lamprey, whom Roger first meets in London, and his wife, Jeanne; Cicely Ford, Edward's ward; Edward Herepath, a villain.

Premise: Roger the Chapman, a former monk, travels about the countryside working as an itinerant peddler and investigating and solving the various crimes and misdemeanors he encounters in fifteenth-century England.

Comment: Each volume is framed by Roger's memoirs, ostensibly written in 1522 ("when I am an old man"), giving further background on his birth and family (particularly in the first volume, *Death and the Chapman*) and providing additional historical references. Although much of the action in these novels takes place "on the road," involving strangers whom Roger meets along the way, the peddler always manages to return to his comfy cottage in Bristol to hole up for the winter, taking his rightful place as man of the house with his long-suffering, ever-patient family.

Literary Crimes & Chimes: Roger's cavalier attitude toward women is a bit off-putting. In *The Hanged Man*, he unceremoniously beds the virgin daughter of the woman who has nursed him back to health, noting that it had been some time since he had had the benefit of female "companionship"; this, he feels, justifies his actions. When the girl turns up pregnant, to his credit he returns and marries her but does not seem overwrought with grief when his new bride dies in childbirth. He leaves his tiny daughter in the care of his mother-in-law and sets out on his travels with little or no qualms about their welfare or safety, returning from time to time to wait out the winter. Later, after his second marriage, in spite of his professed love for Adela, he cannot help but regret the many other loves of his life who "got away." He is always impatient to be on the road again. The other constant in Roger's life is his association with Richard, the Duke of Gloucester, who often calls upon him for assistance with sticky situations. One wonders how likely it is that a lowly peddler would become the bosom buddy of a prince of the realm, even if they do share the same birthday!

THE CASES

1. *Death and the Chapman.* London: Crime Club, HarperCollins, 1991, 190 p.

   BRISTOL, CANTERBURY, AND LONDON, ENGLAND, MAY–SEPTEMBER 1471 (the Prologue is dated 1522). While England's York and Plantagenet families divide the country in an ugly battle for the throne, Roger the Chapman, an itinerant young peddler of insatiable curiosity, pays his way to London by selling trinkets and baubles. Recently released from a Benedictine monastery, the nineteen-year-old is naïve but eager to put his talent for solving puzzles to good use. His wish comes true when a wealthy Bristol alderman asks him to investigate the mysterious disappearance of his only son, Clement Weaver. The young man had last been seen standing only a few feet from London's Crossed Hands Inn, where he was to spend the night. His father believes that Roger, being a "man of the people," might have access to information to which a man of his own class might not be privy. Intrigued, Roger soon discovers that Clement was not the only wealthy traveler to vanish without a trace on the same street in London, and he can't resist a quick look around. There are two competing inns on this street, both of unsavory reputation, and it seems likely that one or the other of them is involved in the disappearances. Determined to find the truth, Roger edges closer and closer to London and the mysterious inn—and to the villainy entertained within. Associates: Alfred; Alison; William; Timothy; Gilbert; Philip; Jeanne. Historical Figures: British King Edward IV; Queen Margaret of Anjou, wife of British King Henry VI; Anne Neville, her daughter; Richard, Duke of Gloucester, who loves Anne.

2. *The Plymouth Cloak.* London: Crime Club, HarperCollins, 1992, 192 p.

   EXETER, AND ON THE ROAD TO PLYMOUTH, ENGLAND; BRITTANY, SEPTEMBER 1473. An uneasy peace between England's houses of Lancaster and York has begun to unravel yet again. Rumors of invasion are rife, and Richard of Gloucester, the King's brother (who will someday become Richard

III of England) is determined to put a stop to the treacherous plots. To that end, he dispatches a royal messenger to Duke Francis of Brittany with a secret letter. Meanwhile, Roger the Chapman, the strapping twenty-one-year-old itinerant peddler, is making his way to Exeter in the hopes that a stop in that thriving city will help his trade. Richard calls upon Roger to accompany his messenger, Philip Underdown, to a Brittany-bound ship at Plymouth. A devious fellow, Philip has more than his fair share of enemies and is, Richard believes, in need of protection. Roger arms himself with a stout cudgel, known in underworld parlance as a "Plymouth Cloak." Although his distaste with Philip's behavior intensifies, especially when he learns that Philip has been a slaver dealing in dwarfs, then all the rage in European courts, Roger keeps to his assignment and successfully foils several attackers. When the two seek shelter in a castle, Philip sneaks out to keep an apparent amorous tryst and is fatally beaten and stabbed. Roger must sort through all the usual suspects in order to wrap up the case and see that Richard's message is delivered safely. Associate: Timothy. Historical Figures: Richard, Duke of Gloucester; George, Duke of Clarence; Earl of Oxford; British King Edward IV; Brittany Duke Francis.

3. *The Hanged Man.* London: Headline, 1993, 248 p. As: *The Weaver's Tale.* New York: St. Martin's Press, 1994, 248 p.

BRISTOL, ENGLAND, CHRISTMAS 1473–NOVEMBER 1474. Roger has collapsed with fever after wandering the roads of western England, peddling his wares amid December's snow and freezing rain. Sheer exhaustion forces him to stop and rest at the lodgings of the widow Margaret Walker and her daughter Lillis, in the ancient trading port of Bristol. He awakens, weak but well on the road to recovery, to find himself embroiled in yet another mystery. His kind hostesses, who have nursed him gently back to health, will not hear of him leaving the comfort of their modest cottage until spring. But Roger's keen senses soon detect the shadow of tragedy looming over the house. The two women seem mistrusting of the villagers and uneasy even in their home. He learns that Margaret's father, William Woodward, had vanished mysteriously and was presumed to have been murdered. Through circumstantial evidence, Robert Herepath, younger brother of Edward Herepath, Woodward's employer, was found guilty and hanged for the crime. Incredibly, two months later the "victim" wandered back into town, alive and well, although suffering from amnesia and unable to account for his disappearance. The town has hanged an innocent man; compounding the mystery, soon after his return the old man's corpse is discovered—and this time it really is murder. Prompted by his own curiosity, not to mention his amorous attentions toward Lillis, Roger agrees to stay and root out the evil at work in a town plagued by secret allegiances and rivalries among its merchants, churchmen, and leading families. Associates: Margaret; Lillis; Alfred; Cicely; Edward. Historical Figure: Richard, Duke of Gloucester.

4. *The Holy Innocents*. London: Headline, 1994, 280 p.

BRISTOL, AND TOTNES, ENGLAND, FEBRUARY–APRIL 1475. With the War of the Roses a distant backdrop, Roger is eager for the open road after having settled for more than a year in Bristol. He leaves the cottage of his mother-in-law, Margaret Walker, and ventures forth to sell his wares. It is a sad parting, as he reflects on his wife's untimely death while giving birth to his tiny daughter, Elizabeth. On a shadowy morning in April 1475, he approaches the thriving village of Totnes. A pack of cutthroats wanders the forest at night, stealing and pillaging in the surrounding villages. Roger barely escapes the marauding band himself and once in the village, hears further tales of their brutal raids. The situation captures the curiosity of Roger's nose for detection, especially when he is asked to guard a house in the absence of its owner, Eudo Colet. A tavern keeper, intimating witchcraft, tells Roger about the strange disappearance and deaths of Mary and Andrew, Colet's stepchildren, who had recently lost their mother, heiress Rosamund Crouchback. The children's nurse, a poor cousin of the dead heiress, hates Colet and asks Roger to investigate the sad case. It is believed that the children, whose mutilated bodies were discovered in the river, could not have left the house unobserved. At the time of their disappearance, Colet had been in the company of a town notable, an excellent alibi. Probing beneath the *façade* of the seemingly prosperous and contented village society, Roger must uncover deep pockets of greed and jealousy if he is to uncover the truth. Associates: Margaret; Elizabeth; Thomas Cozin, Warder of Totnes; Oliver Cozin, his twin, a lawyer.

5. *The Eve of Saint Hyacinth*. London: Headline, 1995, 280 p.

TOTNES, AND LONDON, ENGLAND; CALAIS, FRANCE DURING THE CAMPAIGN, MAY–SEPTEMBER 1475. Roger returns to London for a few badly needed days of rest and entertainment after a busy spring spent peddling wares—and solving two murders—along England's southern coast. His conscience tells him he should be visiting his mother-in-law, Margaret Walker, who is caring for Roger's six-month-old daughter, Elizabeth, but the pleasures of the big city beckon. In the meantime, King Edward IV is about to invade France with a great show of force, although rumors abound that the king is reluctant to undertake the enterprise. As the campaign approaches, a spy is discovered in the household of Roger's mentor, the Duke of Gloucester; all information indicates that the infiltrator is part of a conspiracy to assassinate the duke before the invasion—on the Eve of Saint Hyacinth. Roger, the only person Richard trusts to uncover the traitor, must work quickly to prevent the assassination and prove his loyalty to Gloucester. Associates: Timothy; Philip; Elizabeth; Margaret. Historical Figures: British King Edward IV; French King Louis XI; Richard, Duke of Gloucester; George, Duke of Clarence.

6. *The Wicked Winter.* London: Headline, 1996, 282 p.

BRISTOL, AND CEDERWELL MANOR ON THE RIVER SEVERN, ENGLAND, JANUARY 1476. Despite the wintry weather, Roger is once again relishing the freedom of his calling. As he journeys west, he finds himself following in the footsteps of an itinerant preacher, Brother Simeon, whose fiery sermons are the talk of the countryside. Roger, who has met the Dominican, finds his zeal wearying and is less than enthused when they meet up at Cederwell Manor, where the peddler has hopes of selling his wares. Instead, the two men find the Lady of the manor, Jeanette Cederwell, dead, sprawled on the frozen earth beneath the ancient tower she had converted into a chapel. Roger is convinced her death is murder and begins to investigate. Before he can identify the killer, however, two more people are killed. Three bodies are enough for any mystery, and Roger must bring all of his skills into play in order to discover the identity of the vicious killer. Associates: Margaret; Elizabeth.

7. *The Brothers of Glastonbury.* London: Headline, 1997, 279 p.

GLASTONBURY, ENGLAND, AUGUST 1476. Roger is happy to be nearing the end of his seasonal travels. As much as he enjoys being on the road, he's looking forward to spending the winter with his mother-in-law and daughter. God has other plans for the Chapman, however. Roger's path crosses that of one of his old acquaintances, the Duke of Clarence, and he is asked to do the Duke a favor, an offer he can't refuse. One of the Duke's retainers, William Armstrong, has a difficulty. His daughter Cicely's *fiancé*, Peter Gildersleeve (who is also her cousin), had planned to collect her from the Duke's residence to take her home for their wedding, but he has failed to appear. Her father cannot leave the Duke's service, so Roger is asked to escort young Cicely home to Glastonbury. Roger grudgingly complies but is uncomfortable with the situation he finds when they arrive. Peter has vanished without a trace, and the local villagers are looking askance at her family and muttering about witchcraft. Peter's brother, Mark, hints that he might know where Peter is, but when he goes to search for him, Mark also disappears. Roger feels duty-bound to stay and help the family find the reasons behind the mysterious disappearances. Indeed, he is ideally suited for the task, since he was once a novice at Glastonbury Abbey and is well acquainted with the community. He is startled to discover his investigations involve an ancient manuscript that could lead straight to the Holy Grail! Associates: Margaret; Elizabeth. Historical Figures: George, Duke of Clarence; Isabel, Duchess of Clarence; Bishop Robert Stillington.

8. *The Weaver's Inheritance*. London: Headline, 1998, 247 p.

BRISTOL, ENGLAND, CHRISTMAS 1476–JANUARY 1477. After a hard winter hawking his wares through the ice and rain, Roger is looking forward to spending Christmas in Bristol, enjoying the warm hearth and good food of his mother-in-law, Margaret, even if he must endure her constant matchmaking. However, Margaret has barely introduced him to her cousin, Adela, when Roger's attentions are demanded elsewhere. Clement, the long-lost son of Roger's old mentor, Alderman Weaver, and presumed murdered six years earlier, has reappeared, to the joy of his elderly father, but to the indignation of his sister, Alison *née* Weaver Burnett, who refuses to believe the bedraggled stranger's story. When Alison's violent objections provoke the alderman into disinheriting her, she appeals to Roger to prove her suspicions are correct. Associates: Margaret; Elizabeth, Adela (Woodward) Juett, Margaret's cousin, who becomes Roger's second wife; her son, Nicholas; Alfred; Alison; William; Richard Manifold, the local sheriff, who also finds Adela of interest; Timothy; Jack Nym, the alderman's carter. Historical Figures: British King Edward IV; Richard, Duke of Gloucester; George, Duke of Clarence.

9. *The Saint John's Fern*. London: Headline, 1999, 246 p.

BRISTOL, AND PLYMOUTH, ENGLAND, AUGUST–OCTOBER 1477. Twenty-five-year-old Roger has been married to Adela for four months. All seems to be going well with his little family, especially since his daughter Elizabeth ("Bess") and Adela's son Nicholas ("Nick"), both three-year-olds, seem to be accepting each other just fine. His mother-in-law from his first marriage, Margaret Walker, has also settled into the arrangement, as a kinswoman of Adela. Poor Roger's restless nature takes hold of him once again, however, and sensing somehow that he is "needed" in Plymouth, he hitches a ride with Peter Threadgold, who is traveling there to visit his daughter, Joanna. Roger learns from Joanna that someone has viciously beaten her neighbor, Master Capstick, to death. What's more, witnesses saw the victim's great-nephew, Beric Gilford, leaving the scene of the crime. When the King's men come to arrest the man, however, he has vanished, and the townspeople suspect witchcraft, through the application of Saint John's fern, which has made Beric invisible. Roger begins to investigate, and his questions lead to several attempts on his life, not to mention the growing rumors that he was involved in a second homicide. Associates: Margaret; Adela; Elizabeth "Bess" and Nicholas "Nick," their children. Historical Figures: British King Edward IV; George, Duke of Clarence.

10. *The Goldsmith's Daughter*. Sutton, Surrey: Severn House, 2001, 214 p.

BRISTOL, AND LONDON, ENGLAND, CHRISTMAS 1477–FEBRUARY 1478. King Edward IV trembles as he tries to decide the fate of his younger and treacherous sibling, George, the Duke of Clarence. And Richard, Duke of Gloucester, the other brother, is desperate to find some way to save George from being put to death. When the Duke spies his old and loyal servant, monk-turned-peddler Roger the Chapman, among the crowd at a trial he pounces on the opportunity. If only Roger can prove that Isolda Bonifant, daughter of a well-established London goldsmith and kinswoman of the King's favorite mistress, didn't poisoned her taciturn husband, Gideon, she could be proved innocent and her name cleared. Then Edward's chief mistress, Jane Shore, a cousin of the accused Isolda, would be more than a little willing to do the wily Duke's bidding. But Roger must act quickly. In such a delicate case and with Richard of Gloucester breathing down his neck, he cannot rely simply on his intuition but must bring all his skills into play. Associates: Adela; Elizabeth; Nicholas; Margaret; Jack; Richard; Timothy; Philip and Jeanne Lamprey. Historical Figures: British King Edward IV; Richard, Duke of Gloucester; George, Duke of Clarence.

11. *The Lammas Feast.* Sutton, Surrey: Severn House, 2002, 250 p.

BRISTOL, ENGLAND, JULY 1478. Business is good for Bristol's bakers during the days leading up to Lammastide, "Loaf-Mass," the ancient harvest festival. But the shady Jasper Fairbrother's baking days are over when he's found facedown with a knife in his back. Suspicion immediately falls on a mysterious Breton who had arrived that day and who had been observed arguing with Fairbrother. But when it emerges that the Breton is also a suspected Lancastrian spy, Roger the Chapman wonders if suspicion of murder is merely a convenient pretext for the authorities to hunt down the suspicious stranger. Although there is no good reason for Roger to take an interest in the case, especially when he should be peddling his wares in order to provide for his new baby, his insatiable curiosity and sense of justice are piqued; and before he can discover the identity of the murderer, he is destined to become personally involved when the people nearest and dearest to his heart are threatened. At the end of the story, Roger and Adela inherit a new house (and a dog) for their growing family. Associates: Adela; Nicholas; Adam, Roger's newborn child; Margaret; Richard; Cecily, now a lay sister at the Magdalen Nunnery; Timothy; Philip; Hercules, the dog Roger inherits. Historical Figure: Richard, Duke of Gloucester.

12. *Nine Men Dancing.* Sutton, Surrey: Severn House, 2003, 252 p.

LOWER BROCKHURST, ENGLAND, JANUARY–MARCH 1478. It is bitter winter, and Roger the Chapman is suffering from "cabin fever." He leaves the lovely new house he's inherited (and furnished with the gold coins given him by the Duke of Gloucester), and takes to the roads once again to sell his wares. His long-suffering wife, Adela, is just as glad to see him go but exacts a promise from him to return by the feast of St. Patrick in March.

Roger has a successful, but uneventful, journey; having sold most of his goods, he begins the long trek homeward, keen on surprising Adela by arriving early for once. However, after taking an unfamiliar path and losing his way, he stumbles upon the tiny village of Lower Brockhurst, where he is immediately made welcome at the local tavern. While he rests and eats, he overhears conversations regarding the recent disappearance of a local girl. Roger's investigative instincts are instantly aroused, and he determines to solve the mystery. Has she really just vanished? But Roger soon realizes there is more to the girl's story than meets the eye and that the village harbors dark secrets that some people would do anything to prevent being discovered. At the end of the story, Roger must resist temptation in the form of Rosamund Bush, the alehouse owner's comely young daughter. He does and returns to Adela and his comfortable new home by St. Patrick's Day. Associates: Adela; Elizabeth; Nicholas; Adam; Margaret; Hercules. Historical Figure: Richard, Duke of Gloucester.

13. *The Midsummer Rose.* Sutton, Surrey: Severn House, 2004, 249 p.

BRISTOL, ENGLAND, 1478? Roger the Chapman is not a superstitious man. He hears stories of murders and haunted houses around the market town of Bristol and chooses to believe the more prosaic explanation every time. But when Roger is himself attacked in the very house where a woman murdered her violent husband thirty years previously, he is forced to admit something strange is going on, particularly when everybody he encounters denies seeing or hearing anything untoward in the notorious house that stormy night. And when even his own wife refuses to believe his story, he begins to worry that he is losing his mind. Indignant and instinctively curious, Roger puts his detective skills into action once again to find out who made the attempt on his life. He soon learns more and more about the strange old house and about the people of the market town of Bristol, some of whom have much more to hide than he would ever have believed. Associates: Adela; Nicholas; Elizabeth; Adam; Margaret.

STEVENS, Rosemary (Anne) (1935–). American.

BEAU BRUMMEL SERIES

Scene of the Crime: England, beginning in 1805. The author has stated, in a *Crescent Blues* interview, that she will end the series before 1811, when Brummell fell from favor in real life.

Detective: George "Beau" Brummell (born 1778) has made his reputation in society as a man of wit, loyalty, and impeccable taste, rising through his friendship with the Prince of Wales (later King George IV). He sets the fashion in England, moving men from powdered wigs, makeup, and extravagantly colored clothing to a more sober style that includes frequent baths (and hence, less scent), and clothing of excellent cut rather than extravagant decoration. As depicted in these books, he will go to any lengths to assist his friends and is the soul of kindness, having empathy with people who are less fortunate than himself and willing to stand with them as their protector.

Known Associates: A number of historical figures are depicted in these books, including the Duchess of York (Freddie), the Prince of Wales (Prinny), Viscount Petersham (one of Beau's closest friends), Robinson (Beau's manservant), and John Lavender (of the Bow Street Runners). Fictional characters include John Lavender's daughter, Miss Lydia Lavender, who runs the Haven of Hope shelter for abused and abandoned women; Lionel, whom Miss Lavender hires in *The Bloodied Cravat*; Sylvester Fairingdale, a popinjay who is eager to cause trouble for Beau; and Chakkri, a Siamese cat given to Beau when he leaves the field open for the ambassador from Siam to purchase a Perronneau painting of a cat in *Death on a Silver Tray*.

Premise: A gentleman solves crimes in early nineteenth-century England.

Comment: Brummell's grandfather had rented lodgings to members of the British aristocracy. He saved enough money as landlord to educate his son (Beau's father), who rose to the position of private secretary to Prime Minister Lord North. He saw to it that Beau received a gentleman's education but could not provide him with a gentleman's wealth. Beau's reputation is his fortune, however; it allows him to live on credit and on his friendship to the Prince of Wales. His impeccable personal style has made him a leader in society. He's smart and observant of details but has no intention of becoming involved in solving crimes, until the woman he worships, the Duchess of York, asks for his help. These are light reads, reminiscent of Regency romances, with a touch of the supernatural being provided by Chakkri the cat, who does his best to communicate the solutions to Beau. Beau is a likable character with somewhat self-deprecating humor. He seems to regard himself as nothing more than an arbiter of fashion and to desire that everyone around him see him as just that. He does his best to conceal his tender heart, while helping those around him. This manifests itself in everything from dancing with girls that were (previously) unpopular, to clearing the reputations of those wrongfully accused of crimes.

Literary Crimes & Chimes: These books are very well researched; the author provides historical notes on the characters at the beginning of each book. Even some of the more outlandish rumors about Beau Brummell are recognized. For example, the author has Brummell laugh and encourage his manservant to support the silliest of the rumors, partly for amusement and partly to keep his name on the lips of the *Beau Monde*. The fascination with fashion and with ideal comportment does not overwhelm the narrative. Beau's occasional worries over gambling debts, living beyond his means, and the fickleness of royal favor foreshadow his ultimate fate without belaboring it.

THE CASES

1. *Death on a Silver Tray*. New York: Berkley Prime Crime, 2000, 277 p.

LONDON, ENGLAND, 1805. Beau's contemplation of a painting that he intends to purchase is disrupted by an unpleasant scene, the harridan Lady Wrayburn berating her gentle companion Miss Ashton. The next morning Lady Wrayburn is found poisoned. The Duchess of York asks Beau to clear Miss Ashton's name. Associate: Penelope. Historical Figure: Freddie, Duchess of York.

2. *The Tainted Snuff Box*. New York: Berkley Prime Crime, 2001, 292 p.

BRIGHTON, ENGLAND, 1805. Petersham doesn't realize that he's in danger of being accused of attempted regicide, when the snuff that he has offered to the Prince of Wales causes Sir Simon, the Prince's self-appointed food-taster, to die. Beau must attempt to clear his friend but runs the risk of social ruin if the Prince does not like the truths that are uncovered. Associates: Lord and Lady Perry; Tallarico. Historical Figure: George, Prince of Wales.

3. *The Bloodied Cravat*. New York: Berkley Prime Crime, 2002, 291 p.

OATLANDS, ENGLAND, 1806. Highwaymen waylay Robinson's coach as he travels to Oatlands with Beau's luggage. Along with the clothing, they get Beau's most precious possession, an indiscreet letter written by the Duchess of York. An associate of the robbers soon makes himself known by blackmailing the Duchess; when he is found dead and the letter is not in his possession, Beau has two mysteries to solve. Associates: Lord and Lady Perry, Tallarico, Penelope. Historical Figure: Freddie, Duchess of York.

4. *Murder in the Pleasure Gardens*. New York: Berkley Prime Crime, 2003, 241 p.

LONDON, ENGLAND, 1807. When Beau opens his own gaming club (with food superior to White's), he has no idea that his responsibilities would include saving young men from their folly, excusing their gambling debts, talking them out of suicide, or calming them before they issue challenges. Lieutenant Nevill may take more saving than Beau can provide, when the man who called him out (the well-respected Mr. Jacombe) turns up dead in the Pleasure Gardens at Vauxhall. Who will save Beau, who, in a fit of fury when Jacombe insults Miss Lavender, agrees to stand as Lieutenant Nevill's Second? Associate: Tallarico.

STEWARD, Barbara, and Dwight Steward. American.

EDGAR ALLAN POE SERIES

Scene of the Crime: Washington, DC, 1865, and France, 1889.

Detective: Edgar Allan Poe, the American writer, born 1809, supposedly died in 1849, living in Washington, DC, in 1865 and in Europe in 1889.

Known Associates: Elizabeth Cleone, young American actress (*The Lincoln Diddle*); Wilmot Rufus Griswold, young American salesman traveling in France (*Evermore*).

Premise: The well-known mystery and horror author Edgar Allan Poe has staged his own death in Baltimore in 1849 and then lives in the United States and Europe under his new *nom de guerre*, Henri Le Rennet, becoming a practitioner of phrenology and similar pseudosciences and conducting discrete investigations and solving crimes for the rich and famous.

Comment: Neither Le Rennet/Poe nor Griswold are attractive characters, with the former coming across as a cantankerous old goat, and Griswold (on all too many occasions) as a fool. Cleone is a typical second-rate ingenue. In the first book in the series, Poe solves the mystery of the death of Prince Rudolph, heir to the throne of Austria; in the second, he tackles the assassination of President Abraham Lincoln.

Literary Crimes & Chimes: Both books appear historically faithful to their periods, bringing in numerous obscure and little-known curiosities into the narratives. The solution of *Evermore* is ingenious, although one scarcely can gain enough enthusiasm even to clap at the *dénouement*. Neither case is directly connected to the other, save for the character of Poe himself and through the introduction of *The Lincoln Diddle*, in which Cleone corresponds with Griswold in 1901/1902 to transmit her written remembrances of the 1865 case.

THE CASES

1. *The Lincoln Diddle*. New York: William Morrow, 1979, 251 p.

WASHINGTON, DC, 1865. Elizabeth Cleone, an aspiring young actress on the American stage, recounts the story of her brief affair with Henri Le Rennet and how they were both (together with writer Walt Whitman) drawn into investigating the assassination of President Lincoln through their some-time association with John Wilkes Booth. In the end, Elizabeth comes to the conclusion that Le Rennet is indeed the supposedly deceased writer Edgar Allan Poe, who demonstrates his genius once again by coming to a startling reassessment of Lincoln's murder. Historical Figures: Walt Whitman; John Wilkes Booth; President Abraham Lincoln.

2. Evermore. New York: William Morrow, 1978, 202 p.

FRANCE, 1889. Wilmot Griswold, the Baltimore nephew of a biographer of the late Edgar Allan Poe, is amazed to discover the writer himself resident while on a business trip to France in 1889. When the *émigré* author is petitioned by Empress Elisabeth of Austria to solve the supposed murder of her only son, Crown Prince Rudolph, Griswold becomes Poe's sidekick and narrator during the ensuing chase. The Afterword by Griswold, providing a summation of the events, is dated 1900. Historical Figures: Austrian Empress Elisabeth; Austrian Crown Prince Rudolph.

TODD, Charles (pseud. of David Todd Watjen and Carolyn L. Teachey Watjen). American.

INSPECTOR IAN RUTLEDGE SERIES

Scene of the Crime: England, beginning in 1919.

Detective: Inspector Ian Rutledge was an extraordinary policeman in 1914; his intuition, coupled with the understanding that it takes hard evidence to gain a conviction, made him a rising star at Scotland Yard. Then he went to war. In 1916 an exploding shell nearly buried him alive. He was found under the body of Corporal Hamish MacLeod and was sent back into battle, with the voice of the dead Hamish as his constant companion. His fear of living is greater than his fear of dying, so he put himself into danger again and again and was bitterly amused to find himself hailed as a hero. After the war, in 1919, he returns to Scotland Yard, afraid to rely on his intuition, partly because it seems akin to the voice in his head, which has been diagnosed as a manifestation of shell shock. He is tall and thin, drawn and weary; afraid that others will consider him insane and take him away from his work, which is all that is keeping him sane.

Known Associates: Corporal Hamish MacLeod, killed in the trenches in France but still Rutledge's constant companion in his brain; Chief Superintendent Bowles, Rutledge's superior, a man so eaten up with envy that he prays and schemes for Rutledge's failure; Frances, his advocate, his supporter, and his nagging sister; Jean, his *fiancée*, who was so frightened of the man that he had become that she broke off the engagement; he still compares all other women to her.

Premise: A shell-shocked policeman solves crimes and deals with his own internal demons in early twentieth-century Britain.

Comment: The caustic, irreverent voice of Corporal Hamish MacLeod continually haunts Inspector Rutledge. He has discovered that he cannot silence the ghost through any act of will, and so he lives in an uneasy stalemate with his dead companion. As the series opens, Rutledge is trying to gather together the shards of his life, no longer sure that he has the skill or the nerve to continue, afraid that his comrades will realize that he suffers from shell shock and take his work away from him. The demands of his job, the concentration it takes to understand each crime and find the murderer, brings exhaustion and dreamless sleep. These are the things that keep his madness at bay. Throughout the books the villains, witnesses, and bystanders are people who have been scarred, mentally and physically, by the "Great War." Men like Rutledge are unable to escape their experience of the horror. The women who spent the war years in fear that their husbands or lovers would never return must now cope with the damaged individuals who have returned to them. The men who proudly claim that a badly maimed brother or cousin is doing "just fine" will never be troubled by the memories of those who survived the trenches. The lingering effects of the war on the survivors pervades the series.

Literary Crimes & Chimes: Rutledge is, at the outset, a sympathetic character, simply because he is so quietly and desperately engaged in so many private battles with himself. From the outset the reader can feel the pettiness of Bowles, Rutledge's superior on the force. Bowles takes pleasure in giving Rutledge assignments that are political minefields. Another cross that Rutledge faces on a daily basis is the constant verbal duel with the voice of Hamish, whom the Inspector saw killed in the trenches and who now lives on in his memories. The authors portray the actions and reactions of the members of small communities particularly well. Gossip is a force to be reckoned with, and the community can close its doors against outsiders at any time—even a member of Scotland Yard. These are tough, compelling fictions, as stark at times as anything available in the literature, but well worth the investment of a little time and effort on the part of the reader.

THE CASES

1. "The Man Who Never Was," in *Malice Domestic 9*, ed. by Joan Hess. New York: Avon Books, 2000, p. 141–149.

NEAR THE FRONT IN FRANCE DURING WORLD WAR I. Private Romney has died, not of a bullet but of a hole in his gas mask. As his commanding officer, Ian Rutledge sorts through Romney's personal possessions preparatory to sending them home, he makes a disquieting discovery. Who was Romney, and how and why did his gas mask fail? Associate: Corporal Hamish MacLeod (alive).

2. *A Test of Wills.* New York: St. Martin's Press, 1996, 282 p.

WARWICKSHIRE, ENGLAND, JUNE 1919. Everyone (well, almost everyone) admires, likes, and respects Colonel Harris; no one in the village can understand why anyone would have shot him out of his saddle at point-blank range. The case becomes a political hot potato when it is discovered that a witness saw the local war hero arguing with a colonel just before the murder. The witness is a badly shell-shocked veteran; Rutledge knows that the man's reputation and also knows that his mind would be shredded by the hero's defense counsel. He must find a solution before the case comes to trial. Associates: Miss Catherine Tarrant; MacLeod.

3. *Wings of Fire.* New York: St. Martin's Press, 1998, 294 p.

CORNWALL, ENGLAND, JUNE 1919. A serial killer is hunting in London, and Bowles wants Rutledge, the golden boy, out of the way. When the Home Office asks the Yard to look into three well-explained and investigated deaths, Rutledge is sent to Cornwall. Everyone expects Rutledge to certify the conclusions of the local police; instead, he finds a trail of murder, vengeance, and evil traversing decades and almost destroying one family. Associates: O. A. Manning (Olivia Alison Marlowe); MacLeod; Bowles.

4. *Search the Dark.* New York: Thomas Dunne Books, 1999, 279 p.

DORSET, ENGLAND, AUGUST 1919. Bert Mowbray was told that his wife and children had died in London, while he was away fighting the war in France. Years later, he spots them unexpectedly at a train station and goes into a fury when he believes that his wife faked her own death so that she could take the children and leave him. When she is found dead, Rutledge feels that the most pressing problem is to discover what happened to the children who were with her at the station. Associate: MacLeod.

5. *Legacy of the Dead: An Inspector Ian Rutledge Mystery.* New York: Bantam Books, 2000, 308 p.

DURHAM, SCOTLAND, SEPTEMBER 1919. A campaign of anonymous letters turns the town against one young woman. Then they try to take her child away, and then she is accused of a crime that would send her to the gallows. Rutledge is brought into the case on behalf of both the living and the dead. Associates: Fiona; David Trevor; MacLeod.

6. *Watchers of Time: An Inspector Ian Rutledge Mystery.* New York: Bantam Books, 2001, 339 p.

NORFOLK, ENGLAND, OCTOBER 1919. A dying man (thought to be a good Anglican) shocks his family by demanding to see a priest. A few weeks later the priest is murdered and his study ransacked, and the paltry parish funds pilfered. The local police believe that Father James was a chance casualty of a panicked burglar, not the target of a murderer. The Bishop is concerned enough to ask Scotland Yard to send someone to look into what seems an open-and-shut case. Associates: Marianna Elizabeth Trent (May); Arthur Sedgwick; MacLeod.

7. *A Fearsome Doubt: An Inspector Ian Rutledge Mystery.* New York: Bantam Books, 2002, 395 p.

KENT, ENGLAND, NOVEMBER 1919. As England nears the anniversary of the armistice, ghosts from the past plague Rutledge. He is faced with evidence that a man he once helped convict may have been innocent, and he catches a momentary glimpse of a soldier he had believed dead. Rutledge has always taken his duty to the dead very seriously; now he must investigate to find some peace for the living and some justice for the dead. A powerful man is determined to thwart his case. Associates: Elizabeth Mayhew; Melinda Crawford; MacLeod.

TOURNEY, Leonard D(on) (1942–). American.

MATTHEW AND JOAN STOCK SERIES

Scene of the Crime: Chelmsford, Essex, and London, England, beginning in 1595.

Detective: County Constable Matthew Stock, a humble clothier by trade, and his practical-minded wife, Joan, the real brains behind their team. Their shop in Chelmsford is located on High Street. Stock is appointed Acting Constable of Chelmsford in 1595, after his predecessor dies, and is soon confirmed in that position.

Known Associates: British Queen Elizabeth I (who dies March 1603); Elizabeth Stock, daughter of Matthew and Joan; Peter Bench, assistant shopkeeper to Matthew Stock; Sir Robert Cecil, son of Lord Burleigh, Principal Secretary to the Queen and Matthew's employer.

Premise: A county constable and his wife solve crimes in Renaissance England, while serving as agents for Sir Robert Cecil, Principal Secretary and minister to Queen Elizabeth I.

Comment: The Joan and Matthew Stock series began as fairly standard small-town mysteries set in a closed environment but gradually evolved into something very different, as Matthew began serving as an agent for Sir Robert Cecil, Queen Elizabeth's righthand man. The last few books in the sequence, particularly *Witness of Bones,* ratchet up the tension significantly, with

Matthew being accused of murder and Cecil unable to help him during the final chaotic days of Queen Bess' reign. Matthew is a fairly stolid detective, as befits his chosen profession; it's Joan who has the flashes of insight needed to solve many of these cases, and it's Joan who manages to save her husband in the final novel in the sequence.

Literary Crimes & Chimes: The final years of Queen Elizabeth I's reign were filled with plots and counterplots, and Tourney does an excellent job of navigating through the morass of Papists, Protestants, and politicos, all seeking to establish and enable their own agendas in the power vacuum soon to come. The Stocks represent, even through their rather mundane surnames, the good country "stock" that sustains Olde Engelonde in times of crisis. Sir Robert Cecil is portrayed as a man walking a political tightrope, trying to avoid falling into the abyss as his patron is dying. Tourney has the details of this period just right; the tension that filled public and private life, when everyone had constantly to watch his or her back, comes through very well indeed. Some of the plots are less than sterling, but overall, these novels deserve a new resurrection by the publishing world. Recommended.

THE CASES

1. *Frobisher's Savage: A Joan and Matthew Stock Mystery.* New York: St. Martin's Press, 1994, 264 p.

LONDON, AND CHELMSFORD, ESSEX, ENGLAND, FEBRUARY 1595 (the Prologue is dated 1576). In 1576 Sir Martin Frobisher made the first of three voyages in search of a Northwest Passage. He got as far as Canada and brought back to England two "proofs" that he had reached Cathay: some black stones that he claimed contained gold and an Eskimo. Frobisher's Eskimo is given the name "Adam Nemo" and is set down on the estate of a wealthy landowner as a servant. He learns the strange language of his captors, performs his duties most conscientiously, but keeps to himself. And then everything changes. Visiting his only friend on a nearby farm, a deaf and mute youth named Nicholas, Adam finds the boy cowering in a corner. Everywhere he sees signs of a bloody massacre. When the townsmen whom Adam summons arrive, they discover the mutilated bodies of the farmer, his wife, and their two youngest children. Merchant Matthew Stock, in his first role as recently appointed Acting County Constable, tries to counteract the town's growing hysteria, which fastens itself upon those that they consider strangers—the "savage" and the "idiot." Matthew and his forthright wife, Joan, are firmly convinced of the pair's innocence and are determined that the rule of law shall prevail. There is more than one hair-raising episode, and a breathless pursuit through a snowstorm, before Joan Stock finally unearths the evidence to identify the real murderer. The usual associates are absent here.

2. ***The Players' Boy Is Dead.*** New York: Harper & Row, 1980, 192 p.

LONDON AND CHELMSFORD, ESSEX, ENGLAND, OCTOBER 1600–APRIL 1601. They were a small players' troupe come to perform for a lord and his lady, and none of the ragtag group shone more than the young players' boy, with his flaxen hair and fine features. Indeed, he had won a scullery maid's heart, and it was she who, at cock's crow, went searching for him in the stables where he slept. But, alas, she found him dead, murdered most gruesomely. And now Constable Matthew Stock must search high and low, from a lord's castle to a disreputable inn, to find the person who dealt such an ungodly blow. Historical Figure: Sir Robert Cecil.

3. ***Low Treason.*** New York: Dutton, 1982, 233 p.

LONDON AND CHELMSFORD, ESSEX, ENGLAND, SPRING 1601. Matthew Stock's young relation, Thomas, leaves home to apprentice himself to Castell, a jeweler in London. Then he disappears. Castell writes to say Thomas has gone to sea, but Stock decides that he must investigate the matter himself; such a move is quite unlike the boy. While Stock is away, Thomas returns and tells Joan how the jeweler tried to have him killed. He had discovered that Castell is blackmailing high-ranking members of Elizabeth's court. Joan must rush to London to warn her husband of the danger. For Matthew has no idea of the peril he is in, as he questions the ruthless Castell about Thomas' fate. Associates: Elizabeth; Thomas Ingram. Historical Figure: Sir Robert Cecil.

4. ***The Bartholomew Fair Murders.*** New York: St. Martin's Press, 1986, 232 p.

CHELMSFORD, ESSEX, AND LONDON, ENGLAND, JUNE–SEPTEMBER 1601. Queen Elizabeth the Great will go to Bartholomew Fair—and a wondrous fair it is, drawing people from all over the land, among them the goodly couple Matthew and Joan Stock. But their initial pleasure in the hurly-burly is tempered by the murder of a puppeteer on the road to the fairgrounds. This is an odd murder indeed, for the killer has left strange markings on the dead man's forehead. But the real target of the killer is Queen Bess herself! Historical Figures: British Queen Elizabeth I; Sir Robert Cecil.

5. ***Familiar Spirits.*** New York: St. Martin's Press, 1984, 230 p.

LONDON, AND CHELMSFORD, ESSEX, ENGLAND, SEPTEMBER–OCTOBER 1602. The town of Chelmsford is going mad with the frenzy of witch-hunting. Neighbors accuse one another with no cause, hysterical at the sudden death of a townsman and sightings of an apparition of a dead young woman. But Constable Matthew Stock will have none of it. Sensible, down-to-earth, and aided by the quiet intelligence of his good wife, Joan, he doubts the accusers but seems helpless to save the accused. As the village becomes inflamed with terror, Matthew cleverly begins to piece together a deceptively simple tale of innocence and guilt, heaven and hell, to reveal the long-hidden secrets behind the strange bewitching. The usual associates are absent here.

6. *Old Saxon Blood: A Novel.* New York: St. Martin's Press, 1988, 250 p.

LONDON AND CHELMSFORD, ESSEX, ENGLAND, NOVEMBER 1602 (the Prologue is dated 1601). The Coroner's verdict was death by misadventure, but to Matthew Stock and his wife, Joan—Queen Bess' secret investigators—it's clear that Sir John Challoner was murdered, for no man drowns and then climbs back into his own boat. But finding the killer is thorny work. The castle servants are sullen, the neighboring gentry abusive. When someone hides the headless body of a serving maid in their chamber, even the level-headed Stocks fear the strange spirit of evil that haunts the castle. Before long, the bone-chilling outlines of something much deeper and darker than mere murder begin to take shape. Historical Figures: British Queen Elizabeth I; Sir Robert Cecil.

7. *Knaves Templar.* New York: St. Martin's Press, 1991, 282 p.

LONDON, ENGLAND, DECEMBER 1602–JANUARY 1603. Someone is killing the law students of Temple Bar, making their murders appear suicides. Constable Matthew Stock is called in to investigate the mysterious deaths, posing as a gentleman whose son is seeking admission to study at the prestigious Middle Temple. At first, Matthew's wife, Joan, wants nothing more than to leave London and return to the Stocks' home in Chelmsford in time for Christmas. But the case piques her curiosity, and she stays to play her own part in the circuitous investigation, despite Matthew's enjoining that the Inns of Court and their environs are no fit place for a woman. While Matthew pursues the traditional avenues of inquiry among the denizens of the Inns of Court, Joan does detective work of a different kind in Elizabethan London's seedier quarters and has some harrowing experiences among the bawdy, brawling patrons of the infamous Gull Tavern. Historical Figure: Sir Robert Cecil.

8. *Witness of Bones.* New York: St. Martin's Press, 1992, 262 p.

CHELMSFORD, ESSEX, AND LONDON, ENGLAND, MARCH 1603. The merchant constable Matthew Stock and his likable wife, Joan, have just returned home from London after successfully solving a most heinous series of murders. Eager to resume their relatively peaceful existence in Chelmsford, they are nonetheless immediately immersed in another adventure, their most consequential one yet. As the end draws nigh for British Queen Elizabeth I, various factions are maneuvering to seize control of the throne of England and all the power, wealth, and glory it entails. The most devious scheme begins with a "resurrection" in the graveyard of a controversial church and continues with the murder of a priest, a murder for which Matthew is deliberately framed! With Matthew's life at stake, the Stocks must bring all their powers of detection and deduction to the fore. Historical Figure: Sir Robert Cecil.

WILLIAM SHAKESPEARE SERIES

Scene of the Crime: London and elsewhere in England, beginning in 1603.

Detective: William Shakespeare, the real-life British poet and playwright (1564–1616).

Known Associates: Anne Shakespeare, the poet's wife; the Dark Lady; Sir Robert Cecil, minister to King James I; Ben Jonson, the playwright.

Premise: A British playwright investigates crimes in seventeenth-century London.

Comment: When Shakespeare is contacted by his "dark lady," the former love of his life, he is excited to see her again, but the illusion is soon shattered: disease-ridden and near death, she intends to blackmail him, threatening to expose their former affair to the world unless he pays her physician's bills. A sudden fire cuts short both their meeting and her life. The writer soon learns that the conflagration was no accident, that he is being stalked by someone obsessed with ruining his life. Hope arrives in the person of a small boy who happened to witness the crime. Then the lad is also killed, with Shakespeare the prime suspect. Now out on bail, the poet must fight a race with his own potential death to find the culprit and clear his good name.

Literary Crimes & Chimes: Tourney knows his period well, and he makes good use of the people, places, and things of post-Elizabethan England. One has a sense of actually being there, of experiencing the sorrows and joys of the playwright as he experiences his ordeal. The one problem with the novel, and it's a major one, is that the story is told by Shakespeare himself in the first person. Anyone with a knowledge of English literature knows Shakespeare's voice, has heard it over and over it again echoing throughout his plays and verse. Tourney's voice, while compelling, is not Shakespeare's, not even close, and the difference and distinction are far more jarring than they would have been with any other playwright the writer might have chosen. With anyone else, the reader could have made the leap to suspend disbelief willingly. Alas and alack, that it cannot be so here.

THE CASE

1. *Time's Fool: A Mystery of Shakespeare.* New York: Forge, 2004, 320 p.
LONDON, AND ELSEWHERE IN ENGLAND, DECEMBER 1603. See commentary in this series.

TREMAYNE, Peter (pseud. of Peter Berresford Ellis) (1943–). British.

SISTER FIDELMA SERIES

Scene of the Crime: Ireland, beginning in 664.

Detective: Sister Fidelma was born in 636, the youngest daughter of King Faílbe Fland of Muman (Munster), who died in 637. A former member of the community of St. Brigid of Kildare, she becomes an advocate of the ancient courts of Ireland under the system known as the Brehon Laws. As such, it is her duty to investigate crimes, serve as prosecutor or defender in the courts, and, where necessary, render final judgment.

Known Associates: Saxon Brother Eadulf, Fidelma's faithful companion, who becomes her husband under Irish law (from *The Haunted Abbot*); Colmán, Chief Professor of the Blessed Finnbarr's College in Cork; Colgú mac Failbe Faland, Fidelma's brother.

Premise: Sister Fidelma and her companion, Brother Eadulf (who becomes her husband halfway through the series), investigate crimes and solve mysteries in seventh-century Ireland, Britain, and Europe.

Comment: It should be remembered, while reading this series, that Sister Fidelma is not simply a religieuse, a former member of the community of St. Brigid of Kildare but also a qualified advocate of the ancient law courts of Ireland. Seventh-century Ireland was governed by a system of sophisticated regulations known popularly as the Brehon Laws. Under these, women occupied a unique place, enjoying rights and protection not available in any other Western legal code until modern times. Women could, and did, aspire to all offices and professions as co-equals to their brethren. They could command their people in battle and serve as physicians, magistrates, lawyers, and judges. They were protected by law against sexual harassment, discrimination, and rape. They had the right of divorce with equitable separation laws, and they had the right to inherit personal property. This background, with its strong contrast to Ireland's neighbors, puts Sister Fidelma's position in perspective. She was trained in the laws of her land and is thus qualified by law to practice as an advocate. Her main role is to gather and assess the evidence in a case, independent of the police or government. At times, she can be called upon to serve as a prosecutor or defender in the court or even to render judgment herself. At this time, celibacy, while encouraged, was not yet universal in the Irish or Celtic Church. The condemnation of the "sins of the flesh" was an alien concept to the Celts. In Fidelma's world, both sexes inhabited the abbeys and monastic foundations, which were commonly known as "conhospitae," or "double houses," where men and women lived, cohabited, and raised their children in the service of Jesus Christ.

Literary Crimes & Chimes: Sister Fidelma is one of the most compelling of the historic detectives covered. It is disconcerting from a modern sensibility to realize that this seventh-century woman had, in many ways, more freedom, privileges, and rights than many in our modern world. The series must be read with a full comprehension of the customs and laws of the world through which Fidelma and her companion, Eadulf, move, particularly when, halfway through the series, the two marry with the full blessing of church and state. The dichotomy between the liberal Celtic community and its more rigid Saxon neighbor (dominated by the Church of Rome) becomes even more tangible when Fidelma suffers her own crisis of conscience; she is finally forced to admit to herself that she would not be able to conduct her affairs so freely in her husband's homeland, should they ever have to return there to live. This "thoroughly modern" lady must balance her public life against her private one, making her character one with which many of her fans can identify. Tremayne includes helpful historical notes and pronunciation guides in his books.

THE CASES

1. *Absolution by Murder: A Sister Fidelma Mystery.* London: Headline, 1994, 274 p.

NORTHUMBRIA, ENGLAND, SPRING 664. As the leading churchmen and women gather at the Synod of Whitby to debate the rival merits of the Celtic and Roman Churches, tempers fray. When the Abbess Etain, the chief spokeswoman for the Celtic group, is found murdered in her cell, suspicion immediately falls on the heavily partisan Roman faction. Sister Fidelma is called upon to investigate the murder with the assistance of handsome Brother Eadulf, a supporter of the Romans. Then the Archbishop of Canterbury dies. Associates: Eadulf; Abbess Hilda; Colmán. Historical Figures: Northumbrian King Oswy; Deusdedit, Archbishop of Canterbury.

2. *Shroud for the Archbishop: A Sister Fidelma Mystery.* London: Headline, 1994, 340 p.

ROME, ITALY, FALL 664. Wighard, Archbishop Designate of Canterbury, has been discovered garrotted in his chambers in the Lateran Palace in Rome. The palace guards arrest an Irish *religieux*, Brother Ronan Ragallach, as he flees from Wighard's chambers. Sister Fidelma and Brother Eadulf are called in to conduct an independent investigation. But more deaths follow before the pieces of this strange puzzle of evil and vengeance are finally put together. Associates: Eadulf; Colmán; Colgú mac Failbe Faland. Historical Figure: Roman Pope Vitalian.

3. *Suffer Little Children: A Sister Fidelma Mystery.* London: Headline, 1995, 339 p.

IRELAND, WINTER 664. The Venerable Dacan, a much respected and beloved scholar of the Celtic Church, has been found murdered while on a visit to a remote abbey in the Irish kingdom of Muman (or Munster). When Dacan's foul death is used by a neighboring kingdom to demand reparation from Muman, bloody war seems imminent. Summoned by Muman's king to investigate, Sister Fidelma is asked to solve the brutal killing and by doing so somehow prevent the seemingly inevitable conflict from breaking out between the two opposing Irish kingdoms. Associate: Colgú mac Failbe Faland.

4. *The Subtle Serpent: A Celtic Mystery.* London: Headline, 1996, 339 p.

IRELAND, JANUARY 666. A headless female corpse is found in the drinking well of a remote abbey in Ireland. A merchant ship is encountered under full sail off the coast, but the crew and cargo have vanished. Are these bizarre events somehow connected? It is up to Sister Fidelma and Brother Eadulf to investigate. Associates: Eadulf; Captain Ross.

5. *The Spider's Web: A Celtic Mystery.* London: Headline, 1997, 337 p.

IRELAND, MAY 666. Eber is not a man to make enemies; he has a reputation for kindliness and generosity. One night his household is aroused by a scream from his chamber. The servants burst in to find Moen, a young man to whom Eber had extended his protection, crouched over the bloody body of the chieftain. There seems no doubt of the youth's culpability, but why did Moen kill the gentle and courteous Eber? The problem is exacerbated by the fact that Moen himself cannot tell them—for he is deaf, dumb, and blind. Sister Fidelma finds herself tackling her most difficult case yet, with the help of the long-suffering Eadulf. Associate: Eadulf.

6. *Valley of the Shadow: A Celtic Mystery.* London: Headline, 1998, 269 p.

IRELAND, JULY 666. Sister Fidelma, accompanied by her companion, Saxon Brother Eadulf, is sent to Gleann Geis—known as the "forbidden valley"—in order to negotiate permission with the locals to erect a Christian Church there. When the pair discover thirty-three murdered men placed in a sun-shaped circle, they fear some sort of ritual sacrifice has taken place and embark upon an inquiry fraught with evil and danger. Associates: Eadulf; Muman King Colgú.

7. *The Monk Who Vanished: A Celtic Mystery.* London: Headline, 1999, 272 p.

IRELAND, SEPTEMBER 666. Calamity has struck the Abbey of Imleach. Not only has an elderly brother disappeared, but the holy relics of St. Ailbe have vanished as well. These sacred icons are not just the concern of the religious community but a significant political symbol for the entire kingdom. Who would have dared to take them? Sister Fidelma and Brother Eadulf are asked to investigate, and it seems there is more to the disappearances than meets the eye. Associates: Eadulf; Muman King Colgú.

8. *Act of Mercy: A Celtic Mystery.* London: Headline, 1999, 268 p.

ON PILGRIMAGE AT SEA, OCTOBER 666. Sister Fidelma sets out on a pilgrimage to reflect on her commitment to the religious life and on her growing relationship with the Saxon monk, Brother Eadulf, whom she leaves behind. Complications arise during her first night on the ship when one of her fellow pilgrims is apparently swept overboard. The grisly discovery of a blood-stained robe raises the question of murder, and Fidelma finds herself once again having to put her personal concerns aside in order to focus all her abilities on solving the mystery. Death haunts the tiny band of pilgrims huddled within the close confines of the ship, but it is not until the Holy Shrine is nearly within sight that the amazing truth is uncovered. The usual associates are absent here.

9. *Our Lady of Darkness: A Novel of Ancient Ireland.* London: Headline, 2000, 270 p.

IRELAND, NOVEMBER 666. Arriving home from her pilgrim voyage, Sister Fidelma is startled to learn that her faithful companion, Brother Eadulf, has been sentenced to death for the murder of a young girl, with the execution set to take place within twenty-four hours. She hastens to the capital of Laigin, where he is being held, determined to appeal the verdict. The crime had occurred at the Abbey of Fearna, where Fidelma clashes with the sinister Abbess Fainder. The evidence against Eadulf seems overwhelming. Can he actually be guilty? And will Fidelma's emotional involvement blind her desperate search for the truth? Associate: Eadulf.

10. *Smoke in the Wind.* London: Headline, 2001, 267 p.

DYFED, WALES, WINTER 666. Sister Fidelma and Brother Eadulf are on their way to visit the new Archbishop of Canterbury when their ship is blown off course during a storm. Eadulf is knocked unconscious, and they are forced to land on the coast of modern Wales in the kingdom of Dyfed. The pair is given sanctuary and hospitality by King Gwlyddien and Abbot Tryffin of the Abbey of Dewi Sant; in the course of their discussions, they are asked to solve the mystery of how an entire monastic community, including the King's eldest son, could vanish into thin air. While investigating this puzzle, Fidelma and Eadulf are confronted with the shocking murder of a girl from the village. It's not long before the trail leads to death and treachery in high places, and Fidelma and Eadulf are faced with one of the most sinister and baffling mysteries they've ever been asked to investigate. Note: the appointment of an Archbishop of Canterbury in this and subsequent novels appears to be at odds with the actual history of the period. Associates: Brother Eadulf; Dyfed King Gwlyddien; Prince Cathen, his son.

11. *The Haunted Abbot.* London: Headline, 2002, 298 p.

GREAT BRITAIN, DECEMBER 666. Sister Fidelma of Cashel, daughter and sister to kings, is in the land of the South Folk in the Kingdom of the East Angles (East Anglia) in England, accompanied by her Saxon husband, Brother Eadulf. Having now completed their business with the Archbishop of Canterbury, they make one final detour before returning home. At the insistence of Brother Botulf, a childhood friend of Eadulf, the pair visit his home village, arriving at Aldred's Abbey at midnight on the night of the festival of Yule. There they find Botulf's dead body, his head caved in. As Fidelma and Eadulf soon learn, murder isn't the only danger that faces the abbey. The ghost of a young woman resembling Abbot Cild's dead wife haunts the cloister shadows, and the man suspects Fidelma of using witchcraft to cause the apparition! Now it will require all of Fidelma's skill as an advocate to unravel the mystery and uncover the truth behind these events before the secrets destroy more lives. Complicating matters further for Fidelma, she is beginning to question her personal decisions. She and Eadulf have been married under Irish law for a year, but she has come to realize that she can never live happily in Eadulf's homeland among the South Folk, where women are treated as chattel without the power to question witnesses or give testimony in trials. Associate: Brother Eadulf.

12. *Badger's Moon.* London: Headline, 2003, 265 p.

IRELAND, 667? A series of horrific murders has brought terror to the Kingdom of Muman. The victims, all young girls, have been slaughtered on the nights of three consecutive full moons. Suspicion falls on three dark strangers from the distant land of Aksum (Ethiopia), who are guests at the Abbey of Finbarr. A panic-stricken mob attacks the abbey, leaving the religious community in fear for their lives. Sister Fidelma and her husband, Brother Eadulf, are called in to restore order and find the killer, but it soon becomes clear that the three mysterious strangers are indeed hiding a dark secret. And what about the aging Laig, a hermitlike apothecary, who is known to have instructed all three victims in the magical arts and the power of the moon; what sinister truths are hiding in his woodland dwelling? As Fidelma struggles to repair her faltering relationship with Eadulf, can she uncover the truth before the killer strikes again on the next night of the full moon? Associate: Brother Eadulf.

13. *The Leper's Bell.* London: Headline, 2004, 276 p.

IRELAND, 667? A servant has been murdered and the baby in her charge has been abducted. Fidelma of Cashel has solved even more horrendous crimes in her career, but this case is significantly different because of the personal emotions involved. The baby who has been abducted is their son. What is the motive for the kidnapping? Fidelma and Eadulf have made many enemies during their pursuit of justice. Could someone be seeking vengeance? Ignoring protests that they might be too personally involved to undertake the investigation, Fidelma and Eadulf set out on what proves to be one of their most dangerous cases. Associate: Brother Eadulf.

14. *Hemlock at Vespers: A Collection of Celtic Mysteries.* London: Headline, 2000, 336 p.

IRELAND AND ELSEWHERE, 660s. The first collection of Sister Fidelma mysteries. CONTENTS: "Introduction"; "Murder in Repose"; "Murder by Miracle"; "Tarnishing Halo"; "Abbey Sinister"; "Our Lady of Death"; "Hemlock at Vespers" (Kildare, Ireland); "At the Tent of Holofernes" (Durrow, Ireland); "A Canticle for Wulfstan" (Durrow, Ireland); "The High King's Sword" (Tara, Ireland, 664); "The Poisoned Chalice" (Rome, 664); "Holy Blood" (Seneffe, Belgium, 664/665); "A Scream from the Sepulcher" (Tara, Ireland, 665); "The Horse That Died for Shame" (Kildare, Ireland, 665); "Invitation to a Poisoning" (666); "Those Who Trespass" (666); "Acknowledgements"; "About the Author." The usual associates are absent here.

15. *Whispers of the Dead: A Collection of Ancient Irish Mysteries.* London: Headline, 2004, 307 p.

IRELAND, 650s–660s. The second collection of Sister Fidelma mysteries. CONTENTS: "Introduction"; "Whispers of the Dead"; "Corpse on a Holy Day"; "The Astrologer Who Predicted His Own Murder"; "The Blemish" (650s); "Dark Moon Rising"; "Like a Dog Returning . . ."; "The Banshee"; "The Heir-Apparent"; "Who Stole the Fish?"; "Cry 'Wolf'!"; "Scattered Thorns"; "Gold at Night"; "Death of an Icon"; "The Fosterer"; "The Lost Eagle" (Canterbury, England, 666); "Acknowledgements"; "About the Author." Associate: Brother Eadulf, who appears only in the final story.

WINSPEAR, Jacqueline (1955–). British.

Scene of the Crime: England, beginning in 1929.

Detective: A young woman uses a combination of deduction and empathy to solve crimes in post World War I England.

Known Associates: Francis (Frankie) Dobbs, her father; Lady Rowan Compton, her first employer and her champion; Maurice Blanche, her mentor; Captain Simon Lynch, a doctor who captured her heart while they worked together in the war; Billy Beale, one of Simon's last patients, initially a friend of Maisie's; by *Birds of a Feather* he's the young woman's employee.

Comment: Maurice Blanche, now retired, was employed by both private clients and governments. He was a detective, but was also much more than that. He not only discovered exactly what had happened and who had committed an offense, he also discovered why. He did not present his clients with solutions to crimes, he presented his clients with solutions to the underlying problems. When his *protégée*, Maisie Dobbs, tells him that she wants to do the same kind of work, he takes her as his apprentice. The moral structure he gave her includes the idea that, once she takes a case, she is responsible for the welfare of all parties concerned (including the person suspected of the crime). Her job is to reach a deep understanding, not just of what happened, but also of why it happened and to bring about the most healing solution possible. The methods and, even more than that, the gentle wisdom employed by Maisie are fascinating. She applies inductive and deductive reasoning, in a manner worthy of Sherlock Holmes; but that is blended with empathy; empathy used as a tool to gain an understanding of all the people involved in the crime, and used to bring about healing, so that everyone involved is strengthened and is moving forward on a better path than the one they were on before her intervention. Jacqueline Winspear won a Best First Novel Agatha Award and an Alex Award for *Maisie Dobbs*.

Literary Crimes & Chimes: This series is wonderful, combining timeless wisdom with period detail. The human cost of the war continues to reverberate through everything; no one was left untouched. It is the unspoken element that has shaped the world and the lives of everyone in it. People go about daily lives that are imbued with feelings of grief, guilt, and rage. The first book, *Maisie Dobbs*, uses one of her first cases as a frame to tell her backstory. In fact, each of the books brings out another unresolved element from her own life. Maurice has told her many times that "each case has a way of shining a light on something we need to know about ourselves." She finds that he was right. In the first book she begins to come to terms with her feelings for the man she loved, a man who was essentially destroyed by the war. Similarly, in the second book, Maisie works to heal relationships in a family in which the daughter has fled home. In working through the problems in that family Maisie faces some of the truths about her own relationship with her father.

THE CASES

1. *Maisie Dobbs: a Novel.* New York: Soho, 2003, 294 p.
   ENGLAND, 1929 (with flashbacks including WWI). Maisie is disappointed when the first client of her new business is a suspicious husband; but that case leads her to uncover the schemes of a madman, one who is preying on those who were wounded in the war. Associates: Frankie Dobbs; Lady Rowan; Maurice Blanche; Enid, Priscilla Evernden; Captain Simon Lynch; Iris Rigson; Billy Beale; Mr. Christopher Davenham; Celia Davenham; Detective Inspector Stratton.

2. *Birds of a Feather.* New York: Soho, 2004, 311 p.
   ENGLAND, 1930. Maisie is hired by a wealthy self-made man; his daughter has fled his home. Where some would see a spoiled, bored heiress Maisie finds a deeply troubled young woman, wracked with guilt and in fear for her life. In the midst of Maisie's investigation she realizes that Billy is in serious difficulty and that he may be beyond her help. Then her father is grievously injured and Maisie rushes to his side. The police make an arrest and Maisie

is certain that they not only have the wrong man, but have also not discovered all the crimes she knows are connected. After that she is in a race with the killer, trying to save the next victim. Associates: Frankie Dobbs; Lady Rowan; Maurice Blanche; Billy Beale; Captain Simon Lynch; Detective Inspector Stratton; Joseph Waite; Charlotte Waite; Dame Constance, Abbess of Camden Abbey; Doreen Beale; Dr. Andrew Dene; Smiley Rackham.

"And Further Deponent Sayeth Not"

Author Index

The Author Index also includes Editors.

Series Index

Title Index

Major Character Index

Setting Index

About the Author

MICHAEL BURGESS is Head of Collection Development at California State University, San Bernardino; and professional writer and editor. He has written and edited hundreds of books and thousands of articles, many in the areas of literature and popular reading interests.

JILL H. VASSILAKOS is Head of Technical Services and Government Documents Librarian at California State University, San Bernardino.